EUROPEAN POLITICAL FACTS,

HISTORICAL AND POLITICAL FACTS

Jack Babuscio and Richard Minta Dunn
EUROPEAN POLITICAL FACTS, 1648–1789

Chris Cook and John Paxton
EUROPEAN POLITICAL FACTS, 1789–1848
EUROPEAN POLITICAL FACTS, 1848–1918
EUROPEAN POLITICAL FACTS, 1918–1990

Ken Powell and Chris Cook
ENGLISH HISTORICAL FACTS, 1485–1603

Chris Cook and John Wroughton
ENGLISH HISTORICAL FACTS, 1603–1688

Chris Cook and John Stevenson
BRITISH HISTORICAL FACTS, 1688–1760

Chris Cook and John Stevenson
BRITISH HISTORICAL FACTS, 1760–1830

Chris Cook and Brendan Keith
BRITISH HISTORICAL FACTS, 1830–1900

David Butler and Gareth Butler
BRITISH POLITICAL FACTS, 1900–1994

European Political Facts, 1900–1996

Fourth Edition

Chris Cook

and

John Paxton

Published in Great Britain by
MACMILLAN PRESS LTD
Houndmills, Basingstoke, Hampshire RG21 6XS and London
Companies and representatives throughout the world

A catalogue record for this book is available from the British Library.

ISBN 0–333–69629–8 hardcover
ISBN 0–333–69630–1 paperback

Published in the United States of America by
ST. MARTIN'S PRESS, INC.,
Scholarly and Reference Division,
175 Fifth Avenue, New York, N.Y. 10010

ISBN 0–312–21231–3

Library of Congress Cataloging-in-Publication Data
Cook, Chris, 1945–
European political facts, 1900–1996 / Chris Cook and John Paxton.
— 4th ed.
p. cm.
Includes bibliographical references and index.
ISBN 0–312–21231–3 (cloth)
1. Europe—Politics and government—1871–1918—Handbooks, manuals,
etc.   2. Europe—Politics and government—1918–1945—Handbooks,
manuals, etc.   3. Europe—Politics and government—1945– –
–Handbooks, manuals, etc.   4. International agencies—Handbooks,
manuals, etc.   I. Paxton, John.   II. Title.
JN12.C637 1998
320.94'02'02—dc21   97–41061
                                                                    CIP

First edition (*European Political Facts, 1918–73*) 1975
Second edition (*European Political Facts, 1918–84*) 1986
Third edition (*European Political Facts, 1918–90*) 1992
Fourth edition (*European Political Facts, 1900–1996*) 1998

This book is printed on paper suitable for recycling and made from fully managed and
sustained forest sources.

10   9   8   7   6   5   4   3   2   1
07   06   05   04   03   02   01   00   99   98

Printed and bound in Great Britain by
Antony Rowe Ltd, Chippenham, Wiltshire

To Tim Farmiloe
with affection

CONTENTS

Preface   ix

1 International Organizations   1
    The United Nations (UN)   1
    The League of Nations   6
    Bank for International Settlements (BIS)   10
    International Labour Organization (ILO)   11
    European Trade Union Confederation (ETUC)   12
    International Confederation of Free Trade Unions (ICFTU)   12
    World Confederation of Labour (WCL)   12
    Organization for Economic Co-operation and
      Development (OECD)   13
    North Atlantic Treaty Organization (NATO)   14
    Western European Union (WEU)   16
    Council of Europe   17
    European Union (EU)   19
    European Free Trade Association (EFTA)   23
    Commonwealth of Independent States (CIS)   24
    The Warsaw Pact   26
    Council for Mutual Economic Assistance (COMECON
      or CMEA)   27
    Organization for Security and Co-operation in Europe
      (OSCE)   29
    European Bank for Reconstruction and Development
      (EBRD)   30
    Other European Organizations   31

2 Heads of State   32

3 Parliaments   59

4 Ministers   100

5 Elections   163

6 Political Parties   278

7 Justice   329

8 Defence and Treaties   356

CONTENTS

9 Dependencies   373

10 Population   389

11 New Countries   403

Glossary of Terms   407

Index   426

PREFACE

Nearly a quarter of a century has elapsed since the first edition of this book was published in 1973. During this period, the face of European politics has seen a dramatic transformation. In Eastern Europe communism has collapsed. The Soviet Union itself is no more. Such states as Czechoslovakia and Yugoslavia have split apart, while new nation states have arisen in their place. With the creation of the European Union, many of the democracies of Western Europe are exploring ways of achieving ever closer political, economic and social co-operation. Against this background, there remains a clear and increasing need for readily accessible facts concerning the changing history of modern Europe in the twentieth century. This has been our prime aim in compiling *European Political Facts, 1900–1996*.

Our coverage once again is from the Atlantic to the Urals and in adopting this broad, outward-looking concept of Europe we have, naturally, encountered considerable editorial difficulties. The general aim is comparability between countries. This was not always easy to achieve and in some cases impossible, particularly for comparisons between 'East' and 'West' Europe. This new edition has also expanded chronologically, beginning in 1900 to give a wealth of data on the whole period of the present century. Space provides a natural limit to the information which can be presented for so many countries for so many years.

We are grateful to many people and organizations for their help and advice. In the first place we should like to acknowledge our debt to David Butler, who was a pathfinder with his highly successful *British Political Facts* (Macmillan).

Gratitude also goes to Sheila Fairfield and Dione Daffin for hours of work digging for facts; to Brian Hunter for tremendous help on Eastern European countries; and to Stephen Brooks, Harry Harmer and James Robinson.

We have to thank Penny White and Linda Hollingworth for excellent typing and sharp eyes for inconsistencies.

But some error and inconsistency can still appear in a work of this kind and the editors are solely responsible. We do ask readers to alert us if they spot errors, and constructive and informed criticism will be welcome for future editions.

Chris Cook
John Paxton

1 INTERNATIONAL ORGANIZATIONS

THE UNITED NATIONS
(UN)

The United Nations is an association of states which have pledged themselves, through signing the Charter, to maintain international peace and security and to co-operate in establishing political, economic and social conditions under which this task can be securely achieved. Nothing contained in the Charter authorizes the organization to intervene in matters which are essentially within the domestic jurisdiction of any state.

The United Nations Charter originated from proposals agreed upon at discussions held at Dumbarton Oaks (Washington, DC) between the USSR, US and UK from 21 Aug to 28 Sep, and between the US, UK and China from 29 Sep to 7 Oct 1944. These proposals were laid before the United Nations Conference on International Organization, held at San Francisco from 25 Apr to 26 Jun 1945, and (after amendments had been made to the original proposals) the Charter of the United Nations was signed on 26 Jun 1945 by the delegates of 50 countries. Ratification of all the signatures had been received by 31 Dec 1945.

The United Nations formally came into existence on 24 Oct 1945, with the deposit of the requisite number of ratifications of the Charter with the US Department of State. The official languages of the United Nations are Chinese, English, French, Russian, Spanish and Arabic.

The headquarters of the United Nations is in New York City, USA.

Membership. Membership is open to all peace-loving states whose admission will be effected by the General Assembly upon recommendation of the Security Council.

The Principal Organs of the United Nations are: 1. The General Assembly 2. The Security Council 3. The Economic and Social Council 4. The Trusteeship Council 5. The International Court of Justice 6. The Secretariat.

1. The General Assembly consists of all the members of the United Nations. Each member has one vote. The General Assembly meets regularly once a year, commencing on the 3rd Tuesday in September; the session normally lasts until mid-December and is resumed for some weeks in the new year if this is required. Special sessions may be convoked by the Secretary-General if requested by the Security Council, by a majority of the members of the United Nations or by one member concurred with by the majority of the members. The General Assembly elects its President for each session.

The first regular session was held in London from 10 Jan to 14 Feb and in New York from 23 Oct to 16 Dec 1946.

The work of the General Assembly is divided between six main committees and the special political committee, on each of which every member has the right to be represented by one delegate. I. Political Security. II. Economic and Financial. III. Social, Humanitarian and Cultural. IV. Trust and Non-Self-Governing Territories. V. Administrative and Budgetary. VI. Legal.

In addition there is a General Committee charged with the task of co-ordinating the proceedings of the Assembly and its Committees; and a Credentials Committee which verifies the credentials of the delegates. The General Committee consists of 29 members, comprising the President of the General Assembly, its 17 Vice-Presidents and the Chairmen of the six main committees. The Credentials Committee consists of nine members, elected at the beginning of each session of the General Assembly. The Assembly has two standing committees – an Advisory Committee on Administrative and Budgetary Questions and a Committee on Contributions. The General Assembly establishes subsidiary and *ad hoc* bodies when necessary to deal with specific matters.

The General Assembly may discuss any matters within the scope of the Charter, and with the exception of any situation or dispute on the agenda of the Security Council, may make recommendations on any such questions or matters. For decisions on important questions a two-thirds majority is required, on other questions a simple majority of members present and voting. If the Security Council, because of lack of unanimity of the permanent members, fails to exercise its primary responsibility for the maintenance of international peace and security in any case where there appears to be a threat to the peace, breach of the peace or act of aggression, the General Assembly shall consider the matter immediately with a view to making appropriate recommendations to members for collective measures, including in the case of a breach of the peace or act of aggression the use of armed force when necessary, to maintain or restore international peace and security.

The General Assembly receives and considers reports from the other organs of the United Nations, including the Security Council. The Secretary-General makes an annual report to it on the work of the organization.

2. The Security Council consists of 15 members, each of which has one vote. There are five permanent and ten non-permanent members elected for a two-year term by a two-thirds majority of the General Assembly. Retiring members are not eligible for immediate re-election. Any other member of the United Nations will be invited to participate without vote in the discussion of questions specially affecting its interests.

The Security Council bears the primary responsibility for the maintenance of peace and security. It is also responsible for the functions of the United Nations in trust territories classed as 'strategic areas'. Decisions on procedural questions are made by an affirmative vote of nine members. On all other matters the affirmative vote of nine members must include the concurring votes of all permanent members (in practice, however, an abstention by a permanent member is not considered a veto), subject to the provision that when the Security Council is considering methods for the peaceful settlement of a dispute, parties to the dispute abstain from voting.

For the maintenance of international peace and security the Security Council can, in accordance with special agreements to be concluded, call on armed forces, assistance and facilities of the member states. It is assisted by a Military Staff Committee consisting of the Chiefs of Staff of the permanent members of the Security Council or their representatives.

The Presidency of the Security Council is held for one month in rotation by the member states in the English alphabetical order of their names.

The Security Council functions continuously. Its members are permanently represented at the seat of the organization, but it may meet in any place that will best facilitate its work.

The Council has three standing committees, of Experts, on Council Meetings away from headquarters and on the Admission of New Members. In addition, from time to time, it establishes *ad hoc* committees and commissions such as the Truce Supervision Organization in Palestine.

Permanent Members: China, France, Russia, UK, USA.

3. The Economic and Social Council is responsible under the General Assembly for carrying out the functions of the United Nations with regard to international economic, social, cultural, educational, health and related matters.

The Economic and Social Council consists of 54 member states elected by a two-thirds majority of the General Assembly. Retiring members are eligible for immediate re-election. Each member has one vote. Decisions are made by a majority of the members present and voting.

The Council nominally holds two sessions a year, and special sessions may be held if required. The President is elected for one year and is eligible for immediate re-election.

The Economic and Social Council has the following commissions:

Regional Economic Commissions: ECE (Economic Commission for Europe); ESCAP (Economic Commission for Asia and the Pacific; Bangkok); ECLAC (Economic Commission for Latin America and the Caribbean; Santiago, Chile); ECA (Economic Commission for Africa; Addis Ababa); ESCWA (Economic Commission for Western Asia; Baghdad). These Commissions have been established to enable the nations of the major regions of the world to co-operate on common problems and also to produce economic information.

Eleven functional commissions on: Crime and Criminal Justice; Social Development; Human Rights; Narcotic Drugs; Science and Technology for Development; Status of Women; Statistics; Sustainable Development; Human Settlements; New and Renewable Sources of Energy and Energy for Development; Population and Development.

The Economic and Social Council has the following standing committees: the Committee on Non-Governmental Organizations; the Committee for Programme and Co-ordination; the Committee on Natural Resources, the Committee for Development Planning; the Committee of Experts on the Transport of Dangerous Goods.

Other special bodies are the International Narcotics Control Board and the Administrative Committee on Co-ordination to ensure (1) the most effective implementation of the agreements entered into between the United Nations and the specialized agencies, and (2) co-ordination of activities.

4. The Trusteeship Council. The Charter provides for an international trusteeship system to safeguard the interests of the inhabitants of territories which are not yet fully self-governing and which may be placed thereunder by individual trusteeship agreements. These are called trust territories.

All the original eleven trust territories had become independent or had joined independent countries by 1996.

5. The International Court of Justice was created by an international treaty, the Statute of the Court, which forms an integral part of the United Nations Charter. All members of the United Nations are *ipso facto* parties to the Statute of the Court.

The Court is composed of independent judges, elected regardless of their nationality, who possess the qualifications required in their countries for appointment to the highest judicial offices, or are jurisconsults of recognized competence in international law. There are 15 judges, no two of whom may be nationals of the same state. They are elected by

4

the Security Council and the General Assembly of the United Nations sitting independently. Candidates are chosen from a list of persons nominated by the national groups in the Permanent Court of Arbitration established by Hague Conventions of 1899 and 1907. In the case of members of the United Nations not represented in the Permanent Court of Arbitration, candidates are nominated by national groups appointed for the purpose by their governments. The judges are elected for a nine-year term and are eligible for immediate re-election. When engaged on business of the Court, they enjoy diplomatic privileges and immunities.

The Court elects its own President and Vice-Presidents for three years and remains permanently in session, except for judicial vacations. The full court of 15 judges normally sits, but a quorum of nine judges is sufficient to constitute the Court. In 1993 the Court formed a seven-member Chamber for Environmental Matters. It may form chambers of three or more judges for dealing with particular categories of cases, and forms annually a chamber of five judges to hear and determine, at the request of the parties, cases by summary procedures.

Competence and Jurisdiction. Only states may be parties in cases before the Court, which is open to the states party to its Statute. The conditions under which the Court will be open to other states are laid down by the Security Council. The Court exercises its jurisdiction in all cases which the parties refer to it and in all matters provided for in the Charter, or in treaties and conventions in force. Disputes concerning the jurisdiction of the Court are settled by the Court's own decision.

The Court may apply in its decision: (a) international conventions; (b) international custom; (c) the general principles of law recognized by civilized nations; and (d) as subsidiary means for the determination of the rules of law, judicial decisions and the teachings of highly qualified publicists. If the parties agree, the Court may decide a case *ex aequo et bono.* The Court may also give an advisory opinion on any legal question to any organ of the United Nations or its agencies.

Procedure. The official languages of the Court are French and English. At the request of any party the Court will authorize the use of another language by this party. All questions are decided by a majority of the judges present. If the votes are equal, the President has a casting vote. The judgment is final and without appeal, but a revision may be applied for within ten years from the date of the judgment on the ground of a new decisive factor. Unless otherwise decided by the Court, each party bears its own costs.

Judges. The judges of the Court are elected by the Security Council and the General Assembly.

'National' Judges. If there is no judge on the bench of the nationality of the parties to the dispute, each party has the right to choose a judge.

5

Such judges shall take part in the decision on terms of complete equality with their colleagues.

The Court has its seat at The Hague, but may sit and exercise its functions elsewhere whenever it considers this desirable. The expenses of the Court are borne by the United Nations.

6. The Secretariat is composed of the Secretary-General, who is the chief administrative officer of the organization, and an international staff appointed by him under regulations established by the General Assembly. However, the Secretary-General, the High Commissioner for Refugees and the Managing Director of the Fund are appointed by the General Assembly.

The Secretary-General acts as chief administrative officer in all meetings of the General Assembly, the Security Council, the Economic and Social Council and the Trusteeship Council.

Secretaries-General:

Trygve Lie (Norway)	1 Feb 1946–10 Apr 1953
Dag Hammarskjöld (Sweden)	10 Apr 1953–17 Sep 1961
U Thant (Burma)	
[Acting Secretary-General 1961–2]	3 Nov 1961–31 Dec 1971
Kurt Waldheim (Austria)	1 Jan 1972–31 Dec 1981
Javier Perez de Cuellar (Peru)	1 Jan 1982–31 Dec 1991
Boutros Boutros-Ghali (Egypt)	1 Jan 1992–31 Dec 1996
Kofi Annan (Ghana)	1 Jan 1997–

The Secretary-General is assisted by Under-Secretaries-General and Assistant Secretaries-General

THE LEAGUE OF NATIONS

The League of Nations formally came into existence on 10 Jan 1920, through the coming into force at that date of the Treaty of Versailles. The two official languages of the League were English and French. The seat of the League was Geneva, Switzerland.

The League of Nations was an association of states which had pledged themselves, through signing the Covenant (*i.e.* the constitution of the League) not to go to war before submitting their disputes with each other, or states not members of the League, to arbitration or enquiry and a delay of from three to nine months. Furthermore, any state violating this pledge was automatically in a state of outlawry with the other states, which were bound to sever all economic and political relations with the defaulting state.

Secretaries-General of the League:

| Sir Eric Drummond [Earl of Perth] (Britain) | 1919–1932 |
| Joseph Avenol (France) | 1933–1940 |

On Joseph Avenol's resignation, 26 Jul 1940, Sean Lester (Irish Republic) became Acting Secretary-General.

Membership. The following European states joined the League on the dates given below:

Albania[1]	16 Dec 1920
Belgium	10 Jan 1920
Bulgaria	16 Dec 1920
Czechoslovakia	10 Jan 1920
Denmark	8 Mar 1920
Estonia[1]	22 Sep 1921
Finland	16 Dec 1920
France	10 Jan 1920
Germany	8 Sep 1926
Greece	30 Mar 1920
Hungary	18 Sep 1922
Irish Free State	10 Sep 1923
Italy	10 Jan 1920
Latvia[1]	22 Sep 1921
Lithuania[1]	22 Sep 1921
Luxembourg	16 Dec 1920
Netherlands	9 Mar 1920
Norway	5 Mar 1920
Poland	10 Jan 1920
Portugal	8 Apr 1920
Romania	8 Apr 1920
Spain	10 Jan 1920
Sweden	9 Mar 1920
Switzerland	8 Mar 1920
Turkey	18 July 1932
USSR	18 Sep 1934
UK	10 Jan 1920
Yugoslavia	10 Feb 1920

[1] Made declarations putting the protection of their national minorities under League auspices as a condition of their entry into the League.

7

The following European states withdrew from the League: Spain on 8 Sep 1926, Germany on 21 Oct 1933, Italy on 11 Dec 1937, and Hungary on 11 Apr 1939, announced their withdrawal from the League; according to Art. 1, par. 3, of the Covenant the notice of withdrawal only came into force two years after it had been given. On 22 Mar 1928, Spain resolved to continue as a member of the League.

Austria ceased to be a member after her annexation by Germany in Mar 1938.

The League was formally dissolved at its final meeting on 8 Apr 1946, but in practice it had not met since 1939.

THE ORGANS OF THE LEAGUE

The Primary Organs of the League were: 1. The Council, 2. The Assembly, 3. The Secretariat, 4. The Permanent Court of International Justice (at The Hague).

1. The Council was originally composed of four permanent members (the British Empire, France, Italy and Japan) and four non-permanent members to be elected every year by a majority of the Assembly. The first non-permanent members, appointed by the Peace Conference and named in the Covenant before the first Assembly met, were Belgium, Brazil, Greece and Spain. With the approval of the majority of the Assembly, the Council was able to appoint new permanent and non-permanent members. At the Assembly of Sep 1926 Germany was admitted to the League and given a permanent seat on the Council. At the same time the number of non-permanent seats, already increased to six in 1922, was further increased to nine, the period of office to be three years. In order to institute the new system of rotation, three were elected for one year, three for two years, and three for three years, so that at all subsequent Assemblies three members retired instead of nine at once. Furthermore, the rule was established that a retiring member was ineligible for re-election for three years unless specially declared re-eligible. The number of members elected after being declared re-eligible could not exceed three. Hitherto the only states to secure a declaration of re-eligibility had been Poland and Spain. Both countries applied for re-eligibility in 1937, but neither of them obtained the necessary majority for re-election during the 18th Assembly, Sep 1937. China re-entered the Council in 1936 as a result of such a declaration. Owing to complaints that a number of members of the League were in practice unable to enter the Council, a tenth non-permanent seat was created for three years in 1933, and in 1936 this seat was continued in existence for another three years and an eleventh non-permanent seat created for three years (*i.e.* till 1939). Any member of the League not represented on the Council was invited to send a representative to sit on it at any meetings at which matters especially affecting it were being discussed. A similar invitation could be extended to states not members of the League.

The Council met on the 3rd Monday in January, the 2nd Monday in May, and just before and after the Assembly in September.

2. The Assembly. Every member state of the League was entitled to be represented by a delegation to the Assembly composed of not more than three delegates and three substitute delegates, but it had only one vote. It met at the seat of the League (Geneva) on the second or, in certain circumstances, the first Monday in September. It could meet at other places than Geneva; extraordinary sessions could be called to deal with urgent matters.

The President was elected at the first meeting of the session, and held office for the duration of the session.

The Assembly divided itself into the following seven principal committees, on each of which every member state of the League had the right to be represented by one delegate:

   I. Juridical.
  II. Technical Organizations.
 III. Disarmament.
 IV. Budget and Staff.
  V. Social Questions.
 VI. Political Questions and admission of New Members.
VII. As an experiment, the General Committee of the 19th Assembly decided to set up a Seventh Committee to deal with questions of Health, Opium and Intellectual Co-operation.

The decisions of the Assembly had to be voted unanimously, except where the Covenant or the Peace Treaties provided otherwise. As a general principle decisions on questions of procedure were voted by majority, or in some cases by a two-thirds majority.

3. The Secretariat was a permanent organ composed of the Secretary-General and a number of officials selected from among citizens of all member states and from the United States of America. The Secretary-General, who took office in Jul 1933, was M. Joseph Avenol (France). The other officials were appointed by the Secretary-General with the approval of the Council.

The Under-Secretaries-General as from 1 Feb 1937 were:
      Sean Lester (Ireland) Deputy-Secretary-General
      F. Walters (UK)

Vladimir Sokoline (USSR) as from 20 Feb 1937
Podesta Costa (Argentine) as from Jan 1938

4. Permanent Court of International Justice. The Permanent Court at The Hague was created by an international treaty, the Statute of the Court, which was drafted in 1920 by a committee appointed by the Council of the League of Nations and revised in 1929 with amendments which came into force in 1936. The revised Statutes adopted at the 10th Assembly provided for 15 judges for the Court, and stipulated that the Court should remain permanently in Session except for such holidays as it may decide. The judges were elected jointly by the Council and the Assembly of the League for a term of nine years.

On the dissolution of the League of Nations and the establishment of the United Nations Organization, the Court was superseded by the International Court of Justice.

The Secondary Organs of the League were:

  (a) The Technical Organizations
     1. Economic and Financial
     2. Health
     3. Communications and Transit
  (b) Advisory Committees
     1. Military, Naval and Air Commission
     2. Commission of Enquiry for European Union
     3. Mandates Commission
     4. Opium Committee
     5. Social Committee
     6. Committee of Experts on Slavery
  (c) Committees on Intellectual Co-operation
  (d) International Institutes
     1. Institute of Intellectual Co-operation (Paris)
     2. Institute of Private Law (Rome)
  (e) Administrative Organization High Commissioner for Free City of Danzig

BANK FOR INTERNATIONAL SETTLEMENTS
(BIS)

Founded in 1930, originally to settle the question of German First World War reparations, the BIS is the 'central banks' bank'. It aims to promote co-operation between central banks, to provide facilities for international financial operations and act as agent or trustee in international financial settlements. Its assets are owned by 32 central banks, and the headquarters are in Basle, Switzerland.

The Board of Directors consists of the governor of the central bank and one other appointee from Belgium, France, Germany, Italy, the UK and the USA. Governors of not more than nine central banks are eligible for election.

INTERNATIONAL LABOUR ORGANIZATION
(ILO)

The ILO was constituted in 1919 as an autonomous organization of the League of Nations. Its aim is to improve labour conditions through international action. Membership of the League carried with it membership of the Organization. In 1946 the Organization was recognized as a specialized agency of the United Nations.

One of the ILO's principal functions is the formulation of international standards in the form of International Labour Conventions and Recommendations. Member countries are required to submit Conventions to their competent national authorities with a view to ratification. If a country ratifies a Convention it agrees to bring its laws into line with its terms and to report periodically how these regulations are being applied. More than 6000 ratifications of 176 Conventions had been deposited by mid-1995. Machinery is available to ascertain whether Conventions thus ratified are effectively applied.

Recommendations do not require ratification, but member states are obliged to consider them with a view to giving effect to their provisions by legislation or other action. By the end of 1995 the International Labour Conference had adopted 183 recommendations.

The ILO consists of the International Labour Conference, the Governing Body and the International Labour Office.

In 1960 the ILO established in Geneva the International Institute for Labour Studies. The Institute specializes in advanced education and research on social and labour policy. It brings together for group study experienced persons from all parts of the world – government administrators, trade-union officials, industrial experts, management, university and other specialists. The International Training Centre of the ILO, in Turin, was set up in 1965 to lead the training programmes implemented by the ILO as part of its technical co-operation activities. Member States and the UN system also call on its resources and experience. A UN Staff College was established on the Turin Campus in 1996.

11

EUROPEAN TRADE UNION CONFEDERATION
(ETUC)

The ETUC was formally established in Feb 1973 with some 29m. members from 14 EEC and EFTA countries (Austria, Belgium, Denmark, Finland, France, Federal Republic of Germany, Iceland, Italy, Luxembourg, Netherlands, Norway, Sweden, Switzerland, UK) and the proscribed *Unión General de Trabajadores* of Spain. Membership in 1994 was 45m. from 21 countries.

INTERNATIONAL CONFEDERATION OF
FREE TRADE UNIONS
(ICFTU)

The ICFTU was founded in London in Dec 1949. The amended constitution provides for co-operation with the UN and the ILO and for regional organizations to promote trade unionism, especially in developing countries.

The Congress of the Confederation meets every four years and elects the Executive Board of 50 members nominated on an area basis for a four-year period; the Board meets at least once a year. There are joint committees with the International Trade Secretariat. In 1994 there was a membership of about 123m. from 188 affiliated organizations in 135 countries.

WORLD CONFEDERATION OF LABOUR
(WCL)

The International Federation of Christian Trade Unions was established in 1920 as a mainly Catholic organization; it ceased to exist in 1940 through Fascist and Nazi suppression, most of its members being Italian or German. It was reconstituted in 1945 and renamed World Confederation of Labour in 1968. Its policy is based on the papal encyclicals *Rerum novarum* (1891) and *Quadragesimo anno* (1931), but it claims some Protestant members in Europe.

The Christian International is federative, leaving wide discretion to the autonomy of its constituent unions. Its governing body is Congress, which meets every three years. The General Council, meeting at least once a year, is composed according to the proportion of membership of Congress. Congress elects the Executive Committee of at least 12 members which appoints the Secretary-General.

A total membership of 11m. in about 90 countries is claimed. The largest group is the Confederation of Christian Trade Unions of Belgium with a membership of 1.2m.

ORGANIZATION FOR ECONOMIC CO-OPERATION AND DEVELOPMENT
(OECD)

On 30 Sep 1961 the Organization for European Economic Co-operation (OEEC) was replaced by the Organization for Economic Co-operation and Development. The change of title marks the Organization's altered status and functions: with the accession of Canada and the USA as full members it ceased to be a purely European body; while at the same time it added development aid to the list of its other activities. The member countries were (1996) Australia, Austria, Belgium, Canada, the Czech Republic, Denmark, Finland, France, Federal Republic of Germany, Greece, Iceland, Ireland, Italy, Japan, Luxembourg, Mexico, the Netherlands, New Zealand, Norway, Portugal, Spain, Sweden, Switzerland, Turkey, UK and USA. The EU Commission generally takes part in OECD work.

Objectives are to promote economic and social welfare throughout the OECD area by assisting its member governments in the formulation of policies designed to this end and by co-ordinating these policies; and to stimulate and harmonize its members' efforts in favour of developing countries.

The supreme body is the Council composed of one representative for each member country. It meets either at Heads of Delegations level (about twice a month) under the chairmanship of the Secretary-General, or at ministerial level (usually once a year) under the chairmanship of a minister of a country elected annually to assume these functions. Decisions and Recommendations are adopted by mutual agreement of all members of the Council.

The Council is assisted by an Executive Committee composed of 14 members of the Council designated annually by the latter. The major part of the Organization's work is, however, prepared and carried out in specialized committees, working parties and sub-groups, of which there exist over 200.

In 1990 the Centre for Co-operation with European Economies in Transition (CCET) was established to act as OECD's point of contact for Central and East European countries seeking guidance in moving towards a market economy.

Four autonomous or semi-autonomous bodies also belong to the

Organization: The International Energy Agency (IEA); the Nuclear Energy Agency (NEA); the Development Centre and the Centre for Educational Research and Innovation (CERI). Each one of these bodies has its own governing committee.

The Council, the committees and the other bodies are serviced by an international Secretariat. The Council is chaired by a minister from each country elected in annual rotation.

All member countries have established permanent Delegations to OECD, each headed by an ambassador.

NORTH ATLANTIC TREATY ORGANIZATION (NATO)

On 28 Apr 1948 the Canadian Secretary of State for External Affairs broached the idea of a 'security league' of the free nations, in extension of the Brussels Treaty of 17 Mar 1948. The United States Senate, on 11 Jun, recommended 'the association of the United States with such regional and other collective arrangements as are based on continuous self-help and mutual aid, and as affect its national security'. Detailed proposals were subsequently worked out between the Brussels Treaty powers, the USA and Canada.

On 4 Apr 1949 the foreign ministers of Belgium, Canada, Denmark, France, Iceland, Italy, Luxembourg, the Netherlands, Norway, Portugal, the UK and the USA met in Washington and signed a treaty, the first article of which read as follows:

The parties undertake, as set forth in the Charter of the United Nations, to settle any international disputes in which they may be involved by peaceful means in such a manner that international peace and security and justice are not endangered, and to refrain in their international relations from the threat or use of force in any manner inconsistent with the purposes of the United Nations.

The Treaty came into force on 24 Aug 1949. Greece and Turkey acceded to the Treaty in 1952, the Federal Republic of Germany in 1955 (the reunified Germany in 1990), and in 1982 Spain. Total 16 members.

The Atlantic Alliance was established as a defensive political and military alliance of independent countries in accordance with the terms of the UN Charter. It provides common security for its members through co-operation and consultation in political, military and economic as well as scientific and other non-military fields. The Alliance also links the security of North America to that of Europe. NATO is the organization which

14

enables the goals of the Alliance to be implemented. With the demise of the Warsaw Pact in 1991 and the end of the Cold War, the Atlantic Alliance has undertaken a fundamental transformation of its structures and policies, following the London (Jul 1990), Rome (Nov 1991) and Brussels (Jan 1994) Summits, to meet the new security challenges in Europe.

The initiatives taken at the Brussels Summit in Jan 1994 include endorsement of the concept of Combined Joint Task Forces (CJTFs) and other measures to support the development of a European Security and Defence Identity. CJTFs will provide separable military capabilities which could be employed either by NATO or, in some circumstances, by the Western European Union. They could also enable non-NATO member nations to participate in military operations.

The Brussels Summit reaffirmed that the Alliance remains open to new member states, as part of an evolutionary process; and it launched a major new initiative, which goes beyond dialogue and co-operation, called Partnership for Peace. The states participating in the NACC and other CSCE countries able and willing to contribute to this programme have been invited to join the NATO member states in this Partnership. The Partnership for Peace programme seeks to expand and intensify political and military co-operation throughout Europe. Depending on the capacity and desire of each participating state, Partners work towards transparency in defence budgeting, promoting democratic control of defence ministries, joint planning, joint military exercises, and creating an ability to operate with NATO forces in such fields as peacekeeping, search and rescue and humanitarian operations. Moreover, NATO will consult with any active Partner that perceives a direct threat to its territorial integrity, political independence, or security.

Twenty-five Central and Eastern European and other CSCE countries have joined Partnership for Peace: Albania, Armenia, Austria, Azerbaijan, Belarus, Bulgaria, the Czech Republic, Estonia, Finland, Georgia, Hungary, Kazakhstan, Kyrgyzstan, Latvia, Lithuania, Moldova, Poland, Romania, Russia, Slovakia, Slovenia, Sweden, Turkmenistan, Ukraine and Uzbekistan.

Headquarters: B-1110 Brussels, Belgium.
Secretary-General: Javier Solana Madariaga (Spain).

The Secretary-General takes the chair at all Council meetings, except at the opening and closing of Ministerial sessions, when he gives way to the Council President. The office of President is held annually by the Foreign Minister of one of the Treaty countries.

The Military Committee is composed of the Chiefs of Staff or their representatives of all the member countries except France, which in 1966 withdrew from the Military Committee while remaining a member of the Council. (Iceland, having no military establishment, may be represented by a civilian). It meets at Chiefs of Staff level at least twice a year as required, but remains in permanent session at the level of military representatives and is assisted by an integrated international military staff. It provides general policy guidance of a military nature to the Council.

The area covered by the North Atlantic Treaty was divided among three commands: The Atlantic Ocean Command, the European Command and the Channel Command. These were replaced by two commands in Jul 1994: the European and the Atlantic.

The *Canada–US Regional Planning Group*, which covers the North American area, develops and recommends to the Military Committee plans for the defence of this area. It meets alternately in Washington and Ottawa.

WESTERN EUROPEAN UNION
(WEU)

On 17 Mar 1948 a 50-year treaty 'for collaboration in economic, social and cultural matters and for collective self-defence' was signed in Brussels by the Foreign Ministers of the UK, France, the Netherlands, Belgium and Luxembourg.

On 20 Dec 1950 the Western Union defence organization was merged with the North Atlantic Treaty command.

After the rejection by France of the European Defence Community on 30 Aug 1954 a conference was held in London from 28 Sep to 3 Oct 1954, attended by Belgium, Canada, France, Federal Germany, Italy, the Netherlands, Luxembourg, the UK and the USA, at which it was decided to invite the Federal Republic of Germany and Italy to accede to the Brussels Treaty, to end the occupation of Western Germany and to invite the latter to accede to the North Atlantic Treaty; the Federal Republic agreed that it would voluntarily limit its arms production, and provision was made for the setting up of an agency to control the armaments of the seven Brussels Treaty powers; the UK undertook not to withdraw from the Continent her four divisions and the Tactical Air Force assigned to the Supreme Allied Commander against the wishes of a majority, *i.e.* four, of the Brussels Treaty powers, except in the event of an acute overseas emergency. The Union was formally inaugurated on 6 May 1955.

Members in Feb 1995: Belgium, France, Germany, Greece, Italy, Luxembourg, the Netherlands, Portugal, Spain and the UK. Denmark and Ireland are observers, Iceland, Norway and Turkey are associated members and Bulgaria, the Czech Republic, Estonia, Hungary, Latvia, Lithuania, Poland, Romania and Slovakia are associate partners.

The *Council of WEU* consists of the Foreign Ministers of the member countries or their representatives. An Assembly, composed of the WEU delegates to the Consultative Assembly of the Council of Europe, meets twice a year, usually in Paris. An *Agency for the Control of Armaments* and a *Standing Armaments Committee* have been set up in Paris. The social and cultural activities were transferred to the Council of Europe on 1 Jun 1960.

Headquarters: 4 rue de la Régence, B-1000, Brussels, Belgium.
Secretary-General: José Cutileiro (Portugal).

COUNCIL OF EUROPE

In 1948 the 'Congress of Europe', bringing together at The Hague nearly 1000 influential Europeans from 26 countries, called for the creation of a united Europe, including a European Assembly. This proposal, examined first by the Ministerial Council of the Brussels Treaty Organization, then by a conference of ambassadors, was at the origin of the Council of Europe. The Statute of the Council was signed in London on 5 May 1949 and came into force two months later. The founder members were Belgium, Denmark, France, Ireland, Italy, Luxembourg, the Netherlands, Norway, Sweden and the UK. Turkey and Greece joined in 1949, Iceland in 1950, the Federal Republic of Germany in 1951 (having been an associate since 1950), Austria in 1956, Cyprus in 1961, Switzerland in 1963, Malta in 1965, Portugal in 1976, Spain in 1977, Liechtenstein in 1978, San Marino in 1988, Finland in 1989, Hungary in 1990 and Czechoslovakia (after partitioning the Czech Republic and Slovakia rejoined in 1993) and Poland in 1991, Bulgaria in 1992, Estonia, Lithuania, Romania and Slovenia in 1993, Andorra in 1994 and Albania, Latvia, Macedonia, Moldova and the Ukraine in 1995.

Membership is limited to European states which 'accept the principles of the rule of law and of the enjoyment by all persons within (their) jurisdiction of human rights and fundamental freedoms'. The Statute provides for both withdrawal (Art. 7) and suspension (Arts 8 and 9). Greece withdrew from the Council in Dec 1969 and rejoined in Nov 1974.

Structure. Under the Statute two organs were set up: an inter-governmental *Committee of* (Foreign) *Ministers* with powers of decision and of recommendation to governments, and an inter-parliamentary deliberative body, the *Parliamentary Assembly* – both of which are served by the Secretariat. In addition, a large number of committees of experts have been established, two of them, the Council for Cultural Co-operation and the Committee on Legal Co-operation, having a measure of autonomy; on municipal matters the Committee of Ministers receives the recommendations from the European Local Authorities Conference. The Committee of Ministers meets usually twice a year, their deputies monthly.

The Parliamentary Assembly consists of 263 persons elected or appointed by their national parliaments; it meets three times a year. The work of the Assembly harmonizes relations between the two organs.

Under the European Convention of 1950 a special structure has been established for the protection of human rights. A European Commission investigates alleged violations of the Convention submitted to it either by states or, in some cases, by individuals. Its findings can then be examined by the European Court of Human Rights (set up in 1959), whose obligatory jurisdiction has been recognized by 20 states, or by the Committee of Ministers, empowered to take binding decisions by two-thirds majority vote.

For questions of national refugees and over-population, a Special Representative has been appointed, responsible to the governments collectively.

Aims and Achievements. Art 1 of the Statute states that the Council's aim is 'to achieve a greater unity between its members for the purpose of safeguarding and realizing the ideals and principles which are their common heritage and facilitating their economic and social progress'; 'this aim shall be pursued . . . by discussion of questions of common concern and by agreements and common action'. The only limitation is provided by Art 1 (d), which excludes 'matters relating to national defence'.

It has been the task of the Assembly to propose action to bring European countries closer together, to keep under constant review the progress made and to voice the views of European public opinion on the main political and economic questions of the day. The Ministers' role is to translate the Assembly's recommendations into action, particularly as regards lowering the barriers between the European countries, harmonizing their legislation or introducing where possible common European laws, abolishing discrimination on grounds of nationality and undertaking certain tasks on a joint European basis.

In May 1966 the Committee of Ministers approved a programme designed to streamline the activities of the Council of Europe. It comprises projects for co-operation between member governments in economic, legal, social, public health, environmental and educational and scientific matters; and is to be reviewed every year.

18

Some 152 conventions and agreements have been concluded, covering such matters as social security, patents, extradition, medical treatment, training of nurses, equivalence of degrees and diplomas, cultural affairs, protection of archaeological heritage, conservation of European wild life and natural habitat, innkeepers' liability, compulsory motor insurance, the protection of television broadcasts, adoption of children, transportation of animals and *au pair* replacement. A *Social Charter* sets out the social and economic rights which all member governments agree to guarantee to their citizens.

The official languages are English and French.

Headquarters: Palais de l'Europe, Strasbourg, France.

EUROPEAN UNION
(EU)

In May 1950, Belgium, France, the Federal Republic of Germany, Italy, Luxembourg and the Netherlands started negotiations with the aim of ensuring continual peace by a merging of their essential interests. The negotiations culminated in the signing in 1951 of the Treaty of Paris creating the European Coal and Steel Community (ECSC). After it was found impossible to create European Communities covering Defence and Foreign Affairs, two more communities with the aims of gradually integrating the economies of the six nations and of moving towards closer political unity, the European Economic Community (EEC) and the European Atomic Energy Community (EAEC or Euratom) were created in 1957 by the signing of the Treaties of Rome.

On 30 Jun 1970 membership negotiations began between the Six and the United Kingdom, Denmark, Ireland and Norway. On 22 Jan 1972 those four countries signed a Treaty of Accession, although this was rejected by Norway in a referendum in Nov 1972. On 1 Jan 1973 the UK, Denmark and Ireland became full members. On 28 May 1979 the Greek Treaty of Accession was signed, and Greece joined the Community on 1 Jan 1981; Spain and Portugal on 1 Jan 1986, and Austria, Finland and Sweden on 1 Jan 1995.

In Dec 1985 the Treaties were amended again by the Single European Act. In a consultative referendum held on 24 Feb 1982, Greenlanders voted by 12 615 to 11 180 to withdraw from the European Community and this was achieved in 1985.

The institutional arrangements of the Communities provide for an independent executive with powers of proposal (the Commission), various consultative bodies, and a decision-making body drawn from the governments (the Council). Until 1967 the three Communities were completely distinct, although they shared some non-decision-making bodies: from that date the executives were merged in the European Commission, and the decision-taking bodies in the Council. The institutions and organs of the Communities are as follows:

The **Commission** consists of 20 members appointed by the member states to serve for 4 years. Austria, Belgium, Denmark, Finland, Greece, Ireland, Luxembourg, the Netherlands, Portugal, and Sweden all have one Commissioner each, whilst France, Germany, Italy, Spain and the UK have two each. The Commission acts independently of any country in the interests of the Community as a whole, with as its mandate the implementation and guardianship of the Treaties. In this it has the right of initiative (putting proposals to the Council for action); and execution (once the Council has decided); and can take the other institutions or individual countries before the Court of Justice should any of these renege upon their responsibilities.

Presidents of the High Authority of the European Coal and Steel Community:

1952	Jean Monnet
1955	René Mayer
1958	Paul Finet
1959	Piero Malvestiti
1963	Dino Del Bo

Presidents of the Commission of the European Economic Community:

1958	Walter Hallstein

Presidents of the Commission of the European Atomic Energy Community:

1958	Louis Armand
1959	Étienne Hirsch
1962	Pierre Chatenet

The Institutions of the three Communities were merged on 1 Jul 1967.
Presidents of the European Communities/European Union:

1967	Jean Rey
1970	Franco-Maria Malfatti
1972	Sicco Mansholt
1973	François-Xavier Ortoli
1977	Roy Jenkins

1981	Gaston Thorn
1985	Jacques Delors
1995	Jacques Santer

The **Council of the European Union** consists of ministers from the 15 national governments and represents the national as opposed to the Community interests. It is the body which has the power of decision in the Community.

Each member state has the following votes at the Council, making a total of 87:

Austria	4	Italy	10
Belgium	5	Luxembourg	2
Denmark	3	Netherlands	5
Finland	3	Portugal	5
France	10	Spain	8
Germany	10	Sweden	4
Greece	5	United Kingdom	10
Ireland	3		

The qualified majority is 62, simple majority 44, blocking majority 26.

The Presidency of the Council rotates every six months, in January and July, and is as follows for 1995–2002:

1995	France and Spain	1999	Germany and Finland
1996	Italy and Ireland	2000	Portugal and France
1997	Netherlands and Luxembourg	2001	Sweden and Belgium
1998	United Kingdom and Austria	2002	Spain and Denmark

The **European Parliament** consists of 626 members elected by all member states. The division of the seats (1997) was as follows:

Austria	21	Italy	87
Belgium	25	Luxembourg	6
Denmark	16	Netherlands	31
Finland	16	Portugal	25
France	87	Spain	64
Germany	99	Sweden	22
Greece	25	United Kingdom	87
Ireland	15		

21

The Parliament has a right to be consulted on a wide range of legislative proposals, and forms one arm of the Communities' Budgetary Authority.

The **Court of Justice** is composed of 13 judges and 6 advocates general, is responsible for the adjudication of disputes arising out of the application of the treaties, and its findings are enforceable in all member countries.

President: Gil Carlos Rodríguez Iglesias (Spain).

Address: Palais de la Cour de Justice, Kirchberg, Luxembourg.

The office of European Union **Ombudsman** was established in 1995.

Ombudsman: Jacob Söderman (Finland)

The **Economic and Social Committee** has an advisory role and consists of 189 representatives of employers, trade unions, consumers, etc.

The **Court of Auditors** was established by a Treaty of 22 Jul 1975 which took effect on 1 Jun 1977. It consists of 12 members and was raised to the status of a full EU institution by the 1993 Maastricht Treaty. It audits all income and current and past expenditure of the EU.

The **European Investment Bank** (EIB) was created in 1958 by the EEC Treaty to which its statute is annexed. Its governing body is the Board of Governors consisting of ministers designated by member states. Its main task is to contribute to the balanced development of the common market in the interest of the Community by financing projects; for developing less-developed regions; modernizing or converting undertakings; or developing new activities.

The **European Monetary Institute** based in Frankfurt, Germany was established in 1993 by the Maastricht Treaty. It is planned that this institution will develop into a European central bank responsible for issuing and administering a single currency.

The **Schengen Agreement** was signed in 1990 by France, Federal Republic of Germany, Belgium, Luxembourg and the Netherlands. The Agreement committed the signatories to abolishing internal border controls. Spain and Portugal later became members and in Mar 1995 removal of frontier, passport, customs and immigration controls came into force, but France re-introduced border controls in Jun 1995. France was refused a longer period of trial. Austria joined in 1995, Italy and Greece in 1996.

Other bodies include:

The Committee of Regions
European Drug Agency
European Medical Evaluation Agency
European Agency for Health and Safety
European Office of Veterinary and Plant Health Inspection
European Trademark Office
European Drugs Observatory
European Foundation for Training
European Centre for the Development of Vocational Training
European Environment Agency
European Translation Agency

EUROPEAN FREE TRADE ASSOCIATION
(EFTA)

The Stockholm Convention establishing the Association entered into force on 3 May 1960. Founder members were Austria, Denmark, Norway, Portugal, Sweden, Switzerland and the UK. With the accession of Austria, Denmark, Finland, Portugal, Sweden and the UK to the EU, EFTA was reduced to four member countries by 1996: Iceland, Liechtenstein, Norway and Switzerland.

Free trade in industrial goods among members was achieved by 1996. Co-operation with the EU began in 1972 with the signing of free trade agreements and culminated in the establishment of a European Economic Area (EEA), encompassing the free movement of goods, services, capital and labour throughout EFTA and EU countries. The EEA Agreement was signed by all members of the EU and EFTA on 2 May 1992, but was rejected by Switzerland in a referendum on 6 Dec 1992. Entry into force took place on 1 Jan 1994.

Its main provisions are: Free movement of products within the EEA from 1993 (special arrangements to cover food, energy, coal and steel); EFTA to assume EU rules on company law, consumer protection, education, the environment, research and development and social policy; EFTA to adopt EU competition rules on antitrust matters, abuse of a dominant position, public procurement, mergers and state aid; EFTA to create an EFTA Surveillance Authority and an EFTA Court; individuals to be free to live, work and offer services throughout the EEA, with mutual recognition of professional qualifications; capital movements to be free with some restrictions on investments; EFTA countries to maintain their own domestic agricultural policies if they wish.

COMMONWEALTH OF INDEPENDENT STATES
(CIS)

The Commonwealth of Independent States (CIS) is a multilateral grouping of independent states which proclaimed itself the successor to the Union of Soviet Socialist Republics (USSR) in some aspects of international law and affairs. The member states are the founders, Russia, Belarus and the Ukraine, and nine subsequent adherents: Armenia, Azerbaijan, Georgia, Kazakhstan, Kyrgyzstan, Moldova, Tajikistan, Turkmenistan and Uzbekistan. The common affairs of the CIS are conducted on a multilateral, interstate basis rather than by central institutions. It provides a framework for military, foreign policy and economic co-ordination.

Extended negotiations in the USSR in 1990 and 1991, under the direction of President Gorbachev, sought to establish a 'renewed federation' or, subsequently, to conclude a new union treaty that would embrace all the 15 constituent republics of the USSR at that date. According to a referendum conducted in Mar 1991, 76 per cent of the population (on an 80 per cent turn-out) wished to maintain the USSR as a 'renewed federation of equal sovereign republics in which the human rights and freedoms of any nationality would be fully guaranteed'. In Sep 1991 the three Baltic republics, Estonia, Latvia and Lithuania, were nonetheless recognized as independent states by the USSR State Council, and subsequently by the international community. Most of the remaining republics reached agreement on the broad outlines of a new 'union of sovereign states' in Nov 1991, which would have retained a directly elected President and an all-union legislature, but which would have limited central authority to those powers specifically delegated to it by the members of the union.

A referendum in the Ukraine in Dec 1991, however, showed overwhelming support for full independence, and following this Russia, Belarus and the Ukraine concluded an agreement on 8 Dec 1991 establishing a Commonwealth of Independent States (CIS) with its headquarters in Minsk. The USSR, as a subject of international law and a geopolitical reality, was declared no longer in existence, and each of the three republics individually renounced the 1922 treaty through which the USSR had been established.

The CIS declared itself open to other former Soviet republics, as well as to states elsewhere that shared its objectives, and on 21 Dec 1991 in Alma Ata a further declaration was signed by representatives of the three original members and of eight other republics: Armenia, Azerbaijan, Kazakhstan, Kyrgyzstan, Moldova, Tajikistan, Turkmenistan and Uzbekistan. The declaration committed those who signed it to recognize the independence and sovereignty of other members, to respect human rights including those of national minorities, and to the observance of existing boundaries. Relations among the members of the CIS were to be conducted on an equal, multilateral basis, but it was agreed to endorse the principle of unitary control of strategic nuclear arms and the concept of a 'single economic space'. Members pledged themselves to discharge the obligations that arose from the international treaties and agreements to which the USSR had been a party. In a separate agreement the heads of member states agreed that Russia should take up the seat at the United Nations formerly occupied by the USSR, and a framework of inter-state and inter-government consultation was established. Following these developments, Mikhail Gorbachev resigned as USSR President on 25 Dec 1991 and on 26 Dec the USSR Supreme Soviet voted a formal end to the treaty of union that had been signed in 1992 and dissolved itself.

The 'supreme organ' of the CIS is a **Council of Heads of States**; associated with its work is a **Council of Heads of Government**. At a summit meeting of heads of all the states except Azerbaijan in Jul 1992, agreements were reached on the formation of a CIS peacekeeping force, the establishment of an economic arbitration court and a way to divide former Soviet assets abroad, and some progress was made towards the creation of economic co-ordinating structures. At their subsequent meeting in Jan 1993 Russia, Belarus, Armenia, Kazakhstan, Kyrgyzstan, Turkmenistan and Uzbekistan agreed on a charter to establish a defence alliance, an economic co-ordination committee and an inter-state court. Three participants (Ukraine, Moldova and Tajikistan) agreed only to a declaration that any state would be free to sign the charter in future, and that an inter-state bank should be set up.

On 24 Sep 1993 Russia, Armenia, Azerbaijan, Belarus, Kazakhstan, Kyrgyzstan, Moldova, Tajikistan and Uzbekistan signed an agreement to form an economic union, with Ukraine and Turkmenistan as associated members. Georgia signed some provisions.

A summit meeting in Dec 1993 established a **Council of CIS Foreign Ministers**. In Mar 1994 the CIS was accorded observer status in the United Nations.

In Dec 1993 the **CIS Inter-State Bank** was set up to facilitate multilateral clearing of CIS inter-state transactions with a starting capital of 5000m. roubles.

The former USSR railway network is administered by the **CIS Railway Council** through operating authorities set up in 1991 in each member country.

Meeting in Jul 1992, representatives of the defence and foreign ministries of member states agreed on the creation of a peacekeeping force (white helmets) to be deployed in intra-CIS conflicts at the request of member states, and with the consent of the parties to the conflict. CIS members contribute to this force in proportion to the size of their armed forces; the commander is appointed on each occasion by the CIS heads of state.

The *administrative centre* is in the Supreme Soviet, Minsk, Belarus.

THE WARSAW PACT

On 14 May 1955 the USSR, Albania, Bulgaria, Czechoslovakia, the German Democratic Republic, Hungary, Poland and Romania signed, in Warsaw, a 20-year treaty of friendship and collaboration, after the USSR had (on 7 May) annulled the 20-year treaties of alliance with the UK (1942) and France (1944).

The main provisions of the Treaty were as follows:

Article 4. In case of armed aggression in Europe against one or several States party to the pact by a State or group of States, each State member of the pact ... will afford to the State or States which are the object of such aggression immediate assistance ... These measures will cease as soon as the Security Council takes measures necessary for establishing and preserving international peace and security.

Article 5. The contracting Powers agree to set up a joint command of their armed forces to be allotted by agreement between the Powers, at the disposal of this command and used on the basis of jointly established principles. They will also take over agreed measures necessary to strengthen their defences.

Article 9. The present treaty is open to other States, irrespective of their social or Government regime, who declare their readiness to abide by the terms of the treaty in order to safeguard peace and security of the peoples.

Article 11. In the event of a system of collective security being set up in Europe and a pact to this effect being signed – to which each party to this treaty will direct its efforts – the present treaty will lapse from the day such a collective security treaty comes into force.

In 1988 (estimate) the armed forces of the Warsaw Pact countries totalled 3 090 000, compared with 2 213 593 NATO forces.

From 1962 Albania was no longer invited to the Warsaw Pact meetings but was not formally expelled. On 8 Jun 1990 Hungary announced that it would cease to participate in Warsaw Pact military activities and would leave the alliance at the end of 1991. East Germany formally withdrew from the Pact on 24 Sep 1990.

On 19 Nov 1990 the Warsaw Pact nations signed the Conventional Forces in Europe Treaty in Paris.

The Warsaw Pact was formally disbanded on 31 Mar 1991.

COUNCIL FOR MUTUAL ECONOMIC ASSISTANCE
(COMECON OR CMEA)

Membership. Founder members, in 1949, were USSR, Bulgaria, Czechoslovakia, Hungary, Poland and Romania. Later admissions were Albania (1949; ceased participation 1961), Cuba (1972), German Democratic Republic (1950), Mongolia (1962) and Vietnam (1978). From 1964 Yugoslavia enjoyed associated status with limited participation. Afghanistan, Angola, Ethiopia, Laos, Mozambique, Nicaragua and Yemen sent observers to some CMEA bodies.

The Charter consisted of a preamble and 17 articles.
Extracts from the Charter:

Article 1 *Aims and Principles*: '(1) The purpose of the Council is to facilitate, by uniting and coordinating the efforts of its member countries, the planned development of the national economy, acceleration of economic and technical progress in these countries, a rise in the level of industrialization in countries with less developed industries, uninterrupted growth of labour productivity and a steady advance of the welfare of the peoples. (2) The Council is based on the principles of the sovereign equality of all member countries.'

Article 2 *Membership* 'open to other countries which subscribe to the purposes and principles of the Council'.

Article 3 *Functions and Powers* to (a) 'organize all-round ... cooperation of member countries in the most rational use of natural resources and acceleration of the development of their productive forces', (b) 'foster the improvement of the international socialist division of labour by coordinating national economic development plans, and the specialization and cooperation of production in member countries', (d) to 'assist ... carrying out joint measures for the development of industry and agriculture ... transport ... principal capital investments ... [and] trade'.

Article 4 *Recommendations and Decisions* '. . . shall be adopted only with the consent of the interested member countries'.

The supreme authority was the *Session* of all members held (usually annually) in members' capitals in rotation. All decisions were unanimous. The Executive Committee was made up of one representative from each member state of deputy premier rank. It met at least once every three months and had a *Bureau for Common Questions of Economic Planning*. The administrative organ was the *Secretariat*.

In 1988 the Secretariat and its subordinate committees and permanent commissions were reduced in size and reorganized. Decision-making on trade matters was delegated to enterprise level.

There were 6 Committees: for Co-operation in Planning; for Scientific and Technical Co-operation; for Co-operation in Engineering; for Co-operation in the Agro-Industrial Complex; for Electronics; and for Co-operation in Foreign Economic Relations. There were 11 Permanent Commissions.

The *International Bank for Economic Co-operation* was founded in 1963 with a capital of 300m. roubles and started operating on 1 Jan 1964. It undertook multilateral settlements in 'transferable roubles' (*i.e.* used for intra-COMECON clearing accounts only) and advanced credits to finance trading and other operations.

The *International Investments Bank* was founded in 1970 and went into operation on 1 Jan 1971 with a capital of 1071m. transferable roubles.

COMECON was founded in Jan 1949, partly in response to such Western initiatives as the Marshall Plan, and ostensibly to promote economic development through the joint utilization and co-ordination of resources. In its early years, however, member states were dominated by the Stalinist drive to autarky and the Council remained a façade, functioning merely as a registration agency for bilateral foreign trade and credit agreements. The mid-1950s brought the first attempts to reduce the parallelism in member states' economies, and the Council began to function as a discussion centre for long-term plan co-ordination, a process perhaps hastened by the signature of the Treaty of Rome in 1957.

In 1962 Khrushchev, with the support of the more industrialized members (Czechoslovakia, East Germany, Poland) attempted to convert COMECON from a trade organization into a supra-national authority under which member states' economies would be integrated according to the 'international socialist division of labour'.

Integration plans failed at this stage, partly owing to domestic developments in the USSR (dismissal of Khrushchev), and partly owing to the obstructionist attitude of Romania, who objected to the status of non-industrialized raw-material producer.

28

In the aftermath of the USSR's invasion of Czechoslovakia, renewed Soviet pressure in 1969 for integration encountered rather less intransigence. Romania refused to adhere to the International Investments Bank when it was first mooted in 1970, but joined eventually in 1971. Hungary and Poland propounded a view that a free trade area with preferential tariffs should be formed and individual currencies should ultimately be made convertible.

On 10 Jan 1990 COMECON agreed gradually to adopt a free-market approach to their trading policies, and in a final communiqué stressed the need for 'renewal of the whole system of mutual co-operation'. COMECON finally collapsed in 1991 after the revolutions in Eastern Europe.

ORGANIZATION FOR SECURITY AND CO-OPERATION IN EUROPE
(OSCE)

Initiatives from both NATO and the Warsaw Pact culminated in the first summit Conference on Security and Co-operation in Europe (CSCE) attended by heads of state and government in Helsinki on 30 Jul–1 Aug 1975, which adopted a 'Final Act' laying down ten principles concerning human rights, self-determination and the inter-relations of the participant states. Conferences followed in Belgrade (1977–1978), Madrid (1980–1983), Stockholm (1984–1986) and Vienna (1986–1989). At the Paris summit of 19–21 Nov 1990, the members of NATO and the Warsaw Pact signed a Treaty on the Reduction of Conventional Forces in Europe (CFE) and a declaration that they were 'no longer adversaries' and did not intend to 'use force against the territorial integrity or political independence of any state'. All the 34 participants adopted the Confidence and Security-Building Measures (CSBMs), applying to the exchange of military information, verification of military installations, objection to unusual military activities etc., and signed the Charter of Paris.

On 1 Jan 1995 the CSCE changed its name to the Organization for Security and Co-operation in Europe (OSCE).

Members. In 1996 the 55 member nations were: Albania, Andorra, Armenia, Austria, Azerbaijan, Belarus, Belgium, Bosnia-Hercegovina, Bulgaria, Canada, Croatia, Cyprus, the Czech Republic, Denmark, Estonia, Finland, France, Georgia, Germany, Greece, Hungary, Iceland, Ireland, Italy, Kazakhstan, Kyrgyzstan, Latvia, Liechtenstein, Lithuania, Luxembourg, Macedonia, Malta, Moldova, Monaco, Netherlands, Norway, Poland, Portugal, Romania, Russia (succeeding USSR), San Marino, Slovakia,

Slovenia, Spain, Sweden, Switzerland, Tajikistan, Turkey, Turkmenistan, Ukraine, UK, USA, Uzbekistan, Vatican and Yugoslavia.

The *Charter* sets out principles of human rights, democracy and the rule of law to which all the signatories undertake to adhere, lays down the bases for east–west co-operation and other future action, and institutionalizes the OSCE. The *Council of Foreign Ministers* is the highest decision-making body and meets at least once a year. The Council's agent is the Committee of Senior Officials. It meets four times a year at the Secretariat in Prague. There is also a *Conflict Prevention Centre* in Vienna and an *Office for Democratic Institutions and Human Rights* in Warsaw. The Parliamentary Assembly is formally independent, but maintains close links with the OSCE process. Meetings take place annually in OSCE capitals in rotation. It has a secretariat in Copenhagen. The High Commissioner on National Minorities has the duty of early and impartial evaluation of ethnic conflicts and recommendation of action. There is an office in The Hague.

In Jul 1992 the member nations unanimously agreed to set up an armed peacekeeping force.

Secretary-General: Wilhelm Hoynck (Federal Republic of Germany).

EUROPEAN BANK FOR RECONSTRUCTION AND DEVELOPMENT
(EBRD, BERD)

A treaty to establish the EBRD was signed in May 1990; it was inaugurated on 15 Apr 1991. It had 41 original members: the European Commission, the European Investment Bank, all the EEC countries and all the countries of East Europe except Albania. Albania became a member in Oct 1991, and all the republics of the former USSR in Mar 1992, bringing membership to 59 in 1996.

Its founding capital was of ecu 10m., of which the USA contributed 10 per cent, the UK, France, Germany, Italy and Japan 8.5 per cent each, and the USSR 6 per cent. It was established to lend funds at market rates to Central and Eastern European companies and countries 'which are committed to, and applying, the principles of multi-party democracy and market economics'. Facilities were extended to the countries of the former USSR in 1992.

In 1991 the initial emphasis was placed on programmes to support the creation and strengthening of infrastructure; privatization, reform of the financial sector, including development of capital markets and privatization of commercial banks; development of productive competitive private sectors of small and medium-sized enterprises in industry, agriculture and services; restructuring industrial sectors to put them on a competitive basis; encouraging foreign investment and cleaning up the environment.

There is a Board of Governors with full management powers, and a 23-member Board of Directors which is involved in day-to-day operations.

President: Jacques de Larosière (France).

OTHER EUROPEAN ORGANIZATIONS

	founded
Economic Commission for Europe (ECE)	1947
Brussels Treaty Organization	1948
Danube Commission	1949
Inter-governmental Committee for European Migration	1952
Nordic Council	1952
European Conference of Ministers of Transport (ECMT)	1953
European Organization of Nuclear Research (CERN)	1953
European Civil Aviation Conference (CEAC)	1955
European Nuclear Energy Agency (ENEA)	1957
Benelux Economic Union	1958
European Conference of Postal and Telecommunications Administrations (CEPT)	1959
European Organization for the Safety of Air Navigation (EUROCONTROL)	1963
European Space Agency (ESA)	1975

2 HEADS OF STATE

ALBANIA

Declared independent 1912, invaded by Austria in 1916. Italian C.-in-C. in Albania proclaims independence again on 3 Jun 1917. A provisional republican government ruled until 1921, followed by government under a Council of Regents until Jan 1925, when Albania was proclaimed a Republic.

PRESIDENT

Ahmed Beg Zogu   31 Jan 1925–30 Aug 1928

Albania was proclaimed a monarchy on 1 Sep 1928 and the President became King Zog I.

KING

Zog I, m. Countess Geraldine Apponyi   1 Sep 1928–13 Apr 1949
                                         (formally deposed *in absentia*
                                                              2 Jan 1946)
Victor Emmanuel III of Italy (*see* Italy)   14 Apr 1939–30 Nov 1943
                                   (reigned following Italian invasion until
                                  Italian cabinet nullified his Albanian title)

Between 1 Dec 1943 and 1 Dec 1945 there were provisional governments with no head of state. The Republic was proclaimed 12 Jan 1946.

PRESIDENT

Omer Nishani	13 Jan 1946–24 Jul 1953
Haxhi Lleshi	24 Jul 1953–22 Nov 1982
Ramiz Alia	22 Nov 1982–8 Apr 1992
Sali Berisha	9 Apr 1992–

The President is a nominal Head of State; power was held by the First Secretary of the Central Committee: Enver Hoxha, who died 11 Apr 1985, when Ramiz Alia became First Secretary.

ANDORRA

Under the 1993 Constitution, Andorra became an independent, democratic parliamentary co-principality with sovereignty vested in the people rather than the two co-princes, the President of France and the Bishop of Urgel. The co-princes remain heads of state but with limited powers.

ARMENIA

Independence from the USSR was declared on 30 Sep 1991.

PRESIDENT

L. Ter-Petrosyan   16 Oct 1991–

AUSTRIA

EMPEROR

Ferdinand I, succeeded his father	2 Mar 1835–2 Dec 1848 (abdic.)
Francis Joseph I, m. Elizabeth of Bavaria, succeeded his uncle	2 Dec 1848–21 Nov 1916
Karl, m. Zita of Bourbon-Parma, succeeded his great-uncle	21 Nov 1916–11 Nov 1918 (deposed)

The Republic was proclaimed on 12 Nov 1918.

PRESIDENT

X. Seits (President of the National Assembly and stood in for a head of state)	12 Nov 1918–9 Nov 1920
M. Hainisch	9 Dec 1920–4 Dec 1928
Dr W. Miklas	5 Dec 1928–13 Mar 1938

Austria was incorporated into the German Reich on 12 Mar 1938. For 1938–1945 *see* Germany. A provisional government was installed on liberation, 28 Apr 1945.

PRESIDENT

K. Renner	20 Dec 1945–31 Dec 1950
T. Körner	27 May 1951–4 Jan 1957

A. Schárf	5 May 1957–28 Feb 1965
F. Jonas	23 May 1965–23 Apr 1974 (died)
B. Kreisky	24 Apr 1974–8 Jul 1974 (interim)
R. Kirchschläger	8 Jul 1974–8 Jun 1986
K. Waldheim	8 Jun 1986–8 Jul 1992
T. Klestil	8 Jul 1992–

BELARUS

Belarus became independent in Aug 1991.

PRESIDENT

S. Shuskevich	Sep 1991–28 Jan 1994
M. Hryb	28 Jan 1994–10 Jul 1994
A. Lukashenko	20 Jul 1994–

BELGIUM

KING

Leopold II, m. Marie of Austria, succeeded his father	17 Dec 1865–17 Dec 1909
Albert I, m. Elizabeth of Bavaria, succeeded his uncle Leopold II	17 Dec 1909–17 Feb 1934
Leopold III, m. (i) Astrid of Sweden (ii) Mlle Lilian Baels, succeeded his father	23 Feb 1934–20 Sep 1944
Regency	21 Sep 1944–21 Jul 1950
Leopold III	22 Jul 1950–16 Jul 1951 (abdic.)
Baudouin, m. Fabiola de Mora y Aragón, succeeded his father	17 Jul 1951–31 Jul 1993
Albert II, m. Paola Ruffo di Calabria, succeeded his brother	9 Aug 1993–

BOSNIA–HERCEGOVINA

Bosnia–Hercegovina was recognized as an independent state by the USA and European Union in Apr 1992.

34

PRESIDENT

A. Izetbegovic   Dec 1990–

BULGARIA

KING

Ferdinand of Saxe-Coburg-Gotha
  (elected), m. (i) Marie Louise
  of Parma
  (ii) Eleonore of Reuss Köstritz   7 Jul 1887–4 Oct 1918 (abdic.)
Boris III, m. Giovanña of Savoy,
  succeeded his father   4 Oct 1918–28 Aug 1943
Simeon II, succeeded his father   28 Aug 1943–8 Sep 1946

On 8 Sep 1946 a plebiscite ended the monarchy and established a Republic, which was proclaimed on 15 Sep, but had no head of state until the new constitution came into force on 4 Dec 1947.

PRESIDENT (Chairman of the Presidium)

M. Netchev   9 Dec 1947–27 May 1950
G. Damianov   27 May 1950–27 Nov 1958
D. Ganev   30 Nov 1958–20 Apr 1964
G. Traikov   23 Apr 1964–7 Jul 1971
T. Zhivkov   7 Jul 1971–10 Nov 1989
P. Mladenov   10 Nov 1989–6 Jul 1990
Z. Zhelev   1 Aug 1990–23 Jan 1997
P. Stoyanov   23 Jan 1997–

CROATIA

Croatia declared its independence from Yugoslavia on 30 May 1991.

PRESIDENT

F. Tudjman   19 May 1990–

CYPRUS

From 1918 until 1959 Cyprus was a British dependency; for heads of state *see* United Kingdom. An independent Republic came into being on 16 Aug 1960, the President having been previously elected.

PRESIDENT

Archbishop Makarios[1]	14 Dec 1959–3 Aug 1977 (died)
Spyros Kyprianou	3 Aug 1977–28 Feb 1988
George Vassiliou	28 Feb 1988–28 Feb 1993
Glafcos Clerides	28 Feb 1993–

A Turkish Cypriot Federated State with Rauf Denktash as President was proclaimed 13 Feb 1975.

[1] Nicos Sampson assumed the Presidency on the temporary overthrow of Archbishop Makarios; he was succeeded by Glafcos Clerides on 23 Jul 1974 until 7 Dec 1974.

CZECHOSLOVAKIA

An independent state was founded on 14 Nov 1918, formed from four provinces of the Austrian Empire: Bohemia, Moravia, Silesia, Slovakia. (Hungarian Slovakia and Ruthenia joined the Czechoslovak state in 1920.)

PRESIDENT

Tomas G. Masaryk	14 Nov 1918–13 Dec 1935
Edvard Beneš	18 Dec 1935–4 Oct 1938
Emil Hácha	1 Dec 1938–1 Jun 1945

Edvard Beneš continued as President of the Czech government in exile after Czechoslovakia was proclaimed a German protectorate on 16 Mar 1939. He returned to Prague in 1945. (Slovakia: *see* separate entry.)

PRESIDENT

Edvard Beneš	2 Jun 1945–7 Jun 1948
K. Gottwald	14 Jun 1948–14 Mar 1953
A. Zápotecký	21 Mar 1953–13 Nov 1957
A. Novotný	19 Nov 1957–22 Mar 1968
L. Svoboda	30 Mar 1968–27 May 1975
G. Husák	29 May 1975–10 Dec 1989
V. Havel	29 Dec 1989–31 Dec 1992

The federation of Czechoslovakia was dissolved on 31 Dec 1992.

CZECH REPUBLIC

PRESIDENT

V. Havel   2 Feb 1993–

DENMARK

KING

Christian IX, m. Louise of Hesse-Cassel, formerly Prince Christian of Schleswig-Holstein-Sonderburg-Glücksburg, and appointed heir by the Treaty of London on 8 May 1852	15 Nov 1863–29 Jan 1906
Frederick VIII, m. Louise of Sweden, succeeded his father	29 Jan 1906–14 May 1912
Christian X, m. Alexandrine of Mecklenburg, succeeded his father Frederick VIII	14 May 1912–20 Apr 1947
Frederick IX, m. Ingrid of Sweden, succeeded his father	20 Apr 1947–14 Jan 1972

QUEEN

Margrethe II, m. Henri de Morpezat,
  succeeded her father   14 Jan 1972–

ESTONIA

Proclaimed an independent state 24 Feb 1918. The constitution came into force on 20 Dec 1920, with a provisional government in power. On formation of the cabinet in 1923 the Prime Minister was given powers of head of state.

PRIME MINISTER AND HEAD OF STATE

I. Kukk	25 Nov 1923–15 Dec 1924
M. Jaakson	16 Dec 1924–14 Dec 1925
J. Teemant	15 Dec 1925–8 Dec 1927
M. Toenisson	9 Dec 1927–3 Dec 1928

A. Rei	4 Dec 1928–8 Jul 1929
O. Strandmann	9 Jul 1929–11 Feb 1931
C. Paets	12 Feb 1931–20 Feb 1932
J. Teemant	21 Feb 1932–31 Oct 1932
C. Paets	1 Nov 1932–26 Apr 1933

A new constitution, setting up the office of President, was adopted on 3 Oct 1934. Constantin Paets was appointed President.

The USSR incorporated Estonia as a member on 7 Aug 1940.

On 20 Aug 1991 Estonia declared an end to the transition period to independence from the USSR and this was recognized by the USSR on 6 Sep 1991.

CHAIRMAN OF THE SUPREME COUNCIL

A. Rüütel	– – 1988	– 5 Oct 1992

PRESIDENT

L. Meri	5 Oct 1992–

FINLAND

Proclaimed independent on 6 Dec 1917, and a Regent installed. Republican constitution came into force on 14 Jun 1919.

PRESIDENT

K.J. Ståhlberg	1 Aug 1919–15 Feb 1925
L. Relander	16 Feb 1925–15 Feb 1931
P.E. Svinhufvud	16 Feb 1931–14 Feb 1937
K. Kallio	15 Feb 1937–30 Nov 1940
R. Ryti	19 Dec 1940–4 Aug 1944
C.G.E. Mannerheim	4 Aug 1944–9 Mar 1945
J. Paasikivi	9 Mar 1945–15 Feb 1956
U. Kekkonen	15 Feb 1956–26 Jan 1982
M. Koivisto	26 Jan 1982–1 Mar 1994
M. Ahtisaari	1 Mar 1994–

FRANCE

PRESIDENT OF THE REPUBLIC

E. Loubet	18 Feb 1899–18 Feb 1906
C.A. Fallières	18 Feb 1906–17 Jan 1913
R. Poincaré	17 Jan 1913–17 Jan 1920
P. Deschanel	17 Jan 1920–23 Sep 1920
A. Millerand	23 Sep 1920–10 Jun 1924
G. Doumergue	13 Jun 1924–31 May 1931
P. Doumer	31 May 1931–7 May 1932
A. Lebrun	10 May 1932–11 Jul 1940

Marshal Pétain on 11 Jul 1940 took over the powers of President and added them to his own as Prime Minister. He then appointed a Chief of State.

CHIEF OF STATE

Adm. Darlan	10 Feb 1941–16 Nov 1942
P. Laval	17 Nov 1942–12 May 1945 (left France)

A Government of National Unity was formed on 1 Dec 1945, with Gen. Charles de Gaulle as head of state. He resigned on 2 Feb 1946. A new constitution came into force on 24 Dec 1946 (Fourth Republic).

PRESIDENT OF THE REPUBLIC

V. Auriol	16 Jan 1947–23 Dec 1953
R. Coty	24 Dec 1953–5 Oct 1958

A new constitution came into force on 5 Oct 1958 (Fifth Republic).

PRESIDENT OF THE REPUBLIC

C. de Gaulle	8 Jan 1959–28 Apr 1969
A. Poher	28 Apr 1969–20 Jun 1969 (interim)
G. Pompidou	20 Jun 1969–2 Apr 1974
A. Poher	2 Apr 1974–27 May 1974 (interim)
V. Giscard d'Estaing	27 May 1974–21 May 1981
F. Mitterrand	21 May 1981–17 May 1995
J. Chirac	17 May 1995–

GEORGIA

Proclaimed an independent state 26 May 1918.

PRESIDENT

N. Jordania	26 May 1918–

Georgia was occupied by Soviet forces in 1921, and became a member of the USSR. Georgia became independent of the USSR on 9 Apr 1991.

PRESIDENT

Z. Gamsakhurdia	May 1991–6 Jan 1992
E. Shevardnadze, Chairman of State	
Council from 10 Mar 1992	6 Nov 1992–

GERMANY

The German Empire was established on 18 Jan 1871 with King Wilhelm of Prussia as Emperor. From then until 9 Nov 1918 the Kings of Prussia were Emperors of Germany.

EMPEROR

Wilhelm II, m. Augusta of Schleswig-	15 Jun 1888–9 Nov 1918
Holstein, succeeded his father	(abdicated)

The Republic was proclaimed on the abdication of Kaiser Wilhelm II.

PRESIDENT

F. Ebert	11 Feb 1919–28 Feb 1925
P. von Hindenburg	26 Apr 1925–2 Aug 1934

CHANCELLOR AND FÜHRER

A. Hitler	2 Aug 1934–30 Apr 1945
C. Doenitz	30 Apr 1945–5 Jun 1945

All power was transferred to the Allied Control Council on the surrender of Germany at the end of World War II on 5 Jun 1945. The constitution of the Federal Republic of Germany came into force on 21 Sep 1949 and reunification with the German Democratic Republic occurred on 3 Oct 1990.

PRESIDENT

T. Heuss	12 Sep 1949–1 Jul 1959
H. Lübke	1 Jul 1959–30 Jun 1969
G. Heinemann	1 Jul 1969–30 Jun 1974
W. Scheel	1 Jul 1974–30 Jun 1979
K. Carstens	1 Jul 1979–30 Jun 1984
R. von Weizsäcker	1 Jul 1984–30 Jun 1994
R. Herzog	1 Jul 1994–

The constitution of the German Democratic Republic came into force on 7 Oct 1949; the Republic ceased to exist on 3 Oct 1990.

PRESIDENT

Wilhelm Pieck	11 Oct 1949–7 Sep 1960

The office of President was replaced by the Council of State on 12 Sep 1960.

CHAIRMAN OF THE COUNCIL OF STATE

Walter Ulbricht	12 Sep 1960–1 Aug 1973
Willi Stoph	3 Oct 1973–29 Oct 1976
E. Honecker	29 Oct 1976–18 Oct 1989
E. Krenz	24 Oct 1989–3 Dec 1989
M. Gerlach	6 Dec 1989–5 Apr 1990
S. Bergmann	5 Apr 1990–3 Oct 1990

GREECE

KING

Gëorgios of Schleswig-Holstein-Sonderburg-Glücksburg (elected) m. Olga of Russia	30 Mar 1863–18 Mar 1913
Konstantinos XII, m. Sophia of Prussia, succeeded his father	18 Mar 1913–11 Jun 1917 (abdic.)
Alexandros, succeeded on the expulsion of his father, Konstantinos	12 Jun 1917–25 Oct 1920
Konstantinos XII, recalled by plebiscite to succeed his son	5 Dec 1920–27 Sep 1922 (abdic.)
Gëorgios II, m. Elizabeth of Romania, succeeded his father	27 Sep 1922–18 Dec 1923 (expelled)

A Republic was established by plebiscite on 13 Apr 1924.

PROVISIONAL PRESIDENT

Adm. Konduriotis   20 Dec 1923–18 Mar 1926

DICTATOR

Gen. Pangalos   18 Mar 1926–22 Aug 1926

PROVISIONAL PRESIDENT (Reappointed)

Adm. Konduriotis   4 Dec 1926–14 Dec 1929

PRESIDENT

A. Zaimis   14 Dec 1929–3 Nov 1935

By a plebiscite on 3 Nov 1935 the Republic ended and the monarchy was restored.

KING

Gëorgios II, returned   25 Nov 1935–1 Apr 1947
Paul I, m. Frederika Louise of Brunswick,
    succeeded his brother   1 Apr 1947–6 Mar 1964
Konstantinos XIII, m. Anne-Marie
    of Denmark, succeeded his father   6 Mar 1964–1 Jun 1973

The King handed over his powers to a Regent on 13 Dec 1967 and left Greece. The monarchy was declared abolished on 1 Jun 1973.

PROVISIONAL PRESIDENT

G. Papadopoulos   1 Jun 1973–25 Nov 1973

PRESIDENT

P. Ghizikis   25 Nov 1973–14 Dec 1974
M. Stassinopoulos   18 Dec 1974–20 Jun 1975
K. Tsatsos   20 Jun 1975–12 May 1980
K. Karamanlis   15 May 1980–10 Mar 1985
C. Sartzetakis   29 Mar 1985–5 May 1990
K. Karamanlis   5 May 1990–10 Mar 1995
K. Stefanopoulos   10 Mar 1995–

HUNGARY

The Austrian Emperors ruled Hungary as Emperors until the Dual Monarchy on 12 Jun 1867, when they became separately Emperors of Austria and Kings of Hungary. The Emperor Karl renounced his power in the government of Hungary on 13 Nov 1918.
An independent Republic was proclaimed on 16 Nov 1918.

PROVISIONAL PRESIDENT

Count M. Károlyi   16 Nov 1918–22 Mar 1919

The Soviet Hungarian Republic was proclaimed by Béla Kun's government on 22 Mar 1919, and was followed by a counter-revolutionary régime under Admiral Horthy. In Jun 1920 Hungary was proclaimed a monarchy.

REGENT

Adm. M. von Nagybánya Horthy   1 Mar 1920–16 Oct 1945

A Regency Council was appointed after Horthy's resignation and ruled until the setting up of the Provisional National Government on 24 Dec 1945.
A new republican constitution came into force on 1 Feb 1946.

PRESIDENT

Z. Tildy   1 Feb 1946–30 Jul 1948
A. Szakasits   3 Aug 1948–24 Apr 1950
S. Rónai   8 May 1950–1 Aug 1952

CHAIRMAN OF THE PRESIDIUM

I.M. Dobi   1 Aug 1952–14 Apr 1967

CHAIRMAN OF THE PRESIDING COUNCIL

P. Losonczi   14 Apr 1967–25 Jun 1987
K. Nemeth   28 Jun 1987–29 Jun 1988
B.F. Straub   29 Jun 1988–18 Oct 1989
M. Szuros   18 Oct 1989–3 Aug 1990
A. Göncz   3 Aug 1990–

ICELAND

A sovereign state came into being on 1 Dec 1918, still acknowledging the Danish King as head.

KING

Christian X (*see* Denmark)   1 Dec 1918–24 May 1944

The link with the crown was ended and a republic came into being on 17 Jun 1944.

PRESIDENT

Sveinn Björnssen	17 Jun 1944–24 Jan 1952
Ásgeir Ásgeirsson	1 Jul 1952–1 Aug 1968
Kristján Eldjárn	1 Aug 1968–1 Aug 1980
Vigdis Finnbogadóttir	1 Aug 1980–29 Jun 1996
Olafur Ragnar Grimsson	29 Jun 1996–

IRELAND

By the Irish Free State Agreement Act of 1922 Ireland obtained the status of a self-governing Dominion, still recognizing the British sovereign as head of state.

KING

George V (*see* United Kingdom)
Edward VIII (*see* United Kingdom)
George VI (*see* United Kingdom)

The constitution of the Irish Free State as an independent sovereign state came into force on 29 Dec 1937.

PRESIDENT

Dubhglas de hIde (Dr Douglas Hyde)	25 Jun 1938–24 Jun 1945
S.T. Ó Ceallaigh (S.T. O'Kelly)	25 Jun 1945–24 Jun 1959
Éamon de Valéra	25 Jun 1959–24 Jun 1973
Erskine Childers	25 Jun 1973–17 Nov 1974
Cearbhall Ó Dalaigh	3 Dec 1974–22 Oct 1976
Patrick Hillery	3 Dec 1976–3 Dec 1990
Mary Robinson	3 Dec 1990–

ITALY

KING

Victor Emmanual III, m. Elena of Montenegro,
  succeeded his father Umberto   29 Jul 1900–9 May 1946 (abdic.)
Umberto II, succeeded his father   9 May 1946–13 Jun 1946 (abdic.)

(On 30 Mar 1938 King Victor Emmanual gave unlimited powers to Benito Mussolini to hold in time of war and in the name of the King. Mussolini resigned these powers on 25 Jul 1943.)
  A Republic was proclaimed on 18 Jun 1946.

PRESIDENT

L. Einaudi	10 May 1948–29 Apr 1955
G. Gronchi	29 Apr 1955–6 May 1962
A. Segni	6 May 1962–28 Dec 1964
G. Saragat	28 Dec 1964–29 Dec 1971
G. Leone	29 Dec 1971–15 Jun 1978
A. Fanfani	15 Jun 1978–8 Jul 1978
A. Pertini	9 Jul 1978–3 Jul 1985
F. Cossiga	3 Jul 1985–28 Apr 1992
O.L. Scalfaro	28 May 1992–

LATVIA

Proclaimed a sovereign state on 18 Nov 1918.

PRESIDENT

J. Tschakste	18 Nov 1918–8 Apr 1927
G. Zemgals	8 Apr 1927–8 Apr 1930
A. Kviesis	9 Apr 1930–11 Apr 1936
K. Ulmanis	12 Apr 1936–21 Jul 1940

The USSR agreed to accept Latvia on 6 Aug 1940. The USSR recognized the independence of Latvia on 10 Sep 1991.

CHAIRMAN OF THE SUPREME COUNCIL

A. Gorbunovs   –7 Jul 1993

PRESIDENT

G. Ulmanis   7 Jul 1993–

LIECHTENSTEIN

PRINCE

John II, succeeded his father	12 Nov 1858–11 Feb 1929
Francis I, succeeded his brother	11 Feb 1929–25 Aug 1938
Francis Joseph II, succeeded his great-uncle	26 Jul 1938–13 Nov 1989
Hans-Adam II,[1] succeeded his father	13 Nov 1989–

[1] Prince Hans-Adam II exercised the prerogatives to which the sovereign is entitled from 24 Aug 1984.

LITHUANIA

Proclaimed an independent state 16 Feb 1918
  Constituent assembly elected an acting president on 15 Apr 1920.

ACTING PRESIDENT

A. Stulginskis   15 Apr 1920–8 Jun 1926

PRESIDENT

Dr Grinius	8 Jun 1926–19 Dec 1926
M. Smetona	19 Dec 1926–30 Jun 1940

On 21 Jul 1940 Lithuania voted to become a member of the USSR. The USSR recognized the independence of Lithuania on 10 Sep 1991.

PRESIDENT

A. Brazanskas (Formerly President
  of the Supreme Council and acting
  President)   14 Feb 1993–

LUXEMBOURG

GRAND DUKE

Adolf William of Nassau	23 Nov 1890–17 Nov 1905
William, succeeded his father	17 Nov 1905–25 Feb 1912

GRAND DUCHESS

Marie-Adelaide, succeeded her father	
Grand Duke Willem	26 Jun 1912–15 Jan 1919 (abdic.)
Charlotte, m. Felix of Bourbon	
Parma, succeeded her sister	15 Jan 1919–12 Nov 1964 (abdic.)

GRAND DUKE

Jean, m. Joséphine Charlotte of Belgium,	
succeeded his mother	12 Nov 1964–

MACEDONIA
(FORMER YUGOSLAVIA)

Independence from Yugoslavia was declared on 18 Sep 1991.

PRESIDENT

K. Gligorov	27 Jan 1991–

MALTA

A Republic was established on 13 Dec 1974 with a president.

PRESIDENT

Sir A. Marno	13 Dec 1974–27 Dec 1976
A. Buttigieg	27 Dec 1976–16 Feb 1982
A. Barbara	16 Feb 1982–15 Feb 1987
P. Xuereb (acting)	15 Feb 1987–4 Apr 1989
C. Tabone	4 Apr 1989–4 Apr 1994
U.M. Bonnici	4 Apr 1994–

MOLDOVA

In Aug 1991 Moldova declared its independence from the USSR.

PRESIDENT

M. Snegur   8 Dec 1991–

MONACO

PRINCE

Albert, m. (i) Lady Mary Douglas Hamilton, (ii) Alice, Dowager Duchess de Richelieu, succeeded his father	10 Sep 1889–26 Jun 1922
Louis II, succeeded his father	26 Jun 1922–9 May 1949
Rainier III, m. Miss Grace Kelly, succeeded his grandfather	9 May 1949–

MONTENEGRO

PRINCE-BISHOP

Nicholas I,[1] succeeded his uncle   Aug 1860–26 Nov 1918

[1] On 28 Aug 1910 Nicholas declared himself King.

THE NETHERLANDS

QUEEN

Wilhelmina, m. Henry of Mecklenburg Schwerin, succeeded her father	23 Nov 1890–4 Sep 1948 (abdic.)
Juliana, m. Bernhard of Lippe-Besterfeld, succeeded her mother	4 Nov 1948–30 Apr 1980 (abdic.)
Beatrix, m. Claus von Amsberg, succeeded her mother	1 May 1980–

NORWAY

KING

Haakon VII, formerly Prince Carl of Denmark, m. Maud of Great Britain, elected to the throne	18 Nov 1905–21 Sep 1957

Olav V, m. Märtha of Sweden,
  succeeded his father   21 Sep 1957–17 Jan 1991
Harald V, m. Sonja Haraldsen,
  succeeded his father   17 Jan 1991–

POLAND

Independent state proclaimed on 5 Nov 1918.

PRESIDENT

J. Piłsudski	11 Nov 1918–9 Dec 1922
Gabriel Narutowicz	9 Dec 1922–16 Dec 1922 (assassinated)
S. Wojciechowski	20 Dec 1922–15 May 1926
I. Moscicki	1 Jun 1926–29 Mar 1939

On 29 Mar 1939 the German occupation of Poland began.

PRESIDENT, HEAD OF THE POLISH GOVERNMENT IN EXILE

W. Raczkiewicz   30 Sep 1939–28 Jun 1945

PRESIDENT

Boleslaw Bierut   28 Jun 1945–21 Jul 1952

On 22 Jul 1952 a new constitution replaced the office of President with a Council of State.

CHAIRMAN OF THE COUNCIL OF STATE

A. Zawadski	20 Nov 1952–7 Aug 1964
E. Ochab	12 Aug 1964–8 Apr 1968
M. Spychalski	10 Apr 1968–23 Dec 1970
J. Cyrankiewicz	23 Dec 1970–28 Mar 1972
H. Jabloński	28 Mar 1972–6 Nov 1985
Gen. W. Jaruzelski[1]	6 Nov 1985–22 Dec 1990

PRESIDENT

L. Walesa	22 Dec 1990–23 Dec 1995
A. Kwásniewski	23 Dec 1995–

[1] On 19 Jul 1989 Jaruzelski was elected President of Poland.

PORTUGAL

KING

Carlos I, m. Maria Amalia of Bourbon-
Orleans, succeeded his father   19 Oct 1889–1 Feb 1908
Manuel II, succeeded his father   1 Feb 1908–5 Oct 1910 (deposed)

Republic proclaimed 5 Oct 1910.

PRESIDENT

T. Braga	5 Oct 1910–19 Jun 1911
–. Braachamp	19 Jun 1911–24 Aug 1911
M. de Arriga	24 Aug 1911–7 Aug 1915
B. Machado	7 Aug 1915–28 Apr 1918
S. Paes	28 Apr 1918–14 Dec 1918 (assassinated)
J. Antunes	16 Dec 1918–5 Oct 1919
A. de Almeida	5 Oct 1919–5 Oct 1923
M.T. Gomes	5 Oct 1923–11 Dec 1925
B.L. Machado Guimarâes	11 Dec 1925–1 Jun 1926

A provisional government was in power from 1 Jun 1926 until 29 Nov 1926.

Marshal A.O.F. Carmona	29 Nov 1926–18 Apr 1951
Marshal F.H.C. Lopes	22 Jul 1951–9 Aug 1958
Rear-Adm. A. de D.R. Tomás	9 Aug 1958–25 Apr 1974
Gen. Antonio de Spinola	15 May 1974–30 Sep 1974
Gen. Francisco da Costa Gomes	30 Sep 1974–27 Jun 1976
Gen. Antonio R. Eanes	14 Jul 1976–16 Feb 1986
M. Soares	16 Feb 1986–9 Mar 1996
J. Sampaio	9 Mar 1996–

ROMANIA

KING

Carol I, elected	14 Mar 1881–10 Oct 1914
Ferdinand I, m. Marie of Saxe-Coburg- Gotha, succeeded his uncle	11 Oct 1914–21 Jul 1927
Mihai (Michael) I, succeeded his grandfather since his father Carol had renounced his rights	21 Jul 1927–8 Jun 1930

Carol II, m. Helen of Greece, succeeded his son by act of parliament	8 Jun 1930–6 Sep 1940 (abdic.)
Mihai (Michael) I, proclaimed on abdication of his father	6 Sep 1940–30 Dec 1947 (abdic.)

As a result of a plebiscite a Republic was established and the King abdicated.

PRESIDENT OF THE PRESIDIUM

C.I. Parhon	13 Apr 1948–23 Jan 1952
P. Groza	2 Jun 1952–7 Jan 1958
I.G. Maurer	11 Jan 1958–21 Mar 1961
G. Gheorghiu-Dej	21 Mar 1961–19 Mar 1965
C. Stoica	22 Mar 1965–9 Dec 1967
N. Ceauçescu	9 Dec 1967–22 Dec 1989
I. Iliescu	3 Jan 1990–

RUSSIA

TSAR

Nicholas II, m. Alexandra of Hesse-Darmstadt, succeeded his father	1 Nov 1894–16 Jul 1918 (murdered)

See USSR

After the dissolution of the USSR in Dec 1991 Russia became a member of the Commonwealth of Independent States and was recognized as an independent state by USA and the European Union in Jan 1992.

PRESIDENT

B. Yeltsin	10 Jul 1991–

SAN MARINO

No titular head of state; co-regents are annually elected.

SERBIA

Serbia became independent of Turkey by the Treaty of Berlin on 13 Jul 1878.

KING

Milan IV Obrenovitch (formerly Prince),
    created King   6 Mar 1882–6 Mar 1889 (abdic.)
Alexander I Obrenovitch, m. Draga   6 Mar 1889–10 Jun 1903
    Mascin   (murdered)
Provisional government   11 Jun 1903
See Yugoslavia.

SLOVAKIA

Slovakia was declared an independent country 14 Mar 1939.

PRESIDENT

J. Tiso   26 Oct 1939–1 Apr 1945

Slovakia was re-incorporated with Czechoslovakia in Apr 1945. The Czechoslovakian Federation was dissolved on 31 Dec 1992.

PRESIDENT

M. Mečiar   15 Feb 1993–

SLOVENIA

Independence from the Yugoslav Federation was declared on 25 Jun 1991.

PRESIDENT

M. Kučan   22 Apr 1990–

SPAIN

KING

Alphonso XIII, m. Victoria Eugenie Battenberg, succeeded his father at his birth	17 May 1886–14 Apr 1931 (abdic.)

A republic was proclaimed on 14 Apr 1931.

PRESIDENT

N.A. Zamora y Torres	10 Dec 1931–7 Apr 1936
M. Azaña	10 May 1936–4 Mar 1939

CHIEF OF THE SPANISH STATE

Gen. Francisco Franco	9 Aug 1939–20 Nov 1975

Prince Juan Carlos de Borbòn y Borbòn, grandson of Alphonso XIII, was sworn in as successor to the Chief of State in Jul 1969.

KING

Juan Carlos, I. m. Sophia of Greece	22 Nov 1975–

SWEDEN

KING

Gustaf V, m. Victoria of Baden, succeeded his father Oscar II	8 Dec 1907–29 Oct 1950
Gustaf IV Adolf, m. (i) Margaret Victoria of Connaught, (ii) Lady Louise Mountbatten, succeeded his father	29 Oct 1950–16 Sep 1973
Carl XVI Gustaf, m. Silva Renate Sommerlath, succeeded his grandfather	16 Sep 1973–

SWITZERLAND

PRESIDENTS (Elected for an annual term)

1900 Walter Hauser	1902 Josef Zemp
1901 Ernest Brenner	1903 Adolf Deucher

1904 Robert Comtesse	1947 Philipp Etter
1905 Marc Ruchet	1948 Enrico Celio
1906 Louis Forrer	1949 Ernst Nobs
1907 Eduard Müller	1950 Max Petitpierre
1908 Ernest Brenner	1951 Eduard von Steiger
1909 Adolf Deucher	1952 Karl Kobelt
1910 Robert Comtesse	1953 Philipp Etter
1911 Marc Ruchet	1954 Rudolphe Rubattel
1912 Louis Forrer	1955 Max Petitpierre
1913 Eduard Müller	1956 Markus Feldmann
1914 Artur Hoffman	1957 Hans Streuli
1915 Giuseppe Motta	1958 Thomas Holenstein
1916 Camille Decoppet	1959 Paul Chaudet
1917 Edmond Schultess	1960 Max Petitpierre
1918 F. Ludwig	1961 Friedrich Trangott Wahlen
1919 Gustave Ador	1962 Paul Chaudet
1920 Giuseppe Motta	1963 Willy Spühler
1921 Edmund Schulthess	1964 Ludwig von Moos
1922 Robert Haab	1965 Hanspeter Tschudi
1923 Karl Scheurer	1966 Hans Schattner
1924 Ernest Chuard	1967 Roger Bonvin
1925 Jean M. Musy	1968 Willy Spühler
1926 Henri Häberlin	1969 Ludwig von Moos
1927 Giuseppe Motta	1970 Hanspeter Tschudi
1928 Edmund Schulthess	1971 Rudolf Gnägi
1929 Robert Haab	1972 Nello Celio
1930 Jean M. Musy	1973 Roger Bonvin
1931 Henri Häberlin	1974 Ernst Brugger
1932 Giuseppe Motta	1975 Pierre Graber
1933 Edmund Schulthess	1976 Rudolf Gnägi
1934 Marcel Pilet-Golaz	1977 Kurt Furgler
1935 Rudolf Minger	1978 Willi Ritschard
1936 Albert Meyer	1979 Hans Hürlimann
1937 Giuseppe Motta	1980 Georges-André Chevallaz
1938 Johannes Baumann	1981 Kurt Furgler
1939 Philipp Etter	1982 Fritz Honegger
1940 Marcel Pilet-Golaz	1983 Pierre Aubert
1941 Ernst Wetter	1984 Léon Schlumpf
1942 Philipp Etter	1985 Kurt Furgler
1943 Enrico Celio	1986 Alphons Egli
1944 Walter Stampfi	1987 Pierre Aubert
1945 Eduard von Steiger	1988 Otto Stich
1946 Karl Kobelt	1989 Jean-Pascal Delamuraz

1990 Arnold Koller
1991 Flavio Cotti
1992 René Felber
1993 Adolf Ogi

1994 Otto Stich
1995 Kaspar Villiger
1996 Jean-Pascal Delamuraz

TURKEY

SULTAN

Abd el Hamid II, succeeded his brother	30 Aug 1876–27 Apr 1909
Mohammed V, succeeded his brother	27 Apr 1909–3 Jul 1918
Mohammed VI, succeeded his brother	3 Jul 1918–1 Nov 1922

The office of Sultan was abolished on 1 Nov 1922 and only that of Caliph (held by the Sultans) retained, to be filled by election from the Osman princes.

CALIPH

Prince Abdul Medjid   17 Nov 1922–2 Mar 1924

A republic was proclaimed on 29 Oct 1923.

PRESIDENT

M. Kemal Atatürk	29 Oct 1923–10 Nov 1938
I. Inönü	11 Nov 1938–21 May 1950
C. Bayar	22 May 1950–27 May 1960
C. Gursel	26 Oct 1961–27 Mar 1966
Cevdet Sunay	28 Mar 1966–28 May 1973
Fahri Korutürk	6 Apr 1973–6 Apr 1980
Ihsan Sabri Caglayangil	6 Apr 1980–12 Sep 1980
Gen. Kenan Evren	12 Sep 1980–9 Nov 1989
T. Özal	9 Nov 1989–17 Apr 1993
H. Cindoruk (acting)	17 Apr 1993–16 May 1993
S. Demirel	16 May 1993–

UKRAINE

Ukraine declared itself independent of the USSR, subject to a referendum, in Aug 1991. At the referendum held on 1 Dec 1991, 90 per cent of the electorate voted for independence.

PRESIDENT

L. Kravchuk	1 Dec 1991–19 Jul 1994
L. Kuchma	19 Jul 1994–

UNION OF SOVIET SOCIALIST REPUBLICS
(USSR)

Constitution for the Federal Republic adopted on 10 Jul 1918, by a government which took office on 8 Nov 1917.

PRESIDENT OF THE COUNCIL OF PEOPLE'S COMMISSARS

V.I. Ulianov-Lenin	8 Nov 1917–29 Dec 1922

A new constitution of 30 Dec 1922 replaced this office by a Central Executive Committee with four chairmen.

A new constitution came into force on 5 Dec 1936 establishing the office of Chairman of the Presidium of the Supreme Soviet of the USSR, as head of state.

CHAIRMAN

M.I. Kalinin	5 Dec 1936–27 Jul 1946
N.M. Shvernik	19 Mar 1946–6 Mar 1953
Marshal K.E. Voroshilov	6 Mar 1953–7 May 1960
L.I. Brezhnev	7 May 1960–15 Jul 1964
A.I. Mikoyan	15 Jul 1964–9 Dec 1965
N.V. Podgorny	9 Dec 1965–16 Jun 1977
L.I. Brezhnev	16 Jun 1977–10 Nov 1982
Y.V. Andropov	16 Jun 1983–9 Feb 1984
K.U. Chernenko	11 Apr 1984–10 Mar 1985
A. Gromyko	14 Mar 1985–30 Sep 1988
M. Gorbachev[1]	1 Oct 1988–25 May 1989

Negotiations in 1990 and 1991 under President Gorbachev attempted to establish a 'renewed federation' and to conclude a new Union Treaty, but these failed and the Union was declared 'no longer in existence' in Dec 1991.

---

[1] On 25 May 1989 M. Gorbachev was elected President of the USSR by the newly constituted 2250-member Congress of People's Deputies.

56

UNITED KINGDOM

QUEEN

Victoria, m. Albert of Saxe-Coburg-Gotha, succeeded her uncle	20 Jun 1837–22 Jan 1901

KING

Edward VII, m. Alexandra of Schleswig-Holstein-Sonderburg-Glücksburg, succeeded his mother	22 Jan 1901–6 May 1910
George V, m. Victoria Mary of Teck, succeeded his father Edward VII	6 May 1910–20 Jan 1936
Edward VIII, succeeded his father	20 Jan 1936–10 Dec 1936 (abdic.)
George VI, m. Lady Elizabeth Bowes-Lyon, succeeded on the abdication of his brother	10 Dec 1936–6 Feb 1952

QUEEN

Elizabeth II, m. Philip of Greece, succeeded her father	6 Feb 1952–

VATICAN

SUPREME PONTIFF

Leo XIII	3 Mar 1878–20 Jul 1903
Pius X	9 Aug 1903–20 Aug 1914
Benedict XV	3 Sep 1914–22 Jan 1922
Pius XI	6 Mar 1922–13 Feb 1939
Pius XII	2 Mar 1939–9 Oct 1958
John XXIII	28 Oct 1958–3 Jun 1963
Paul VI	21 Jun 1963–6 Aug 1978
John Paul I	26 Aug 1978–28 Sep 1978
John Paul II	16 Oct 1978–

YUGOSLAVIA

The state was founded on 29 Dec 1918 as the Serb, Croat and Slovene State (Montenegro joined on 1 Mar 1921). The name was changed to Yugoslavia on 3 Oct 1929.

KING

Peter I, m. Zorka of Montenegro,
elected king   2 Jun 1903–6 Aug 1921
Alexander I, m. Marie of Romania,   6 Aug 1921–9 Oct 1934
succeeded his father   (assassinated)
Peter II, succeeded his father   9 Oct 1934–29 Nov 1945 (abdic.)

On 29 Nov 1945 King Peter abdicated and a Republic was proclaimed.

PRESIDENT OF THE PRESIDIUM

Dr I. Ribar   2 Dec 1945–13 Jan 1953

PRESIDENT OF THE REPUBLIC

Marshal J. Broz-Tito   14 Jan 1953–4 May 1980

HEAD OF THE COLLECTIVE PRESIDENCY

L. Kolisevski   4 May 1980–15 May 1980
C. Mijatović   15 May 1980–15 May 1981
S. Krajger   15 May 1981–15 May 1982
P. Stambolić   15 May 1982–15 May 1983
M. Spiljak   15 May 1983–15 May 1984
V. Djuranović   15 May 1984–15 May 1985
R. Vlajković   15 May 1985–15 May 1986
S. Hasani   15 May 1986–15 May 1987
L. Mojsov   15 May 1987–15 May 1988
R. Dizdarević   15 May 1988–15 May 1989
J. Drnovsek   15 May 1989–15 May 1990
B. Jovic   15 May 1990–15 May 1991
S. Mešić   15 May 1991–15 Jun 1992

FORMER YUGOSLAVIA
(SERBIA AND MONTENEGRO)

Serbia and Montenegro announced on 22 Apr 1992 the formation of
the Federal Republic of Yugoslavia, constituted by themselves, as the
legal successor to the former Socialist Federal Republic of Yugoslavia.

PRESIDENT

D. Cosic   15 Jun 1992–1 Jun 1993
Z. Lilic   25 Jun 1993–

3 PARLIAMENTS

ALBANIA

From 1920 until the Italian invasion Albania had a parliamentary system of government with a single elected chamber, but neither under the Republic nor under the monarchy did this function effectively. Under the Republic formed in 1946 there has been one chamber, the People's Assembly, elected on universal suffrage of all over 18, and sitting for a four-year term. The Assembly elects its Presidium and Council of Ministers. The Chairman of the Presidium is also the head of the state, and the Chairman of the Council of Ministers the Prime Minister. The Assembly, the Council and the Presidium operated on the Soviet pattern; the Assembly sits for short sessions, the Presidium more or less permanently, although the Assembly must meet twice a year. The assembly has one member for each 8000 voters. The Presidium has a chairman and three deputy chairmen, a secretary and ten members. The initiation and passing of legislation, and the exercise of legislative and executive power is the same as in the Soviet Union.

Following anti-government demonstrations after Jul 1990, the political structure of Albania changed. In Dec 1990 a decree was adopted by the People's Assembly legalizing opposition parties (see p. 279). A new constitution was promulgated on 26 Apr 1991. The supreme legislative body is the single-chamber National Assembly of 140 deputies, directly elected for 4-year terms.

A draft new constitution, submitted to a referendum in Nov 1994, was rejected by 53.8 per cent of votes cast.

ARMENIA

Following the collapse of the Soviet Union, the Supreme Soviet in Armenia adopted a declaration of sovereignty in Aug 1990. It voted to unite Armenia with Nagorno-Karabakh and renamed Armenia the 'Republic of Armenia'. A popular vote in Sep 1991 resulted in a 99 per cent majority support for a fully independent status.

On 16 Oct 1991 Levon Ter-Petrosyan was elected the republic's first President in a popular ballot by 83 per cent of votes cast against 5 opponents. Turn-out was 73 per cent.

AUSTRIA

On 12 Nov 18 the Austrian members of the Austro-Hungarian imperial Reichsrat, having constituted themselves the German National Assembly, declared that Austria was a Republic. The following January a Constituent Assembly was elected as supreme authority for the purposes of framing a new constitution which came into operation in Nov 20. The Assembly had one chamber and was elected on universal adult suffrage. The new constitution provided for a bi-cameral federal legislature. The National Council was elected by proportional representation for four years, and could be adjourned only by its own decision. It could be summoned immediately on the request of at least a quarter of its members, or of the government. The Federal Council was elected by the Provincial Diets, having representatives from each province who sat for the length of term of their Diet. The Federal Council could initiate bills through the government; a bill passed by the National Council would be passed to the Federal Council and, if amended by them, reconsidered by the National Council and passable by a majority in that house. The Federal Council had no power to amend estimates.

The President was elected by both houses in joint session, for four years; his duties were mainly ceremonial and symbolic and all acts of government were the responsibility of ministers. The ministers were elected by the National Council on a motion submitted by its Principal Committee, and were not allowed to continue as Council members, if they were, or to become Council members while in office. Legislature and Executive were widely separate. The government suspended parliament in 1933 and in 1934 dissolved the Socialist Party; after strong reaction a new constitution, with socialist leanings, was brought in in 1935, but parliament worked with increasing difficulty until the integration with Germany in 1938, when it virtually ceased to operate.

A constitution similar to that of 1920 was restored in 1945. The state has now a Nationalrat with deputies elected on the original suffrage and a Bundesrat of deputies elected by the Provincial Diets. Bills must pass both houses. In 1996 the Nationalrat had 183 deputies and the Bundesrat 64; of the latter there may be not more than 12 members for any one Province, and not less than three. Bundesrat members are not necessarily members of the Provincial Diets, but they must be eligible to be so; they are elected for varying terms, whereas Nationalrat members sit for four years, two regular sessions being convened each year in spring and autumn. An extraordinary session may be held if the government or one-third of the members of either house demand it.

Bills must pass both houses; they may be initiated by either house or by the government but must be presented in the National Council. There is provision also for the popular initiative; every proposal signed by 200 000 Länder voters or half the voters in each of the three Länder must be submitted to the National Council. The National Council may also request a referendum on a bill which it has assented to. All bills go secondly to the Federal Council which may object to them within eight weeks; the bill becomes law if the National Council reaffirms it with half its members present.

BELARUS

Belarus adopted a declaration of independence from the Soviet Union on 25 Aug 1991. The name 'Republic of Belarus' was adopted in Sep 1991.

A new constitution was adopted on 15 Mar 1994. It provides for a president who must be a citizen of at least 35 years of age, have resided for 10 years in Belarus and whose candidacy must be supported by the signature of 70 deputies or 100 000 electors. Presidential elections were held on 23 Jun 1994. Alyaksandr Lukashenka was elected in the run-off on 11 Jul 1994 with 80 per cent of the votes cast.

BELGIUM

Belgium is a constitutional monarchy with two legislative chambers, the Chamber of Representatives and the Senate. The King shares legislative powers with the two chambers and exercises the executive power in conjunction with his ministers; he may not act alone. He appoints ministers from among members of parliament, and sanctions laws. The Chamber of Representatives consisted until 1995 of 212 members – the maximum was one for every 40 000 inhabitants – elected on proportional representation for four-year terms. Members must be at least 25. The Senate members must be at least 40 and are elected as follows: one member for every 200 000 inhabitants, elected by the provincial councils on proportional representation; half the number of Chamber deputies elected by the same electorate. Constitutionally the Chamber and the Senate both have equal powers; bills may be introduced in both houses and must pass both before being signed by the King. Traditionally the legislature possessed considerable control over the cabinet, since all legislation passes through a strong committee system in both houses. In the years between the two world wars particularly this provided stability when political life was disrupted by Fleming-Walloon or Catholic–Protestant differences.

In 1921 the length of service for members of the Senate was reduced from eight years to four, and the franchise was extended to all men over 21, together with women who were war-widows or war-sufferers. Before 1921 there was a system of plural votes on grounds of property or income. The franchise was extended to women in 1948.

Senate and Chamber meet annually in October (November until 1921) and must sit for at least forty days. the government, through the King, has power to dissolve either chamber separately or both chambers at once. In the latter case a new election must take place within forty days and a meeting of the Chambers within two months; no adjournment for longer than one month may be made without the consent of both Chambers.

Money bills originate in the Chamber of Representatives. There is also a strong subsidiary body – the Court of Accounts – with members appointed by the Chamber with authority to control all treasury work and all provision for revenue and expenditure. By an Act 23 Dec 1946 a Council of State was also set up, with separate sections for legislation and administration on constitutional matters.

In the 1990s Belgium faced a growing constitutional crisis. In Feb 1992, legislation for the first stage of an eventual federal state was introduced in parliament. In Sep 1992, constitutional changes were made to devolve more power to the regions (i.e., to the parliaments of Dutch-speaking Flanders and French-speaking Wallonia). Meanwhile the royal power to accept or refuse prime-ministerial resignations has been ended, as has the monarch's absolute right to dissolve parliament after a vote of no confidence. Further pressure for constitutional change grew after the child sex scandal of 1996.

BOSNIA-HERCEGOVINA

Bosnia-Hercegovina seceded from the Yugoslav federation in Mar 1992, following a referendum which supported full independence. Bosnian independence was recognized by its admission to the United Nations in May 1992, but civil war continued (see p. 358). A provisional agreement for a new constitution was signed on 30 Jul 1993 by all three sides. This was overtaken by a new agreement between the Bosnian government and the Bosnian Croat leadership in Feb 1994. A new Federation of Bosnia and Hercegovina was established in March. The new federal constitution provided for a balance of power between Muslims and Croats in a federation divided according to a cantonal system.

BULGARIA

The constitution of 1879 was still in operation in 1918, after amendment in 1911. The legislature was a single chamber, the National Assembly (Sobranje). Members were elected by universal manhood suffrage; one member for every 20 000 inhabitants. All literate men over 30 were eligible to sit, except for soldiers, clergy and those deprived of civil rights. The term was four years, but the Assembly could be dissolved at any time by the King, and elections held within two months. There was a second, but not permanent, chamber, the Grand Sobranje; this had twice the membership of the Sobranje but was elected only for special purposes. It sat to decide questions on territory, changes to the constitution or the succession to the throne. Both houses were elected on proportional representation. Laws passed by the National Assembly required the assent of the King, who might himself initiate legislation through his ministers. After 1911 the King might also make treaties with foreign powers without having the Assembly's consent; he might also issue regulations and take emergency measures in time of danger, although it was the cabinet who assumed responsibility for such measures. Cabinet members were chosen by the King. They were required to countersign royal acts and were responsible both to the King and to the Assembly.

In Oct 1937 an electoral law fixed the number of Sobranje members at 160 (it had previously had 227) and the size of constituencies to at least 20 000 electors, comprising all men and all married women over 21.

A Republic was proclaimed in Sep 1946 and a new constitution drawn up in Dec 1947 which was replaced, but not significantly altered, by a new one in 1971; it provided for a parliament on the Russian model, except that there was only one assembly, as before, consisting of deputies elected by secret, direct and universal suffrage of all inhabitants over 18, one deputy for every 30 000 – later every 20 000 – inhabitants. The Assembly elected its Presidium of chairman, two deputy chairmen, secretary and 15 members; this was the most powerful organ of the state. There was also a Council of Ministers elected by the National Assembly. The relation of the three bodies to each other was on the Russian pattern.

In Jan 1990 the National Assembly instituted 21 constitutional reforms, including the abolition of the Communist Party's right to be the only governing party. This was followed in Apr 1990 by amendments which created an executive presidency, permitted free multi-party elections, and removed the words 'socialist' and 'communist' from the constitution.

A new constitution was adopted at Turnovo in Jul 1991. The president is directly elected for not more than 2 5-year terms. Candidates for the presidency must be at least 40 years old and have lived for the last 5 years in Bulgaria. Presidential elections were held in Jan 1992.

The 240-member National Assembly is directly elected by proportional representation.

CROATIA

Following the secession from Yugoslavia, Croatia adopted a new constitution on 21 Dec 1990. The president is elected directly for a 5-year term. Parliament consists of the 138-member Sabor, elected by a combination of proportional representation and first-past-the-post methods, and an upper house, the 68-member Chamber of Counties, composed of representatives of counties elected by proportional representation, and 5 members nominated by the President. The role of the Chamber of Counties is primarily consultative.

CYPRUS

An independent Republic was set up in 1960 with a unicameral parliament, the House of Representatives. The House had 50 members, 35 Greek and 15 Turkish, who were directly elected within their respective communities. The communities also had their own Communal Chambers, to which certain domestic issues were reserved. The franchise was universal and the term for members five years. Greek members elected a Greek President of the House, Turkish members a Turkish Vice-President. The Prime Minister and Council of Ministers were appointed by the President of the Republic. In practice the office of President and Prime Minister were combined.

In Dec 1963 the Turkish members ceased to attend parliament. On 13 Feb 1975 a Turkish Cypriot Federated State was formed, having its own legislative assembly and executive council.

CZECHOSLOVAKIA

The constitution of the Republic was put into operation in 1920. It provided for a two-chamber parliament, the National Parliament, which consisted of a Chamber of Deputies and a Senate, elected on proportional representation by all citizens over 21. The Chamber was elected for six years and had 300 deputies; the Senate sat for eight years and had 150 members. Legislation might be introduced by the government or by either of the chambers. Bills passed by the deputies were passed to the Senate for consideration. A bill rejected by the Senate could still become law if passed again with an absolute majority by the deputies. If the Senate rejected it by a three-quarters majority then it required a three-fifths majority to pass in the Chamber. A bill initiated in the Senate died if it was dismissed twice by an absolute majority in the Chamber. Bills relating to money and defence could only be initiated by the deputies. The legislature had no strong control over the government; if the National Parliament rejected a government bill the government could still decide (unanimously) to put the bill to a referendum, provided it was not an amendment to the constitution.

The President (Dr Masaryk) was in fact elected for life, but the constitution provided that in future the President would be elected by the National Parliament for a seven-year term. His election would need the attendance of an absolute majority of the parliament and a three-fifths majority of votes. He was to be head of state, but the government would be responsible for the exercise of his powers. He could not declare war without parliamentary approval. He could dissolve both chambers, but not during the last six months of his presidency. He might return a bill to parliament with his observations on it, when it could only be carried if an absolute majority of all members adhered to it.

The parliament did not operate effectively after Czechoslovakia became a German Protectorate in 1939.

A new constitution of Jun 1948 provided for a single-chamber National Assembly with 300 members elected for six years. In 1953 a Presidium on the Soviet model was set up, with a Chairman (Prime Minister) and ten deputies; later in the same year the number of deputies was reduced to four and the Presidium considerably reduced in power. In 1969 the state became a federation; the new Federal Assembly consisted of the Chamber of Nations, with 75 Czech and 75 Slovak delegates elected by the National Councils of the Czechs and Slovaks, and the Chamber of the People which had 200 deputies elected by national suffrage.

The Federal Assembly had overall responsibility for constitutional and foreign affairs, defence and the federal economy. Other matters fell to the National Councils; the Czech had 200 deputies and the Slovak 150. After 1971 all Deputies, federal and national, were elected for a five-year term.

The Communist Party's monopoly of political power was abolished by the Federal Assembly on 30 Nov 1989 and independent parties were legalized. In Mar 1990 the Assembly passed election laws allowing for free multi-party elections with proportional representation. Assembly deputies were to be elected for two-year terms. In Apr 1990 the state was renamed the Czech and Slovak Federative Republic. On 25 Nov 1992 the Czechoslovak Federal Parliament approved (by three votes) the creation of independent Czech and Slovak states from 1 Jan 1993. These states are now the Czech Republic and Slovakia.

CZECH REPUBLIC

The newly-independent Czech Republic came into existence on 1 Jan 1993. The constitution provides for a parliament comprising a 200-member House of Representatives, elected for 4-year terms by proportional representation, and an 81-member Senate elected for 6-year terms in single-member districts, 27 senators being elected every 2 years.

The president of the republic is elected for a 5-year term by both chambers of parliament. He or she must be at least 40 years of age. The president names the prime minister at the suggestion of the speaker.

There is a Constitutional Court at Brno whose 15 members are nominated by the president and approved by the senate for 10-year terms.

DENMARK

The constitutional Charter of 1915 provided that the legislative power should be held by the King and the Rigsdag (parliament) jointly, and that the executive power be held by the King and exercised through his ministers, although he could not declare war or sign a peace treaty without parliament's consent. There were two chambers: the Folketing (lower house) had 149 members, 117 of them elected by proportional representation and 31 additional seats divided among parties who had insufficient votes to win any. It sat for a four-year term but might be dissolved by the King. There was no specific ruling that the ministers who formed the King's Council of State and who were appointed and dismissed by him, were responsible to the Folketing in the parliamentary sense. The King normally presided over the Council of State; he had the right to object to its decisions and to re-introduce the matter at a future meeting. In his absence the Prime Minister presided. The Landsting had 78 members indirectly elected and sat for a term of eight years; those members elected in the Landsting electoral districts sat for four years, when there was a further election for half of their number; members elected by the former Landsting sat for the whole eight years; there were 56 members elected in the districts and 19 by the Landsting. Parliament was obliged to meet annually in October. Ministers had access to both houses but could only vote in the chamber of which they were members.

The constitutional Charter of Jun 1953 abolished the Landsting. The Folketing remained with 179 members, 135 of them elected in the districts, and 40 additional seats. The Council of State continued to operate as a cabinet, ministers being individually and collectively responsible to the Folketing for their actions. The legislative power is still the joint prerogative of the Queen and the Folketing, and the executive power is still vested in the Queen acting through her ministers. The cabinet is only called the Council of State when the Queen is presiding.

Any member may initiate a bill. Bills are approved or not after three readings. If one-third of members request it, a bill that has been passed may be subject to a referendum. A bill that is to be subject to referendum may be withdrawn within five weeks of its being passed. The referendum is held and its result acted upon in accordance with the Prime Minister's decision. Since 1978 the franchise, formerly of men and women over 21, has been extended to those over 18 years.

ESTONIA

The Constitutional Assembly of 1918 formulated a constitution which came into force in 1920. This provided for a republican state with a State Assembly elected by all citizens over 25, by proportional representation, and sitting for three years.

The Assembly had 100 members, and elected its own chairman and officers from among them. The Assembly appointed a government responsible to it and consisting of the head of state and his ministers. The executive prepared the budget and submitted it to the Assembly for approval. Bills passed in the Assembly might remain unpromulgated for two months if one-third of the Assembly demanded it; within that period a referendum could be demanded, or the bill's adoption recommended, by 25 000 citizens entitled to vote.

A second constitution was framed in 1934 and a third in 1938, when the main changes were made. A President was to be popularly elected for a term of six years. Parliament had two chambers, the first having 80 members directly elected by the national electorate for a five-year term. The second – the State Council – had 40 members all over 40 years of age and elected by organizations and public bodies. The Prime Minister, no longer head of state, was chosen by the President and formed his own cabinet which was responsible to parliament. He did not automatically resign on a vote of no confidence; it was the President's decision whether the cabinet should be dismissed or parliament dissolved.

After 1940 Estonia was a constituent republic of the USSR. However, in Sep 1991, the independence of Estonia was recognized by the European Community, United States and USSR.

Following the declaration of independence from the Soviet Union of 20 Aug 1991, a draft constitution drawn up by a constitutional assembly was approved by 91 per cent of votes cast at a referendum on 28 Jun 1992. The constitution came into effect on 4 Jul 1992. It defines Estonia as a 'democratic state guided by the rule of law, where universally recognized norms of international law are an inseparable part of the legal system'. It provides for a 101-member national assembly (Rigikogu) elected by proportional representation.

FINLAND

The constitutional law of 1919 provided for a republican state with a President and a single-chamber parliament. The President is elected indirectly for a six-year term. He ratifies or withholds consent to new laws, dissolves the Diet and orders new elections and conducts foreign affairs. In all this he must act through his ministers, who are individually and collectively responsible to the Diet, and must take all his decisions in meetings of the cabinet. He has a strong veto power on legislation, and if he does not give the necessary approval within three months the bill dies. In this event, if the new Diet accepts the bill exactly as it was after new elections, it becomes valid without his assent.

Every citizen over 18 may vote and every citizen over 20 may be elected to the Diet, which has 200 members and is elected by proportional representation for a four-year term (originally a three-year term). The House meets annually for at least 120 days after which it determines the date of its own rising. The President, as embodying the supreme executive power, initiates legislation by introducing bills into the Diet; the Diet with the President has power to propose a new law or to repeal or amend an existing one. New bills are drafted by the Council of State (cabinet), and may be passed for opinion to the Supreme Court or Supreme Administrative Court. Bills adopted by the House are submitted to the President. The Council of State has no fixed size but consists of as many ministers as are necessary, and always includes a Chancellor of Justice and a deputy who have the right to assist at all sessions of the Council of State and of tribunals and public departments, with free access to their minutes. These may not be members of the Diet. There is a strong system of Diet committees which must be constituted within five days of the opening of a session. Standing committees are the Committees on Fundamental Laws, Laws, Foreign Affairs, Finance and a Bank Committee. The Grand Committee must also be established within the same period, having 45 members elected by the Diet. No member of the government may be a committee member. The Grand Committee serves as a body to consider bills which have had their first reading and previously been passed to one of the specialist committees for opinion. The opinion of the Grand Committee is heard at the second reading.

FRANCE

The Third Republic kept the constitution of 1875 until it ended in 1940. This provided for two chambers, a Chamber of Deputies and a Senate. The Chamber of 26 members was elected for four years by manhood suffrage on proportional representation. The Senate had 314 members elected for nine years, one third retiring every three. Both houses assembled annually in January, and were obliged to remain in session for at least five months of the twelve. Bills could be presented in both houses either by the government or by private members, except financial bills which were solely the concern of the deputies. There was also a Council of State presided over by the Minister of Justice and other members all appointed by the President. It gave opinion on any question of administration put to it by the government.

The President was a symbolic head of state, theoretically with many powers but in practice not exercising them. He had the right to dissolve the Chamber, but did not use it after 1877; the suspensory veto over acts of parliament was never used. His role in lawmaking and the determination of policy was controlled by the cabinet.

The government's executive power lay with the ministers who were not necessarily members of either house and were chosen by the President in conjunction with the Prime Minister. They were responsible to both houses and were obliged to countersign (individually) every act of the President. Political dissension between many small parties made for weakness in the executive which had on several occasions to be offset by a grant of special powers made by parliament to the ministers. Special powers to proceed by decree for budgetary and taxation measures were granted in 1926; special powers were also granted in 1934, 1935, 1937 and 1938 and over a hundred decrees issued. Similarly ministers seldom felt strong enough to ask for a dissolution and election on the defeat of a measure; they normally resigned. Between 1870 and 1934 France had 88 ministries with an average life of less than nine months.

The constitution for the Fourth Republic was submitted to the vote in 1946. The Senate was replaced by the Council of State as a purely advisory body, the Chamber by the National Assembly as the legislative body. The executive had limited power to dissolve parliament, and popular sovereignty was invested in the referendum. In 1954, by a constitutional amendment, the Council of the Republic had some power restored to it as a delaying body, with power to hold up National Assembly action in public matters for 108 days. It could also initiate bills and pass them to the National Assembly. The Assembly then had 627 members, 544 of them from Metropolitan France, elected all at the same time for a five-year term. The position of the President was similar to that under the

Third Republic, except that the President of the Council of Ministers (Prime Minister) had taken over some of his powers, principally the power to propose legislation to parliament and to issue edicts to supplement the law. The programme of the cabinet had to be approved by public vote by an absolute majority of the National Assembly before the Council of Ministers could be appointed. Once appointed they were responsible to the Assembly but not to the Council of the Republic. The Prime Minister in theory had considerable powers; he assured the execution of all national laws, directed the armed forces and appointed most civil and military officials. In practice, however, he spent much of his time trying to maintain a cohesive executive when no one party was ever strong enough to govern alone.

Under the Fifth Republic the President is head of the government as well as head of state. He can dissolve parliament, negotiate treaties and deal with emergencies without counter-signature. He appoints (rather than formally nominating) the Prime Minister. He is indirectly elected for a seven-year term, but there is no bar to re-election. He may submit matters to the Constitutional Council for opinion, ask parliament to reconsider bills, give ruling on proposals to submit bills to referendum. Before acting outright in an emergency he must consult both executive and legislature, but he is not bound to their advice. Nor is he bound to accept the resignation of the government if the National Assembly has caused it to resign.

The Constitutional Council is appointed for nine years, one-third of its members retiring every three years. The National Assembly now has 577 members directly elected for five years (555 from Metropolitan France) and neither the Prime Minister nor any of the cabinet are allowed to hold seats in it. The Council of the Republic continues as the Senate, and all bills go to it. The Senate has 321 members (296 from Metropolitan France), indirectly elected for nine years, one-third retiring every three years. Both houses sit for about five months of the year, one session beginning in October, and the second in April. Sessions are shorter than before, the number of private members' bills is considerably fewer – an average of 2000 a year under the Fourth Republic, 200 a year under the fifth – and the programme of the National Assembly is determined by the government and not by the house.

GEORGIA

With the collapse of the Soviet Union, nationalist pressures in Georgia gathered strength. On 9 Apr 1991, following a 98.9 per cent popular vote in favour, the Supreme Soviet unanimously declared the republic an independent state based on the treaty of independence of May 1918. In May 1991 an armed insurrection led to control falling to a military council. In presidential elections in 1992, Edward Shevardnadze became *de facto* head of state. The 234-member parliament is elected by a system combining single-member districts with proportional representation based on party lists.

GERMANY

In Jan 1919 a National Assembly was elected by proportional representation, the franchise being of all over 20. This assembly elected the first President of the Republic in Feb 1919, and laid down that future presidents were to be elected by direct vote, for seven years. A constitution was promulgated on 11 Aug 1919 by which a new federal republic was provided with a bicameral federal parliament, to be responsible for defence, foreign relations, tax, customs and railways. The upper house (Reichsrat) had 55 members representing the component states and each member had an individual vote. All bills had to be approved by the Reichsrat before being introduced into the lower house (Reichstag). Members of the Reichstag were elected by proportional representation on a franchise of all over 20, for a four-year term. There was a cabinet appointed by the President but requiring the confidence of the Reichstag.

The President initiated orders and decrees, although they had still to be countersigned, appointed all national officials, decided the sessions and dissolutions of the Reichstag and ordered referenda. Without consulting the government or the legislature he could, in time of danger, suspend the national authorities and appoint a national commissioner in their place, employ the armed forces and suspend certain fundamental rights. By 1932 his emergency powers had been used 233 times, the Reichstag having the right to repeal any measures taken when the emergency was over.

By the law of 14 Jul 1933 all political parties except the National Socialist German Workers' Party were declared illegal; the Reichstag did not operate normally from that date. Its meetings became shorter until they were limited to sessions of two or three days, and it met infrequently. It remained virtually dead until 1949.

Note: The constitution of 1919 provided for popular election of the president, but Paul von Hindenburg was the only president so elected. President Ebert was elected by the Constituent Assembly itself, and Adolf Hitler assumed the Presidency by incorporating it with his own office of Chancellor.

FEDERAL REPUBLIC OF GERMANY

A Constituent Assembly met in 1948 and devised a Basic Law which was approved by the parliaments of the separate states of the federation and came into force in 1949 as the first constitution of the Federal Republic. Parliament consists of the Federal Council (Bundesrat) which is composed of members of governments of the Länder.

The Bundesrat originally had 49 members and 22 non-voting members for Berlin. Since re-unification the Bundesrat has had 68 members. Elections for a new Bundestag take place in the last three months of its term, or in the case of its dissolution after not more than 60 days. The new house meets not more than 30 days after election. The President of the Bundestag may convene the house at any time and must do so if asked by one-third of its members or by the Federal President or Federal Chancellor.

Meetings are public, but the public may be excluded. Members of the Bundesrat or of the government have free access to the Bundestag meetings and committee meetings and must be heard at any time; the same is true of Bundestag members at meetings of the Bundesrat, and either house may demand the presence of any member of the Federal Government.

The governments of the Länder appoint and recall those of their members who make up the Bundesrat, or they may appoint other members to represent them. Each Land has at least three votes; Länder with over 2m. inhabitants have four, those with over 6m. have five. Each Land has as many members as it has votes, and the votes may only be given as a block. The government has an obligation to keep the Bundesrat informed of the conduct of Federal affairs.

Bills are introduced in the Bundestag either by the government or by members of either house. Government bills go to the Bundesrat first, and the house must give an opinion within three weeks. A bill adopted in the Bundestag then goes to the Bundesrat, which may within two weeks demand a joint committee to consider it. Bills altering or adding to the constitution require Bundesrat approval before they may be passed; such bills need a two-thirds majority in both houses. For other bills the Bundesrat has a power of veto, but even then a veto adopted by a majority of Bundesrat votes may be rejected by a majority of Bundestag votes. There is provision for a state of legislative emergency for a bill which the Bundestag has rejected despite the government declaring it urgent, or a bill which has been put forward with a request for a vote of confidence.

The Federal Chancellor is elected by the Bundestag on the proposal of the Federal President. Ministers are appointed and dismissed by the President on the Chancellor's proposal. The Chancellor determines and assumes responsibility for general policy, and within that policy the ministers run their own departments on their own responsibility. The President is elected by indirect vote for a five-year term; immediate re-election is allowed once. His orders and instructions require countersignature by the Chancellor or by a minister.

Major constitutional implications followed the approach of German reunification. The two German states' economic and monetary systems were unified on 1 Jul 1990. On 31 Aug 1990 East and West Germany signed a treaty covering some political and social aspects of German unity, leaving others to be decided by an all-German parliament. On 20 Sep 1990 both states ratified unification terms by which East Germany would merge with the Federal Republic under Art. 23 of the West German Basic Law on 3 Oct 1990. The Basic Law was amended to prevent future claims on former German territory now under Polish or Soviet Union control. In December all-German elections were held for a single German parliament.

GERMAN DEMOCRATIC REPUBLIC

In 1948 the Soviet-occupied zone of Germany had a People's Council: this was converted into a People's Chamber in 1949 and on 7 Oct 1949 the Chamber enacted a constitution for the Democratic Republic. A new constitution was approved by referendum on 6 Apr 1968.

The Chamber had 500 deputies who were directly elected for four years. It assured the enforcement of its own laws and decisions and laid down the principles to which the Council of State, the Council of Ministers, the National Defence Council, the Supreme Court and the Procurator General should adhere. No one could limit the rights of the Chamber. It could hold plebiscites, declare a state of defence when necessary, and approve and terminate state treaties. In between its sessions it authorized the Council of State to fulfil all tasks resulting from the Chamber's laws and decisions. The Council was elected for four years. It dealt with bills to be submitted to the Chamber and submitted them for discussion by the Chamber's committees; it convened the Chamber either on request or on its own initiative; it issued decrees and decisions with the force of law; it had power to interpret existing law; it issued the writs for elections; its Chairman represented the Republic in international relations. (The Council was formed to replace the office of President abolished in 1960.) The Council was an organ of the Chamber and was responsible to it.

The Council of Ministers was also an organ of the Chamber and was elected by it. Its Chairman was proposed to the Chamber by the Chairman of the Council of State. It functioned collectively in the exercise of executive power; from within its ranks it appointed a Presidium; the Chairman of the Council was also the Chairman of the Presidium. The Chamber reached decisions by majority vote. Bills were presented by the deputies of the parties or mass organizations represented, by the committees of the Chamber, the Council of State, the Council of Ministers or by the Confederation of Free German Trade Unions. The bill's conformity with the constitution was examined by the Council of State; the bill was then discussed in committee and comments submitted to the Chamber in plenary session. Drafts of basic laws, prior to their being passed, were submitted to the electorate for discussion.

The Chamber could be dissolved before the end of its electoral term only on its own decision taken on a two-thirds majority. After the end of an electoral term the Council of Ministers and the Council of State continued their work until the new Chamber elected new Councils.

The German Democratic Republic ceased to exist following reunification in 1990. See Federal Republic of Germany (pp. 72–3).

GREECE

The constitution of 1911 continued in force until 1925 when it was replaced temporarily by a new one; this was abandoned in 1935 and the original reinstated although some parts of the second constitution were substituted for some of the original clauses later in the year. The constitution of 1952 further amended that of 1911, and remained in force until 1968 when a new one was adopted after a referendum. In 1973 the Monarchy ended and a Republic came into being, with a President as head of state. The 1952 constitution was reintroduced in modified form in 1974, and a new one was promulgated in 1975. All constitutions except the 1925 have provided for a single-chamber parliament, the House of Representatives. This has been the sole or joint source of legislation except during periods of rule by military junta (1967–1973, 1973–1974).

The House had at least 150 members elected by direct universal suffrage for four years. It met annually in October for each regular session, which had to be for at least three months. It sat in public but the public could be excluded, if the majority of members so decided. It shared with the King or his Regent the legislative power and the right of proposing laws; this second right the King or the Regent exercised through his ministers. Their countersignature was necessary for all his acts, and through them his executive power was exercised. If no minister consented to sign the decrees dismissing an entire ministry and appointing a new one, they could be signed by the President of the new ministry whom the King had appointed. He could suspend the work of a session once only; he could dissolve the house, but the decree of dissolution had to include the convocation of the electors within 45 days and of the new house within three months. He had no power to delay the operation of the law. A bill was at first accompanied by an explanatory report and sent to a committee of the house; it was brought in for discussion when the committee had reported, or when the time allowed for such report had elapsed. No proposal was considered accepted unless it had been discussed and voted on twice at separate sittings. A bill could be passed in one sitting provided the committee to which it was submitted had agreed, and provided less than twenty representatives objected before the close of the debate, Ministers had free access to debates and could demand a hearing at any time; they voted only if they were members. They were individually responsible to the House, and no order from the King could release them from their responsibility.

The 1925 Republican constitution provided for a Senate as well as a Chamber of Representatives, and a President. The President was elected for five years by both houses in joint session. The Chamber had between 200 and 300 directly elected members and the Senate 120 members indirectly elected. The ministers were responsible to both houses for the actions of the executive, *i.e.* the President. Bills could be introduced by members of both houses and by the government; the Senate had power to delay legislation but the Chamber could pass a bill by majority vote over the Senate's opposition after three months or earlier at a joint session if the Senate requested one. The budget was initiated in the Chamber and the Senate was obliged to pronounce on it within one month. The President required ministerial countersignature for all his acts.

The unicameral parliament provided by other constitutions had members directly elected by universal adult suffrage, for four years. Under the monarchy there were at least 150 members, under the presidency, at least 200.

The House shares with the President the legislative power and the right to propose laws; this second right the President exercises through his ministers. Their countersignature is necessary for all his acts, and through them his executive power is exercised. He has no power to delay the operation of the law. Ministers have free access to debates and may demand a hearing at any time; they vote only if they are members. They are individually responsible to the House.

75

HUNGARY

The first permanent Parliament set up after the end of the Austro-Hungarian monarchy was the National Assembly of 1920. The head of the state was Admiral Horthy who held the title of Regent; he had power of suspensive veto over laws passed by the Assembly and power to dissolve the house provided a newly elected Assembly met within 90 days. When the Assembly ended in 1922 a law was passed by government decree (*i.e.* by the Regent's ministers) making the 200 seats in rural constituencies subject to open and not secret voting. Men over 24 who had completed the course at elementary school, and women over 30 with certain qualifications received the vote. The government's supporters were returned in strength, but the working of parliament became disorderly and difficult. In 1924 the government was granted extraordinary powers for a two-year period of reconstruction.

In 1926 a second chamber was formed, comprising male members of the former reigning house, elected representatives of hereditary members of the former Upper House, about 50 members elected by town and county municipalities, about 31 members as religious representatives, about 40 members elected by institutions and organizations and some life members appointed by the head of the state. It ceased functioning after 1944. In 1937 the Regent was made no longer responsible to parliament. In 1938 the number of deputies in the Assembly was increased from 245 to 260. The Assembly proclaimed a Republic in 1946.

In 1949 a further – Communist – constitution was set up with parliament electing a Presidium on the Soviet model; the Presidium was in continual session and had power to dissolve government bodies and to annul legislation. The Assembly had 352 deputies, and after 1967 more than one candidate was allowed to stand for election in each constituency provided they supported the policies of the Patriotic Front and received 30% of the votes cast at pre-election nominations. Members were elected for four years until 1975, when the term was changed to five years. The Assembly also elected a Council of Ministers with a chairman as Prime Minister. The relationship between Assembly, Council and Presidium was on the Soviet model.

Parliament approved a new constitution on 18 Oct 1989 dissolving the People's Republic, removing the right of any party to sole governing powers, and instituting parliamentary democracy. A Hungarian Republic was proclaimed on 23 Oct 1989.

Under the 1989 constitution, the single-chamber National Assembly has 386 members, 120 elected by proportional representation. Members are elected for a four-year term. The head of state is the president of the Republic.

ICELAND

The constitution in force in 1900 was based on the Charter of 1874. Executive power belonged to the King (who was King of both Denmark and Iceland as two separate sovereign states) and was exercised through ministers responsible to him and to parliament (the Althing). The legislative power rested conjointly with the Althing and the King. The Althing had 40 members, 34 of them elected by universal suffrage in constituencies and the remaining 6 elected for the whole country on proportional representation. The 34 sat for 6 years, the rest for 12. The Althing had an Upper House of 14 members – *i.e.* the 6 described above and 8 others elected by the whole Althing from among the 34. The remaining 26 members formed the Lower House. The Althing met every other year in July, and could not sit for longer than four weeks without royal sanction. Ministers had free access to both houses, but could only vote in the house of which they were members. Budget bills had to be introduced in the Lower House, but all other bills could be introduced in either. If the houses could not agree on a bill they assembled in common sitting and the decision was by a two-thirds majority except in the case of a budget bill, for which a simple majority was enough.

In the Charter of 1920 and its amendments of 1934 some alterations were made to the composition of the Althing: the number of members had not to exceed 49, of whom 38 were elected from the constituencies, each electing candidates by simple majority except for the capital which elected 6 on proportional representation. Not more than 11 supplementary seats were distributed among parties having insufficient seats in proportion to their electors. The Upper House was composed of one-third of Althing members elected by both houses in common sitting. The Althing met every year. The electoral law of 1959 provided for an Althing of 60 members, of whom 49 were elected in 8 constituencies by proportional representation, with 11 supplementary members chosen as before. The republic was proclaimed in 1944 and a President elected to exercise executive power through the ministers. He serves for four years.

IRELAND

There are two houses in the Irish parliament, the House of Representatives (Dáil) and the Senate. The House had 166 members in 1996 elected by universal adult suffrage. The Senate had 60 members of whom 11 are nominated by the Prime Minister, 6 elected by the universities and 43 elected by a college from representatives of the public services and interests. The President is elected for a seven-year term and may be re-elected for consecutive terms. The constitution in force is that of 1937. The constitution formed by Dáil Eireann in 1919 was a temporary one, not intended as a permanent basis for a fully operating government. It provided for a chairman for the Dáil, a Prime Minister and other ministers; it defined the competence of the Dáil and made provision for audit and budgeting. The constitution of the Irish Free State in 1922 provided for a constitutional monarchy with responsible government by a cabinet of ministers. In order to restrict the power of the executive there was also provision for referendum and popular initiative, and for the direct election by the Dáil of ministers who were not Dáil members or members of the cabinet. All these measures, however, had lapsed or been removed within five years.

Note: The 1937 constitution did not declare a Republic. It provided instead for a continuation of the arrangements made at the abdication of Edward VIII, when the mention of the Crown was removed from the previous constitution and an ordinary statute (The Executive Authority (External Relations) Act) put in its place to provide an organ for the state in the conduct of its external affairs. In 1948 it was therefore possible to create the Republic by ordinary legislation and not by changing the constitution. The President appoints the Prime Minister on the nomination of the Dáil, and the other ministers on the nomination of the Prime Minister, with the previous approval of the Dáil. The Prime Minister holds office until he chooses to resign, in which case the government is deemed also to have resigned, until he loses majority support or until he himself secures dissolution by asking the President. Appointment to the government is distinct from appointment to a department. Members of the government may include members of the Senate (but in practice have only done so twice). There is provision for ministers without portfolio.

Bills are proposed mainly by the government in planned legislative programmes. There is provision for private members' bills, but few are initiated. The Senate has power to delay legislation while the Dáil reconsiders its previous decision. Bills can be discussed at parliamentary party meetings either between their preparation and presentation to the House, or between presentation and second reading.

There may be no amendment to the constitution without a referendum, though this was possible before 1930.

ITALY

Italy is a Republic, with a President and a parliament consisting of a Chamber of Deputies and a Senate. The Chamber is elected for five years by direct and universal suffrage (changed in 1993) with one deputy for every 80 000 inhabitants. The Senate is elected for six years with at least six senators for each Region – one for every 200 000 inhabitants – except for the Valle d'Aosta which has only one. The President can nominate five senators for life, and may himself become a senator for life upon retiring from the Presidency.

Parliament may be dissolved by the President. A cabinet need resign only on a motivated motion of censure.

A joint session of Chamber and Senate is needed to elect a President, with an additional three delegates from each Regional Council (one from the Valle d'Aosta). The presidential term is seven years.

The Republic was established in 1946, following a referendum on 2 Jun and the consequent abdication of King Umberto II on 13 Jun. The republican constitution came into force on 1 Jan 1948.

The constitution prior to 1948 was an expansion of the Statuto fondamentale del Regno of 1848. The executive power belonged to the sovereign and was exercised through responsible ministers; legislative power rested in King and parliament, which consisted of a Senate and a lower chamber. This latter was the Chamber of Deputies until 1938; it was elected by universal adult male suffrage for five years with one deputy for every 71 000 of the population. The King had power to dissolve it at any time provided he ordered new elections and convoked a new meeting within four months. In 1938 the Chamber was replaced by the Chamber of Fasci and Corporations which had first met in 1929. Membership of this consisted of the Duce and the members of the Grand Fascist Council, a third body whose approval was needed for all constitutional measures and which consisted of original members of the Fascist Party on its coming to power, who were appointed for an indefinite period, ministers and other dignitaries appointed for the duration of their terms of office and other members appointed for three years by the Duce. The Duce as Prime Minister was responsible to the King.

Suffrage in 1919 was by proportional representation. In 1923 this was replaced by a system of election in fifteen constituencies, with two-thirds of seats allotted to whichever party gained at least 25% of total votes. In 1925 there was a further alteration introducing single-member constituencies, by-elections and suffrage for all over 25. Parliament, however, did not function normally after the Fascist ministry took power in 1922, as the Fascists were the only effective party.

In 1993, against a background of political scandals, and as a result of the Apr 1993 referendum, the Italian parliament voted to revise the proportional representation system.

Under the new electoral system (first used in the Mar 1994 elections), three-quarters of the members of each house (472 deputies and 232 senators) are elected by a majority 'winner-takes-all' system. The remaining quarter of senators and deputies are still elected by the old proportional representation (PR) system. A party requires 4 per cent of the national proportional vote to be awarded any of the PR seats. Constituencies now average 120 000 population for the Chamber of Deputies and 244 000 for the Senate.

LATVIA

The constitution came into force in 1922 and provided for a republican state with a single house of parliament (the Saeima). The house had 100 representatives directly elected on universal adult suffrage by proportional representation for a term of three years. The house elected the state President by absolute majority for a three-year term. The President chose the Prime Minister, who appointed the cabinet. The cabinet was responsible to the house. The President had the right to dissolve parliament only after the proposal to dissolve it had been voted on and confirmed by the electorate. If he did not obtain this confirmation he was obliged to resign. In 1934 the parliament was disbanded and a government set up which combined executive and legislative power in the former Council of Ministers. This government was led by the former Prime Minister Karlis Ulmanis. He combined his office with that of President in 1936. From 1940 to 1991 Latvia was a constituent republic of the USSR.

In May 1990 the Latvian Supreme Soviet declared that the Soviet occupation of Latvia on 17 Jun 1940 was illegal. It resolved to re-establish the 1922 Constitution. The declaration of independence of 21 Aug 1991 stated that Latvia was an independent, democratic republic as set out in the 1922 constitution. The president is elected by parliament.

LIECHTENSTEIN

The constitution of 1921 provides for a Diet of 15 members in one house, elected on universal suffrage and proportional representation. They sit for four years. The Prince convokes, closes and dissolves the Diet, and may adjourn it for three months provided the adjournment is announced before the full Diet. Convocation may be demanded by 400 citizens, and dissolution decided by plebiscite on the demand of 600. The Diet supervises the entire administration of the state. Bills may be initiated by the Diet, the Prince acting through the government, and the citizens (400 or three communes). To be valid a law must be passed by an absolute majority of at least two-thirds of members. If the Diet rejects a bill submitted to it by popular initiative, it is obliged to submit the bill to referendum, when it can be passed by the citizens even if the Diet disagrees. The government is appointed by the Prince with the approval of the Diet; he acts through them, but all his actions must be countersigned and it is his ministers who are responsible.

LITHUANIA

The constitution was adopted in 1922 and provided for a single-chamber parliament elected for three years by universal suffrage and proportional representation. Elections for a new house had to take place before the expiration of the previous term. The President of the Republic was elected by parliament for three years and by absolute majority; he could run for two successive terms but no third term without a break. He appointed the Prime Minister, and confirmed the ministers chosen by him, and also appointed the State Comptrollers (with auditing powers), but all bodies appointed could only function with the confidence of the house. He had power to return a bill to the house for reconsideration within twenty-one days of the passage; but was then bound to accept it if it was passed again by an absolute majority. His power of delay could be cancelled by a declaration of urgency by the house. He presided at and took part in cabinet meetings.

Any amendment to the constitution could be brought forward by the house, the government, or 50 000 citizens, but needed a three-fifths majority of the total number of deputies for adoption. After that a referendum could be demanded on it. Ministers had individual and collective responsibility.

In 1926 the democratic system was brought to an end by political confusion. Further constitutional changes were made in 1928 and 1938 on authoritarian lines. By 1938 a dictatorship had been established and the house was no longer operating normally. In 1940 Lithuania became a constituent republic of the USSR.

The independence of Lithuania was recognised by the Soviet Union on 6 Sep 1991. Earlier, in a referendum of Feb 1991, over 90 per cent of those voting were in favour of independence. A draft constitution was published in Apr 1991. Parliament (the *Seimas*) comprises 141 members. It is elected by a system partly proportional and partly constituency-based, with 70 seats allocated to parties according to their share of the vote (with a 4 per cent threshold except for ethnic parties). The 71 constituency seats require candidates to poll more than 50 per cent of the vote, otherwise there are run-off ballots.

LUXEMBOURG

The constitution of 1868 was amended in 1919, 1948 and 1956. In 1919 it was decided that sovereign power was vested in the people and that deputies to the single Chamber of Deputies were to be elected on universal suffrage by the list system of proportional representation. The Chamber of Deputies had 48 members in 1919. They were elected for a six-year term, half of them being re-elected every three years. The head of state shared legislative power with the Chamber and exercised the executive power through the cabinet. The constitution allowed the sovereign to organize the government. The sovereign also chose the 15 members of the permanent Council of State who served for life. The Council discussed proposed legislation and was obliged to give an opinion on any matter referred to it by the sovereign or the representatives of the law.

In 1956 the term of office for deputies was altered to five years.

The Grand Duke names and dismisses the government, which must consist of at least three members who may not be members of the Chamber, and who are responsible collectively and individually.

Bills are passed after two readings with an interval of three months approved by an absolute majority.

MACEDONIA

The independence of Macedonia was proclaimed on 20 Nov 1992. It was admitted to the United Nations on 8 Apr 1993 under the name of 'Former Yugoslav Republic of Macedonia' a decision acceptable to Greece. On 20 Nov 1992 parliament had promulgated a new constitution which asserted Macedonia's independence. The president is directly elected for 5-year terms. Candidates must be citizens aged at least 40 years. The parliament is a 120-member single-chamber assembly (*Sobranie*), elected by universal suffrage for 4-year terms. The *Sobranie* has power to adopt and amend the constitution, enact laws and gives interpretations thereof, adopts the budget of the republic, decides on war and peace and chooses the government. The assembly may also call for a referendum.

MOLDOVA

With the collapse of the Soviet Union, Moldova declared itself an independent republic in Aug 1991. A new constitution became effective on 27 Aug 1994. It defined Moldova as an independent, democratic and unitary state. However, in the predominantly Russian-speaking areas of Transdniestria a self-styled republic was established in Sep 1991, and approved by a local referendum in Dec 1991. Under the Moldovan constitution, parliament has 104 seats and is elected for 4-year terms. There is a 4 per cent threshold for election; votes falling below this are redistributed to successful parties. The president is elected for 4-year terms. Elections were held in 1994 (see p. 226).

MONACO

The constitution of 1911 lasted until 1959; it provided for a National Council of 18 members elected for a five-year term by 30 delegates of municipalities and 21 electors chosen by adult male suffrage. Legislative power was exercised by the Prince and the Council, executive power by a Minister of State and a three-member Council of Government under the Prince.

In 1959 the Prince suspended this constitution and dissolved the National Council, which was then revived in 1962 as a directly elected body with a five-year term. Executive power is still vested in the Prince, the Minister of State who represents him, and the Council. The Minister directs all administration and presides over the Council with the casting vote. The Council consists of three members named by the Prince (members for the Interior, Finance and Public Works). The Council takes its decisions after deliberation and prepares drafts and ordinances for the Prince's consideration. Legislative power is vested in the Prince and the National Council. The Assembly of the National Council chooses a Bureau, with President and Vice-President. The Assembly sits for two sessions a year, each of 15 days at most; the Prince may convoke and dissolve it. He communicates with the assembly through the Minister of State, who, together with the councillors, may attend at his own wish and must attend when asked. The initiative rests with the Prince, but the National Council may submit draft proposals to him and ask him to initiate them. The National Council controls the budget, which is submitted to it by the Council, and has sole right to levy direct taxation.

THE NETHERLANDS

The parliament consists of two chambers. The Upper House has had 75 members since 1956, prior to which it had 50. They are elected by members of the Provincial States. The Second Chamber has had 150 deputies since 1956 (100 before that) and they are directly elected on universal suffrage and proportional representation. The Second Chamber shares legislative power with the sovereign, who has power to dissolve both chambers provided elections take place within 40 days and the new house or houses be convoked within three months.

The Upper House is elected for six years, and half the members retire every three years. The Lower House members are elected for four years.

Bills are proposed either by the Sovereign, acting through responsible ministers, or by a member of the Lower House. The Upper House has power only to approve or reject them without amendment; the houses must ultimately agree. Ministers and Secretaries of State attend sessions of both houses either at their own or parliament's wish, but they may not be members of either house. The constitution can only be revised if the bill for its revision is passed and confirmed again by a second parliament after the dissolution of the first.

The constitutional amendments of 1922 provided that the Upper House should be elected for six years and not for nine as formerly. Until 1922 the right to declare war and to conclude and ratify treaties with foreign powers was a royal power, exercised in conjunction with the cabinet. Since then, the exercise of these powers has depended on previous parliamentary sanction. The constitution allows considerable royal initiative, but in practice the operation of the cabinet system has set this aside. There is also a Council of State of not more than 16 members which sits as an advisory body on all legislative matters and is consulted by the Crown, the government or parliament.

NORWAY

Norway's constitution dates from 1814; although there have been amendments since, the nature of the Storting (Parliament) is virtually the same as then provided. The state is a constitutional monarchy; in default of male heirs the King proposes a successor to parliament which has the right to select another. The King also has power of veto which may be exercised twice; a bill which passes three parliaments formed by three elections becomes law without his assent.

Parliament assembles in October every year for a session of no fixed duration. Once the house is assembled it divides in two by electing one-quarter of its members to form the Lagting or Upper House; the remaining three-quarters forming the Odelsting or Lower House. There is a president nominated for each house and for the joint house. Most questions are decided by the joint house, but legislation must be considered by both houses separately. If they disagree, then the bill must be decided by parliament as a whole and the decision taken on a two-thirds majority (of voters, not of total membership). The same majority is needed for constitutional amendments.

The executive is represented by the Crown acting through the Prime Minister and cabinet of 14 ministers. The ministers attend sessions of parliament and take part in discussions, but they do not vote. They do initiate bills.

There is a strong committee system through which all proposed legislation must pass before submission to the house. All bills are proposed in the Odelsting, and if accepted are sent to the Lagting. The Lagting may either approve a bill as it stands or reject it as it stands and give its reasons. If rejected it is returned to the Odelsting which will send it once more, either in an amended or original form, to the Lagting. If still rejected the joint session must take place to pass it.

The Crown has no power of dissolution, nor can it summon parliament to meet. The dates of meeting are decided by parliament itself. Election is direct, by all citizens over 20 and by proportional representation. The 150 members are elected for a three-year term.

POLAND

The constitution of the Republic came into operation in 1920. The legislature consisted of a Diet and a Senate. Diet members were elected on universal suffrage for a five-year term. The Senate was elected on universal suffrage of all citizens over 30 and by proportional representation in the provincial districts. It sat also for five years. National minorities represented 20 per cent of Diet membership.

The Diet had the power of initiating legislation, and had to submit every bill it passed to the Senate. The Senate was obliged to refer a bill back within 30 days if it was suggesting amendments; otherwise the bill was promulgated. If the Diet accepted the Senate's amendments by a simple majority or rejected them by a majority of eleven-twentieths, the bill was passed in the form it left the Diet for the second time.

A President was elected by parliament as a whole for a term of seven years. His position was largely symbolic and his actions required the consent of parliament. He might dissolve the Diet if he had the consent of the Senate, but the Senate in so consenting determined its own dissolution. He exercised the executive power through a council of ministers responsible to the Diet.

There was also a Supreme Court of Control which made independent and judicious survey of the government's provincial administration. Its president was a minister, not a member of the Council of Ministers but responsible to the Diet.

The constitution could only be amended by a two-thirds majority of at least half the number of deputies and senators fixed by law. It might be revised once every 25 years by simple majority of a joint session.

The constitution of 1935 made radical changes in the office of President and the composition of the houses. The working of the original Diet was frequently disrupted by party differences; now there were to be no political parties in the Diet or the Senate. The Senate was to have one-third of its 96 Senators nominated by the President of the Republic and the remaining two-thirds elected by colleges.

The President was chosen by referendum from two candidates, one elected by the two houses together and the other nominated by the retiring President. He could now exercise without countersignature his right to nominate and dismiss the Prime Minister and the Inspector-General of the armed forces, to nominate judges and senators, and to dissolve the Diet and the Senate before the end of their term. If the Diet and the Senate demanded the dismissal of a minister or of the cabinet, the President might concur or dissolve the houses.

The next constitution was adopted in 1952. There was now one chamber which sat for four years and was elected by all citizens over 18. It elected, on the Russian pattern, a Council of Ministers with a Chairman as Prime Minister, and a Council of State composed of a Chairman, a Secretary and 14 members, which sat in almost permanent session and exercised the power of a Presidium.

Round-table talks were held in Feb 1989 between Solidarity and the government. Fundamental changes to the constitution were proposed. These included a new office of State President, and the establishment of a new bicameral National Assembly with a newly-created Senate acting as the Upper House. The Senate would not have power to initiate legislation, but would have a power of veto over the Sejm.

Constitutional changes continued to be demanded by Solidarity after 1990. These constitutional reforms (known as the 'Small Constitution') took place in Aug 1992. Under them, the authority of the republic is vested in the Sejm (Parliament) of 460 members, elected by proportional representation for 4 years by all citizens over 18. There is a 5 per cent threshold for parties and 8 per cent for coalitions, but seats are reserved for representatives of ethnic minorities even if their vote falls below 5 per cent. The Sejm elects a Council of State and a Council of Ministers. There is also an elected 100-member upper house, the Senate. The Senate has a power of veto which only a two-thirds majority of the Sejm can override. The head of state is the president. The prime minister is chosen by the president with the approval of the Sejm.

PORTUGAL

By the republican constitution of 1911, legislative power was given to a Congress with a Chamber of Deputies and a Senate. There were 164 deputies elected for three years by male suffrage. The Senate had 71 members elected by electoral colleges formed from the Municipal Councils, and sat for six years with half the number retiring every three years. The Chamber of Deputies had priority in the discussion of financial bills, bills promoted by the government and of those relating to the armed forces. The Senate might amend or reject, but both houses had to agree, by joint session if necessary, before a bill could be promulgated by the President.

The President was elected by joint session of both houses for a four-year term. He had no power of veto but did have power of dissolution after consulting the cabinet. The cabinet was responsible for his acts. For the period of the first constitution the cabinet was extremely weak owing to differences between numerous small parties. Its power to advise dissolution was used frequently and both houses were dissolved for long periods.

The constitution of 1933 remained in force until 1974. It provided for a President directly elected by citizens with literacy or financial qualifications. The National Assembly was to have one chamber with 90 deputies elected for four years by direct suffrage. There was to be a Privy Council of ten members to assist the President. In practice one party took over the National Assembly and retained control. In 1959 the constitution was amended to provide for indirect election of the President by an electoral college made up of members of the National Assembly and of the Corporative Chamber. On 25 Apr 1974 the Government was overthrown and a Junta of National Salvation installed. The dissolution of the National Assembly and of the Council of State followed.

A new constitution was adopted in 1976 and revised in 1982. The President was now elected by popular vote for a five-year term. He was to appoint the Prime Minister and, on the latter's recommendation, the other ministers. A new National Assembly was provided with 250 members, still elected by direct vote for a four-year term. In 1982 the effective ruling junta was abolished and replaced by a Council of State and a Constitutional Tribunal.

ROMANIA

The constitution of 1866 continued in force with amendments until 1923. It provided for a monarchy acting through responsible ministers, and a two-chamber parliament. The Chamber of Deputies was elected by three classes of electors whose franchise depended on property and educational qualifications. The Senate was elected by two classes with property qualifications higher than those required for electors to the Chamber. By the 1923 constitution the King's powers were defined as those of a constitutional monarch, sharing legislative power with the Chamber and the Senate. All three had the right of initiating measures.

The Chamber of Deputies was elected in universal suffrage by all over 21, by proportional representation and compulsory ballot. The Senate was composed of elected and *ex officio* members, some elected on a similar system to members of the Chamber, some by electoral colleges of local councillors with one senator for each Department (the largest local government unit), and some by members of Chambers of Commerce, institutes of agriculture and commerce, etc., and by the universities. The *ex officio* members included church officials, members of learned institutions, former political and parliamentary figures. All bills, initiated by either the chamber or the King, passed before a Legislative Council which gave help in drafting and co-ordinating measures. It was consulted in all cases except those concerning the budget. The King had power of suspensive veto.

A constitution was adopted in 1938 which introduced Senate members nominated by the King, equal in number to those elected. Senators sat for nine years and deputies for six, and the election of deputies was now by all citizens of 30 years and over engaged in manual work, agriculture, commerce, industry or intellectual work. Senators were elected by the same professions, but the age limit was 40. In 1939 the Principal Council and the Grand Council were instituted, to elect eight representatives from each of three classes – agriculturists, free professions and workers. The Principal Council would have executive power and the Grand Council would be an advisory body. By that time the parliament had been in dissolution for over a year, having been dissolved in Dec 1937. In Dec 1947 the state became a republic. A new constitution was passed in 1948 providing for one chamber, the Grand National Assembly, which is elected by all over 18 years, for four years with one deputy for every 40 000 inhabitants. This body sat in short sessions twice a year. It elected a Presidium which sat almost permanently and to which its legislative powers were delegated. The Presidium had a chairman, who was head of state, four vice-chairmen, a secretary and 22 members. There was also a Council of Ministers, but all ministerial policies were shaped by deliberative collegiate bodies of which the minister was chairman. The Council of Ministers and the Presidium (or Council of State) related to the Assembly as on the Russian pattern. In 1972 the National Assembly's term was changed from four years to five.

Following the revolution of Dec 1989 and the fall of the Ceauçescu regime, the National Salvation Front assumed sweeping power pending the drafting of a new constitution. The leading role of the Communist Party was abolished by decree and multi-party elections were held.

The National Assembly drafted a new constitution in Nov 1991 which was approved by referendum on 8 Dec 1991. Under this constitution, the National Assembly consists of a 341-member Chamber of Deputies and a 143-member Senate. Both are elected for 4-year terms from 41 constituencies by modified proportional representation, the number of seats won in each constituency being determined by the proportion of the total vote. There is a 3 per cent threshold for admission to either house.

RUSSIA

At the time of the collapse of the Soviet Union, the Russian constitution was a heavily amended version of the 1977 Soviet constitution (see Union of Soviet Socialist Republics). In Dec 1991 President Boris Yeltsin (elected on 12 Jun 1991) was given power by the Congress of People's Deputies to rule by decree. An attempt to cancel this power failed in Apr 1992. A referendum was held on 25 Apr 1993 to test support for the basic principles of a new constitution.

A constitutional conference opened in Jun 1993 but the situation remained fluid as the president and the Congress continued to disagree. The abrogation of the constitution and dissolution of the Congress of People's Deputies by Yeltsin, in Sep 1993, was followed by the announcement that a new constitution would be written and new parliamentary elections held before the end of 1993 (see p. 249) followed by a presidential election.

The referendum of 12 Dec 1993 approved the new Basic Law, replacing the 1978 constitution passed under Brezhnev. The new constitution greatly strengthens the powers of the president, who is elected for four years and can serve no more than two terms. The new powers as head of state include the right to pass decrees without reference to parliament (although they can be vetoed by a two-thirds majority); the right to declare a state of emergency (with parliamentary consent); the appointment of military commanders, diplomats and senior judges; the right to reject legislation passed by the lower house (the State Duma); and the right to call parliamentary elections. The president can be impeached after court decisions followed by a two-thirds majority in each house of parliament. There is no provision for a vice president.

Parliament consists of two chambers. The lower house, the State Duma, has 450 deputies, half elected by the 'first-past-the-post' system and the remainder by proportional representation from party lists. The Duma approves legislation but can only draft laws affecting the budget with government consent. The upper house, the Federation Council, has 178 representatives, two from each member state of the federation. The council cannot be dissolved by the president and approves Duma legislation.

Among the constitution's provisions, which mark a decisive break with the Communist past, are affirmation of the freedom of worship, speech and travel, as well as a free press. Private property is enshrined as an inalienable right and all mention of a state ideology vanished. Parliament can only make constitutional changes by a two-thirds majority in each house.

SLOVAKIA

Under the constitution adopted on 1 Sep 1992 for an independent Slovakia (which came into being on 1 Jan 1993), parliament is the National Council. This consists of 150 members elected by proportional representation.

Citizenship belongs to all citizens of the former federal Slovak Republic; other residents of 5 years standing may apply for citizenship. Slovakia grants dual citizenship to Czechs.

SLOVENIA

Slovenia declared its complete independence of former Yugoslavia on 8 Oct 1991. Its independence was recognised by Germany on 23 Dec 1991 and by the European Communities on 15 Jan 1992. Under the constitution enacted by the Assembly in Dec 1991, there is a bicameral parliament consisting of a 90-member National Assembly elected for 4-year terms by proportional representation with a 3 per cent threshold; and a 40-

member State Council, elected for 5-year terms by interest groups. It has veto powers over the National Assembly.

SPAIN

Spain was a constitutional monarchy until the system was virtually set aside by the military *coup d'état* under General Primo de Rivera in 1923. The constitution had provided for legislative power being exercised by the parliament of two chambers and the King; both chambers were equal in authority, and ministers were responsible to them. Parliamentary life was frequently disrupted and always weakened by political confusion, and no single strong authority emerged.

The military and civil dictatorships which followed abolished the parliament temporarily, together with the post of Prime Minister and other Ministries except War and Foreign Affairs. In 1925 a civilian cabinet was restored, but the parliament was still in dissolution.

The constitution of 1931 provided a single-chamber parliament, Congress, and republican state under a President. The Congress was elected for four years by universal suffrage on proportional representation. Electors and deputies had to be over 23. Executive power was held by the head of state, through a Council of Ministers headed by a Prime Minister whom he appointed. There was a Council of the Realm of 16 members, of whom 10 were elected by the Cortes (parliament), and a National Council which was partly elected and partly appointed. The Cortes consisted of members of the government; national councillors; presidents of the supreme court of justice, the council of the realm, the supreme military tribunal, the court of exchequer and the national economic council; 150 representatives of trade unions; representatives of municipalities and provincial councils elected by their respective corporations; 100 deputies (2 from each province) elected by the heads of families; 30 representatives of universities, learned societies, chambers of commerce. Its function was to prepare and pass laws, working through commissions and through plenary session. The Commissions were arranged and appointed by the President of the Cortes in agreement with the government. President and government also arranged the agenda. Laws once passed were sent to the head of state who might within one month return them to the Cortes for fresh deliberation.

A new constitution came into force in 1978, establishing a parliamentary monarchy. The new Cortes was bicameral. The upper house or Senate had 208 senators, 4 each for the 47 peninsular provinces and others elected by the insular provinces, Ceuta and Melilla and the autonomous communities. The lower house or Congress of Deputies had 300–400 members, elected by proportional representation. Suffrage for both houses is universal and direct; the term of both houses is four years. Executive power is vested in the Prime Minister, who is elected by the Congress, and his cabinet.

SWEDEN

The constitution in force in 1900 was that of 1809, under which executive power lay with the King who exercised it through the Council of State with the Prime Minister at its head. All members of the Council of State were responsible for the acts of the government. The ministers prepared bills for the Diet, issued general directives and made higher appointments but did not as a rule take individual administrative decisions. This was done by central boards, whose organization depended on the appropriations granted by the Diet. The King in Council might ask the advice of the boards, but was not bound to follow it. All members of the Council of State were also members of parliament.

Until 1971 there were two chambers of the legislature, the Upper and Lower Houses. The Upper House had members elected by proportional representation, candidates being chosen on property or income qualifications. They sat for eight years and were elected by members of county councils, the electors of Stockholm and five other large towns. The Lower House had 230 members elected by proportional representation. In 1921 women were given the franchise like men at the age of 23. Also in 1921 the two houses gained the right to appoint their own speakers, with an elected substitute to take his place if necessary. Formerly speakers were appointed by the king. In the same year the King's prerogative of consulting a private committee on important questions of foreign relations was modified; a Foreign Affairs Committee was set up consisting of 16 members from each house and appointed by the parliament, and the King was bound to take its advice. All foreign agreements of importance were submitted to parliament for ratification.

Bills passed by the houses passed through a strong committee system which provided opinion on all except finance bills. If the houses disagreed on any bill, the matter would go to each house separately; the houses would then sit together and decide by majority. Both houses had equal powers in framing laws.

Since 1971 the Diet has consisted of one chamber. It has 349 members directly elected by universal suffrage for three years. All over 19 have the vote, and proportional representation is used in 28 constituencies from which 310 members are elected. The remaining 39 seats are distributed to parties receiving at least 4% of votes.

In 1975 a new constitution made parliament the central organ of government, in which the King no longer has any powers.

SWITZERLAND

The constitution is that of 1874, and under it the highest authority is vested in the electorate. This consisted of all male citizens over 20 until 1971 when the franchise was extended to women. The electorate has power through referenda to vote on amendments to or revision of the constitution. Referenda are also held on laws and international treaties if 30 000 voters or eight cantons request them, and the electorate can also initiate constitutional amendments if 50 000 voters support the initiative. The legislature consists of two chambers, the Council of States and the National Council. The Council of States has 46 members chosen and paid by the 23 cantons; election procedures depend on which canton they represent. The National Council has 200 councillors directly elected for four years in proportion to the population of the cantons, with at least one member for each canton or half-canton. Members are paid not by the cantons but from federal funds.

Laws to be submitted to popular vote must have been agreed by both chambers. The chief executive authority lies with the Bundesrat or Federal Council. It has seven members elected from seven different cantons by a joint session of both chambers. It sits for a four-year term. The members must not hold any other office in the cantons or the Confederation. The President of the Federal Council is the President of the Confederation. He and his vice-president are first magistrates of the state. They are elected by a Federal Assembly for one year only. The seven members of the Council act as ministers and heads of the seven administrative departments.

Bills can be introduced in parliament by a member, by either of the houses or by the Federal Council.

TURKEY

In Apr 1920 the Grand National Assembly declared itself the sole sovereign representative of the nation, and repudiated the authority of the Sultan and the old parliament at Constantinople. The Assembly consisted of one chamber and every citizen over 18 voted for its members, who had to be at least 30. Members sat for two years then (from 1924) for four years. The house sat annually and could not be in recess for more than four months of the year. Special sessions could be convened at the request of one-fifth of the members, the President of the Council or the President of the Republic. The Assembly was responsible for preparing, framing and passing laws, concluding conventions and treaties of peace, making declarations of war, examining and ratifying laws presented to it by the Commission on the Budget, coining money and administering punishment and pardon. A law passed by the Assembly was passed to the President of the Republic. He might return it for further consideration within ten days, but the Assembly could override his objections and re-vote the law. On bills concerning the budget or the constitution there was no power of veto. The President was elected by the Assembly for its own term, and might be re-elected. All his acts required countersignature by the President of the Council and the minister concerned. The President appointed the President of the Council (Prime Minister) who in turn designated members of his council from among members of the Assembly. Within a week of his appointment he was obliged to offer a programme and ask for a vote of confidence. Ministers were collectively and individually responsible to the Assembly.

There was also a Council of State elected from among suitably qualified men by the Assembly. This gave advice on legislation.

In 1934 the age for the franchise was altered to 23 and the age for deputies to 31.

In 1937 the principles of the Republican People's Party were incorporated into the constitution; from then on only this party was active in parliament, although there were independent members. Opposition parties came into being again in 1945. The Grand National Assembly was dissolved by the military *coup d'état* of 1960.

The Constitution of 1961 provided for a seven-year term for the President, who might not be re-elected. He was elected by joint session of two houses, the National Assembly and the Senate, which had 150 members directly elected, 15 nominated by the President and 18 life senators. Laws were only initiated by the Assembly and the Council of Ministers. Bills were debated first in the Assembly and then referred to the Senate. If the houses did not agree on the bill, the decision was made by a joint committee which prepared another draft for submission to the Assembly. The Assembly then accepted either this draft or the one previously passed to the Senate, or the one amended by the Senate. If the Senate had amended by absolute majority, the Assembly could only revert to its unamended draft, also by absolute majority. Any bill which the Assembly rejected but the Senate adopted was returned to the Assembly for review.

In Sep 1980 the Assembly was dissolved and power passed to a National Security Council. A new constitution was drafted and came into force in 1982. All who were members of parliament on 1 Jan 80 were banned from political life for five years. The new Assembly was to have 400 members sitting for a four-year term. A deputy could be expelled, and prevented from standing again for his new party, if he changed sides. The Assembly could also force the resignation of the Council of Ministers by a vote of no confidence. The President was to be elected by a two-thirds majority of the Assembly. He would appoint the Prime Minister, who would then appoint a cabinet. Presidential decrees must be countersigned by the Prime Minister, who assumes responsibility for them. The President was to be advised by a 20-member State Consultative Council which he appointed himself.

The number of deputies was increased from 400 to 450 in Jun 1987 and further increased to 550 in constitutional changes in Jul 1995.

UKRAINE

With the collapse of the Soviet Union, the independence of Ukraine was declared on 5 Dec 1991 (having been preceded by a referendum on 1 Dec 1991 in which 90.3 per cent of votes were cast in favour of independence). Under the terms of the constitution parliament (the Supreme Council) has 450 seats. Turn-out in each electoral district must reach 50 per cent for an election to be valid. The State Council is chaired by the president.

UNION OF SOVIET SOCIALIST REPUBLICS (USSR)

The Union of Soviet Socialist Republics was formally constituted on 6 Jul 23. The central executive power was the Council of the Union together with the Council of Nationalities, the latter being composed of five representatives from each of the autonomous and allied republics and one representative from each of the autonomous regions. The supreme authority, however, lay with the Central Executive Committee which was elected by the Congress of Soviets of the Union. This was the source of all legislation and its decrees and resolutions were sovereign. Between its sessions authority was exercised by the Presidium, which was self-electing and nearly identical in membership with the Presidium of the Russian Socialist Federal Soviet Republic. The Central Executive Committee met infrequently and for short terms; the power of the Presidium was therefore considerable. By 1926 the Executive Committee numbered about 300 and met three times a year. The Presidium prepared the order of business and executed the resolutions passed, being itself in almost continuous session.

The Central Executive Committee also elected the Council of People's Commissars. Originally this had greater power than the Presidium and acted as a cabinet of ministers responsible for departments, but by 1923 its power as a body had been considerably weakened. The Presidium had power to ratify or to stay the executions of the Council's resolutions, to be a court of appeal for any Commissar against the Council as a whole, and to require quarterly reports of all proceedings and instructions of the Council.

A new constitution was formed on 5 Dec 1936 and remained in force until 1977. Under it there existed the Council (or 'Soviet') of the Union and the Soviet of Nationalities; their legislative rights were equal; they were elected for a term of four years, the Soviet of the Union by citizens of the USSR on the basis of one deputy for every 300 000 inhabitants, the Soviet of Nationalities by citizens voting by Union and Autonomous Republics, Autonomous Regions and National Areas. The latter Soviet had 32 deputies from each Union Republic, 11 from each Autonomous Republic, 5 from each Autonomous Region and 1 from each National Area. The Council of Ministers (previously called People's Commissars) was appointed by the Supreme Soviet. It was the highest executive and administrative organ but had no legislative power. It executed laws already made and co-ordinated departmental administration. The Chairman of the Council was equivalent to a Prime Minister. It had two First Deputy Chairmen with no departmental responsibility, and four vice-chairmen of whom one had a departmental responsibility. It was itself responsible to the Supreme Soviet or to the Presidium when the Soviet was not in session.

The Presidium of the Supreme Soviet had 39 members including a chairman (the President of the USSR), 5 vice-chairmen (one from each union republic) 21 members and a secretary. It was the practice to elect the chairmen of the presidia of the Union Soviets from among the vice-chairmen. Members of the Council of Ministers could not be elected to the Presidium. The Presidium convened the sessions of the Supreme Soviet, dissolved it in the event of a deadlock and arranged new elections. It had the power to conduct referenda, to rescind the decisions and orders of the Council of Ministers if they were not in accordance with the law and constitution. The Presidium itself was empowered to interpret the law and constitution. Ministers were appointed and removed by the Presidium, but normally at the instance of the Council of Ministers. The Presidium commanded the armed forces and had the power to declare war.

The constitution of 1977 defined the separation of powers between the central government and the constituent republics with their own Supreme Soviets, Councils of Ministers and Presidia. The Law on Elections to the Supreme Soviet of the USSR, 1978, laid down procedures for choosing candidates, who stood either as Communists or as 'non-party' candidates, and were elected by universal adult suffrage and direct ballot, following a preliminary selection conference.

On 13 Mar 1990 the Soviet Congress of People's Deputies repealed Art. 6 of the constitution, ending the Communist Party's monopoly of political power. It also strengthened the powers of the presidency, combining the posts of head of government and head of state. The president could be subject to a parliamentary veto and was prohibited from declaring a state of emergency in any of the Soviet republics without the agreement of local officials. Mikhail Gorbachev, the sole candidate, was elected president by the Congress on 15 Mar 1990. The president would be chosen by popular election in 1995. In Oct 1990 the Supreme Soviet passed a law giving political parties equivalent legal status to the Communist Party, opening the way for a multi-party democracy. At the same time the Communist Party's authority over Soviet institutions – including the armed forces, the KGB, and the official trade unions – was removed. The constitutional position was, however, complicated by 9 of the USSR's 15 constituent republics having declared by Jun 1990 that their own laws had precedence over those of central government. The attempted coup of Aug 1991 transformed the constitutional position once again and precipitated the collapse of the Soviet Union. The Soviet Union ceased to exist on 31 Dec 1991 after the formation of the Commonwealth of Independent States (see p. 24).

For Russia, see p. 89. See also entries for Armenia, Belarus, Moldova, Ukraine, etc.

UNITED KINGDOM

Parliament has two houses, the House of Lords and the House of Commons. The Commons are elected directly by universal adult suffrage for a five-year term. In 1918 the franchise was for men over 21 and women over 30; it was extended to women over 21 in 1928, and in 1970 the voting age was lowered to 18 years. The Lords is composed of hereditary peers and peeresses, those on whom peerages have been conferred for life, 2 archbishops and 24 bishops.

No English or Scottish peer may sit in the Commons unless he has disclaimed his title for life; Irish peers may sit.

The executive power lies nominally with the Crown, but in fact is exercised through the cabinet of responsible ministers, headed by the Prime Minister who recommends the appointment of other ministers. Ministers are members of either house.

In 1918 the House of Lords was as it had been reorganized by the Parliament Act of 1911. Bills certified by the Speaker of the House of Commons as money bills were to receive the royal assent one month after being sent to the House of Lords, whether the Lords had approved them or not. Any other public bill (except for one extending the life of parliament) passed by the Commons in three successive sessions and rejected by the Lords was to receive the royal assent nevertheless, provided two years had elapsed between the second reading in the first session of the Commons and the third reading in the third session. The 1949 Parliament Act reduced the delaying powers of the upper house to two sessions and one year. In 1958 the parliamentary balance of the house was improved by the introduction of peerages given for life to men and women by the Sovereign on the advice of the Prime Minister. Opposition party leaders are able to convey their own recommendations for peerages through the Prime Minister to the Queen.

Parliament sits from September or October to the same time of the following year, with a summer recess beginning in July. During adjournments the Speaker or the Lord Chancellor may give notice of an earlier meeting if it is in the national interest. All sessions end by prorogation, and all bills not passed by then lapse. Bills (including private members' bills) may originate in either House unless they deal with finance or representation, when they are introduced in the Commons. Until 1939 private members generally had precedence for bills and motions on some 22 days in each session, of which some 13 days would be Fridays and shorter than other working days. Since 1967 private members have had precedence on 20 Fridays in each session. The United Kingdom has no written constitution.

YUGOSLAVIA

The Republic was established in 1945, with a President in place of the King. The constitution framed in 1953 provided for a parliament of two houses, the Federal Council and the Council of Producers, the latter being composed of one deputy for every 70 000 of the active population – that is, all engaged in production, transport and commerce. The houses sat separately except for joint sessions to elect officers, including the President of the Republic.

In 1963 a new Federal Assembly was established, with five chambers: Federal, Economic, Education and Culture, Social Welfare and Health, Organizational-Political. Each had 120 deputies and the Federal Chamber also had 70 members delegated by the six republics and two autonomous provinces; they sat as a Chamber of Nationalities. All members were elected for four years, half their number being renewed every two years; no one could be elected successively as a member of the same chamber or of the Federal Executive Council.

The Federal Chamber elected the Federal Executive Council from among its own members, to act as the Assembly's political executive organ; it consisted of a President, two Vice-Presidents and 14 members. The President of the Republic was elected by the Assembly in joint session of all its chambers.

In 1974 a new constitution set up a system of assemblies, based on work-place, employment or community, and at its apex a new bicameral legislature, the Assembly, consisting of the Federal Chamber and the Chamber of Republics and Provinces. The Federal Chamber had 30 delegates from self-managing organizations, communities and socio-political organizations from each Republic, and 20 from each Autonomous Province. The Chamber of Republics and Provinces had 12 from each Republican Assembly and 8 from each Provincial Assembly. The Federal Executive Council had a Chairman (prime minister), 14 members, 8 Federal Secretaries and 6 Chairmen of Federal Committees. The Republics were equally represented, with corresponding representation of the Autonomous Provinces. The prime minister was proposed by the President and elected by the Assembly, who also elected the other ministers at the proposal of the prime minister.

There was a State Presidency of eight members elected every five years; the annual President was Head of State.

The suffrage was for all over 18 years (16, if employed).

Against a background of increasing demands for secession, in Dec 1989 a constitutional change gave the central government more power to deal with unrest. Constitutional changes in the constituent republics (especially Slovenia and Croatia) increased the likelihood that the country would fall apart.

Following the disintegration of Yugoslavia, and the emergence of the independent states of Slovenia, Croatia, Bosnia-Hercegovina and Macedonia, the two remaining constituents of Yugoslavia (Serbia and Montenegro) announced on 27 Apr 1992 the formation of a federal republic of Yugoslavia constituted by themselves as the legal successor to the former Socialist Federal Republic of Yugoslavia. Under the 1992 constitution, the head of state is the Federal President, elected by both chambers of the federal parliament.

The federal parliament consists of two chambers. The Chamber of the Republics has 40 members, 20 each elected from the assemblies of Montenegro and Serbia. Its assent is necessary to all legislation. The Chamber of Citizens has 138 members, elected by universal suffrage.

4 MINISTERS

ALBANIA

Turham Pasha was Prime Minister from 1918–1920. S. Delvin, 1920 and in Dec 1920 H. Prishtina was P.M. for a few days. P. Evangheli, Jul–Dec 1921; X. Ypi, Dec 1921–Dec 1922. A. Zogu (later King Zog) Dec 1922–Feb 1924; S. Verlaci, Feb 1924–Jun 1924; F. Noli, Jun–Dec 1924; K. Kotta, Dec 1924–Mar 1930.

Date of taking office	Prime Minister	Foreign Minister	Finance Minister
12 Jan 1933	P. Evangheli	X. Vila	A. Dibra

In Apr 1939 Italy invaded Albania and in Jun the office of Foreign Minister was abolished.

Date of taking office	Prime Minister	Foreign Minister	Finance Minister
12 Apr 1939	S. Verlazi	X. Dino	
3 Dec 1941	M. Kruja		
19 Jan 1943	E. Libohova		
13 Feb 1943	M. Bushati		
12 May 1943	E. Libohova		
2 Dec 1945	E. Hoxha	N. Miskane	
24 Mar 1946		E. Hoxha	
		Gen. M. Shehu	
24 Jul 1953		B. Shtylla	T. Jakova
20 Jul 1954	Gen. M. Shehu		A. Kellezi
4 Jun 1956			A. Verli
18 Mar 1966		N. Nase	
29 Oct 1974			L. Gogo
13 Nov 1976			H. Toska
14 Jan 1982	A. Çarçani		Q. Mihali
1 Jul 1982		R. Malile	
17 Feb 1984			N. Gjyzari
17 Jul 1986			A. Nako
22 Feb 1991	F. Nano		
5 Jun 1991	Y. Bufi		
10 Dec 1991	V. Ahmeti		
13 Apr 1992	A. Meksi	A. Serreqi	G. Rulli

ALBANIA (*continued*)

Date of taking office	Prime Minister	Foreign Minister	Finance Minister
1994			P. Dishnica
1995			D. Vrioni
1996		T. Shehu	R. Bode
1997	B. Fino		

ARMENIA

Date of taking office	Prime Minister	Foreign Minister	Finance Minister
1992	K. Arutyunyan	R. Hovannisyan	
Nov 1992		A. Kirakosyan	
Feb 1993	H. Bagratian		
5 Jul 1995		V. Papazian	L. Barkhoudarin
21 Mar 1997	R. Kocharyan		

AUSTRIA

MINISTERS FOR AUSTRIA

Date of taking office	Prime Minister	Finance Minister
21 Dec 1899	H. von Wittek	A. von Jorkasch-Koch
19 Jan 1900	E. von Kœrber	E. Bohm von Bawerk
26 Oct 1904		M. Kosel
1 Jan 1905	P. Gautsch von Frankenthurn	
2 May 1906	K. von Hohenlohe-Waldenburg-Schillingsfürst	
2 Jun 1906	M.W. von Beck	W. von Korytowsky
14 Nov 1908	R. von Bienerth	Baron von Jorkasch-Koch
10 Feb 1909		L. von Biliński
9 Jan 1911		R. Meyer
28 Jun 1911	P. Gautsch von Frankenthurn	
3 Nov 1911	K. von Stürgkh	
19 Nov 1911		Count von Zaleski
8 Oct 1913		A. Engel von Mainfelden
3 Nov 1915		K. von Leth
31 Oct 1916	E. von Kœrber	K. Marek

101

AUSTRIA (*continued*)

Date of taking office	Prime Minister	Finance Minister
20 Dec 1916	H. von Clam-Martinitz	A.B. Spitzmüller
23 Jun 1917	E. Seidler von Feuchtenegg	Baron von Wimmer
25 Jul 1918	M. Hussarek von Heinlein	
27 Oct 1918	H. Lammasch	J. Redlich

MINISTERS FOR COMMON AFFAIRS

Date of taking office	Prime Minister	Foreign Minister	Finance Minister
4 Jun 1882			B. von Kállay
16 May 1895	A. Golochowski	A. Golochowski	
14 Jul 1903			A. Golochowski
24 Jul 1903			S. Burián
24 Oct 1906	A. Lexa d'Aerenthal	A. Lexa d'Aerenthal	
17 Feb 1912	L. Berchthold	L. Berchthold	
20 Feb 1912			L. von Bilińsky
13 Jan 1915	S. Burián	S. Burián	
7 Feb 1915			E. von Kœrber
2 Dec 1916			K. von Hohenlohe-Waldenburg-Schillingsfürst
22 Dec 1916	O. Czernin	O. Czernin	S. Burián
16 Apr 1918			A.B. Spitzmüller
24 Oct 1918	J. Andrássy		
2 Nov 1918	L. von Flotow		
4 Nov 1918			Baron von Kuh-Chrobak
12 Nov 1918	K. Renner	K. Renner	R. Reisch
25 Jun 1920	M. Mayr	M. Mayr	F. Grimm
21 Jun 1921	J. Schober	Baron Hennet	A. Gurtler
31 May 1922	I. Seipel	A. Grunberger	V. Kienbock
17 Nov 1924	K. Ramek	H. Mataja	J. Ahrer
15 Jan 1926	I. Seipel	I. Seipel	V. Kienbock
3 May 1929	E. Streeruwitz		
26 Sep 1929	J. Schober	J. Schober	O. Juch
25 Sep 1930	M. Vaugoin		
3 Dec 1930	O. Ender		
20 Jun 1931	K. Buresch		

AUSTRIA (*continued*)

Date of taking office	Prime Minister	Foreign Minister	Finance Minister
29 Jan 1932		K. Buresch	E. Weidenhoffer
20 May 1932	E. Dollfuss	E. Dollfuss	
10 May 1933			K. Buresch
30 Jul 1934	K. Schuschnigg	E. Berger-Waldenegg	
18 Oct 1935			L. Draxler
3 Nov 1936		G. Schmidt	H. Neumayer
13 Mar 1938	A. Seyss-Inquart	W. Wolf	
25 May 1938			M. Fischbock

Note: The cabinet was limited in size after the union with the German Third Reich. The Foreign Ministry was carried on in Berlin by the German Foreign Minister. The Seyss-Inquart cabinet was dissolved on the Allied occupation of Austria, and a provisional government under Dr K. Renner took office on 28 Apr 1945.

Date of taking office	Prime Minister	Foreign Minister	Finance Minister
18 Dec 1945	L. Figl	L. Figl	G. Zimmerman
1 May 1946		K. Gruber	
7 Nov 1949			E. Margaretha
23 Jan 1952			R. Kamitz
2 Apr 1953	J. Raab		
25 Nov 1953		L. Figl	
16 Jul 1959		B. Kreisky	
9 Jun 1960		E. Heilingsetzer	
11 Apr 1961	A. Gorbach	B. Kreisky	J. Klaus
27 Mar 1963			F. Korinek
2 Apr 1964	J. Klaus		W. Schmitz
18 Apr 1966		L. Toncic-Sorinj	
18 Jan 1968		K. Waldheim	S. Koren
21 Apr 1970	B. Kreisky	R. Kirschlager	H. Androsch
25 Jun 1974		E. Bielka-Karttrev	
29 Oct 1976		W. Pahr	
14 Jan 1981			H. Salcher
24 May 1983	F. Sinowatz	E. Lane	
10 Sep 1984		L. Gratz	F. Vranitzky
9 Jun 1986	F. Vranitzky	P. Jankowitsch	F. Lacina
21 Jan 1987		A. Monk	
12 Mar 1996		W. Schuessel	V. Klima
19 Jan 1997	V. Klima		R. Edlinger

BELARUS

Belarus became independent in Aug 1991.

Date of taking office	Prime Minister	Foreign Minister	Finance Minister
1991	V. Kebich		
Aug 1994	M. Chyhir	U. Syanko	
1995			P. Dzik

BELGIUM

Date of taking office	Prime Minister	Foreign Minister	Finance Minister
26 Mar 1894	J. de Burlet		P. de Smet de Nayer
26 Feb 1896	P. de Smet de Nayer	M. de Favereau	
24 Jan 1899	J. Vandenpeereboom		
5 Aug 1899	P. de Smet de Nayer		
2 May 1907	J. de Trooz	J. Davignon	J. Liebaert
9 Jan 1908	F. Schollaert		J. Renkin
Nov 1908			J. Liebaert
14 Jun 1911	M. Levie		
13 Jul 1911	Ch. de Broqueville		
27 Feb 1914			A. Burggraf van de Vyvere
21 Jan 1916		E. van Beyens	
30 Jul 1917		Ch. de Broqueville	
Jan 1918		P. Hymans	
3 Jun 1918	G. Cooreman		
21 Nov 1918	L. Delacroix	P. Hyams	L. Delacroix
20 Nov 1920	H. Carton de Wiart	H. Jaspar	G. Theunis
14 Dec 1921	G. Theunis		
13 May 1925	M. van de Vijvere		
17 Jun 1925	Viscomte Poullet	E. Vandervelde	Baron Houtart
22 Nov 1927		P. Hyams	
24 Nov 1929	L. Delacroix		
6 Jun 1931	J. Renkin	P. Hyams	
19 Feb 1932			J. Renkin
23 Oct 1932	Ct de Brocqueville		H. Jaspar

BELGIUM (*continued*)

Date of taking office	Prime Minister	Foreign Minister	Finance Minister
12 Jun 1934		H. Jaspar	M. Sap
25 Mar 1935	P. van Zeeland	P. van Zeeland	M.L. Gérard
13 Jun 1936		P.H. Spaak	H. de Man
24 Nov 1937	P.E. Janson		
9 Mar 1938			M. Merlot (*ad interim*)
1 May 1938			E. Soudan
15 May 1938	P.H. Spaak		M.L. Gérard
3 Dec 1938			A. Jannsen
21 Jan 1939		P.E. Janson	
20 Feb 1939	H. Pierlot	E. Soudan	C. Gutt
18 Apr 1939		H. Pierlot	
4 Sep 1939		P.H. Spaak	
11 Feb 1945	A. van Acker		G. Eyskens
31 Mar 1946			F. de Vogel
19 Mar 1947	P.H. Spaak		G. Eyskens
10 Aug 1949	G. Eyskens	P. van Zeeland	H. Liebaert
8 Jun 1950	J. Duvieusart		J. van Houtte
15 Aug 1950	J. Pholien		
15 Jan 1952	J. van Houtte		Baron Janssen
12 Apr 1954	A. van Acker	P.H. Spaak	H. Liebaert
11 May 1957		V. Larock	
25 Jun 1958	G. Eyskens	P. Wigny	J. van Houtte
25 Apr 1961	T. Lefevre	P.H. Spaak	A. Dequae
28 Jul 1965	P. Harmel		G. Eyskens
20 Mar 1966	P. van den Boeynants	P. Harmel	R. Henrion
18 Jun 1968	G. Eyskens		Baron J. Snoy et d'Oppuers
20 Jan 1972			A. Vlerick
22 Jan 1973	E. Le Burton	R. van Elslande	W. de Clercq
25 Apr 1974	L. Tindemans		
3 Jun 1977		H. Simonet	G. Geens
20 Oct 1978	V. Boeynants		
3 Apr 1979	W. Martens		
18 May 1980		C.-F. Nothomb	R. Henrion
30 Jun 1980			P. Hatry
22 Oct 1980			M. Eyskens

BELGIUM (continued)

Date of taking office	Prime Minister	Foreign Minister	Finance Minister
6 Apr 1981	M. Eyskens		R. Vandeputte
17 Dec 1981	W. Martens	L. Tindemans	W. de Clercq
10 Jan 1985			F. Grootjans
12 Nov 1985			M. Eyskens
2 May 1988			P. Maystadt
10 Jun 1989		M. Eyskens	
7 Mar 1992	J.-L. Dehaene	W. Claes	
Oct 1994		F. Vandenbroucke	
Mar 1995		E. Derycke	

BOSNIA–HERCEGOVINA

Date of taking office	Prime Minister	Foreign Minister	Finance Minister
1990	J. Relivan		
Dec 1992	M. Akmandzić	H. Silajdžić	
25 Oct 1993	H. Silajdžić		
1995			B. Bilić
30 Jan 1996	H. Muratović	J. Prlic	M. Kikanović

BULGARIA

Date of taking office	Prime Minister	Foreign Minister	Finance Minister
18 Jan 1899	T. Ivantchov	T. Ivantchov	M. Tenev
28 Jan 1899	D. Grekov		
12 Oct 1899	T. Ivantchov	T. Ivantchov	
23 Jan 1901	R. Petrov		
14 Mar 1901	P. Karavelov	S. Dánev	P. Karavelov
4 Jan 1902	S. Dánev		
15 May 1903	R. Petrov	R. Petrov	L. Payakov
14 Nov 1906	D. Pétkov	D. Stanciov	
16 Mar 1907	P.J. Gúdev		
29 Jan 1908	A. Málinov	S. Paprikov	J. Sallabechev
1910		A. Málinov	A. Liaptchev

BULGARIA (*continued*)

Date of taking office	Prime Minister	Foreign Minister	Finance Minister
20 Mar 1911	S. Dánev		
29 Mar 1911	J.E. Guéchov	J.E. Guéchov	T. Théodorov
4 Jul 1913	S. Dánev		
18 Jul 1913	V. Radoslavov	N. Ghenadiev	D. Tontchev
1914		V. Radoslavov	
16 Jun 1918	A. Málinov		
14 Oct 1919	A.S. Stamboliiski	A.S. Stamboliiski	R. Daskalov
11 Jan 1922			M. Turlakov
10 Feb 1923			P. Yanev

Note: Premier Stamboliiski was killed during the *coup d'état* of 9 Jun 1923.

Date of taking office	Prime Minister	Foreign Minister	Finance Minister
9 Jun 1923	A. Tsankov	K. Kaltov	P. Todorov
1 Jan 1925	A. Lyapchev	A. Burov	V. Mollov
12 Oct 1931	N. Mushanov	N. Mushanov	S. Stefanov
19 May 1934	K. Georgiev	K. Georgiev	P. Todorov (*coup d'état*)
24 May 1934		K. Batalov	
22 Jan 1935	Gen. P. Zlatev		M. Kalandarov (*coup d'état*)
21 Apr 1935	P.M. Toshev	G. Kyoseivanov	M. Ryaskov (*coup d'état*)
23 Nov 1935	G. Kyoseivanov		K. Gunev
1938			D. Bozhilov
16 Feb 1940	B. Filov	I. Popov	
11 Apr 1942		B. Filov	
9 Sep 1943	D. Bozhilov	S. Kirov	
10 Oct 1943		D. Shishmanov	
1 Jun 1944	I. Bagryanov	I. Bagryanov	D. Savov
12 Jun 1944		P. Draganov	
2 Sep 1944	K. Muraviev	P. Stainov	A. Girginov
9 Sep 1944	K. Georgiev		P. Stoyanov
31 Mar 1946		G. Kulishev	I. Stefanov
22 Nov 1946	G. Dimitrov	K. Georgiev	
11 Dec 1947		V. Kolarov	
21 Jul 1949	V. Kolarov		
6 Aug 1949		V. Poptomov	P. Kunin
8 Oct 1949			K. Lazarov

BULGARIA (*continued*)

Date of taking office	Prime Minister	Foreign Minister	Finance Minister
1 Feb 1950	V. Chervenkov		
27 May 1950		M. Neichev	
17 Apr 1956	A. Yugov		
18 Aug 1956		K. Lukanov	
19 Nov 1962	T. Zhivkov		
27 Nov 1962		I. Bashev	D. Popov
8 Jul 1971	S. Todorov		
16 Dec 1971		P. Mladenov	
16 Jun 1976			B. Beltchev
16 Jun 1981	G. Filipov		
21 Mar 1986	G. Atanasov		
20 Sep 1990	A. Loukanov	L. Gotsev	
20 Dec 1990	D. Popov	V. Valkov	I. Kostov
8 Nov 1991	F. Dimitov	S. Ganev	
30 Dec 1992	L. Berov	S. Daskalov	S. Aleksandrov
1993		S. Pashovski	
17 Oct 1994	R. Indzhova		
25 Jan 1995	Z. Videnov[1]	G. Pirinski	D. Kostov

[1] Resigned 22 Dec 1996.

CROATIA

Date of taking office	Prime Minister	Foreign Minister	Finance Minister
1991	J. Manolić		
1992	F. Greguric	Z. Separović	
8 Sep 1992	H. Sarinić	Z. Škrabalo	Z. Jašić
23 Mar 1993	N. Valentić	M. Granić	B. Prka
4 Nov 1995	Z. Makesa		

CYPRUS

Cyprus was a British dependency until 1960, when it became an independent republic. Ministers were appointed in 1959, pending full independence.

CYPRUS (*continued*)

Date of taking office	Prime Minister (or equivalent)	Foreign Minister	Finance Minister
5 Apr 1959	Archbishop Makarios	Archbishop Makarios	R. Theocarous

In 1960 President Makarios combined the powers of President and Prime Minister, and held both.

Date of taking office	Prime Minister (or equivalent)	Foreign Minister	Finance Minister
22 Aug 1960		S. Kyprianou	
1 Jul 1962			R. Solomides
15 Jun 1968			A. Patsalides
16 Jun 1972		L. Christophides	
16 Jul 1974		D. Dimitrou	
8 Aug 1974		G. Clerides	
14 Jan 1975		L. Christophides	

On the death of President Makarios in 1977 the succeeding Presidents followed this practice regarding the post of Prime Minister.

Date of taking office	Prime Minister (or equivalent)	Foreign Minister	Finance Minister
8 Mar 1978		N. Rolandis	
1 Nov 1979			A. Afxentiou
20 Apr 1982			S. Vassiliou
22 Sep 1983		G. Iacovou	
7 Jan 1985			C. Kittis
29 Jul 1986			C. Mavrellis
28 Feb 1988			G. Syrimis
28 Feb 1993		A. Michaelides	P. Economides
7 Nov 1994			C. Christodoulou

The Turkish Federated State of Cyprus was proclaimed on 13 Feb 1975 with Rauf Denktash as President. A constituent assembly was sworn in on 24 Feb 1975 and elections were held on 20 Jun 1976. A cabinet was appointed after N. Konuk had been appointed Prime Minister on 3 Jul 1976. The State declared itself independent on 15 Nov 1983 as the Turkish Republic of Northern Cyprus.

CZECHOSLOVAKIA

Date of taking office	Prime Minister	Foreign Minister	Finance Minister
14 Nov 1918	K. Kramař (provisional government)		
8 Jul 1919	V. Tusar	E. Beneš	K. Sontag

CZECHOSLOVAKIA (continued)

Date of taking office	Prime Minister	Foreign Minister	Finance Minister
15 Sep 1920	J. Černý		M. Hanošek
26 Sep 1921	E. Beneš		A. Novák
8 Oct 1922	A. Švehla		T. Becka
18 Mar 1926	J. Černý		K. Engliš
12 Oct 1926	A. Švehla		
13 Oct 1927	Mgr. J. Šrámek		
1 Feb 1929	J. Udrzal		B. Vlasek
8 Dec 1929			K. Engliš
16 Apr 1931			K. Trapl
29 Oct 1932	M. Malypetr		
18 Dec 1935		M. Hodža	
29 Feb 1936	M. Hodža	K. Krofta	E. Franke
21 Jul 1937			J. Kalfus
22 Sep 1938	Gen. J. Syrový		
4 Oct 1938		F. Chvalkovský	
30 Nov 1938	R. Beran		

Note: The Ministry of Foreign Affairs was dissolved by the Reich Protectorate, 18 Mar 1939.

27 Apr 1939	Gen. A. Elias		

Note: A government in exile was set up in London following the German invasion.

24 Jul 1940	Mgr. J. Šrámek	J. Masaryk	E. Outrata
27 Oct 1941			L. Feierabend
6 Nov 1945	Z. Fierlinger		V. Šrobár
2 Jul 1946	K. Gottwald		J. Dolansky
15 Jun 1948	A. Zápotocký	V. Clementis	
14 Mar 1950	V. Široký		
31 Jan 1953		V. David	
21 Mar 1953		V. Široký	J. Kabes
15 Sep 1953			J. Duris
22 Sep 1963	J. Lenárt		R. Dvořák
11 Nov 1965			B. Sucharda
1 Apr 1968	O. Černík	J. Hajek	
19 Sep 1968		O. Černík	

110

CZECHOSLOVAKIA (*continued*)

Date of taking office	Prime Minister	Foreign Minister	Finance Minister

Note: On 31 Dec 1968 Czechoslovakia became a federation, with separate governments for the Czech Socialist Republic and the Slovak Socialist Republic. Details below are for the central, federal, government:

Date of taking office	Prime Minister	Foreign Minister	Finance Minister
1 Jan 1969	O. Černík	J. Marko	B. Sucharda
3 Jan 1971	L. Štrougal		R. Rohliček
9 Dec 1971		B. Chňoupek	
14 Dec 1973			L. Lér
29 Nov 1985		J. Žák	
12 Oct 1988	L. Adamec	J. Johanes	J. Stejskal
10 Dec 1989	M. Čalfa	J. Dienstbier	V. Klaus
1 Jul 1992	J. Strasky		

The dissolution of the Czech and Slovak Federal Republic took place on 31 Dec 1992.

CZECH REPUBLIC

Date of taking office	Prime Minister	Foreign Minister	Finance Minister
26 Jan 1993	V. Klaus	J. Zieleniec	I. Kočàrník

DENMARK

Date of taking office	Prime Minister	Foreign Minister	Finance Minister
23 May 1897	K.E. Hørring	N.F. Ravn	K.E. Hørring
27 Apr 1900	H. de Sehested	H. de Sehested	H.W. Scharling
24 Jul 1901	J.H. Deuntzer	J.H. Deuntzer	C.F. Hage
14 Jan 1905	J.C. Christensen	F.C.O. de Raben-Levetzau	V. Lassen
12 Oct 1908	N.T. Neergaard	C.W. de Ahlefeldt-Laurvigen	C. Brun
16 Aug 1909	L. von Holstein-Ledreborg		

DENMARK (continued)

Date of taking office	Prime Minister	Foreign Minister	Finance Minister
28 Oct 1909	C.T. Zahle	E.J.C. de Scavenius	C.E.C. Brandes
5 Jul 1910	K. Berntsen	C.W. de Ahlefeldt-Laurvigen	N.T. Neergaard
21 Jun 1913	C.T. Zahle	E.J.C. de Scavenius	C.E.C. Brandes
4 May 1920	N. Neergard		N.T. Neergard
9 Oct 1922		C.M.T. Cold	
23 Apr 1924	T. Stauning	C.P.O.G. Moltke	C.V. Bramsnaes
29 Apr 1929		P. Munch	
			H.P. Hansen
4 Nov 1935			V. Buhl
		E.J.C. de Scavenius	
4 May 1942	V. Buhl		
16 Jul 1942			M. Andersen
9 Nov 1942	E. Scavenius		J. Koefoed
8 Nov 1945	K. Kristensen	G. Rasmussen	T. Kristensen
13 Nov 1947	H. Hedtoft		H.C. Hansen
30 Oct 1950	E. Erikson	O.B. Kraft	T. Kristensen
30 Sep 1953	H. Hedtoft	H.C. Hansen	V. Kampmann
29 Jan 1955	H.C. Hansen		
9 Oct 1958		J.O. Krag	
19 Feb 1960	V. Kampmann		
1 Mar 1960			K. Philip
5 Sep 1961			H.R. Knudsen
3 Sep 1962	J.O. Krag	P. Haekkerup	
9 Nov 1962			P. Hansen
24 Aug 1965			H. Grünbaum
28 Nov 1966		J.O. Krag	
1 Oct 1967		H. Tabor	
1 Feb 1968	H.T.I. Baunsgard	P. Hartling	P. Moller
17 Mar 1971			E. Ninn-Hansen
9 Oct 1971	J.O. Krag	K.B. Andersen	H. Grünbaum
5 Oct 1972	A. Jørgensen		
19 Sep 1973	P. Hartling	O. Guldberg	A. Andersen
13 Feb 1975	A. Jørgensen	K.B. Andersen	K. Heinesen
30 Aug 1978		H. Christophersen	
26 Oct 1979		K. Olesen	S. Jakobsen
30 Dec 1981			K. Heinesen
10 Sep 1982	P. Schuter	U. Ellemann-Jensen	H. Christophersen

DENMARK (*continued*)

Date of taking office	Prime Minister	Foreign Minister	Finance Minister
23 Jul 1984			P. Simonsen
30 Oct 1989			H. Dyremose
25 Jan 1993	P.N. Rasmussen	N. Helveg	M. Lykketoft

ESTONIA

Date of taking office	Prime Minister	Foreign Minister	Finance Minister
1991	E. Savissar	L. Meri	R. Miller
30 Jan 1992	T. Vähi		
8 Oct 1992	M. Laar	T. Velliste	M. Üürike
Feb 1994		J. Luik	H. Kranich
28 Oct 1994	A. Tarand		A. Iipstok
23 Mar 1995	T. Vähi	T.H. Ilves	M. Opmann
Oct 1995		S. Kallas	

FINLAND

Date of taking office	Prime Minister	Foreign Minister	Finance Minister
26 Nov 1918	L. Ingman	C. Enckell	
18 Apr 1919	K. Castren		
18 Aug 1919	J. Vennola		
15 Mar 1920	M. Erich	E.R.W. Holsti	M. Wartiowaara
1 Mar 1921	J. Vennola		R. Ryti
14 Nov 1922	K. Kallio	J. Vennola	
18 Jan 1924	A.K. Kajander	C. Enckell	H.M.J. Relander
22 Nov 1924	L. Ingman	H. Procopé	P. Pulkkinen
1 Jan 1926	K. Kallio	E.N. Setälä	K. Järvinen
13 Dec 1926	V. Tanner	V. Voionmaa	A. Ryoma
27 Dec 1928	O. Hantere	H. Procopé	H.M.J. Relander
16 Aug 1929	K. Kallio		T.H. Reinekka
20 Mar 1931	J. Sunila	M. Yrsjö-Koskinen	K. Järvinen
14 Dec 1932	T.M. Kivimaki	A.V. Hackzell	H.M.J. Relander
12 Mar 1937	A.K. Kajander	E.R.W. Holsti	V. Tanner

FINLAND (continued)

Date of taking office	Prime Minister	Foreign Minister	Finance Minister
16 Nov 1938		V. Voionmaa	
13 Dec 1938		E. Erkko	
2 Dec 1939	R. Ryti	V. Tanner	M. Pekkala
27 Mar 1940		R. Witting	
4 Jan 1941	J.W. Rangell		M. Pekkala and J. Koivosto (Joint Ministry)
May 1942			V. Tanner
4 Mar 1943	E. Linkomies	H. Ramsay	
8 Aug 1944	A. Hackzell	C. Enckell	M. Hiltonen
21 Sep 1944	U. Castren		
11 Nov 1944	J. Paasikivi		M. Helo
9 Apr 1945			S. Tuomioja
25 Mar 1946	M. Pekkala		R. Törngren
29 Jul 1948	K.A. Fagerholm		O. Hiltunen
18 Mar 1950	U. Kekkonen	A. Gartz	V.J. Sukselainen
17 Jan 1951			O. Hiltunen
20 Sep 1951		S. Tuomioja	V.J. Rantala
9 Jul 1953		R. Törngren	
16 Nov 1953	S. Tuomioja		T. Junnila
5 May 1954	R. Törngren	U. Kekkonen	V.J. Sukselainen
20 Oct 1954	U. Kekkonen	J. Virolainen	P. Tervo
17 Feb 1956	K.A. Fagerholm	R. Törngren	A. Simonen
27 May 1957	V.J. Sukselainen	J. Virolainen	N. Meinander
2 Jul 1957			M. Miettunen
29 Nov 1957	R. von Feiandt	P.J. Hynninen	L. Hietanen
26 Apr 1958	R. Kuuskoski		M.I.O. Nurmela
29 Aug 1958	K.A. Fagerholm	J. Virolainen	P. Hetemäki
13 Jan 1959	V.J. Sukselainen	R. Törngren	W. Sarjala
19 Jun 1959		A. Karjalainen	
14 Jul 1961	M. Miettunen		
13 Apr 1962	A. Karjalainen		
18 Dec 1963	R.R. Lehto	J. Hallama	E.J. Rekola
12 Sep 1964	J. Virolainen	A. Karjalainen	E. Kaitila
27 May 1966	K.R. Paasio		M. Koivisto
29 Dec 1967			E. Raunio
22 Mar 1968	M. Koivisto		
14 May 1968	T. Aura	V. Leskinen	P. Hetemäki

114

FINLAND (*continued*)

Date of taking office	Prime Minister	Foreign Minister	Finance Minister
15 Jul 1970	A. Karjalainen		C.O. Tallgren
29 Oct 1971	T. Aura	O. Mattila	P. Hetemäki
25 Feb 1972	K.R. Paasio	K. Sorsa	M. Koivisto
4 Sep 1972	K. Sorsa	A. Karjalainen	J. Virolainen
			E. Niskanen
13 Jun 1975	K. Liinamaa	O.J. Mattila	H. Tuominen
			T. Varjas
30 Nov 1975	M. Miettunen	K. Sorsa	P. Paavela
			V. Luukka
29 Sep 1976		E. Korhonen	E. Rekola
			J. Loikkanen
17 May 1977	K. Sorsa	P. Väyrynen	P. Paavela
			E. Rekola
25 May 1979	M. Koivisto		A. Pekkala
			P. Työläjärvi
28 May 1981			M. Forsman
			replaced
			P. Työläjärvi as 2nd
12 Feb 1982	K. Sorsa		
17 Feb 1982		P. Stenbäck	
1 Sep 1982			J. Laine replaced
			M. Forsman as 2nd
6 May 1983		P. Väyrynen	P. Vennamo
			replaced
			J. Laine as 2nd
30 Apr 1987	H. Holkeri	K. Sorsa	E. Liikanen
1 Feb 1989		P. Paasio	
3 Jun 1990			M. Louekoski
26 Apr 1991	E. Aho	P. Väyrynen	I. Viinanen
13 Apr 1995	P. Lipponen	T. Halonen	S. Niinistö

FRANCE

Date of taking office	Prime Minister	Foreign Minister	Finance Minister
27 Jun 1898	E.H. Brisson	T. Delcassé	P.L. Peytral
1 Nov 1898	C. Dupuy		

FRANCE (*continued*)

Date of taking office	*Prime Minister*	*Foreign Minister*	*Finance Minister*
22 Jun 1899	P.M. Waldeck-Rousseau		J. Caillaux
7 Jun 1902	E. Combes		M. Rouvier
24 Jan 1905	M. Rouvier		
13 Mar 1906	F. Sarrien	L. Bourgeois	R. Poincaré
23 Oct 1906	G. Clemenceau	S. Pichon	J. Caillaux
24 Jul 1909	A. Briand		G. Cochery
3 Nov 1910			L.L. Klotz
4 Mar 1911	A.E.E. Monis	J. Cruppi	J. Caillaux
27 Jun 1911	J. Caillaux	J. de Selves	L.L. Klotz
14 Jan 1912	R. Poincaré	R. Poincaré	
18 Jan 1913	A. Briand	C. Jonnart	
24 Mar 1913	L. Barthou	S. Pichon	C. Dumont
8 Dec 1913	G. Doumergue	G. Doumergue	J. Caillaux
9 Jun 1914	R. Viviani	L. Bourgeois	E. Clementel
3 Aug 1914		T. Delcassé	A. Ribot
4 Aug 1914		G. Doumergue	
27 Aug 1914		T. Delcassé	
12 Oct 1915		R. Viviani	
29 Oct 1915	A. Briand	A. Briand	
20 Mar 1917	A. Ribot	A. Ribot	J. Thierry
12 Sep 1917	P. Painlevé		L.L. Klotz
17 Nov 1917	G. Clemenceau	S. Pichon	
20 Jan 1920	A. Millerand	A. Millerand	F. Marsal
20 Oct 1920	M. Leygues		
16 Jan 1921	A. Briand	A. Briand	P. Doumer
15 Jan 1922	R. Poincaré	R. Poincaré	M. de Lasteyrie
9 Jun 1924	F. Marsal		
14 Jun 1924	E. Herriot	E. Herriot	E. Clementel
10 Apr 1925	M. Painlevé		
23 Nov 1925	A. Briand		
23 Aug 1926	R. Poincaré	A. Briand	R. Poincaré
11 Nov 1928			H. Cheron
27 Jul 1929	A. Briand		
2 Nov 1929	A. Tardieu	A. Briand	P. Reynaud
13 Dec 1930	M. Steeg		
27 Jan 1931	P. Laval	A. Briand	P.-E. Flandin
14 Jan 1932		P. Laval	
20 Feb 1932	A. Tardieu	A. Tardieu	

FRANCE (*continued*)

Date of taking office	Prime Minister	Foreign Minister	Finance Minister
3 Jun 1932	E. Herriot	E. Herriot	M. Germain-Martin
18 Dec 1932	J. Paul-Boncour	J. Paul-Boncour	H. Cheron
31 Jan 1933	E. Daladier		G. Bonnet
26 Oct 1933	A. Sarraut		
26 Nov 1933	C. Chautemps		
30 Jan 1934	E. Daladier	E. Daladier	R. Piétri
4 Feb 1934			P. Marchandeau
9 Feb 1934	G. Doumergue	L. Barthou	M. Germain-Martin
13 Oct 1934		P. Laval	
8 Nov 1934	P.-E. Flandin		
1 Jun 1935	F. Bouisson		J. Caillaux
7 Jun 1935	P. Laval		
24 Jan 1936	A. Sarraut	P.-E. Flandin	
5 Jun 1936	L. Blum	Y. Delbos	V. Auriol
22 Jun 1937	C. Chautemps		G. Bonnet
18 Jan 1938			P. Marchandeau
13 Mar 1938	L. Blum	J. Paul-Boncour	L. Blum
10 Apr 1938	E. Daladier	G. Bonnet	P. Marchandeau
2 Nov 1938			P. Reynaud
21 Mar 1940	P. Reynaud	P. Reynaud	L. Lamoureux
18 May 1940		E. Daladier	
5 Jun 1940		P. Reynaud	Y. Bouthilier
16 Jun 1940	Marshal P. Pétain	P. Baudouin	
24 Oct 1940		P. Laval	
14 Dec 1940		P.-E. Flandin	
10 Feb 1941		Adm. F. Darlan	
18 Apr 1942	P. Laval	P. Laval	P. Cathala
10 Sep 1944	Gen. C. de Gaulle	G. Bidault	R. Pleven
29 Jan 1946	F. Gouin		A. Philip
24 Jun 1946	G. Bidault		R. Schuman
16 Dec 1946	L. Blum	L. Blum	A. Philip
22 Jan 1947	P. Ramadier	G. Bidault	R. Schuman
24 Nov 1947	R. Schuman		R. Mayer
26 Jul 1948	A. Marie	R. Schuman	P. Reynaud
5 Sep 1948	R. Schuman		C. Pineau
12 Sep 1948	H. Queuille		H. Queuille

FRANCE (*continued*)

Date of taking office	Prime Minister	Foreign Minister	Finance Minister
12 Jan 1949			M. Petsche
28 Oct 1949	G. Bidault		
2 Jul 1950	H. Queuille		
12 Jul 1950	R. Pleven		
10 Mar 1951	H. Queuille		
11 Aug 1951	R. Pleven		R. Mayer
20 Jan 1952	E. Faure		E. Faure
8 Mar 1952	A. Pinay		A. Pinay
8 Jan 1953	R. Mayer	G. Bidault	M. Borgès-Mauoury
28 Jun 1953	J. Laniel		E. Faure
19 Jun 1954	P. Mendès-France	P. Mendès-France	E. Faure
23 Feb 1955	E. Faure	A. Pinay	P. Pflimlin
31 Jan 1956	G. Mollet	C. Pineau	P. Ramadier
5 Nov 1957	F. Gaillard		P. Pflimlin
14 May 1958	P. Pflimlin		
1 Jun 1958	C. de Gaulle		
8 Jan 1959	M. Debré	M. Couve de Murville	A. Pinay
May 1959			M. Baumgartner
15 Apr 1962	G. Pompidou		V. Giscard d'Estaing
9 Jan 1966			M. Debré
12 Jul 1968	M. Couve de Murville	M. Debré	F. Ortoli
22 Jun 1969	J. Chaban-Delmas	M. Schumann	V. Giscard d'Estaing
6 Jul 1972	P. Messmer		
5 Apr 1973		M. Jobert	V. Giscard d'Estaing
27 May 1974	J. Chirac		
28 May 1974		J. Sauvagnargues	J.-P. Fourcade
17 Aug 1976	R. Barre	L. de Guiringaud	R. Barre
30 Mar 1977			R. Boulin
5 Apr 1978			R. Monory
30 Nov 1978		J. François-Poncet	
21 May 1981	P. Mauroy		
22 May 1981		C. Cheysson	J. Delors
17 Jul 1984	L. Fabius		

FRANCE (*continued*)

Date of taking office	Prime Minister	Foreign Minister	Finance Minister
19 Jul 1984			P. Bérégovoy
7 Dec 1984		R. Dumas	
20 Mar 1986	J. Chirac	J.B. Raimond	E. Balladur
23 Jun 1988	M. Rocard	R. Dumas	P. Bérégovoy
15 May 1991	E. Cresson		
2 Apr 1992	P. Bérégovoy		M. Sapin
29 Mar 1993	E. Balladur	A. Juppé	N. Sarkorzy
18 May 1995	A. Juppé	H. de Charette	A. Madelin
7 Nov 1995			J. Arthuis

GEORGIA

Date of taking office	Prime Minister	Foreign Minister	Finance Minister
6 Jan 1992	T. Sigua		
6 Aug 1993	E. Shevardnadze (acting)		
20 Aug 1993	O. Patsatsia	A. Chikvaidze	D. Iakobidze
8 Dec 1995	N. Lekishvili		
1996	Z. Zhvanian	I. Menagarishvili	

GERMANY

Date of taking office	Prime Minister	Foreign Minister	Finance Minister
26 Oct 1894	Prince von Hohenlohe-Schillingsfürst		
20 Oct 1897		B. von Bülow	
17 Oct 1900	B. von Bülow	Baron von Richthofen	
17 Jan 1906		H. von Tschirschky und Bögendorff	
7 Oct 1907		W. von Schoen	
27 Jun 1909	T. Bethmann-Hollweg		

119

GERMANY (continued)

Date of taking office	Prime Minister	Foreign Minister	Finance Minister
28 Jun 1910		A. von Kiderlen-Wächter	
11 Jan 1913		G. von Jagow	
25 Nov 1916		A. Zimmermann	
14 Jul 1917	G. Michaelis		
7 Aug 1917		R. von Kühlmann	
25 Oct 1917	G. von Herling		
9 Aug 1918		P. von Hintze	
4 Oct 1918	Prince Max of Baden	W. Solf	
9 Nov 1918	Friedrich Ebert		
20 Dec 1918		U. von Brockdorff-Rantzau	
13 Feb 1919	P. Scheidemann	U. von Brockdorff-Rantzau	E. Schiffer
21 Jun 1919	G. Bauer		M. Erzberger
28 Mar 1920	M. Müller	Dr A. Köster	J. Wirth
25 Jun 1920	C. Fehrenbach	W. Simons	
10 May 1921	J. Wirth		A. Hermes
31 Jan 1922		W. Rathenau	
22 Nov 1922	W. Cuno	H. von Rosenberg	
13 Aug 1923	G. Stresemann	G. Stresemann	
30 Nov 1923	W. Marx		H. Luther
15 Jan 1925	H. Luther		O. von Schleiben
19 Jan 1926			H. Reinhold
17 May 1926	W. Marx		H. Kohler
28 Jun 1928	H. Müller		R. Hilferding
3 Nov 1929		J. Curtius	
1 Apr 1930	H. Brüning		H.R. Dietrich
9 Oct 1931		H. Brüning	

Note: The Brüning government was dismissed on 30 May 1932.

2 June 1932	F. von Papen	K. von Neurath	L.E. Schwerin von Krosigk
4 Nov 1932	K. von Schleicher		
30 Jan 1933	A. Hitler		
5 Feb 1938		J. von Ribbentrop	

GERMANY (*continued*)

Date of taking office	Prime Minister	Foreign Minister	Finance Minister
30 Apr 1945	C. Doenitz		

Note: Admiral Doenitz surrendered his powers to the allied occupation forces on 5 June 1945.

FEDERAL REPUBLIC OF GERMANY[1]

Date of taking office	Chancellor	Foreign Minister	Finance Minister
20 Sep 1949	K. Adenauer		F. Schäffer
13 Mar 1951		K. Adenauer	
6 Jun 1955		H. von Brentano	
24 Oct 1957			F. Etzel
14 Nov 1961		G. Schröder	H. Starke
11 Dec 1962			R. Dahlgrün
17 Oct 1963	L. Erhard		
1 Dec 1966	K. Kiesinger	W. Brandt	F.J. Strauss
21 Oct 1969	W. Brandt	W. Scheel	A. Möller
13 May 1971			K. Schiller
7 Jul 1972			H. Schmidt
16 May 1974	H. Schmidt	H.-D. Genscher	H. Apel
3 Feb 1978			H. Matthöfer
29 Apr 1982			M. Lahnstein
1 Oct 1982	H. Kohl		
4 Oct 1982			G. Stoltenberg
13 Apr 1989			T. Waigel
18 May 1992		K. Kinkel	

[1] Following the reunification of Germany on 3 Oct 1990 elections were held on 2 Dec 1990.

GERMAN DEMOCRATIC REPUBLIC

Date of taking office	Prime Minister	Foreign Minister	Finance Minister
15 Nov 1950	O. Grotewohl	G. Dertinger	H. Loch
15 Jan 1953		A. Ackermann	

GERMAN DEMOCRATIC REPUBLIC (*continued*)

Date of taking office	Prime Minister	Foreign Minister	Finance Minister
1 Oct 1953		L. Bolz	
24 Nov 1955			W. Rumpf
24 Sep 1964	W. Stoph		
24 Jun 1965		O. Winzer	
13 Jul 1967			S. Bohm
3 Oct 1973	H. Sindermann		
20 Jan 1975		O. Fischer	
3 Nov 1976	W. Stoph		
4 Jun 1980			Dr W. Schmieder
26 Jun 1981			H. Höfner
13 Nov 1989	H. Modrow		
12 Apr 1990	L. de Maizière	M. Meckel	W. Romberg

The German Democratic Republic ceased to exist on 3 Oct 1990.

GREECE

Date of taking office	Prime Minister	Foreign Minister	Finance Minister
14 Apr 1899	G.N. Theotókis	A. Românos	A.N. Simópoulos
12 Nov 1901	A. Zaimis	A. Zaïmis	P. Negris
2 Dec 1902	T. Delyannis		
11 Jul 1903	D.G. Rhallis	D.G. Rhallis	D.G. Rhallis
1 Dec 1903	G.N. Theotókis		
24 Dec 1904	T. Delyannis		
26 Jun 1905	D.G. Rhallis		
21 Dec 1905	G.N. Theotókis	A.G. Skouzès	A.N. Simópoulos
5 Jul 1908	D.G. Rhallis	G. Baltazzi	D. Gunaris
28 Aug 1909	K. Mavromichalis	K. Mavromichalis	–. Evtaxias
7 Feb 1910	S. Dragoumis		
19 Oct 1910	E. Venizelos	J. Gryparis	L. Koromilas
1912		L. Koromilas	A.N. Diomidis
1913		D. Panàs	
1914		E. Venizelos	
7 Mar 1915	D. Gunaris		
15 Oct 1915	A. Zaïmis		
4 Nov 1915	S. Skuludis	S. Skuludis	S. Dragoumis

GREECE (*continued*)

Date of taking office	Prime Minister	Foreign Minister	Finance Minister
8 Apr 1916			D.G. Rhallis
21 Jun 1916	A. Zaïmis	A. Zaïmis	
16 Sep 1916	N. Kalojeropulos		
8 Oct 1916	S. Lambrós		
26 Apr 1917	A. Zaïmis	A. Zaïmis	
27 Jun 1917	E. Venizelos	N. Politis	M. Negropontis
1 Apr 1921	D. Gounaris	J. Baltazzi	M. Protopapadakis
26 Nov 1922	Col. Gonotas	A. Alexandris	M. Kofinas
11 Mar 1924	A. Papanastasiou	A. Papanastasiou	A. Papanastasiou
7 Oct 1924	A. Michalakopoulos	A. Michalakopoulos	C. Gotsis
25 Oct 1925	T. Rangalos	L.R. Canacaris	T. Rangalos
4 Dec 1926	A. Zaïmis	A. Michalakopoulos	C. Gotsis
19 Jul 1928	E. Venizelos	A. Karapanos	G. Maris
23 Dec 1930		A. Michalakopoulos	
23 Apr 1932			K. Varvaressos
26 May 1932	A. Papanastasiou	A. Papanastasiou	
5 Jun 1932	E. Venizelos	A. Michalakopoulos	
3 Nov 1932	P. Tsaldaris	J. Rallys	P. Tsaldaris
13 Jan 1933	E. Venizelos	A. Michalakopoulos	M. Kaphantaris
6 Mar 1933	Gen. Othonais (*ad interim*)		
10 Mar 1933	P. Tsaldaris	D. Maximos	S. Loverdos
5 Mar 1935		P. Tsaldaris	G. Pesmazoglou
9 Oct 1935	Gen. Kondylis	J. Theotokis	Gen. Kondylis
30 Nov 1935	C. Demerdjis	C. Demerdjis	M. Mandjavinos
15 Mar 1936			G. Mantzarinos
21 Jan 1937	J. Metaxas	J. Metaxas	P. Rediadis
11 Feb 1937			M. Apostolides
29 Jan 1941	A. Korizis		
21 Apr 1941	E. Tsouderos	E. Tsouderos	E. Tsouderos
30 Sep 1941			K. Varvaressos
13 Apr 1944	S. Venizelis	S. Venizelis	M. Manzadones
26 Apr 1944	G. Papandreou	G. Papandreou	
8 Jun 1944			P. Kanellopoulos
31 Aug 1944			A. Svolos
3 Jan 1945	Gen. Plastiras	J. Sophianopoulos	G. Sideris
8 Apr 1945	Adm. Voulgaris		G. Mantzarinos
11 Aug 1945		I. Politis	

GREECE (continued)

Date of taking office	Prime Minister	Foreign Minister	Finance Minister
17 Oct 1945	Archp Danaskires		
1 Nov 1945	P. Kanellopoulos	P. Kanellopoulos	Prof. Cassimatis
21 Nov 1945	T. Sofoulis	J. Sophianopoulos	M. Mylonas
29 Jan 1946		C. Rendis	
4 Apr 1946	M. Poulitsas	C. Tsaldaris	S. Stephanopoulos
17 Apr 1946	C. Tsaldaris		D. Helmis
27 Jan 1947	D. Maximos		
29 Aug 1947	C. Tsaldaris		
7 Sep 1947	T. Sofoulis		
30 Jun 1949	A. Diomedes		
6 Jan 1950	J. Theotokis	P. Pipinelis	G. Mantzarinos
23 Mar 1950	S. Venizelis	S. Venizelis	M. Zaimis
15 Apr 1950	Gen. Plastiras	Gen. Plastiras	K. Kartalis
13 Sep 1950	S. Venizelis	S. Venizelis	S. Castopoulos
2 Feb 1951			G. Mavros
8 Aug 1951		I. Politis	
27 Oct 1951	Gen. Plastiras	S. Venizelis	C. Evelpidis
19 Nov 1952	A. Papagos	S. Stephanopoulos	C. Papyannis
15 Dec 1954			D. Eftaxias
6 Oct 1955	C. Karamanlis	S. Theotokis	A. Apostolides
29 Feb 1956			C. Thiraios
27 May 1956		G. Averoff	
5 Mar 1958	M. Georgakoloulos	G. Pesmajogiou	M. Mestikopoulos
17 May 1958	C. Karamanlis	E. Averoff	C. Papaconstantinou
4 Nov 1961			S. Theotokis
19 Jun 1963	P. Pipinelis	P. Pipinelis	
8 Nov 1963	G. Papandreou	S. Venizelis	C. Mitsotakis
30 Dec 1963	J. Paraskevopoulos	C. Xanthopoulos-Palamos	
18 Feb 1964	G. Papandreou	S. Kostopoulos	C. Mitsotakis
20 Jul 1965	G. Athanasiadis-Novas	G. Melas	S. Allamanis
20 Aug 1965	E. Tsirimokos	E. Tsirimokos	
17 Sep 1965	S. Stephanopoulos		G. Melas
11 Apr 1966		S. Stephanopoulos	
11 May 1966		I. Toumboas	
22 Dec 1966	I. Paraskevopoulos	E. Economou-Gouras	P. Stergiotis
3 Apr 1967	P. Kanellopoulos	P. Kanellopoulos	C. Papaconstantinou
21 Apr 1967	C. Kollios	P. Economou-Gouras	A. Adroutsopoulos

GREECE (*continued*)

Date of taking office	Prime Minister	Foreign Minister	Finance Minister
2 Nov 1967		C. Kollios	
20 Nov 1967		P. Pipinelis	
13 Dec 1967	G. Papadopoulos		
1 Jan 1970		G. Papadopoulos	
26 Aug 1971			I. Koulis
8 Oct 1973	S. Markezinis	C. Xanthopoulos-Palamos	
25 Nov 1973	A. Androutsopoulos	S. Tetenes	A. Androutsopoulos
8 Jul 1974		K. Kypreos (provisional)	
24 Jul 1974	K. Karamanlis		
26 Jul 1974		G. Mavros	I. Pesmazoglou

On 8 Oct 1974 a caretaker government was formed, K. Karamanlis and G. Mavros retaining their posts, other ministers replaced by non-political persons. On 15 Oct 1974 D. Bitsios replaced G. Mavros.

Date of taking office	Prime Minister	Foreign Minister	Finance Minister
21 Nov 1974	K. Karamanlis	D. Bitsios	E. Devletoglou
28 Nov 1977		P. Papaligouras	I. Boutos
10 May 1978		G. Rallis	A. Kanellopoulos
9 May 1980	G. Rallis	K. Mitsotakis	M. Evert
21 Oct 1981	A. Papandreou	I. Charalambopoulos	E. Drettakis
2 Jun 1989	Tz. Tzannetakis	G. Papoulias	A. Samaras
23 Nov 1989	X. Zolotas	A. Samaras	G. Souflias
14 Apr 1990	C. Mitsotakis	M. Papaconstantinou	I. Paleokrassas S. Manos
10 Oct 1993	A. Papandreou	K. Papoulias	G. Gennimatas
20 Jan 1996	C. Simitis	Th. Pangalos	A. Papadopoulos

HUNGARY

Date of taking office	Prime Minister	Foreign Minister	Finance Minister
15 Jan 1895			L. von Lukács
25 Feb 1899	K. von Szell		
27 Jun 1903	K. Khuen-Héderváry		
3 Nov 1903	S. von Tisza		
18 Nov 1905	G. Fejérváry-von-Komlos-Keresztes		G. Fejérváry-von-Komlos-Keresztes

HUNGARY (continued)

Date of taking office	Prime Minister	Foreign Minister	Finance Minister
8 Apr 1906	A. Wekerle		A. Wekerle
17 Jan 1910	K. Khuen-Héderváry		L. von Lukács
22 Jan 1912	L. von Lukács		J. Teleszky
10 Jun 1913	S. von Tisza		
15 Jun 1917	M. von Esterhazy		G. Graz
20 Aug 1917	A. Wekerle		
16 Sep 1917			A. Wekerle
11 Feb 1918			A. Popovics
30 Oct 1918	J. von Hadik		
31 Oct 1918	M. von Károlyi		M. von Károlyi
14 Mar 1920	A. Simonyi-Semadam	Ct P. Teleki	Baron F. Korányi
14 Apr 1921	Ct I. Bethlen	Ct D. Banffy	M. Hegedüs
1 Jan 1922			T. Kállay
17 Jun 1922		G. Daruvary	
1 Jun 1924		T. Scitovsky	J. Bud
1 Nov 1925		L. Valkó	
5 Sep 1928			A. Wekerle
1 Oct 1929	Ct J. Károlyi	Ct J. Károlyi	
22 Aug 1931	G. Károlyi	L. Valkó	Ct J. Károlyi
1 Dec 1931			Baron F. Korányi
1 Oct 1932	G. Gömbös	K. Kánya	B. Imrédy
8 Jan 1935			T. Fabinyi
12 Oct 1936	K. Dáranyi		
9 Mar 1938			L. Reményi-Schneller
13 May 1938	B. Imrédy		
28 Nov 1938		B. Imrédy	
10 Dec 1938		Ct S. Csáky	
16 Feb 1939	Ct P. Teleki		
15 Feb 1941		L. Bárdossy	
5 Apr 1941	L. Bárdossy		
10 Mar 1942	I. Kállay		
23 Mar 1944	D. Sztójay	D. Sztójay	
29 Aug 1944	Gen. Lakatos	Fd-Marshal Henvey	
16 Oct 1944	F. Szálasi	Baron Keményi	
21 Dec 1944	Gen. B. Miklos	J. Gyöngyösy	I. Vásáry
10 Jul 1945			M. Ottványi

HUNGARY (*continued*)

Date of taking office	Prime Minister	Foreign Minister	Finance Minister
15 Nov 1945	Z. Tildy		F. Gordon
5 Feb 1946	F. Nagy		L. Dinnyés
13 Mar 1947			M. Nyárády
31 May 1947	L. Dinnyés	M. Mihalyti	
23 Sep 1947		E. Molnár	
5 Aug 1948		L. Rajk	
9 Dec 1948	I. Dobi		E. Gerö
10 Jun 1949		G. Kállai	I. Kossa
24 Feb 1950			K. Olt
13 May 1951		K. Kiss	
14 Aug 1952	M. Rákosi		
16 Nov 1952		E. Molnár	
4 Jul 1953	I. Nagy	J. Bodoczky	
18 Apr 1955	A. Hegedüs		
30 Jul 1956		I. Horváth	
24 Oct 1956	I. Nagy		
4 Nov 1956	J. Kádár		I. Kossa
9 May 1957			I. Antos
27 Jan 1958	F. Münnich		
16 Feb 1958		E. Sík	
16 Jan 1960			R. Nyers
13 Sep 1961	J. Kádár	J. Péter	
27 Nov 1963			M. Timar
28 Jun 1965	G. Kállai		
14 Apr 1967	J. Fock		P. Vályi
13 May 1971			L. Faluvégi
14 Dec 1973		F. Puja	
15 May 1975	G. Lázár		
27 Jun 1980			I. Hetényi
8 Jul 1983		P. Várkonyi	
30 Dec 1986			P. Medgyessy
25 Jun 1987	K. Grósz		
16 Dec 1987			M. Villányi
24 Nov 1988	M. Németh		
10 May 1989		G. Horn	L. Békesi
22 May 1990	J. Antall	G. Jeszensky	F. Rabár
22 May 1991			M. Kupa
24 Feb 1993			I. Szabó

HUNGARY (continued)

Date of taking office	Prime Minister	Foreign Minister	Finance Minister
27 Dec 1993	P. Boross		
15 Jul 1994	G. Horn	L. Kovacs	L. Békesi
28 Feb 1995			L. Bokros
1 Mar 1996			P. Medgyessy

ICELAND

Date of taking office	Prime Minister	Foreign Minister	Finance Minister
25 Feb 1920	J. Magnusson		N. Gudmundsson
15 Mar 1922	S. Egers		M. Jonsson
22 Mar 1924	J. Magnusson		J. Thorlaksson
28 Feb 1927	T. Thorhallsson		N.J. Kristjansson
20 Oct 1931			E. Arnarson
3 Jun 1932	A. Asgeirsson		A. Asgeirsson
29 Jul 1934	H. Jonasson		E. Jonsson
17 Apr 1939			J. Moller
18 Nov 1941		O. Thors	
1942		S. Stefansson	
16 May 1942	O. Thors		
16 Dec 1942	B. Thordarson	V. Thor	B. Olafsson
1 Oct 1944	O. Thors	O. Thors	P. Magnusson
4 Feb 1947	S.J. Stefansson	B. Benediktsson	J.T. Josefsson
14 Mar 1950	S. Steinthorsson		E. Jonsson
13 Sep 1953	O. Thors	K. Gudmundsson	
24 Jul 1956	H. Jonasson	G.I. Gudmundsson	
20 Dec 1958	E. Jonsson		G.I. Gudmundsson
20 Nov 1959	O. Thors		G. Thorodssen
14 Nov 1963	B. Benediktsson		
1 Sep 1965		E. Jonsson	
10 Jul 1970	J. Hafstein		
10 Oct 1970			M. Jonsson
14 Jul 1971	O. Johannesson	E. Ágústsson	H. Sigursson
29 Aug 1974	G. Hallgrímsson	E. Ágústsson	M.A. Mathiesen
31 Aug 1978	Ó. Jóhannesson	B. Groendal	T. Arnasson
15 Oct 1979	B. Groendal		S. Björgvinsson
8 Feb 1980	G. Thoroddsen	O. Jóhannesson	R. Arnalds

ICELAND (*continued*)

Date of taking office	Prime Minister	Foreign Minister	Finance Minister
26 May 1983	S. Hermannsson	G. Hallgrímsson	A. Gudmundsson
16 Oct 1985			Th. Pálsson
24 Jan 1986		M.Á. Mathiesen	
8 Jul 1987	Th. Pálsson	S. Hermannsson	J.B. Hannibalsson
28 Sep 1988	S. Hermannsson	J.B. Hannibalsson	Ó.R. Grímsson
30 Apr 1991	D. Oddsson		F. Sophusson
23 Apr 1995		H. Ásgrímsson	

IRELAND

Date of taking office	Prime Minister	Foreign Minister	Finance Minister
16 Jan 1922	Provisional government: Finance and General Minister Michael Collins, Foreign Affairs Minister Gavan Duffy.		
6 Dec 1922	W. Cosgrave	D. Fitzgerald P. MacGilligan	W. Cosgrave E. Blythe
9 Mar 1932	E. de Valera	E. de Valera	S. MacEntee
27 Sep 1939			S.T. O'Kelly
9 Jun 1944			F. Aiken
18 Dec 1948	J.A. Costello	S. MacBride	P. MacGilligan
30 May 1951	E. de Valera	F. Aiken	A. MacEntee
2 Jun 1954	J.A. Costello	L. Cosgrave	G. Sweetman
20 Mar 1957	E. de Valera	F. Aiken	J. Ryan
23 Jun 1959	S. Lemass		
21 Apr 1965			J. Lynch
9 Nov 1966	J. Lynch		
10 Nov 1966			C. Haughey
2 Jul 1969		P. Hillery	
8 May 1970			G. Colley
14 Mar 1973	L. Cosgrave	G. FitzGerald	R. Ryan
5 Jul 1977	J. Lynch	M. O'Kennedy	G. Golley
11 Dec 1979	C. Haughey	B. Lenihan	M. O'Kennedy
16 Dec 1980			E. FitzGerald
30 Jun 1981	G. FitzGerald	J. Dooge	J. Bruton
9 Mar 1982	C. Haughey	G. Collins	R. MacSharry
14 Dec 1982	G. FitzGerald	P. Barry	A. Dukes

IRELAND (continued)

Date of taking office	Prime Minister	Foreign Minister	Finance Minister
13 Feb 1986			J. Bruton
10 Mar 1987	C. Haughey	B. Lenihan	R. McSharry
24 Nov 1988			A. Reynolds
12 Jul 1989		G. Collins	
11 Feb 1992	A. Reynolds	D. Andrews	B. Ahern
12 Jan 1993		D. Spring	
15 Dec 1994	J. Bruton		R. Quinn

ITALY

Date of taking office	Prime Minister	Foreign Minister	Finance Minister
29 Jun 1898	L. Pelloux	F.N. Canevaro	P. Carcano
14 May 1899		E. Visconti-Venosta	P. Carmine
24 Jun 1900	G. Saracco		B. Chimirri
14 Feb 1901	G. Zanardelli	G. Prinetti	L. Wollemborg
23 Jun 1903		C. Morin	
3 Aug 1903			P. Carcano
3 Nov 1903	G. Giolitti	T. Tittoni	P. Rosano
10 Nov 1903			L. Luzatti
24 Nov 1904			A. Majorana
27 Mar 1905	A. Fortis		
27 Dec 1905		Marquis de San Giuliano	G. Baccelli
8 Feb 1906	S. de Sonnino	F. de Guicciardini	A. Salandra
9 May 1906	G. Giolitti	T. Tittoni	M. Massimini
1906			P. Lacava
10 Dec 1909	S. de Sonnino	F. de Guicciardini	–. Arlotta
30 Mar 1910	L. Luzzatti	Marquis de San Giuliano	L. Facta
27 Mar 1911	G. Giolitti		
21 Mar 1914	A. Salandra		L. Rava
5 Nov 1914		S. de Sonnino	E. Daneo
19 Jun 1916	P. Boselli		F. Meda
30 Oct 1917	V.E. Orlando		
21 Jun 1919	F. Nitti	V. Scialoja	G. de Nava
15 Jun 1920	G. Giolitti	Ct Sforza	F. Tedesco

ITALY (*continued*)

Date of taking office	Prime Minister	Foreign Minister	Finance Minister
25 Feb 1922	L. Facta	Dr C. Schauzer	G. Bertone
30 Oct 1922	B. Mussolini	B. Mussolini	A. de Stefani
30 Aug 1925			Ct G. Volpi
1 Jan 1929			A. Mosconi
12 Sep 1929		D. Grandi	
20 Jul 1932		B. Mussolini	G. Jung
24 Jan 1935			Ct P. Thaon de Reval
9 June 1936		Ct G.C. de Cortellezzo	
6 Feb 1943		B. Mussolini	Baron G. Acerbo
25 Jul 1943	Marshal Badoglio	Baron Guariglea	D. Bartolini
9 Jun 1944	I. Bonomi		M. Siglienti
10 Dec 1944		A. de Gasperi	M. Presenti
19 Jun 1945	F. Parri		M. Scoccimaro
4 Dec 1945	A. de Gasperi		
17 Oct 1946		P. Nenni	
30 May 1947		Ct Sforza	G. Pella
23 May 1948			E. Vanoni
16 Jul 1953		A. de Gasperi	
17 Aug 1953	G. Pella	G. Pella	
18 Jan 1954	A. Fanfani	A. Piccione	A. Zoli
10 Feb 1954	M. Scelba		R. Tremelloni
18 Sep 1954		G. Martino	
6 Jul 1955	A. Segni		G. Andreotti
20 May 1957	A. Zoli	G. Pella	
19 Jun 1958	A. Fanfani	A. Fanfani	L. Preti
16 Feb 1959	A. Segni		P.E. Taviani
25 Mar 1960	F. Tambroni	A. Segni	G. Trabucchi
26 Jul 1960	A. Fanfani		
29 May 1962		A. Piccione	
21 Jun 1963	G. Leone		M. Martinelli
4 Dec 1963	A. Moro	G. Saragat	R. Tremelloni
6 Mar 1965		A. Fanfani	
23 Feb 1966			L. Preti
24 Jun 1968	G. Leone	G. Medici	M.F. Aggradi
12 Dec 1968	M. Rumor	P. Nenni	O. Reale
5 Aug 1969		A. Moro	G. Bosco
27 Mar 1970			L. Preti

ITALY (continued)

Date of taking office	Prime Minister	Foreign Minister	Finance Minister
6 Aug 1970	E. Colombo		
15 Feb 1972	G. Andreotti		G. Pella
26 Jun 1972		G. Medici	A. Valsecchi
8 Jul 1973	M. Rumor	A. Moro	E. Colombo
15 Mar 1974			M. Tanassi
23 Nov 1974	A. Moro	M. Rumor	B. Visentini
12 Feb 1976			G. Stammati
30 Jul 1976	G. Andreotti	A. Forlani	F.M. Pandolfi
13 Mar 1978			F.M. Malfatti
5 Aug 1979	F. Cossiga	M.F. Malfatti	M. Reviglio
14 Jan 1980		A. Ruffini	
4 Apr 1980		E. Colombo	
19 Oct 1980	A. Forlani		F. Reviglio
28 Jun 1981	G. Spadolini		S. Formica
11 Dec 1982	A. Fanfani		F. Forte
4 Aug 1983	B. Craxi	G. Andreotti	B. Visentini
18 Apr 1987	A. Fanfani		G. Guarino
29 Jul 1987	G. Goria		A. Gava
13 Apr 1988	C. de Mita		E. Colombo
23 Jul 1989	G. Andreotti	G. de Michelis	R. Formica
28 Jun 1992	G. Amato		
29 Apr 1993	C. Ciampi	B. Andreatta	F. Gallo
11 May 1994	S. Berlusconi	A. Martino	G. Tremonti
17 Jan 1995	L. Dini	S. Agnelli	A. Fantozzi
17 May 1996	R. Prodi	L. Dini	V. Visco

LATVIA

Date of taking office	Prime Minister	Foreign Minister
18 Aug 1918	K. Ulmanis	Z.A. Meierovics
19 Jun 1921	Z.A. Meierovics	
27 Jan 1923	J. Pauļuks	
28 Jun 1923	Z.A. Meierovics	
27 Jan 1924	V. Zāmuēls	L. Sēja
19 Dec 1924	H. Celmiņš	
Aug 1925		H. Celmiņš

132

LATVIA (*continued*)

Date of taking office	Prime Minister	Foreign Minister
24 Dec 1925	K. Ulmanis	H. Albāts
7 May 1926	A. Alberings	K. Ulmanis
19 Dec 1926	M. Skujenieks	F. Cielēns
24 Jan 1928	P. Juraševskis	A. Balodis
1 Dec 1928	H. Celmiņš	
9 Apr 1930		H. Celmiņš
27 Mar 1931	K. Ulmanis	
6 Dec 1931	M. Skujenieks	
9 Dec 1931		K. Zariņš
24 Mar 1933	A. Bļodnieks	V. Salnais
17 Mar 1934	K. Ulmanis	

Independence was again achieved in Sep 1991.

Date of taking office	Prime Minister	Foreign Minister
7 May 1990	I. Godmanis	
22 May 1990		J. Jurkāns
10 Nov 1992		G. Andrejevs
20 Jul 1993	V. Birkavs	
16 Sep 1994	M. Gailis	V. Birkavs
21 Dec 1995	A. Šķele	

LITHUANIA

Date of taking office	Prime Minister	Foreign Minister	Finance Minister
17 Jan 1991	G. Vagnorius	A. Saudargas	R. Sikorskis
21 Jul 1992	A. Abišala		
30 Jul 1992			A. Misevičius
2 Dec 1992	B. Lubys		
10 Dec 1992			E. Vilkelis
10 Mar 1993	A. Slezevičius	P. Gylus	
10 Feb 1995			R. Šarkinas
13 Feb 1996	M.L. Stankevičius		
28 Nov 1996	G. Vagnorius		
4 Dec 1996		A. Saudargas	R. Matiliauskas
19 Feb 1997			A. Gediminas Šeneta

LUXEMBOURG

Date of taking office	Prime Minister	Foreign Minister	Finance Minister
23 Nov 1890	Separated from the Netherlands; at that date the following ministers were in office:		
	P. Eyschen	P. Eyschen	–. Mongenast
1915	–. Loutsch	–. Loutsch	E. Reiffen
1 Apr 1921	E. Reuter		A. Neyens
1 Mar 1925	P. Pruom		A. Schmit
1 Jul 1926	J. Bech		M. Clemang
1 Aug 1926			P. Dupong
5 Nov 1937	P. Dupong	J. Bech	

Note: On 15 Aug 1940 the government was declared void by the German forces of occupation. A government in exile continued in London.

Date of taking office	Prime Minister	Foreign Minister	Finance Minister
29 Dec 1953	J. Bech	J. Bech	P. Werner
1 Jan 1958	P. Frieden		
25 Feb 1959	P. Werner	E. Schauss	
15 Jul 1964		P. Werner	
23 Dec 1967		P. Gregoire	
29 Jan 1969		G. Thorn	
18 Jun 1974	G. Thorn	G. Thorn	R. Vouel
19 Jul 1976			J. Poos
16 Jul 1979	P. Werner		J. Santer
21 Nov 1980		C. Flesch	
20 Jul 1984	J. Santer	J.F. Poos	
14 Jul 1989			J.-C. Juncker
20 Jan 1995	J.-C. Juncker		

REPUBLIC OF MACEDONIA

Date of taking office	Prime Minister	Foreign Minister	Finance Minister
20 Mar 1991	N. Kljusev	D. Maleski	M. Tosevski
4 Sep 1992			D. Hajredini
6 Jul 1993		S. Crvenkovski	
20 Dec 1994	B. Crvenkovski		J. Miljovski
23 Feb 1996		L. Frckoski	T. Fiti

MALTA

Date of taking office	Prime Minister	Foreign Minister	Finance Minister
4 Nov 1947	Dr P. Boffa		
1 Jan 1950			A. Colombo
26 Sep 1950	E. Mizzi		F. Azzopardi
20 Dec 1950	B. Olivier		
11 Mar 1955	D. Mintoff		D. Mintoff

Note: Mr Mintoff resigned in Apr 1958 and the constitution was suspended.

Date of taking office	Prime Minister	Foreign Minister	Finance Minister
5 Mar 1962	B. Olivier		G. Felice
21 Jun 1971	D. Mintoff	D. Mintoff	J. Abela
9 Jul 1981			J. Cassar
20 Dec 1981		A.S. Trigona	L. Spiteri
22 Dec 1985	C. Mifsud Bonnici		W. Abela
12 Mar 1987	E. Fenech Adami	V. Tabone	G. Bonello Du Puis
1989		E. Fenech Adami	
1990		G. De Marco	
1992			J. Dalli
28 Oct 1996	A. Sant	G. Vella	L. Spiteri

MOLDOVA

Date of taking office	Prime Minister	Foreign Minister	Finance Minister
1 Jul 1992	A. Sangheli	I. Botnaru	K. Vasylivna
Nov 1993		M. Popov	V. Chitan

MONTENEGRO

Date of taking office	Prime Minister	Foreign Minister	Finance Minister

Ministerial government was established in 1907.

Date of taking office	Prime Minister	Foreign Minister	Finance Minister
17 Apr 1907	L. Tomanovitch	L. Tomanovitch	D. Voukotitch
14 Sep 1910			P. Yergovitch
23 Aug 1911		D. Grégovitch	

135

MONTENEGRO (*continued*)

Date of taking office	Prime Minister	Foreign Minister	Finance Minister
1912	M. Martinovitch	M. Martinovitch	D. Drlievitch
8 May 1913	J. Voukotitch	P. Plamenatz	R. Popovitch
1915			-. Mouchkovitch
May 1916	A. Radovitch	A. Radovitch	A. Radovitch
Jan 1917	M. Tomanovitch	M. Tomanovitch	M. Tomanovitch
13 Jun 1917	E. Popovitch	E. Popovitch	E. Popovitch

THE NETHERLANDS

Date of taking office	Prime Minister	Foreign Minister	Finance Minister
26 Jul 1897	N.G. Pierson	W.H. de Beaufort	N.G. Pierson
27 Jul 1901	A. Kuyper	R. Melvil	J.J.I. Harte van Tecklenburg
9 Mar 1905		A.G. Ellis	
22 Apr 1905		W.M. van Weede van Beerencamp	
14 Aug 1905	T.H. de Meester	D.A.W. van Tets van Goudriaan	T.H. de Meester
12 Feb 1908	T. Heemskerk	R. de Marees van Svinderen	M.J.C.M. Kolkman
29 Aug 1913	P.W.A.C. van der Lynden	P.W.A.C. van der Lynden	A.E.J. Bertling
27 Sep 1913		J. Loudon	
24 Oct 1914			M.W.F. Treb
8 Feb 1916			A. van Gijn
22 Feb 1917			M.W.F. Treub
9 Sep 1918	C.J.M.R. de Beerenbroeck	H.A. van Karnebeek	S. de Vries
28 Jul 1921			D.J. de Geer
11 Aug 1923			H. Colijn
31 Jul 1925	H. Colijn		
8 Mar 1926	D.J. de Geer		D.J. de Geer
30 Mar 1927		F.B. van Blokland	
10 Aug 1929	C.J.M.R. de Beerenbroeck		
24 May 1933	H. Colijn	A.C.D. de Graeff	P.J. Oud

THE NETHERLANDS (*continued*)

Date of taking office	Prime Minister	Foreign Minister	Finance Minister
23 Jun 1937		H. Colijn	J.A. de Wilde
14 Sep 1937		J.A.N. Patijn	
21 May 1939			H. Colijn
10 Aug 1939	D.J. de Geer	E.N. van Kleffens	D.J. de Geer
4 Sep 1940	P.S. Gerbrandy		J.I.M. Welter
23 Nov 1941			J.W. Albarda
15 Sep 1942			J. van den Broek
24 Feb 1945			G.W.M. Huysmans
23 Jun 1945	W. Schermerhorn		P. Lieftinck
26 Feb 1946		J.H. van Royen	
13 Jul 1946	L.J.M. Beel	C.G.W.H. Baron van Boetzelaer van Ooterhuit	
7 Aug 1948	W. Drees	D.U. Stikker	
1 Sep 1952		J.W. Beyen J.M.A.H. Luns *Joint Ministry*	J.A. van der Kieft
12 Oct 1956			H.J. Hofstra
22 Dec 1958	L. Beel	J.M.A.H. Luns	J. Zijlstra
19 May 1959	J.E. de Quay		
24 Jul 1963	V.G.M. Marijunen		J.H. Witteveen
12 Apr 1965	J. Cals		A. Vondeling
22 Nov 1966	J. Zijlstra		J. Zijlstra
3 Apr 1967	P.J.S. de Jong		H.J. Witteveen
6 Jul 1971	B.W. Biescheuval	W.K.N. Schmelzer	R.J. Nelissen
11 May 1973	J. den Uyl	M. van der Stoel	W.F. Duisenberg
19 Dec 1977	A. van Agt	C. van der Klaauw	F. Andriessen
4 Mar 1980			A. van der Stee
11 Sep 1981		M. van der Stoel	
29 May 1982		A. van Agt	
4 Nov 1982	R. Lubbers	H. van den Broek	H. Ruding
7 Nov 1989			W. Kok
22 Aug 1994	W. Kok	H.A.F.M.O. van Mierlo	G. Zalm

NORWAY

Date of taking office	Prime Minister	Foreign Minister	Finance Minister

Norway became independent of Sweden on 7 Jun 1905. At that date the following ministers were in office:

Date of taking office	Prime Minister	Foreign Minister	Finance Minister
Since			
11 Mar 1905	P.C.H.K. Michelsen	J.G. Lövland	P.C.H.K. Michelsen
1906			A. Berge
28 Oct 1907	J.G. Lövland		J.M. Helvorsen
1908	G. Knudsen	W. Christopherson	G. Knudsen
1 Feb 1910	W. Konow	J. Irgens	A. Berge
19 Feb 1912	J. Brathé		W. Konow
31 Jan 1913	G. Knudsen	N. Ihlen	A.T. Omhalt
21 Jun 1920	O.B. Halvorsen	C.F. Michelet	E.H. Bull
22 Jun 1921	O.A. Blehr	A.C. Raested	O.A. Blehr
5 Mar 1923	O. Halvorsen	C.F. Michelet	A. Berge
1 May 1923	A. Berge		
7 Jul 1924	J.L. Mowinckel	J.L. Mowinckel	A. Holmboe
4 Mar 1926	I. Lykke	I. Lykke	F.L. Konow
13 Feb 1928	J.L. Mowinckel	J.L. Mowinckel	P. Lund
12 May 1931	N. Kolstad	B. Bradland	F. Sundby
15 Mar 1932	J. Hundseid		
27 Feb 1933	J.L. Mowinckel	J.L. Mowinckel	P. Lund
14 Nov 1934			G. Jan
19 Mar 1935	J. Nygaardsvold	H. Kont	A. Indreboe
			K. Bergsvik
30 Jun 1939			O.F. Torp
21 Feb 1941		T.H. Lie	

Note: The government in exile continued in London.

Date of taking office	Prime Minister	Foreign Minister	Finance Minister
1 Mar 1942			P. Hartmann
24 Jun 1945	E. Gerhardsen		G. Jahn
1 Nov 1945			E. Brofoss
1 Nov 1947			O. Meisdalshagen
16 Nov 1951	O.F. Torp		T. Bratteli
21 Jan 1955	E. Gerhardsen		M. Lid
1 Mar 1957			T. Bratteli
23 Apr 1960			P.J. Bjerve
23 Jan 1963			A. Cappelen
27 Aug 1963	J. Lyng	E. Wikborg	D. Vårvik

NORWAY (continued)

Date of taking office	Prime Minister	Foreign Minister	Finance Minister
24 Sep 1963	E. Gerhardsen	H. Lange	A. Cappelen
12 Oct 1965	P. Borten	J. Lyng	O. Myrvoll
22 May 1970		S. Stray	
13 Mar 1971	T. Bratteli	A. Cappelen	R. Christiansen
7 Oct 1972	L. Korvald		
18 Oct 1972		D. Vårvik	J. Norbom
16 Oct 1973	T. Bratteli	K. Frydenlund	P. Kleppe
9 Jan 1976	O. Nordli		
5 Oct 1979			U. Sand
4 Feb 1981	G.H. Brundtland		
14 Oct 1981	K.I. Willoch	S. Stray	R. Presthus
25 Apr 1986			A. Skauge
9 May 1986	G.H. Brundtland	K. Frydenlund	G. Berge
9 Mar 1987		T. Stoltenberg	
16 Oct 1989	J.P. Syse	K.M. Bondevik	A. Skauge
3 Nov 1990	G.H. Brundtland	T. Stoltenberg	S. Johnsen
2 Apr 1993		J.J. Holst	
24 Jan 1994		B.T. Godal	
25 Oct 1996	T. Jagland		J. Stoltenberg

POLAND

Date of taking office	Prime Minister	Foreign Minister	Finance Minister
19 Jan 1919	I. Paderewski, provisional government.		
14 Dec 1919	L. Skulski	S. Patek	W. Grabski
24 Jun 1920	W. Grabski		
24 Jul 1920	W. Witos	Prince Sapieha	J.K. Steczkowski
23 Sep 1921	A. Ponikowski	K. Skirmunt	J. Michalski
28 Jun 1922	M. Sliwinski		
31 Jul 1922	M. Nowacki		
16 Dec 1922	W. Sikorski	Ct A. Skrzyński	W. Grabski
28 May 1923	W. Witos		
19 Dec 1923	W. Grabski	Ct M. Zamoyski	
		Ct A. Skrzyński	
29 Nov 1925	Ct A. Skrzyński		J. Zdziechowski
9 Jun 1926	K. Bartel		

139

POLAND (continued)

Date of taking office	Prime Minister	Foreign Minister	Finance Minister
2 Oct 1926	J. Piłsudski	A. Zaleski	G. Czechowicz
18 Oct 1928	K. Bartel		M. Grodyński
14 Apr 1929	K. Świtalski		
29 Dec 1929	K. Bartel		
1 Apr 1930	W. Sławek		I. Matuszewski
25 Aug 1930	J. Piłsudski		
4 Dec 1930	W. Sławek		
29 Dec 1930	K. Bartel		
27 May 1931	A. Prystor		J. Piłsudski
7 Sep 1932			Z. Zawadzki
2 Nov 1932		J. Beck	
10 May 1933	J. Jedrzejewicz		
13 May 1934	L. Kozłowski		
28 Mar 1935	W. Sławek		
12 Oct 1935	M. Kosciałkowski-Zyndram		E. Kwiatkowski
16 May 1936	F.S. Składkowski		
20 Sep 1939	W. Sikorski	A. Zaleski	A. Koc

Note: The government in exile continued in Paris and later in London.

1 Jan 1941			H. Strasburger
28 Aug 1941		Ct E. Raczyński	
14 Jul 1943	S. Mikołajczyk	T. Romer	L. Grosfeld
30 Nov 1944	T. Arciszewski	A. Tarnowski	J. Kwapiński
28 June 1945	E. Osobka-Morawski	W. Rzymowski	K. Dabrowski
6 Feb 1947	J. Cyrankiewicz	Z. Modzelewski	
17 Mar 1951		S. Skrzeszewski	
20 Nov 1952	B. Bierut		
19 Mar 1954	J. Cyrankiewicz		
27 Apr 1956		A. Rapacki	
27 Jan 1957			T. Dietrich
16 Nov 1960			J. Albrecht
15 Jul 1968			S. Majewski
22 Dec 1968		S. Jędrychowski	
28 Jun 1969			J. Trendota
23 Dec 1970	P. Jaroszewicz		
22 Dec 1971		S. Olszowski	S. Jędrychowski
21 Nov 1974			H. Kisiel

POLAND (*continued*)

Date of taking office	Prime Minister	Foreign Minister	Finance Minister
2 Dec 1976		E. Wojtaszek	
18 Feb 1980	E. Babiuch		
24 Aug 1980	J. Pińkowski	J. Czyrek	M. Krzak
11 Feb 1981	Gen. W. Jaruzelski		
21 Jul 1982		S. Olszowski	
8 Oct 1982			S. Nieckadz
6 Nov 1985	Z. Messner	M. Orzechowski	B. Samojlik
13 Oct 1988	M. Rakowski	T. Olechowski	A. Wroblewski
12 Sep 1989	T. Mazowiecki	K. Skubiszewski	L. Balcerowicz
4 Jan 1991	J.K. Bielecki		
Dec 1991	J. Olszewski		K. Lutkowski
Feb 1992			A. Olechowski
11 Jul 1992	H. Suchocka		J. Osiatyński
26 Oct 1993	W. Pawlak	A. Olechowski	M. Borowski
Mar 1994			H. Chmielak
May 1994			G. Kołodko
7 Mar 1995	J. Oleksy	W. Bartoszewski	
Dec 1995		D. Rosati	
7 Feb 1996	W. Cimoszewicz		
5 Feb 1997			M. Belka

PORTUGAL

Date of taking office	Prime Minister	Foreign Minister	Finance Minister
7 Feb 1897	J. Luiciano de Castro	H. de Barros Gomes	F. Ressano Garcia
18 Aug 1898		Veiga Beirao	M.A. Espregueira
25 Jun 1900	E.R. Hintze Ribeiro	J. Arroyo	A. Andrade
1901		F. Mattoso	F. Mattoso
28 Feb 1903		W. de Lima	A.T. de Souza
20 Oct 1904	J. Luiciano de Castro	E. Villaça	M.A. d'Espregueira
20 Mar 1906	E.R. Hintze Ribeiro		
19 May 1906	J.F. Franco	L. Magalhães	E.D. Schröter
2 May 1907		L. Monteiro	F.A. Miranda de Carvalho

PORTUGAL (*continued*)

Date of taking office	Prime Minister	Foreign Minister	Finance Minister
5 Feb 1908	F.J. Ferreira de Amaral	W. de Lima	M.A. d'Espregueira
19 Jul 1908	A.A. de Campos Henriques		
2 Apr 1909	S. Tellez		
15 May 1909	W. de Lima	C. di Roma du Bocage	P. Azevedo
22 Dec 1909	F.A. de Veiga Beirâo		
26 Jun 1910	A.T. de Souza		
5 Oct 1910	T. Braga	B. Machado	J. Belvas
2 Sep 1911	J.P. Chagas		
11 Nov 1911	A. de Vasconcellos	A. de Vasconcellos	S. Pais
16 Jun 1912	D. Leite		V. Ferreira
9 Jan 1913	O. Costa	A. Macieira	O. Costa
8 Feb 1914	B. Machado Guimarâes	F. Andrade	-. Santos Lucas
7 Dec 1914	V.H. de Azevudo		
28 Jan 1915	J.P. Continho de Castro	A.L. Vieira Soares	V.M. de Carvalho Guimarâes
14 Feb 1915	J.P. Chagas		
19 May 1915	A. Costa		
20 Jun 1915	J.P. de Castro		
30 Nov 1915	A. Costa		
16 Mar 1916	A.J. d'Almeida	A.L. Vieira Soares	A. Costa
15 Apr 1917	A. Costa		
8 Dec 1917	S. Pais		
12 Mar 1920	A.N. Bapista	X. da Silva	P. Lopes
2 Mar 1921	B. Machado	D. Pereira	A.M. da Silva
9 Feb 1922	A.M. da Silva	M. Barbosa-Magalhaes	M. Puero
1 Jan 1923		D. Pereira	V. Guimarães
18 Dec 1923	A. de Castro		A. de Castro
15 Feb 1925	V. Guimarães	P. Martins	V. Guimarães
18 Dec 1925	A.M. da Silva	V. Borges	A.M. Guedes
9 Jul 1926	A.O. de F. Carmona	A.M. de B. Rodrigues	J.J.S. de Cordes
10 Nov 1928	J.V. de Freitas	M.C.Q. Meireles	A. de O. Salazar
20 Jan 1930	D. de Oliveira	F.A. Branco	
5 Jul 1932	A. de O. Salazar	C. de S. Mendes	

PORTUGAL (*continued*)

Date of taking office	*Prime Minister*	*Foreign Minister*	*Finance Minister*
11 Apr 1933		J.C. da Mata	
23 Oct 1934		A. de M. Guimarães	
18 Jan 1936		A.R. Monteiro	
		A. de O. Salazar	
28 Aug 1940			J.P. da C.L. Lumbrales
4 Feb 1947		J.C. da Mata	
1 Aug 1950		P.A.V. Cunha	A.A. de Oliveira
8 Jul 1955			A.M.P. Barbosa
13 Aug 1958		M.G.N.D. Matias	
3 May 1961		A.M.G.F. Nogueira	
13 Jun 1965			U.C. de A. Cortes
17 Aug 1968			J.A.D. Rosas
26 Sep 1968	M.J. das N.A. Caetano		
1 Apr 1969		M.J. das N.A. Caetano	
14 Jan 1970		R.M. de M. d'E. Patricio	
11 Aug 1972			M.A.C.A. Dias

The Caetano government was overthrown by the armed forces on 25 Apr 1974.

Date of taking office	*Prime Minister*	*Foreign Minister*	*Finance Minister*
16 May 1974	A. da P. Carlos	M. Soares	J. da S. Lopes
17 Jul 1974	V. dos S. Gonçalves		
25 Mar 1975		E.A. de M. Antunes	J.J. Fragoso
8 Aug 1975		M. Ruivo	
29 Aug 1975	J.B.P. de Azevedo		
19 Sep 1975		E.A. de M. Antunes	F.S. Zenha
16 Jul 1976	M. Soares		
23 Jul 1976		J.M. Ferreira	H.M. Carreira
10 Oct 1977		M. Soares	
28 Aug 1978	A.J.N. da Costa	C.G. Gago	J. da S. Lopes
25 Oct 1978	C.A.M. Pinto		
22 Nov 1978		J. de F. Cruz	M.J. Nunes
19 Jul 1979	M. de L. Pintassilgo		
1 Aug 1979			A.S. Franco
29 Dec 1979	F.L. Sá Carneiro		
3 Jan 1980		D.F. do Amaral	A.A. Cavaco e Silva
4 Dec 1980	D.F. do Amaral (interim)		

PORTUGAL (continued)

Date of taking office	Prime Minister	Foreign Minister	Finance Minister
22 Dec 1980	F.J.P. Pinto Balsemão		
9 Jan 1981		A.G. Pereira	J.A.M. Leitão
4 Sep 1981			J.F. Salgueiro
4 Jun 1982		V.G. Pereira	

F.J.P. Pinto Balsemão resigned on 19 Dec 1982. Dr Pereira Crespo was appointed Prime Minister on 27 Dec 1982, but his nominated ministry was not accepted. Pinto Balsemão was recalled on 23 Jan 1983 to lead a caretaker government, with the Foreign and Finance Ministers who were in office at his resignation, pending elections.

Date of taking office	Prime Minister	Foreign Minister	Finance Minister
9 Jun 1983	Dr M. Soares	J. Gama	E. Lopes
6 Nov 1985	A.C. Silva	P.P. de Miranda	M. Cadilhe
17 Aug 1987		J. de D. Pinteiro	
5 Jan 1990			M. Beleza
1992		J.D. Barroso	J.B. de Macedo
1993			E.A. Catrogo
30 Oct 1995	A. Guterres	J. Gama	A.S. Franco

ROMANIA

Date of taking office	Prime Minister	Foreign Minister	Finance Minister
11 Apr 1899	G.C. Cantacuzène	J. Lahovari	G. Manu
7 Jul 1900	P.P. Carp	A. Marghiloman	P.P. Carp
14 Feb 1901	D. Stourdza	D. Stourdza	G.D. Pallade
1902		J.C. Brătianu	E. Costinescu
4 Jan 1905	G. Cantacuzène	J. Lahovari	T. Ionescu
25 Mar 1907	D. Stourdza	D. Stourdza	E. Costinescu
Mar 1909	J.C. Brătianu	A.G. Djuvara	
10 Jan 1911	P.P. Carp	T. Majorescu	P.P. Carp
10 Apr 1912	T. Majorescu		A. Marghiloman
16 Jan 1914	J.C. Brătianu	E. Porumbaru	E. Costinescu
9 Feb 1918	A. Avarescu		
19 Mar 1918	A. Marghiloman	C. Arion	M. Saulescu
16 Mar 1920	A. Avarescu	D. Zamsirescu	C. Argetoianu

144

ROMANIA (*continued*)

Date of taking office	Prime Minister	Foreign Minister	Finance Minister
21 Jun 1920		T. Ionescu	N. Titulescu
19 Jan 1922	I. Brătianu	I. Duca	V. Brătianu
30 Mar 1926	Gen. A. Averescu	M. Mitilineu	I. Lapedatu
27 Mar 1927			Gen. A. Averescu
24 Nov 1927	V. Brătianu	N. Titulescu	V. Brătianu
11 Nov 1928	J. Maniu	G. Mironescu	M. Popovici
Jun 1930			M. Manoilescu
19 Apr 1931	N. Iorga	C. Argetoianu	C. Argetoianu
		Prince D. Ghica	Prince D. Ghica
6 Jun 1932	A. Vaida-Voevod	G. Mironescu	
11 Aug 1932		A. Vaida-Voevod	G. Mironescu
8 Oct 1932		N. Titulescu	
19 Oct 1932	J. Maniu		V. Madgearu
14 Jan 1933	A. Vaida-Voevod		
14 Nov 1933	I. Duca		D. Brătianu
29 Dec 1933	C. Angelescu		
3 Jan 1934	G. Tatarescu		
5 Jan 1935			V. Slăvescu
4 Feb 1935			V. Antonescu
30 Aug 1936		V. Antonescu	M. Cancicov
28 Dec 1937	O. Goga	I. Micescu	E. Savu
11 Feb 1938	M. Cristea	G. Tatarescu	M. Cancicov
30 Mar 1938		N. Petrescu-Comnen	
21 Dec 1938		G. Gafencu	
1 Feb 1939			M. Constantinescu
6 Mar 1939	M. Calinescu		
21 Sep 1939	Gen. Argeseanu		
28 Sep 1939	C. Argetoianu		
24 Nov 1939	G. Tatarescu		
2 Jun 1940		I. Gigurtu	
4 Jul 1940	I. Gigurtu	M. Manoilescu	E. Savu
3 Sep 1940	I. Antonescu		
15 Sep 1940		M. Sturdza	G. Cretzianu
1 Dec 1940		I Antonescu	
27 Jan 1941			N. Stoenescu
16 Oct 1942			A. Neagu
24 Aug 1944	C. Sănătescu	G. Niculescu-Buzeşti	G. Potopeanu
2 Dec 1944	N. Radescu	C. Vişoianu	M. Romniceanu

145

ROMANIA (continued)

Date of taking office	Prime Minister	Foreign Minister	Finance Minister
6 Mar 1945	P. Groza	G. Tatarescu	D. Alimănişteanu
29 Nov 1946			A. Alexandrini
7 Nov 1947		A. Pauker	V. Luca
9 Mar 1952			D. Petrescu
2 Jun 1952	G. Gheorghiu-Dej		
5 Jul 1952		S. Bughici	
2 Oct 1955	C. Stoica	G. Preoteasa	M. Manescu
14 Jul 1957		I.G. Maurer	
11 Jan 1958		A. Bunaciu	
21 Mar 1961	I.G. Maurer	C. Manescu	A. Vijoli
13 Jul 1968			V. Pirvu
19 Aug 1969			F. Dŭmitrescu
18 Oct 1972		G. Macovescu	
29 Mar 1974	M. Manescu		
7 Mar 1978			P. Niculescu
23 Mar 1978		S. Andrei	
30 Mar 1979	I. Verdeţ		
26 Mar 1981			P. Gigea
21 May 1982	G. Dăscălescu		
11 Nov 1985		I. Vaduva	A. Babe
26 Aug 1986		I. Totu	G. Paraschiv
5 Dec 1987			I. Patan
3 Nov 1989		I. Stoian	
24 Dec 1989	P. Roman	S. Celac	T. Stolojan
28 Jun 1990		A. Năstase	E. Dijmărescu
1 Oct 1991	T. Stolojan		G. Danielescu
4 Nov 1992	N. Văcăroiu	T. Mele şcanu	F. Georgescu
12 Dec 1996	V. Ciorbea	A. Severin	M. Ciumara

RUSSIA

Date of taking office	Prime Minister	Foreign Minister	Finance Minister
16 Jun 1895	J.N. Durnovo		
Sep 1896		N.P. Shishkin	
		Count Muraviev	
22 Jun 1900		Count Lamsdorff	

RUSSIA (*continued*)

Date of taking office	Prime Minister	Foreign Minister	Finance Minister
29 Aug 1903	S.J. Witte		
31 Aug 1903			E.D. Pleske
10 Apr 1904			W.N. Kokovtsov
30 Oct 1905			I.P. Shipov
8 May 1906	I.L. Goremykin	A.P. Isvolsky	W.N. Kokovtsov
23 Jul 1906	P.A. Stolypin		
28 Sep 1910		S. Sazonov	
23 Sep 1911	W.N. Kokovtsov		
11 Nov 1914	I.L. Goremykin		P.L. Bark
2 Feb 1916	B.W. Stürmer		
23 Nov 1916	A.F. Trepov	N.N. Pokrovsky	
9 Jan 1917	N.D. Golitsin	P.N. Milyukov	M.I. Tereshchenko
14 Mar 1917	G.J. Lvov		
8 May 1917		M.I. Tereshchenko	
18 May 1917			A.I. Shingaryov
21 Jul 1917	A.F. Kerensky		
6 Aug 1917			N.V. Nekrasov
27 Sep 1917			M.W. Bernatsky

See USSR p. 160.

RUSSIAN FEDERATION

Date of taking office	Prime Minister	Foreign Minister	Finance Minister
1992	B. Yeltsin (acting)		
15 Jun 1992	Y. Gaidar		
14 Dec 1992	V. Chernomyrdin		
Jan 1996		Y. Primakov	

SERBIA

Date of taking office	Prime Minister	Foreign Minister	Finance Minister
23 Oct 1897	V. Djordjević	V. Djordjević	S.D. Prjović
1898			M. Popović
1899			V. Petrović

SERBIA (continued)

Date of taking office	Prime Minister	Foreign Minister	Finance Minister
12 Jul 1900	A.S. Jovanović	A.S. Jovanović	M. Popović
20 Mar 1901	M. Vujić	M. Vujić	
20 Oct 1902	P. Velimirović	V. Antonić	M. Radovanović
18 Nov 1902	-. Zinzar-Marković		
11 Jun 1903	J. Avakumović		
11 Feb 1904	S. Grujić	A. Nikolić	
10 Dec 1904	N. Pašić		
28 May 1905	L. Stojanović	J. Zujović	Dr -. Markovitch
7 Mar 1906	S. Grujić		
28 Apr 1906	N.P. Pašić	N.P. Pašić	L. Patchou
7 Jul 1908	P. Velimirović	M.G. Milanović	M. Popović
24 Feb 1909	S. Novaković		
11 Oct 1909	N.P. Pachitch		S.M. Protić
25 Jun 1911	M.G. Milanović		
2 Jul 1912	M. Trifković		
12 Sep 1912 until 1919	N.P. Pašić	N.P. Pašić	L. Patchou

SLOVAKIA

Date of taking office	Prime Minister	Foreign Minister	Finance Minister
1 Mar 1993	V. Mečiar		J. Tóth
16 Mar 1994	J. Moravcik		
13 Dec 1994	V. Mečiar	J. Schenk	S. Kozlík

SLOVENIA

Date of taking office	Prime Minister	Foreign Minister	Finance Minister
6 Dec 1992	J. Drnovšek		M. Gaspari
1993		L. Peterle	
26 Jan 1995		Z. Thaler	
1996		D. Kračun	
27 Feb 1997		Z. Thaler	

SPAIN

Date of taking office	Prime Minister	Foreign Minister	Finance Minister
4 Mar 1899	F. Silvela	F. Silvela	R.F. Villaverde
23 Oct 1900	M. de Azcárraga y Palmero	M. Aguilar de Campo	M.A. Salazar
26 Feb 1901	P.M. Sagasta		
6 Mar 1901		Duc de Almodóvar del Rio	- Urzaiz
6 Dec 1902	F. Silvela		
20 Jul 1903	R.F. Villaverde		
8 Dec 1903	A. Maura y Montomar		
16 Dec 1904	M. de Azcárraga y Palmero		
27 Jan 1905	R.F. Villaverde		
23 Jun 1905	E. Montero Rios	P. Gullon	J. de Echegaray
20 Dec 1905	S. Moret		
6 Jul 1906	J. Lopez Dominguez		J. Navarro Reverter
25 Jan 1907	A. Maura y Montomar	M.A. Salazar	G.J. de Osma
1908			A. Gonzales Besada
22 Oct 1909	S. Moret	J. Perez Caballero	J. Alvarado
9 Feb 1910	J. Canalejas	G. Prieto	-. Cobian
12 Nov 1912	A. Figueroa y Torres		J. Navarro Reverter
27 Oct 1913	E. Dato	Marquis de Lima	Count de Bugallal
10 Dec 1915	A. Figueroa y Torres	A. Gimeno	S. Alba
19 Apr 1917	M. Garcia-Prieto	J. Alvarado	
11 Jun 1917	E. Dato		
4 Nov 1917	M. Garcia-Prieto		
23 Mar 1918	A. Maura	E. Dato	A. Gonzales-Besada
9 Nov 1918	M. Garcia-Prieto		
5 May 1920	E. Dato	Marquis de Lema	D. Pascual
13 Mar 1921	M. Allendesalazar		M. Arguelles
8 Mar 1922	S. Guerra	F. Prida	M. Bergamin
7 Dec 1922	Marquis de Alhucemas	S. Alba	J.M. Pedregal
3 Dec 1925	P. de Rivera	M. Yanguas	M. Calvo-Sotelo
27 Feb 1927		P. de Rivera	
1 Jan 1930	Gen. Berenguer	Duke of Alba	M. Arguelles
1 Apr 1931	A. Zamora	A. Lervoux	I. Prieto
16 Dec 1931	M. Azana y Diaz	L.Z. Escolano	J.C. Romeu

SPAIN (continued)

Date of taking office	Prime Minister	Foreign Minister	Finance Minister
1 Mar 1933	A.L. Garcia	L.P. Romero	M.M. Ramon
4 Oct 1934		J.J.R. Garcia	
19 Feb 1936	M. Azana y Diaz	A. Barcia y Trelles	G.F. Lopez

A military rebellion under General Francisco Franco forced the civil war of 1936–1939. With the surrender of Madrid in Mar 1939 the Loyalist government fled to France and a corporate state was set up under Franco's dictatorship.

Date of taking office	Prime Minister	Foreign Minister	Finance Minister
4 Sep 1936	F.L. Caballero	J.A. del Vaijo	J. Negrin
17 May 1937	J. Negrin	J. Giralt	
1 Feb 1938	F. Franco	Count de Jornada	M. Amado
10 Aug 1939		J.B. Atienza	J.L. Lopez
17 Oct 1940		R.S. Suner	
20 May 1941			J.B. Burin
3 Sep 1942		F. Gomez-Jordana	
11 Aug 1944		J.F. de Lequerica	
21 Jul 1945		A.M. Artajo	
1 Mar 1952		F. Gomez y de Llano	
1 Feb 1957		F.M. Castialla y Maiz	M. Navarro Rubio
1 Jul 1965			J.J. Espinoza
29 Oct 1969		G.L. Bravo de Costro	A.M. Luque
9 Jun 1973	Adm. L. Carrero Blanco		
11 Jun 1973		L. Lopez Rodo	A. Barrerra de Irimo
2 Jan 1974	C. Arias Navarro		
4 Jan 1974		P. Cortina Mauri	
31 Oct 1974			R. Cabello de Alba y Grac
13 Dec 1975		J.M. de Areilza y Martines Rodas	J.M. Villar Mir
5 Jul 1976	A. Suarez Gonzalez		
8 Jul 1976		M. Oreja Aguirre	E. Carriles Galarraga
5 Jul 1977			F.F. Ordonez
6 Apr 1979			J.G. Anoveros
8 Sep 1980		J.P. Perez-Llorca	
26 Feb 1981	L. Calvo Sotelo y Bustelo		
2 Dec 1982	F. Gonzalez Marquez		

150

SPAIN (*continued*)

Date of taking office	Prime Minister	Foreign Minister	Finance Minister
3 Dec 1982		F. Moran	M. Boyer
5 Jul 1985		F. Fernandez Ordonez	C. Solchaga
1994		J. Solana Madariaga	
Jul 1995		C. Westendorp	P. Solbes Mira
5 May 1996	J.M. Aznar Lopez	A. Juan Matutes	R. de Rato y Figaredo

SWEDEN

Date of taking office	Prime Minister	Foreign Minister	Finance Minister
12 Oct 1889	J.G.N.S. Åkerhielm	C. Lewenhaupt	E. Bull
1890			F. von Essen
24 Feb 1891	E.G. Boström		
1895			E.G. Boström
1896		L.W.A. Douglas	R. Wersäll
1899		C.H.T.A. de Lagerheim	H.H. Wachtmeister
12 Sep 1900	F.W. von Otter		
5 Jul 1902	E.G. Boström		E.F.W. Meyer
13 Apr 1905	J.O. Ramstedt		
2 Aug 1905	C. Lundeberg		
7 Nov 1905	K. Staaff	E.B. Trolle	J.E. Biesèrt
29 May 1906	S.A.A. Lindman		C.J.G. Swartz
11 Jun 1909		A.F. von Taube	
7 Oct 1911	K. Staaff	J.J.A. Ehrensvärd	A.T. von Adelswärd
17 Dec 1914	H. von Hammarskjöld	K.A. Wallenberg	A.F. Vennersten
29 May 1917	K. Swartz	S.A.A. Lindman	M. Carleson
19 Oct 1917	N. Edén	J. Hellner	R.W. Thorsson
10 Mar 1920	H. Branting	Baron Palmstierna	F.W. Thorsson
23 Feb 1921	O.F. von Sydow	Count H. Wrangel	K.J. Beskow
13 Oct 1921	H. Branting	H. Branting	F.W. Thorsson
9 Apr 1923	E. Trygger	Baron Marcks von Wurtemburg	K.J. Beskow
24 Jan 1925	R. Sandler	O. Unden	F.W. Thorsson
8 May 1925			E. Wigforss

SWEDEN (*continued*)

Date of taking office	Prime Minister	Foreign Minister	Finance Minister
7 Jun 1926	C.G. Ekman	E. Lofgren	E. Lyberg
2 Oct 1928	Adm. Lindman	E. Trygger	N. Wohlin
			A. Dahl
7 Jun 1930	C.G. Ekman	S.G.F. Ramel	F.T. Hamrin
7 Aug 1932	F.T. Hamrin		
24 Sep 1932	P.A. Hansson	R.J. Sandler	E. Wigforss
19 Jun 1936	M. Pehrsson	M. Westman	V.S. Ljungdahl
27 Sep 1936	P.A. Hansson	R.J. Sandler	E. Wigforss
12 Dec 1939		C. Gunther	
31 Jul 1945		O. Unden	
10 Oct 1946	T. Erlander		
30 Jun 1949			D. Hall
20 Oct 1949			P.E. Sköld
25 Sep 1955			G. Strang
19 Sep 1962		T. Nilsson	
14 Oct 1969	O. Palme		
29 Jun 1971		K. Wickmann	
31 Oct 1973		S. Andersson	
7 Oct 1976	T. Fälldin		
8 Oct 1976		K. Söder	I. Mundebo
13 Oct 1978	O. Ullsten		
18 Oct 1978		H. Blix	
11 Oct 1979	T. Fälldin		
12 Oct 1979		O. Ullsten	G. Bohman (Economic Affairs) I. Mundebo (Budget)
31 Jul 1980			I. Mundebo (Economic Affairs) R. Wirtén (Budget)
22 May 1981			R. Wirtén (Economic Affairs and Budget)
8 Oct 1982	O. Palme	L. Bodstrom	K.-O. Feldt
17 Oct 1985		S. Andersson	
12 Mar 1986	I. Carlsson		
27 Feb 1990		L. Hjelm-Wallén	A. Larsson
3 Oct 1991	C. Bildt	M. af Ugglas	A. Wibble

SWEDEN (*continued*)

Date of taking office	*Prime Minister*	*Foreign Minister*	*Finance Minister*
1993		B. Lundgren	
7 Oct 1994	I. Carlsson		
1995			G. Persson
Mar 1996	G. Persson	L. Hjelm-Wallén	E. Åsbrink

SWITZERLAND

The Federal Council has an active Vice-President elected for one year, and seven members each responsible for a department, elected for four years.

	Vice-President	*Foreign Affairs*	*Finance Minister*
1935	A. Meyer	G. Motta	A. Meyer
1936	G. Motta		
1937	J. Baumann		
1938	P. Etter		
1939	M. Pilet-Golaz		E. Wetter
1940	H. Obrecht	M. Pilet-Golaz	
1941	P. Etter		
1942	E. Celio		
1943	W. Stampfli		
1944	M. Pilet-Golaz		E. Nobs
1945	K. Koblet	M. Petitpierre	
1946	P. Etter		
1947	E. Celio		
1948	E. Nobs		
1949	M. Petitpierre		
1950	E. von Steiger		
1951	K. Koblet		
1952	P. Etter		M. Weber
1953	R. Rubattel		
1954	J. Escher		H. Streuli
1955	M. Feldmann		
1956	H. Streuli		
1957	T. Holenstein		
1958	P. Chaudet		
1959	G. Lepovi		
1960	F. Traugott Wahlen		J. Bourgknecht

153

SWITZERLAND (*continued*)

Date of taking office	Prime Minister	Foreign Minister	Finance Minister
1961	P. Chaudet		
1962	J. Bourgknecht	F. Traugott Wahlen	
1963	L. van Moos		R. Bonvin
1964	H.P. Schudi		
1965	H. Schaffner		
1966	R. Bonvin	W. Spuhler	
1967	W. Spuhler		
1968	L. van Moos		N. Celio
1969	H.P. Schudi		
1970	R. Gnägi	P. Graber	
1971	N. Celio		
1972	R. Bonvin		
1973	E. Brugger		G.-A. Chevellaz
1974	P. Graber		
1975	R. Gnägi		
1976	K. Furgler		
1977	W. Ritschard		
1978	H. Hürlimann	P. Aubert	
1979	G.-A. Chevallaz		
1980	K. Furgler		W. Ritschard
1981	F. Honegger		
1982	P. Aubert		
1983	G.-A. Chevallaz		
1984	L. Schlumpf		O. Stich
1985	K. Furgler		
1986	A. Egli		
1987	P. Aubert		
1988	O. Stich		
1989	J.-P. Delamuraz	R. Felber	
1990	A. Koller		
1991	R. Felber		
1992	A. Ogi	F. Cotti	
1993	O. Stich		
1994	K. Villiger		
1995	J.-P. Delamuraz		K. Villiger
1996	A. Koller		

TURKEY

Date of taking office	Prime Minister	Foreign Minister	Finance Minister
Nov 1895	Halil Rifat	A. Tewfik	Sabri Rey
1897			A. Nazif
1898			A. Tewfik
1899			Rechad Bey
13 Nov 1901	Said Pasha		
16 Jan 1903	M. Ferid		A. Nazif
1906			Zia Pasha
22 Jul 1908	Said Pasha		
7 Aug 1908	M. Kamil		
31 Mar 1909	A. Tewfik		
May 1909	H. Hilmi	Rifaat Pasha	Djavid Bey
12 Jan 1910	I. Hakki		
4 Oct 1911	Said Pasha	Assim Bey	Nail Bey
22 Jul 1912	G. Ahmed Mukhtar		
30 Oct 1912	M. Kâmil	Gabriel Effendi	Abdurrahman Bey
23 Jan 1913	M. Sevket		
15 Jun 1913	Said Halim	Said Halim	Rifaat Bey
4 Feb 1917	M. Talât	A. Nessimi	Djavid Bey
Oct 1918	A. Izzet		
Nov 1918	A. Tewfik		
5 Apr 1920	(Grand Vizier) Damad Ferid Pasha	Damad Ferid Pasha	Reshai Bey
21 Oct 1920	(Grand Vizier) Tewfik Pasha	Sefa Bey	Abdullah Bey
		Izzet Pasha	Nuzhet Bey
20 Jan 1921	New constitution established a Council of Commissioners instead of a cabinet.		
1 Feb 1923	(President) Reouf Bey	Ismet Pasha	Abdul Halik Bey
30 Oct 1923	Ismet Pasha		
4 Mar 1925		Tewfik Rustu Bey	
			Hassan Bey
			Abdul Halik Bey
2 Nov 1927			S. Saracoglu
28 Sep 1930			Abdul Halik Bey
1 May 1931			Fuad Agrali
1 Mar 1935	Ismet Inönü		

TURKEY (continued)

Date of taking office	Prime Minister	Foreign Minister	Finance Minister
13 Oct 1937	J. Bayar		
12 Nov 1938		S. Saracoglu	
27 Jan 1939	R. Saydam		
11 Mar 1943	S. Saracoglu	N. Menemencioglu	
15 Jun 1944		S. Saracoglu	
14 Sep 1944		H. Saka	N.E. Sumer
7 Aug 1946	R. Peker		H. Nazmikismir
9 Sep 1947	H. Saka	N. Sadak	
11 Jun 1948			S. Adalan
16 Jan 1949	S. Gunaltay		I. Aksal
22 May 1950	A. Menderes	F. Koprulu	H. Ayan
10 Mar 1951			H. Polatkan
15 Apr 1955		A. Menderes	
9 Dec 1955		F. Koprulu	N. Okmen
20 Jun 1956		E. Menderes	
30 Nov 1956			H. Polatkan
25 Nov 1957		F.R. Zorlu	
28 May 1960	C. Gursel	S. Sarpa	E. Alican
24 Dec 1960			K. Kurdas
20 Nov 1961	I. Inönü		S. Inan
25 Jun 1962		F.C. Erkin	F. Melen
21 Feb 1965	S.H. Urguplu	H. Isik	I. Gursan
27 Oct 1965	S. Demirel	I.S. Çağlayangil	
12 Nov 1966			C. Bilgehan
3 Nov 1969			M. Erez
1 Mar 1971	N. Erim	O. Olcay	S.N. Ergin
22 May 1972	F. Melen	U.H. Bayülken	S. Özbek
15 Apr 1973	N. Talû	U.H. Bayülken	S.T. Müftüoglu
25 Jan 1974	B. Ecevit	T. Gunes	D. Baykal
17 Nov 1974	S. Irmak	M. Esenbel	B. Gürsoy
31 Mar 1975	S. Demirel	I.S. Çağlayangil	Y. Ergenekon
21 Jun 1977	B. Ecevit	G. Okçün	B. Üstünel
21 Jul 1977	S. Demirel	I.S. Çağlayangil	C. Bilgehan
5 Jan 1978	B. Ecevit	G. Okçün	Z. Müezzinoğlu
12 Nov 1979	S. Demirel	H. Erkmen	I. Sezgin

The government was overthrown on 12 Sep 1980 and its powers taken over by a National Security Council of the armed forces.

TURKEY (continued)

Date of taking office		Prime Minister	Foreign Minister	Finance Minister
21 Sep	1980	B. Ülüsü	I. Turkmen	K. Erdem
14 Jul	1982			A.B. Kafaoğlu
13 Dec	1983	T. Özal	V. Halefoğlu	V. Arikan
26 Oct	1984			A.K. Alptemoçin
22 Dec	1987		M. Yilmaz	
31 Mar	1989			E. Pakdemirli
9 Nov	1989	Y. Akbulut		
22 Feb	1990		A. Bozer	
29 Mar	1990			A. Kahveci
12 Oct	1990		A.K. Alptemoçin	
23 Jun	1991	M. Yilmaz	S. Giray	
20 Nov	1991	S. Demirel		S. Oral
21 Nov	1991		H. Çetin	
25 Jun	1993	T. Çiller		I. Attila
27 Jul	1994		M. Soysal	
12 Dec	1994		M. Karayalçin	
27 Mar	1995		E. İnönü	
5 Oct	1995		C. Kirca	
30 Oct	1995		D. Baykal	
6 Mar	1996	M. Yilmaz	E. Gönensay	
7 Mar	1996			L. Kayalar
28 Jun	1996	N. Erbakan	T. Çiller	A. Şener

UKRAINE

Date of taking office		Prime Minister	Foreign Minister	Finance Minister
	1992	V. Fokin	V.A. Kravtev	
13 Oct	1992	L. Kuchma	A. Zlenko	
22 Sep	1993	Y. Zvyahisky		
		(until 27 Sep 1993 then vacant)		
16 Jun	1994	V. Masol		
1 Mar	1995	Y. Marchuk	H. Udovenko	P. Hermanchuk
	1996	P. Lazarenko	G. Udovenko	V. Koronevsky

UNITED KINGDOM

Date of taking office	Prime Minister	Foreign Minister	Finance Minister
25 Jun 1895	Lord Salisbury	Lord Salisbury	M. Hicks-Beach
1 Nov 1900		Lord Lansdowne	
12 Jul 1902	A.J. Balfour		
Aug 1902			C.T. Ritchie
5 Oct 1903			J.A. Chamberlain
10 Dec 1905	H. Campbell-Bannerman	E. Grey	H.H. Asquith
6 Apr 1908	H.H. Asquith		D. Lloyd-George
26 May 1915			R. McKenna
6 Dec 1916	D. Lloyd-George		
10 Dec 1916		A.J. Balfour	A. Bonar Law
10 Jan 1919			A. Chamberlain
23 Oct 1919		Lord Curzon	
1 Apr 1921			Sir R. Horne
23 Oct 1922	A. Bonar Law		
24 Oct 1922			S. Baldwin
22 May 1923	S. Baldwin		
27 Aug 1923			N. Chamberlain
22 Jan 1924	J.R. MacDonald	J.R. MacDonald	P. Snowden
4 Nov 1924	S. Baldwin		
6 Nov 1924		Sir A. Chamberlain	W. Churchill
5 Jun 1929	J.R. MacDonald		
7 Jun 1929		A. Henderson	P. Snowden
25 Aug 1931		Marquis of Reading	
5 Nov 1931		Sir J. Simon	N. Chamberlain
7 Jun 1935	S. Baldwin	Sir S. Hoare	
22 Dec 1935		A. Eden	
28 May 1937	N. Chamberlain		Sir J. Simon
21 Feb 1938		Viscount Halifax	
10 May 1940	W. Churchill		
12 May 1940			Sir K. Wood
22 Dec 1940		A. Eden	
24 Sep 1943			Sir J. Anderson
26 Jul 1945	C. Attlee		
27 Jul 1945		E. Bevin	H. Dalton
13 Nov 1947			Sir S. Cripps
19 Oct 1950			H. Gaitskell
9 Mar 1951		H. Morrison	

UNITED KINGDOM (*continued*)

Date of taking office	Prime Minister	Foreign Minister	Finance Minister
26 Oct 1951	Sir W. Churchill	Sir A. Eden	R. Butler
6 Apr 1955	Sir A. Eden		
7 Apr 1955		H. Macmillan	
20 Dec 1955		S. Lloyd	H. Macmillan
10 Jan 1957	H. Macmillan		
13 Jan 1957			P. Thorneycroft
6 Jan 1958			D. Heathcoat Amory
27 Jul 1960		Lord Home	S. Lloyd
13 Jul 1962			R. Maudling
18 Oct 1963	Sir A. Douglas-Home		
20 Oct 1963		R. Butler	
16 Oct 1964	H. Wilson	P. Gordon Walker	J. Callaghan
22 Jan 1965		M. Stewart	
11 Aug 1966		G. Brown	
30 Nov 1967			R. Jenkins
16 Mar 1968		M. Stewart	
19 Jun 1970	E. Heath		
20 Jun 1970		Sir A. Douglas-Home	I. Macleod
25 Jul 1970			A. Barber
4 Mar 1974	H. Wilson	J. Callaghan	D. Healey
5 Apr 1976	J. Callaghan		
8 Apr 1976		A. Crosland	
21 Feb 1977		D. Owen	
4 May 1979	M. Thatcher		
5 May 1979		Lord Carrington	Sir G. Howe
5 Apr 1982		F. Pym	
12 Jun 1983		Sir G. Howe	N. Lawson
24 Jul 1989		J. Major	
26 Oct 1989			J. Major
28 Oct 1989		D. Hurd	
28 Nov 1990	J. Major		
29 Nov 1990			N. Lamont
27 May 1993			K. Clarke
5 Jul 1995		M. Rifkind	
2 May 1997	A. Blair	R. Cook	G. Brown

USSR

Date of taking office	Prime Minister	Foreign Minister	Finance Minister
8 Nov 1917	V.I. Lenin	G.V. Chicherin	N.N. Krestinskii
1 Dec 1922			G.Y. Sokolnikov
1 Jan 1924	A.I. Rykov		
1 Mar 1926			N.P. Bryukhanov
21 Jul 1930		M.M. Litvinov	
1 Jan 1931	V.M. Molotov		G.F. Grinko
1 Aug 1937			V.Y. Chubar

Ministers were called People's Commissars until 1946.

Date of taking office	Prime Minister	Foreign Minister	Finance Minister
19 Jan 1938			A.G. Zverev
3 May 1939		V.M. Molotov	
7 May 1941	J.V. Stalin		
17 Feb 1948			A.N. Kosygin
28 Dec 1948			A.G. Zverev
4 Mar 1949		A.Y. Vyshinski	
6 Mar 1953	G.M. Malenkov	V.M. Molotov	
8 Feb 1955	N.A. Bulganin		
1 Jun 1956		D.T. Shepilov	
15 Feb 1957		A.A. Gromyko	
31 Mar 1958	N.S. Khrushchev		
16 May 1960			V.F. Garbuzov
15 Oct 1964	A.N. Kosygin		
23 Oct 1980	N.A. Tikhonov		
2 Jul 1985		E. Shevardnadze	
27 Sep 1985	N.I. Ryzhkov		
12 Nov 1985			B.I. Grostev
17 Jul 1989			V.S. Pavlov
15 Jan 1991		A. Bessmertnykh	
14 Jan 1991	V.S. Pavlov		
25 Aug 1991	I. Silayev		

The USSR collapsed on 25 Dec 1991.

YUGOSLAVIA

Date of taking office	Prime Minister	Foreign Minister	Finance Minister
12 Feb 1921	S. Protić	M. Trumbić	V. Janković
24 Dec 1921	N. Pasić	M. Ničić	K. Kumanudi
3 Dec 1922			M. Stojadinović
8 Apr 1926	N. Uzunović		N. Uzunović
1 Feb 1927		N. Perić	B. Narković
23 Feb 1928	V. Vukitčević	V. Marinković	
6 Jan 1929	Gen. P. Zivković		S. Svrljuga
4 Apr 1932	V. Marinković		M. Djordjević
11 Jul 1932	M. Serškić	B. Jevtić	
27 Jan 1934	N. Uzunović		
Dec 1934	B. Jevtić		
24 Jun 1935	M. Stojadinović	M. Stojadinović	D. Letica
5 Feb 1939	D. Cvetković	A.C. Marković	V. Juričić
26 Aug 1939			J. Šutej
27 Mar 1941	Gen. D. Simović	M. Ninčić	

In 1941 the Axis powers occupied Yugoslavia. A government-in-exile was established in London in Jun 1941 and eventually moved to Cairo.

11 Jan 1942	S. Jovanović		
Jun 1943	M. Trifimović		
10 Aug 1943	B. Purić		I. Cicin-Sain
7 Mar 1945	Marshal J.B. Tito	I. Subasić	S. Zejević
2 Feb 1946		S. Simić	
6 May 1948			D. Radosavljević
31 Aug 1948		E. Kardelj	
1 Nov 1951			M. Popović
14 Jan 1953		K. Popović	R. Nedelković
1 Jan 1954			N. Bozinović
1 Jan 1957			A. Humo
1 Jan 1959			N. Minčov
1 Jan 1963			K. Gligorov
29 Jun 1963	P. Stambolić		
23 Apr 1965		M. Nikezić	
18 May 1967	M. Spiljak		J. Smole
28 Apr 1969		M. Tepavac	
17 May 1969	M. Ribičić		
30 Jul 1971	D. Bijedić		

161

YUGOSLAVIA (*continued*)

Date of taking office	Prime Minister	Foreign Minister	Finance Minister
1 Nov 1972		J. Petrić	
5 Dec 1972		M. Minić	
17 May 1974			M. Cemović
14 Feb 1977	V. Djuranović		
16 May 1978		J. Vrhovec	P. Kostić
16 May 1982	M. Planinć	L. Mojsov	J. Florijanić
12 Mar 1989	A. Marković	B. Lončar	B. Žekan

FORMER YUGOSLAVIA

Date of taking office	Prime Minister	Foreign Minister	Finance Minister
14 Jul 1992	M. Panić		
Feb 1993	R. Kontić	M. Milutinović	J. Žebić

5 ELECTIONS

ALBANIA

In Mar 1920 the Lushnjë congress elected a National Assembly and a Senate. Political parties began to emerge: a group known as 'liberals' and one known as 'conservatives'.

Elections were held on 4 Feb 1921 to a National Assembly of 77 deputies and a Senate of 18 (6 of whom were appointed). Alternative governments were formed by the conservative feudalistic Progressive Party and the People's Party which itself split into a right-wing faction headed by A. Zogu and a liberal faction (becoming a Democratic party) headed by Bishop Fan Noli.

At the elections of Dec 1923, 40 Progressive and 35 People's Party candidates were returned, together with 20 independents. Fan Noli left the People's Party to form an opposition and seized power on 17 Jun 1924. His government itself split into Radical and National Democrats, and Zogu seized power again in Dec 1924.

By a new constitution of Feb 1925 a bicameral National Assembly was set up with deputies elected every three years and a partly-elected Senate. The President was to be elected by the National Assembly for a seven-year period. In the 1925 elections opposition groups were not permitted to stand and complete victory went to the Zogists. Zogu became President.

By a new constitution of 1 Sep 1928 the Senate was abolished and a National Assembly of 56 set up. Political parties were forbidden and elections were indirect and on a limited suffrage. Government-nominated candidates were presented to the electors for approval. Albania became a monarchy and Zogu its king under the name Zog I. The elections of 1932 and 1937 were held under these conditions.

On 2 Dec 1945 elections were held for a new People's Assembly. 82 candidates stood on the single Democratic Front list for 82 seats. 89.9% of the electorate voted, and 93.16% of votes cast were for the Democratic Front.

At the elections of 28 May 1950 the electorate was 541 241, the turnout 99.43% of whom 98.18% voted for the 121 deputies (1 per 10 000).

Note: Some parties are referred to by initials. *See* Chapter 6, 'Political Parties', for full names.

Turn-out in subsequent elections up to 1970 (30 May 1954; 1 Jun 1958; 3 Jun 1962; 11 Jul 1966; 20 Sep 1970) was never less than 99% and reached (it was claimed) 100% in 1970. One deputy represents 8000 electors. Elections are held every four years. In subsequent elections, in Oct 1974, Nov 1978 and Nov 1982, there was 100% turnout for the 250 candidates of the Democratic Front.

In elections held on 1 Feb 1987, it was reported that 1 830 652 valid votes were cast for 250 candidates, a turnout of 100%. There was one invalid vote.

1991 (Mar–Apr)	Albania Party of Labour (Communists	169
	Democratic Party	75
	Omonia (minority Greek)	5
	National Veterans' Committee	1
	Others (Agrarian Party, Ecology Party, Republican Party)	–
		250

1992 (Mar)

	Seats	%
Democratic Party	92	68
Socialist Party (ex-communists)	38	22
Social Democratic Party	7	4
Omonia (minority Greek)	2	3
Republican Party	1	3

1996 (May/Jun)

The elections of 26 May and 2 Jun 1996 resulted in the Democratic Party claiming 122 seats and 87% of the vote. However the opposition, led by the Socialists, withdrew because of alleged intimidation.

ARMENIA

For elections 1918–1921, see note on p. 268.

Elections in Armenia since independence in 1991 have consisted of the presidential election of 16 Oct 1991 (won by Levon Ter-Petrosyan of the Pan-Armenian National Movement with 87% of the votes cast) and the general election of 5 and 27 Jul 1995. In the 1995 general election, 40 of the 190 seats were filled by proportional representation. The elections were dominated by the Republican bloc (a coalition of the Pan-Armenian National Movement and 5 other parties) which secured 119 of the 190 seats.

At the most recent presidential election, in 1996, President Ter-Petrosyan won 51.75% of the votes cast, Vazgen Manukyan 41.29% and the communist Sergei Badalyan 6.34%.

AUSTRIA

Voting procedures. Direct secret proportional elections in multi-member constituencies. Tyrol and Vorarlberg provinces had compulsory voting by law from 1919, Styria from 1949. Universal adult suffrage for all over 20 (over 21 in 1930 and 1945).

The calculation of aggregate voting figures for the former Austria–Hungary is almost impossible before the elections of 1907, when universal male suffrage was introduced. The results for the last two elections before the dissolution of the Habsburg Monarchy were dominated by the Christian Social Party. The three largest parties on each occasion are given below:

	Party	Seats	% votes
1907 (14 May)	Christian Social Party	94	52.3
	Social Democrats	28	21.0
	German People's Party	15	6.6
1911 (13 Jun)	Christian Social Party	70	45.5
	Social Democrats	33	25.4
	German Freedom Party	15	5.1

Since 1919, elections have been held as follows:

	Electorate	Valid votes	Votes per party		Seats	% of electorate	% of votes
1919	3 554 242	2 973 454	SDP	1 211 814	69	34.1	40.7
			CSP	1 068 382	63	30.0	36.0
			Grossdeutsche Partei	545 938	24	15.4	18.4
1920	3 752 212	2 980 328	CSP	1 245 531	85	33.2	41.8
			SDP	1 072 709	69	28.6	36.0
			GdVP	514 127	28	13.7	17.2
1923	3 849 484	3 312 606	CSP	1 490 876	82	38.7	45.0

	Electorate	Valid votes		Votes per party	Seats	% of electorate	% of votes
			SDP	1 311 870	68	34.1	39.6
			GdVP	422 600	15	11.0	12.8
1927	4 119 626	3 641 526	CSP ⎫ GdVP ⎭	1 756 761[1]	73 12	42.6	41.4 6.8
			SDP	1 539 635	71	37.4	42.3
1930	4 121 282	3 687 082	SDP	1 516 913	72	36.8	41.1
			CSP	1 314 468	66	31.9	35.6
			NWbLb	427 962	19	10.4	11.6
1945	3 449 605	3 217 354	ÖVP	1 602 227	85	46.4	49.8
			SPÖ	1 434 898	76	41.6	44.6
			KPÖ	174 257	4	5.0	5.4
1949	4 391 815	4 193 733	ÖVP	1 846 581	77	42.0	44.0
			SPÖ	1 623 524	67	37.0	38.7
			FPÖ ⎫ WdU ⎭	489 213[1]	16	11.1	11.7
1953	4 586 870	4 318 688	SPÖ	1 818 517	73	39.6	42.1
			ÖVP	1 781 777	74	38.8	41.2
			FPÖ ⎫ WdU ⎭	472 866[1]	14	10.3	10.9
1956	4 614 464	4 351 908	ÖVP	1 999 989	82	43.3	46.1
			SPÖ	1 873 292	74	40.6	43.0
			FPÖ WdU	283 749[1]	6	6.1	6.5
1959	4 696 633	4 362 856	SPÖ	1 953 935	78	41.6	44.8
			ÖVP	1 928 043	79	41.0	44.2
			FPÖ	336 110	8	7.1	7.7
1962	4 805 351	4 456 131	ÖVP	2 024 501	81	42.1	45.4
			SPÖ	1 960 685	76	40.8	44.0
			FPÖ	313 895	8	6.5	7.0
1966	4 886 534	4 531 864	ÖVP	2 191 128	85	44.8	48.4
			SPÖ	1 928 922	74	39.5	42.6
			FPÖ	242 599	6	5.0	5.3
1970	5 045 841	4 588 961	ÖVP	2 051 012	79	40.6	44.7
			SPÖ	22 221 981	81	44.0	48.4
			FPÖ	253 425	5	5.0	5.5
1971	4 984 448	4 556 990	ÖVP	1 964 713	80	39.4	43.1
			SPÖ	2 280 168	93	45.7	50.0
			FPÖ	248 473	10	5.0	5.5
1975	5 019 168	4 610 533	SPÖ	2 324 309	93	46.3	50.4
			ÖVP	1 980 474	80	39.4	42.9
			FPÖ	249 317	10	4.9	5.4
			KPÖ	54 971	–	1.1	1.2
			Others	1 462	–	–	–
1979	5 186 676	4 728 239	SPÖ	2 412 778	95	46.5	51.0
			ÖVP	1 981 286	77	38.1	41.9
			FPÖ	286 644	11	5.5	6.1

[1] Two-party front

166

	Electorate	Valid votes		Votes per party		Seats	% of electorate	% of votes
			KPÖ	45 270		–	0.9	1.0
			Others	2 261		–	–	–
1983	5 316 438	4 750 773	SPÖ	2 270 997		90	42.7	47.8
			ÖVP	2 052 714		81	38.7	43.2
			FPÖ	236 320		12	4.4	5.0
			VGÖ	89 694		–	1.7	1.9
			ALÖ	60 150		–	1.1	1.3
			KPÖ	31 408		–	0.6	0.7
			Others	9 490		–	0.2	0.2

The results of the elections in 1986 and 1990 were:

		Votes per party	Seats	% of votes
1986	SPÖ	2 092 094	80	43.1
	ÖVP	2 003 663	77	41.3
	FPÖ	472 205	18	9.7
	KPÖ	35 104	–	0.7
	Greens	234 028	8	4.8
	Others	15 164	–	0.3
1990	SPÖ	2 012 463	81	42.8
	ÖVP	1 508 226	60	32.1
	FPÖ	782 610	33	16.6
	Greens	224 941	9	4.8
	Others	174 875	–	3.7

The outcome of the Oct 1994 and Dec 1995 elections was as follows:

(Oct) 1994

	Seats	% vote
SPÖ	65	34.9
ÖVP	52	27.7
FPÖ	42	22.5
Greens (GAL)	13	7.3
Liberal Forum	11	6.0
Others	–	1.6

(17 Dec) 1995

	Seats	% vote
SPÖ	71	38.2
ÖVP	53	28.3
FPÖ	40	21.9
Liberal Forum	9	4.8
Greens (GAL)	10	5.5
Others	–	1.4

BELARUS

Following independence, a new constitution was adopted in Mar 1994. In the second round of presidential elections on 10 Jul 1994 Alyaksandr Lukashenka easily defeated Vyacheslav Kebich (85% to 15%). The legislative elections of May 1995 failed to fill sufficient seats in the Supreme Council to form a quorum. The party affiliation of those elected was frequently unclear. Fresh elections were held in 141 seats in Nov and a third phase in Dec. Of 198 elected deputies on this occasion, 95 were without party affiliation. Of the 260 seat Supreme Council, the Party of Communists of Belarus led with 42 seats, the Agrarian Party had 33. No other party reached double figures.

BELGIUM

Voting procedures. Proportional representation in single-member constituencies. Vote for all males over 25 for the Chamber of Representatives and over 30 for the Senate, until the constitutional revision of 1920–1921 set the electoral age at 21. Women received the right to vote in 1948.

Between 1900 and 1918, elections were held on the following occasions for the Chamber of Representatives:

27 May 1900	24 May 1908
25 May 1902	22 May 1910
29 May 1904	2 Jun 1912
27 May 1906	24 May 1914

Only the elections of 1900 and 1912 were general elections for which meaningful figures can be produced. Both elections were dominated by the Catholic Party (86 seats out of 152 with 48.5% of the vote in 1900 and 101 seats out of 186 in 1912 with 51.1% of the vote).

		Votes per party	Seats	% of votes
1919	Catholics	645 462	71	36.62
	Socialists	645 075	70	36.60
	Liberals	310 853	34	17.64
1921	Catholics	715 041	69	37.01
	Socialists	672 445	68	34.80
	Liberals	343 929	33	17.80
1925	Socialists	820 116	78	39.43
	Catholics	751 058	75	36.11
	Liberals	304 467	23	14.64
1929	Socialists	803 347	70	36.02
	Catholics	788 914	71	35.37
	Liberals	369 114	28	16.55

	Votes per party		Seats	% of votes
1932	Catholics	899 887	79	38.55
	Socialists	866 817	73	37.11
	Liberals	333 567	24	14.28
1936	Socialists	758 485	70	32.10
	Catholics	653 717	61	27.67
	Liberals	292 972	23	12.40
	Rexists	271 491	21	11.49
1939	Catholics	764 843	73	32.73
	Socialists	705 969	64	30.18
	Liberals	401 991	33	17.19
1946	Catholics	1 006 293	92	42.53
	Socialists	746 738	69	31.56
	Communists	300 099	23	12.68
	Liberals	211 143	17	8.92
1949	Catholics	2 190 898	105	43.56
	Socialists	1 496 539	66	29.75
	Liberals	767 180	29	15.25
1950	Catholics	2 356 608	108	47.68
	Socialists	1 705 781	77	34.51
	Liberals	556 102	20	11.25
1954	Catholics	2 123 408	95	41.14
	Socialists	1 927 015	86	37.34
	Liberals	626 983	25	12.15
1958	Catholics	2 465 549	104	46.50
	Socialists	1 897 646	84	35.79
	Liberals	585 999	21	11.05
1961	Catholics	2 182 642	96	41.46
	Socialists	1 933 424	84	36.73
	Liberals	649 376	20	12.33
1965	Catholics	1 785 211	77	34.45
	Socialists	1 465 503	64	28.28
	Liberals	1 119 991	48	21.61
1968	Catholics	1 643 785	69	31. 8
	Socialists	1 449 172	59	28.0
	Liberals	1 080 894	47	20.9
1971	Catholics	1 587 195	67	30.1
	Socialists	1 438 626	61	27.2
	Liberals	865 657	34	16.4
1974	Catholics	1 699 233	72	32.3
	Socialists	1 401 288	59	26.7
	Liberals	798 896	30	15.2
	FDF/Rassemblement	575 616	25	11.0
	Volksunie	536 195	22	10.2
	Communists	169 668	4	3.2
	Others	75 758	–	1.4
1977	Catholics	1 459 997	56	26.2
	Socialists/PSC	543 608	24	9.7

169

	Votes per party		Seats	% of votes
	PSB ⎱ BSP ⎰	1 473 329	35 27	13.4 13.0
	PVV	475 912	17	8.5
	PRLW ⎱ PL ⎰	328 571 63 041	14 ⎱ 2 ⎰	7.0
	Volksunie	559 634	20	10.0
	FDF	237 280	10	4.7
	RW	158 559	5	2.4
	Communists	151 421	2	2.7
	Vlaams Blok ⎱ RAD-UDRT ⎰ Others ⎰	122 878	– ⎱ – ⎰ – ⎰	2.2
1978	Catholics (CVP)	1 446 056	57	26.1
	Socialists (PSC)	560 565	25	10.1
	PSB	719 926	32	13.0
	BSP	684 465	26	12.4
	PVV	571 520	22	10.3
	PRLW ⎱ PL ⎰	287 942 42 156	14 1	6.0
	Volksunie	388 368	14	7.0
	FDF	235 152	11	4.2
	RW	158 563	4	2.9
	Communists	180 088	4	3.2
	Vlaams Blok		1	
	RAD-UDRT	258 405	1	4.7
	Others		0	
1981	CVP	1 165 155	43	19.3
	PSC	430 712	18	7.1
	PS	765 055	35	12.7
	SP	744 586	26	12.4
	PRL	516 291	24	8.6
	PVV	776 882	28	12.9
	VU	588 430	20	9.8
	FDF			
	RW	253 703	8	4.2
	Communists	138 992	2	2.3
	UDRT	163 725	3	2.7
	Ecology	289 901	4	4.8
	Vlaams Blok	66 424	1	1.1
	Others	123 250	–	2.1
1985	CVP	1 291 595	49	21.3
	PS	834 488	35	13.8
	SP	883 065	32	14.6
	PRL	619 392	24	10.2
	PVV	650 604	22	10.7
	PSC	482 559	20	8.0
	VU	477 408	16	7.9
	Ecolo	152 481	5	2.5 ⎱
	Agalev	226 998	4	3.7 ⎰
	FDF	72 361	3	1.2 ⎱
	PW	9 294	–	0.2 ⎰
	Vlaams Blok	85 330	1	1.4
	Others	278 840	1	4.6

	Votes per party		Seats	% of votes
1987	CVP	1 194 687	43	19.5
	PS	961 429	40	15.7
	SP	913 975	32	14.9
	PVV	709 137	25	11.6
	PRL	577 897	23	9.4
	PSC	491 839	19	8.0
	VU	494 229	16	8.1
	Agalev	275 307	6	4.5
	Ecolo	157 985	3	2.6
	FDF	71 340	3	1.2
	Vlaams Blok	116 410	2	1.9
	Others	176 977	–	2.9

		Seats	% votes
1991 (24 Nov)	Christian Peoples Party (CVP)	39	16.7
	Socialist Party (PS)	35	13.6
	Socialist Party (SP)	28	12.0
	PVV (later renamed VLD)	26	11.9
	Liberal Reform Party	20	8.2
	Social Christian Party	18	7.8
	Vlaams Blok	12	6.6
	Ecolo	10	5.1
	Agalev	7	4.9
	Others	7	7.3
1995 (21 May)	Christian Peoples Party (CVP)	29	17.2
	Social Christian Party (PSC)	12	7.7
	Flemish Liberals & Democrats (VLD)	21	13.1
	Liberal Reform Party (PRL-FDF)	18	10.3
	Socialist Party (SP)	20	12.6
	Socialist Party (PS)	21	11.9
	Vlaams Blok	11	7.8
	Volksunie	5	4.7
	National Front (FN)	2	2.3
	Agalev	5	4.4
	Ecolo	6	4.0

BOSNIA–HERCEGOVINA

For the complex position of Bosnia after the break-up of Yugoslavia, see p. 403. The elections of Nov–Dec 1990 had the following outcome:

Party of Democratic Action	86
Serbian Democratic Party	72
Croat Democratic Union	44
League of Communists*/Socialist Alliance	20*
Alliance of Reform Forces	13
Others	5
Total	240

* later renamed Socialist Democratic Party

171

As agreed at the Dayton Peace Conference, nationwide elections were to take place in Bosnia–Hercegovina in Sep 1996. The outcome (for the presidential contest) was:

Candidate	Party	Votes
A Izetbegovic	Muslim/Democratic Party of Action	729 034
M Krajisnik	Serb/Serb Democratic Party	690 373
K Zubak	Croat/Croatian Democratic Union	342 007
M Ivanic	Serb/Socialist Party	305 803
H Silajdzic	Muslim/Party for Bosnia–Hercegovina	123 784
I Komsic	United List	38 261

BULGARIA

By 1900 Bulgaria was a constitutional monarchy with an electoral system established by the 1879 Turnovo constitution. The legislature was the unicameral National Assembly, *Narodno Sŭbranie*, of deputies each representing 10 000 electors, elected by universal suffrage at 21 years for three-(later four-) year terms. To pass any constitutional amendment a Grand National Assembly, *Veliko Narodno Sŭbranie*, was elected of twice the usual number of deputies. Elections were on the proportional representation system.

	Votes per party		*Seats*
1923 (23 Apr)	Agrarians	569 000	212
	Communists	204 000	16
	Social Democrats	28 000	2
	Middle class and traditional parties	275 000	15
1923 (18 Nov)	Democratic *entente* in a bloc with		202 ⎫
	Social Democrats	638 675	29 ⎭
	Left-wing-Agrarians in a bloc with		31 ⎫
	Communists	217 607	8 ⎭
	Right-wing Agrarians	42 737	19
	National Liberals	36 507	7

By an electoral law of 1927 proportional representation (abolished in 1923) was restored in a system favourable to the government party, Democratic *entente*, enabling it to win 168 of the 273 seats with 39% of the votes in the election of 29 May 1927:

	Votes per party		*Seats*
Democratic *entente*		504 703	168
'Iron bloc' of Agrarians,			42

Votes per party		Seats
Social Democrats and		10
Artisans	285 758	4
Workers (*i.e.* Communists)	29 210	4
National Liberals		14
Democrats		12
Macedonians		11
Radicals		2

A new proportional representation system was introduced for the elections of 21 Jun 1931, the results of which were:

Votes per party		Seats
Agrarians		69
'Popular bloc' of Democrats		43
Kyorchev Liberals and		32
Radicals	590 000	8
Democratic *entente*		
in a bloc with		63
Smilov Liberals	417 000	15
Workers (*i.e.* Communists)	166 000	33
Macedonians		8
Social Democrats		5

The government was taken over on 19 May 1934 in a *coup d'état* by a group of army officers in alliance with a group of intellectuals associated with the journal *Zveno*. Tsar Boris overthrew this government in turn on 22 Jan 1935 and set up a royal dictatorship.

By an electoral law of 1937 the number of deputies was reduced to 160, political parties were banned and unmarried women disfranchised.

At the election of Mar 1938 Agrarians and Social Democrats stood in opposition to the government in the Bulgarian version of the Popular Front called the 'Constitutional bloc', and won 63 seats. At the elections of 30 Jan 1940 opposition candidates (including 9 Communists) won 20 seats.

On 9 Sep 1944 at the beginning of the Soviet occupation a 'Fatherland Front' government of Communists and anti-fascists was set up.

18 Nov 45 (Opposition boycotted election)	Fatherland Front, 88.2% (85.6% of electorate voted)

A referendum was held on 8 Sep 1946 at which 92.7% of the electorate voted, 3 801 160 for a Republic, and 197 176 to retain the monarchy. 119 168 votes were invalid. A People's Republic was proclaimed on 15 Sep 1946.

The elections of 27 Oct 1946 were for a 'Grand' National Assembly as was necessary to carry a constitutional change. The Communists and their allies stood in a Fatherland Front bloc; the opposition parties campaigned as the 'United opposition'.

	Votes per party		Seats
1946	Fatherland Front	2 980 000	366
	Communists	2 260 000	277
	Obbov Agrarians		67
	Neikov Social Democrats		9
	Zveno group		8
	Radicals		4
	United opposition	1 300 000	99
	Agrarians		89
	Social Democrats		9
	Independent		1

On 4 Dec 1947 the 'Dimitrov' constitution was promulgated. The National Assembly was elected for four-year terms by all citizens of 18 and over. Each deputy represented 20 000 electors. The President was to be elected by the National Assembly.

Before the elections of 1949 the Social Democrats merged with the Communists and the Zveno group dissolved. 99.8% of votes cast were for the single Fatherland Front list of Communist or Agrarian candidates.

	Electorate	Votes per party	% of Votes
1953	5 017 667 (99.48% voted)	Fatherland Front (465 deputies elected)	99.8
1957	5 218 602 (99.77% voted) (Votes = 5 206 428)	Fatherland Front 5 204 027 (number of deputies reduced to 253)	99.95
1962	5 485 607 (99.71% voted) (Votes = 5 466 517)	Fatherland Front (321 deputies elected)	99.9
1966	5 774 251 (99.63% voted) (Votes = 5 752 817)	Fatherland Front 5 744 072 (number of candidates = 416)	99.85
1971	(99.85% voted)	Fatherland Front	99.9

A new constitution was promulgated on 18 May 1971 by which the number of deputies was fixed at 400 and their term of service altered to five years.

In elections in May 1976, of an electorate of 6 378 348, some 6 375 092 voted (99.99%). Of these, 6 369 762 (99.92%) voted for the Fatherland Front, returning 272 members for the Bulgarian Communist Party, 100 for the Bulgarian Agrarian Party and 28 non-party members.

In elections in Jun 1981, of the total electorate some 6 524 086 (99.96%) cast their votes. Of these 6 519 674 (99.93%) were for the Fatherland Front. The members returned comprised 271 Bulgarian Communist Party, 99 Agrarian Union and 30 non-party.

In elections in Jun 1986, of the total registered electorate of 6 650 739 some 6 645 645 (99.92%) cast their votes. The members returned comprised 276 Bulgarian Communist Party, 99 Agrarian Union and 25 nonparty.

Following the fall of the former Communist regime, the first free elections for 58 years were held on 10 and 17 Jun 1990 for the 400-seat Grand National Assembly. Turnout on the first round of voting exceeded 80%. The result was:

Bulgarian Socialist Party (BSP)	211
Union of Democratic Forces (UDF)*	144
Movement for Rights and Freedom (MRF) **	23
Agrarian Party	16
Independents	2
Others	4
	400

* a 16-party opposition alliance.
** the party of the ethnic Turkish minority.

	Party	Seats	% votes
1991 (Oct)	Union of Democratic Forces (UDF)	110	34.4
	Bulgarian Socialist Party	106	33.1
	Movement for Rights and Freedom	24	7.6
	United Bulgarian Agrarian Party	–	3.8
	Others (Independents, smaller parties etc.)	–	21.1
1994 (18 Dec)	Bulgarian Socialist Party (BSP) (former Communists)	125	43.5
	Union of Democratic Forces (UDF)	69	24.2
	Popular Union (Agrarian Party and Democratic Party)	18	6.3
	Movement for Rights and Freedom (Turkish)	15	5.5
	Bulgarian Business Bloc*	13	4.8

* Other parties fell below 4% threshold

CROATIA

Elections were held in independent Croatia for the Sabor (Assembly) on 2 Aug 1992. The outcome was a landslide victory for the Croatian Democratic Union of Franjo Tudjman.

	Seats	% votes
Croatian Democratic Union	85	41.5
Croatian Social Liberal Party	14	18.3
Social Democratic Party/		
Party of Democratic Reform of Croatia	11	5.8
Croatian People's Party	6	6.9
Dalmatian Action ⎫		
Istrian Democratic Assembly ⎬	6	na
Rijeka Democratic Alliance ⎭		
Serbian People's Party	3	na
Others (including Independents)	13	na
	138	

In January 1993 a proportional representation system was introduced.

		Seats	% vote
1995 (29 Aug)	Croatian Democratic Union	75	44.8
	Peasant Party Coalition	16	18.4
	Croatian Social Liberal Party	12	11.6
	Social Democratic Party	10	na
	Croat Right-Wing Party	4	na
	Others	3	na

Electorate 3.6m. Turnout 66%

CYPRUS (GREEK)

		Seats	% vote
1991	Democratic Rally (Disy)	20	35.8
	Akel (Communists)	18	30.6
	Democratic Party (Diko)	11	19.5
	EDEK (Socialists)	7	10.9
1996 (26 May)	Democratic Rally	–	34.5
	Akel	19	33.0
	Democratic Party	9	–
	EDEK (Socialists)	5	–

CYPRUS (TURKISH)

Elections held on 6 May 1990 produced a victory for the National Unity Party, with 34 of the 50 seats. The Democratic Struggle Party (comprising Republican Turkish Party, Communal Liberal Party and New Dawn) won 14 seats. Further elections were held in Dec 1993. In 1996, the Democratic Party had 16 seats in the Assembly, National Unity Party 15, the Republican Turkish Party 13, Communal Liberation 5 and the National Birth Party 1.

CZECHOSLOVAKIA

A National Assembly was set up on 14 Nov 1918 of 260 delegates of the following party composition:

Agrarians	54
Social Democrats	50
Slovaks	50
National Democrats	44
National Socialists	28
Catholics	28
Progressive Liberals	6

Representatives of the German minority refused to take part.

A constitution was promulgated on 29 Feb 1920 providing for a bi-cameral National Assembly, *Národni Shromáždĕni* to be elected by direct universal suffrage on the proportional representation method. The Chamber of Deputies of 300 members was to be elected for six years by citizens over 21; the Senate for eight years by voters over 26, and to have 150 senators.

The head of state was to be a President elected by both chambers for seven years.

Elections to the Chamber of Deputies were held on 18 Apr 1920 and to the Senate on 25 Apr 1920. The electorate was 6 917 956 (for the Chamber of Deputies; the Senate electorate was a proportion of this which remained more or less constant throughout later elections. At this election it was 5 804 134). Turn-out was 89.9 %. Valid votes cast for the Chamber of Deputies: 6 130 318

Pre-war Czechoslovak politics was dominated by the problem of national minorities, and the official classification of voting figures in the 1920 election reflects this preoccupation: Czechoslovak parties polled 4 255 623 votes (68.64% of votes cast) and gained 199 seats in the Chamber of Deputies, and gained 102 seats in the Senate with 70.07 % of votes cast. German parties: 72; 1 586 060 (25.58%) and 37; 26.09%. Hungarian–German parties: 9; 247 901 (4%) and 2; 1.93%. Hungarian parties: 1; 30 734 (0.50%) and 1; 0.77%.

Seats gained and proportion of votes polled by individual, successful parties were:

Chamber of Deputies:		Seats	% of votes
Czechoslovak parties	Social Democrats	74	25.65
	Populist Catholics	33	11.29
	Agrarians	28	9.74
	National Socialists	24	8.08
	National Democrats	19	6.25
	Slovak National Agrarians	12	3.9
	Professional Middle Class	6	1.98
	Working People (Progressive Socialists)	3	0.95

Chamber of Deputies:		Seats	% of votes
German parties	German Social Democrats	31	11.12
	German Electoral Union	15	5.3
	Union of German Peasants	11	3.9
	German Christian Social Party	10	3.44
	German Democratic Liberals	5	1.78
Hungarian-German parties	Hungarian-German Christian Socialists	5	2.25
	Hungarian-German Social Democrats	4	1.75
Hungarian parties	Hungarian Agrarians	1	0.43

Senate		Seats	% of votes
Czechoslovak parties	Social Democrats	41	28.07
	Populist Catholics	18	11.91
	Agrarians	14	10.15
	National Socialists	10	7.15
	National Democrats	10	6.78
	Slovak National Agrarians	6	3.47
	Professional Middle Class	3	2.06
German parties	German Social Democrats	16	11.35
	German Electoral Union	8	5.75
	Union of German Peasants	6	4.03
	German Christian Social Party	4	2.7
	German Democratic Liberals	3	2.26
Hungarian-German	Hungarian-German Christian Socialists	2	1.93
Hungarian	Hungarian Agrarians	1	0.77

At the elections of 15 Nov 1925 all 300 seats in the Chamber of Deputies and all 150 in the Senate were filled by election. The electorate was 7 855 822, the turn-out was 91.4% and 7 105 276 votes were cast.

	Chamber of Deputies			Senate		
	Votes	% of votes	Seats	Votes	% of votes	Seats
(Czechoslovak parties):						
Agrarians	970 489	13.66	45	841 647	13.81	23
Populist Catholics	691 238	9.73	31	618 033	10.14	16
Social Democrats	630 894	8.88	29	537 470	8.82	14
National Socialists	609 195	8.57	28	516 250	8.47	14

	Chamber of Deputies			Senate		
	Votes	% of votes	Seats	Votes	% of votes	Seats
Professional Middle Class	285 928	4.02	13	257 171	4.22	6
National Democrats	284 628	4.01	13	256 360	4.2	7
German Social Democrats	411 040	5.79	17	363 310	6.84	12
German Christian Social Party	314 440	4.43	13	289 055	4.74	7
German Nationalists	240 879	3.39	10	214 589	3.52	5
Nazis	168 278	2.37	7	139 945	2.3	3
Union of German Peasants	571 198	8.04	24	505 597	8.29	12
Hlinka's Populist Slovak Catholics	489 027	6.88	23	417 206	6.84	12
Sub-Carpathian Russian Agrarians	35 674	0.5	1			
Polish People's and Workers' Union	29 884	0.42	1			
Hungarian Christian Social Party	98 383	1.39	4	85 777	1.41	2
Communists	933 711	13.14	41	774 454	12.7	20

At the elections of 27 Oct 1929 the electorate was 8 183 462, the turn-out 91.6% and 7 385 084 votes cast.

	Chamber of Deputies			Senate		
	Votes	% of votes	Seats	Votes	% of votes	Seats
(Czechoslovak parties):						
Agrarians	1 105 429	14.97	46	978 291	15.17	24
Social Democrats	963 312	13.05	39	841 331	13.04	20
National Socialists	767 571	10.39	32	666 607	10.33	16
Populist Catholics	623 522	8.44	25	559 700	8.68	13
National Democrats	359 533	4.87	15	325 023	5.04	8
Professional Middle Class	291 238	3.94	12	274 085	4.25	6
Anti-Electoral Scrutiny	70 857	0.96	3	51 617	0.8	1
German Social Democrats	506 750	5.76	19	446 940	6.93	11
German Electoral Coalition	396 383	5.37	16	359.002	5.57	9
German Christian Social Party	348 097	4.71	14	313 544	4.86	8
Nazis	204 096	2.77	8	171 181	2.65	4
German Nationalist and Sudeten German Union	189 071	2.56	7			
Hlinka's Populist Slovak Catholics	425 052	5.76	19	377 498	5.85	9
Hungarian Christian Socialists	257 231	3.48	9	233 772	3.62	6
Polish and Jewish Union	104 539	1.42	4			
Communists	753 444	10.2	30	644 896	10.00	15

At the elections of 19 May 1935 the electorate was 8 957 572, turn-out was 92.8% and 8 231 412 votes were cast.

179

	Chamber of Deputies			Senate		
	Votes	% of votes	Seats	Votes	% of votes	Seats
(Czechoslovak parties):						
Agrarians	1 176 593	13.29	45	1 042 924	14.33	23
Social Democrats	1 034 774	12.57	38	910 252	12.51	20
National Socialists	755 880	9.18	18	672 126	9.24	14
Populist Catholics	615 877	7.48	22	557 684	7.66	11
Artisans and Tradesmen	448 047	5.44	17	393 732	5.41	8
Fascists	167 433	2.04	6			
National Union	456 353	5.55	17	410 095	5.64	9
Sudeten Germans	1 249 531	15.18	44	1 092 255	15.01	23
German Social Democrats	299 942	3.64	11	271 097	3.73	6
German Christian Social Party	162 781	1.98	6	155 234	2.13	3
Union of German Peasants	142 399	1.73	5			
Autonomous bloc (Hlinka's Slovaks, Poles and Hungarians)	564 273	6.86	22	495 166	6.8	11
Hungarian-German Christian Social bloc	291 831	3.55	9	259 832	3.57	6
Communists	849 509	10.32	30	740 696	10.18	16

With the dismemberment and annexation of Czechoslovakia by Germany in 1938 all political parties were proscribed and two puppet organizations set up: The Party of National Unity and the Party of Labour.

On 3 Apr 1945 Beneš established a provisional government at Košice with a cabinet of seven Communists, three Slovak Democrats, three Populist Catholics, three National Socialists and two Social Democrats. This organized an indirect election in Sep and Oct 1945 of a provisional National Assembly which met on 28 Oct 1945. Four parties were recognized in the Czech lands (Communists, Agrarians, National Socialists, Social Democrats) and allotted 40 deputies each, 2 in Slovakia (Populist Catholics and Slovak Democrats) 50 each, 32 seats went to the Trade Union organization and 8 to outstanding individuals in the cultural sphere, making 300 in all.

At the elections of 26 May 1946 to a Constituent Assembly eight official parties were allowed to stand: no independents, no fascist parties and (at Soviet insistence) no Agrarians. The electorate was 7 583 784 (all citizens over 18) of whom 7 138 694 voted.

Votes per party		Seats
Communists	2 695 915	114
National Socialists	1 298 917	55
Populist Catholics	1 110 920	47
Slovak Democrats	988 275	43
Social Democrats	905 654	36
Slovak Freedom	67 575	3
Slovak Labour	49 983	2

Elections were held on 30 May 1948 in which the electorate of 7 998 035 was invited to vote for a single list of National Front candidates. 7 419 253 votes were cast, 6 424 734 for the National Front.

President Beneš resigned and was succeeded by K. Gottwald.

A new constitution of 9 Jun 1948 provided for a single-chamber National Assembly, *Národni Shromáždĕni*, of 368 deputies elected by universal suffrage of citizens over 18 for a six-year period. The President was to be elected by the National Assembly for seven years.

An electoral law of May 1954 permitted only one candidate to stand per constituency; all candidates had to be nominated by the National Front.

At the elections of 28 Nov 1954 the electorate was 8 783 816, votes cast numbered 8 711 718 (99.18%), of which 8 494 102 (97.89%) were for the National Front. At the elections of 12 Jun 1960, 9 085 432 votes were cast (99.68% of the electorate), of which 9 059 838 (99.86% of votes cast) went to the National Front.

On 11 Jul 1960 a new constitution made Czechoslovakia a 'Socialist' instead of a 'People's' Republic, and fixed the number of National Assembly deputies at 300. The President was henceforth to be elected for a five-year term, the National Assembly for four.

At the elections of 14 Jun 1964, 9 418 349 votes were cast (99.98% of the electorate), 9 412 309 for the National Front (99.99% of votes cast).

Czechoslovakia became a Federal Republic of the Czech lands and Slovakia as of 1 Jan 1969. Each federative republic elected a National Council. The Federal Assembly consisted of two chambers: the Chamber of the People of 200 deputies, and the Chamber of the Nations composed of 75 Czech and 75 Slovak deputies. Elections were held every five years, to coincide with Communist Party congresses.

The elections due in 1968 were postponed until 26–27 Nov 1971. In 1968 a new electoral law had permitted more than one candidate to stand for each seat, but this was annulled in the 1971 elections in which the number of candidates was once again equivalent to the number of seats. The electorate was 10 253 796 of whom 99.45% voted. Votes for candidates: Federal Assembly Chamber of the People, 99.81%; Federal Assembly Chamber of the Nations, 99.77%; Czech National Council, 99.78%; Slovak National Council, 99.94%.

In elections in Oct 1976, of the 10 649 261 voters, 99.7% cast their votes. Of these, 10 605 672 (99.97%) voted for National Front candidates.

In elections in Jun 1981, of the 10 789 574 voters, 99.51% cast their votes. Of these, 10 725 609 (99.9%) voted for the National Front.

In elections in May 1986, of the 10 950 675 registered voters, 99.39% reportedly cast their votes. All 200 candidates of the Communist National Front were elected.

With the fall of the Communist regime in the 'Velvet Revolution' of 1989, free elections subsequently took place on 8–9 Jun 1990. On a turnout of 96% of Czechoslovakia's 11.2 million eligible voters, the main results were:

	Seats	% of votes
Civic Forum/Public Against Violence*	170	46.3
Communists	47	13.6
Christian Democratic Union**	40	11.6
Others (inc. separatist Slovak National Party)	43	28.5
	300	

* Public Against Violence was the sister-party of Civic Forum in Slovakia.
** A conservative coalition of the People's Party and the Czech and Slovak Christian Democratic Parties.

Note:
Prior to the division of Czechoslovakia from 1 Jan 1993, elections to the Czech National Council took place in Jun 1992. The elections were dominated by the Civic Democratic Party–Christian Democratic Party coalition (76 seats, 29.7% of votes cast), followed by the Left Bloc (35 seats, 14% of the vote). The Czechoslovak Social Democratic Party and the Liberal Social Union each took 16 seats with 6.5% of the vote.

CZECH REPUBLIC

The first elections to the Czech Republic, after the separation of Slovakia, were held on 2 Jun 1996.

	Seats	% votes
Civic Democratic Party	68	29.6
Civic Democratic Alliance	13	6.4
CDU–CPP	18	8.1
Czech Social Democratic Party	61	26.4
Communist Party of Bohemia and Moravia	22	10.3
Association for the Republican Party of Czechoslovakia	18	8.0

DENMARK

By 1918, the capital had direct proportional elections, the provinces had direct elections in single-member constituencies with some additional seats allotted in proportion to the vote. From 1920, direct proportional elections in multi-member seats. Suffrage of men and women over 29, except those working as servants and farm helpers without their own household. Age reduced to 25 at the third election of 1920, to 23 in 1953 and to 21 in 1961. From 1915–1953 there was a second chamber, the Landsting. For this there was indirect election, electors being selected by city or parish, voters having one vote per elector allocated. Voters were all men and women over 35. Electors in turn elected 53 (first two elections of the period) of the 66 Landsting members, and 55 of them in the last ten elections.

The main feature of Danish elections from 1900 was the rise of the Social Democrats. Elections were held in 1901, 1903, 1906, 1909, 1910, 1913 and 1915. For this last election no meaningful figures can be obtained. The Liberals dominated each election in terms of seats, but the Social Democrats rose steadily.

	Liberals	Social Democrats
1901	76 (39.4)	14 (19.3)
1903	73 (46.1)	16 (21.6)
1906	56 (31.1)	24 (25.4)
1909	48 (30.0)	24 (29.0)
1910	57 (34.1)	24 (28.3)
1913	44 (28.6)	32 (29.6)

		Votes per party	Seats	% of votes
1918	Liberals	269 005	44	29.4
	Soc. Dem.	262 796	39	29.4
	Rad. Lib.	192 478	33	21.0
	Con.	167 865	22	18.3
1920(1)	Liberals	350 563	48	34.2
	Soc. Dem.	300 345	42	29.3
	Con.	201 499	28	19.7
	Rad. Lib.	122 160	17	11.9
1920(2)	Liberals	343 351	51	36.1
	Soc. Dem.	285 166	42	29.9
	Con.	180 293	26	18.9
	Rad. Lib.	110 931	16	11.6
1920 (3)	Liberals	411 661	51	34.0
	Soc. Dem.	389 653	48	32.2
	Con.	216 733	27	17.9
	Rad. Lib.	147 120	18	12.1
1924	Soc. Dem.	469 949	55	36.6
	Liberals	362 682	44	28.3
	Con.	242 955	28	18.9
	Rad. Lib.	166 476	20	13.0
1926	Soc. Dem.	497 106	53	37.2
	Liberals	378 137	46	28.3
	Con.	275 793	30	20.6

		Votes per party	Seats	% of votes
	Rad. Lib.	150 931	16	11.3
1929	Soc. Dem.	593 191	61	41.8
	Liberals	402 121	43	28.3
	Con.	233 935	24	16.5
	Rad. Lab.	151 746	16	10.7
1932	Soc. Dem.	660 839	62	42.7
	Liberals	381 862	38	24.7
	Con.	289 531	27	18.7
	Rad. Lib.	145 221	14	9.4
1935	Soc. Dem.	759 102	68	46.1
	Liberals	292 247	28	17.8
	Con.	293 393	26	17.8
	Rad. Lib.	151 507	14	9.2
1939	Soc. Dem.	729 619	64	42.9
	Liberals	309 355	30	18.2
	Con.	301 625	26	17.8
	Rad. Lib.	161 834	14	9.5
1943	Soc. Dem.	894 632	66	44.5
	Con.	421 523	31	21.0
	Liberals	376 850	28	18.7
1945	Soc. Dem.	671 755	48	32.8
	Liberals	479 158	38	23.4
	Con.	373 688	26	18.2
1947	Soc. Dem.	834 089	57	40.0
	Liberals	574 895	49	27.6
	Con.	259 324	17	12.4
1950	Soc. Dem.	813 224	59	39.6
	Liberals	438 188	32	21.3
	Con.	365 236	27	17.8
1953(1)	Soc. Dem.	836 507	61	40.4
	Liberals	456 896	33	22.1
	Con.	358 509	26	17.3
1953(2)	Soc. Dem.	894 913	74	41.3
	Liberals	499 656	42	23.1
	Con.	364 960	30	16.8
1957	Soc. Dem.	910 170	70	39.4
	Liberals	578 932	45	25.1
	Con.	383 843	30	16.6
1960	Soc. Dem.	1 023 794	76	42.1
	Liberals	512 041	38	21.1
	Con.	435 764	32	17.9
1964	Soc. Dem.	1 103 667	76	41.9
	Liberals	547 770	38	20.8
	Con.	527 798	36	20.1
1966	Soc. Dem.	1 068 911	69	38.2
	Liberals	539 028	35	19.3
	Con.	522 027	34	18.7

	Votes per party		*Seats*	*% of votes*
1968	Soc. Dem.	974 833	62	34.1
	Liberals	530 167	34	18.6
	Cons.	581 051	37	20.4
1971	Soc. Dem.	1 074 777	70	37.3
	Liberals	450 904	30	15.6
	Cons.	481 335	31	16.7
1973	Soc. Dem.	783 145	46	25.6
	Soc. People's Party	183 522	11	6.0
	Com.	110 715	6	3.6
	Left Soc.	44 843	0	1.5
	Lib. Dem.	374 283	22	12.3
	Rad. Lib.	343 117	20	11.2
	Chr. People's Party	123 573	7	4.0
	Con.	279 391	16	9.2
	Centre Dem.	236 784	14	7.8
	Pro. Party	414 212	24	13.6
	STP	54 067	–	1.8
1975	Soc. Dem.	913 155	53	30.0
	Soc. People's Party	150 963	9	4.9
	Com.	127 837	7	4.2
	Left Soc.	63 579	4	2.1
	Lib. Dem.	711 298	42	23.3
	Rad. Lib.	216 553	13	7.1
	Chr. People's Party	162 734	9	5.3
	Con.	168 164	10	5.5
	Centre Dem.	66 316	4	2.2
	Pro. Party	414 212	24	13.6
	STP	54 067	–	1.8
1977	Soc. Dem.	1 150 355	65	37.0
	Soc. People's Party	120 357	7	3.9
	Com.	114 022	7	3.7
	Left Soc.	83 667	5	2.7
	Lib. Dem.	371 728	21	12.0
	Rad. Lib.	113 330	6	3.6
	Chr. People's Party	106 082	6	3.4
	Con.	263 262	15	8.5
	Centre Dem.	200 347	11	6.4
	Pro. Party	453 782	26	14.6
	STP	102 149	6	3.3
	Pensioners Party	26 889	0	0.9
1979	Soc. Dem.	1 213 456	68	38.3
	Lib. Dem.	396 484	22	12.5
	Con.	395 653	22	12.5
	Pro. Party	349 243	20	11.0
	Soc. People's Party	187 284	11	5.9
	Rad. Lib.	172 365	10	5.4
	Left Soc.	116 047	6	3.7
	Centre Dem.	102 132	6	3.2
	Chr. People's Party	82 133	5	2.6
	STP	83 238	5	2.6
	Com.	58 901	0	1.9
	Com. Workers Party	13 070	0	0.4

185

	Votes per party		Seats	% of votes
1981	Soc. Dem.	1 027 376	59	32.9
	Con. People's Party	450 970	26	14.4
	Soc. People's Party	353 167	21	11.3
	Lib.	353 435	20	11.3
	Pro. Party	278 454	16	8.9
	Centre Dem.	258 720	15	8.3
	Rad. Lib.	159 933	9	5.1
	Left Soc.	82 106	5	2.6
	Chr. People's Party	72 020	4	2.3
	Others	85 744	–	2.7
1984	Soc. Dem.	1 062 602	56	31.4
	Con. People's Party	788 225	42	23.3
	Soc. People's Party	387 115	21	11.4
	Venstre (Lib.)	405 722	22	12.0
	Rad. Lib.	184 634	10	5.5
	Centre Dem.	154 557	8	4.6
	Pro. Party	120 631	6	3.6
	Chr. People's Party	91 633	5	2.7
	Others	191 604	5	5.6
1987	Soc. Dem.	985 906	54	29.3
	Con. People's Party	700 886	38	20.8
	Soc. People's Party	490 176	27	14.6
	Venstre (Lib.)	354 291	19	10.5
	Rad. Lib.	209 086	11	6.2
	Centre Dem.	161 070	9	4.8
	Pro. Party	160 461	9	4.8
	Chr. People's Party	79 664	4	2.4
	Others	221 017	4	6.6
1988	Soc. Dem.		55	29.9
	Con. People's Party		35	19.3
	Soc. People's Party		24	13.0
	Venstre (Lib.)		22	11.8
	Pro. Party		16	9.0
	Rad. Lib.		10	5.6
	Centre Dem.		9	4.7
	Chr. People's Party		4	2.0
	Others		–	4.6
1990	Soc. Dem.		69	37.4
	Con. People's Party		30	16.0
	Lib.		29	15.8
	Soc. People's Party		15	8.3
	Pro. Party		12	6.4
	Centre Dem.		9	5.1
	Rad. Lib.		7	3.5
	Chr. People's Party		4	2.3
	Others		–	5.2
			179*	100.0

* Total of 179 includes 4 from Greenland and the Faroes.

		Seats	% votes
1994	Soc. Dem.	62	34.6
	Lib.	42	23.3
	Con. People's Party	27	15.0
	Soc. People's Party	13	7.3
	Pro. Party	11	6.4
	Soc. Lib. (formerly Rad. Lib.)	9	4.6
	Red–Green Alliance	6	3.2
	Centre Dem.	5	2.8
	Others	1	2.8
		175	100.0

ESTONIA

Elections for a Constituent Assembly were held 7 and 8 Apr 1919, and a coalition government formed headed by the Social Democratic Party. A constitution was adopted on 15 Jun 1920 which provided for a single-chamber parliament (*Riigikogu*) of 100 deputies elected every 3 years by proportional representation. Elections were held in 1920, 1923, 1926, 1929 and 1932. The system favoured the proliferation of political parties. There were also national minority parties: Swedish, German and Russian. The Communist Party was outlawed in Feb 1925 after an abortive *coup*. The fascist ex-servicemen's organization Vaps began to gain influence at a time of increasing dissatisfaction with government instability (between 1919 and 1933 there were 20 coalition governments) and instigated a referendum to amend the constitution in Oct 1933. The amendment was approved by 416 879 votes (56.3% of the electorate), but the President (K. Päts) on 12 Mar 1934 assumed direct control under emergency powers and presented a third constitution to the people in Feb 1936. This was approved by a majority of 76.1% and came into force on 1 Jan 1938. It provided for a new two-chamber parliament: a 40-strong National Council of appointed specialists, and an 80-strong Chamber of Deputies elected every five years on the single-member constituency system. The President was to be directly elected every six years.

At the elections of 24 Apr 1938 the poll was a record 90%. Päts was elected President. 55 members of the pro-Päts Patriotic League were elected. Social Democrats and extreme left-wing groups were in opposition.

Elections were held in independent Estonia on 5 March 1995, with 1265 candidates from 16 parties.

	Seats	% votes
Coalition Party/Rural Union	41	32.2
Reform Party/Liberals	19	16.2
Centre Party	16	14.2

	Seats	% votes
Fatherland Alliance	8	7.9
Moderate Party	6	6.0
Our Home is Estonia (Russian)	6	5.9
Right Wing	5	5.0

EUROPEAN UNION
EUROPEAN PARLIAMENT

DIRECT ELECTIONS 1979[†]

	Votes per party	Seats	% of votes
Belgium			
CVP	1 607 925	7	29.5
PSC	445 940	3	8.2
BSP	698 892	3	12.8
PSB	575 886	4	10.6
PVV	512 355	2	9.4
PRL	372 857	2	6.9
FDF/RW	414 412	2	7.6
Volksunie	324 569	1	6.0
Others	490 031	–	9.0
Turnout 91.4%			
Denmark*			
People's Movement against EEC	365 760	4	20.5
Social Democrats	382 487	3	21.5
Liberal Democrats	252 767	3	14.2
Conservatives	245 309	2	13.8
Centre Democrats	107 790	1	6.1
Progress Party	100 702	1	5.7
Socialist People's Party	81 991	1	4.6
Left Socialists	60 964	0	3.4
Single Tax Party	59 379	0	3.3
Radical Liberals	56 944	0	3.2
Christian People's Party	30 985	0	1.7
Others	36 426	0	2.0
Turnout 47.8%			

[†] Figures are set out in the EU *Handbooks* for each election and also the invaluable *Times Guide to the European Parliament* (1979, 1984, 1989, 1994).
* In Greenland, with 1 seat, the successful candidate was from the ruling SIUMUT (Socialist) Party. The turnout was 33.5%

	Votes per party	Seats	% of votes
Federal Republic of Germany			
SPD	11 377 818	35	40.8
CDU	10 890 355	34	39.1
CSU	2 816 758	8	10.1
FDP	1 663 506	4	6.0
Greens	893 510	–	3.2
Others	109 026	–	0.8
Turnout 65.9%			
France			
UFE	5 588 026	26	27.6
PS/MRG	4 764 341	21	23.5
Communists	4 154 512	19	20.5
DIFE	3 302 131	15	16.3
Europe-Ecologie	887 863	–	4.4
Others	1 545 543	–	7.6
Turnout 60%			
Ireland			
Fianna Fail	464 451	5	34.7
Fine Gael	443 652	4	33.1
Labour Party	193 129	4	14.5
Independents	193 898	2	14.4
Others	43 942	–	3.3
Turnout 63.6%			
Italy			
DC (+ SVP)	12 971 528	30	36.5
PCI (+ PDUP)	10 768 000	25	30.7
PSI	3 866 946	9	11.0
MSI/DN	1 909 055	4	5.4
PSDI	1 514 272	4	4.3
PR	1 285 065	3	3.7
PLI }	1 271 159	3	3.6
PRI }	896 139	2	2.6
DP	252 342	1	0.7
Others	505 303	0	1.3
Turnout 85.5%			
Luxembourg			
PCS	352 296	3	36.2
PD	274 307	2	28.1
LSAP	211 106	1	21.7
PC	48 813	–	4.9
Others	14 570	–	9.2
Turnout 88.9%			
Netherlands			
CDA	2 017 692	10	35.6
PvdA	1 721 949	9	30.4

	Votes per party	Seats	% of votes
VVD	914 661	4	16.4
D-66	511 590	2	9.0
SGP	126 397	–	2.2
Others	373 933	–	6.5
Turnout 57.8%			

United Kingdom*

Conservative	6 508 512	60	50.7
Labour	4 253 117	17	33.1
Liberal	1 690 598	–	13.2
Scottish Nationalist	219 142	1	1.7
Plaid Cymru	83 399	–	0.6
Others	88 486	–	0.7
Turnout 32%			

* In Ulster, where the single-transferable vote system was used, the results were one representative each for the Democratic Unionists, Official Unionists and the SDLP.

DIRECT ELECTIONS 1984

	Votes per party	Seats	% of votes
Belgium			
PS	762 377	5	13.3
SP	980 668	4	17.1
CVP	1 134 012	4	19.8
PSC	436 126	2	7.6
PRL	540 597	3	9.4
PVV	494 585	2	8.6
Volksunie	484 925	2	8.5
Agalev	246 879	1	4.3
Ecologistes	220 704	1	3.9
FDF	142 871	–	2.5
RW	51 899	–	0.9
Others	230 194	–	4.0
Turnout 92.0%			
Denmark*			
Conservatives	414 175	4	20.8
People's Movement (against EEC)	413 807	4	20.8
Social Democrats	387 098	3	19.4
Liberal Democrats	248 497	2	12.5
Socialist People's Party	183 589	1	9.2
Centre Democrats	131 984	1	6.6
Progress Party	68 747	–	3.5
Radical Liberals	62 558	–	3.1

* Greenland also elected one EEC MP, not included in above figures.

190

	Votes per party	Seats	% of votes
Christian People's Party	54 624	–	2.7
Left Socialists	25 305	–	1.3
Turnout 52.3%			

Federal Republic of Germany

CDU	9 306 775	34	37.5
SPD	9 294 916	33	37.4
CSU	2 104 590	7	8.5
Die Grünen	2 024 801	7	8.2
FDP	1 192 138	–	4.8
Others	918 082	–	3.6
Turnout 56.8%			

France

UDF/RPR	8 683 596	41	43.0
PSF	4 188 875	20	20.8
PCF	2 261 312	10	11.2
National Front	2 210 334	10	11.0
Others	2 836 817	–	14.0
Turnout 56.7%			

Greece

PASOK	2 451 409	10	41.6
ND	2 246 896	9	38.1
KKE (ext)	685 387	3	11.6
KKE (int)	200 531	1	3.4
Others	311 997	1	5.3
Turnout 77.2%			

Ireland

Fianna Fail	438 946	8	39.2
Fine Gael	361 034	6	32.2
Independents	113 067	1	10.1
Labour Party	93 656	–	8.4
Sinn Fein	54 672	–	4.9
Others	59 141	–	5.3
Turnout 47.6%			

Italy

PCI/PDUP	11 624 183	27	33.3
DC	11 532 342	26	33.0
PSI	3 909 027	9	11.2
MIS-DN	2 265 619	5	6.5
PLI/PRI	2 131 457	5	6.1
PSDI	1 208 071	3	3.5
PR	1 193 141	3	3.4
Others	1 043 395	3	3.0

	Votes per party	Seats	% of votes
Luxembourg			
PCS	345 363	3	35.3
POSL	295 993	2	30.3
PD	206 763	1	21.2
Others	129 266	–	13.2
Turnout 87.0%			
Netherlands			
PvdA	1 785 399	9	33.7
CDA	1 590 601	8	30.0
VVD	1 002 825	5	18.9
GPA	296 516	2	5.6
CC	275 824	1	5.2
Dem 66	120 848	–	2.3
Others	225 608	–	4.3
Turnout 50.5%			
United Kingdom			
Conservative	5 426 796	45	40.8
Labour	4 865 220	32	36.5
Liberal/SDP Alliance	2 591 657	–	19.5
Scottish Nationalists	230 590	1	1.7
Plaid Cymru	103 031	–	0.8
Ecology Party	74 176	–	0.6
Others	21 348	–	0.2
Turnout 32.0%			

DIRECT ELECTIONS 1989[†]

	Votes per party	Seats	% of votes
Belgium			
Socialist (SP – Flanders)	733 247 ⎫	3	26.9 ⎫
Socialist (PS – Wallonia)	854 148 ⎭	5	⎭
Christian People's (CVP – Flanders)	1 247 090 ⎫	5	29.2 ⎫
Social Christian (PSC – Wallonia)	476 802 ⎭	2	⎭
Reform and Freedom (PRL – Flanders)	625 566 ⎫	2	17.8 ⎫
Freedom and Progress (PVV – Wallonia)	423 511 ⎭	2	⎭
People's Union, Flanders (VU – Eva)	318 146	1	5.4
Ecologists (Agalev – Flanders)	446 524 ⎫	1	13.9 ⎫
Ecologists (Ecolo – V – Wallonia)	371 053 ⎭	2	⎭
Walloon Rally (PWE)	85 870	–	1.5
Vlaams Blok (Flemish National Pty)	241 117	1	4.1
Others	76 211	–	1.2
Turnout 90.7%	5 899 285	24	100.0

[†] *Source: Times Guide to the European Parliament* (1990).

	Votes per party	Seats	% of votes
Denmark*			
Social Democratic Party	417 076	4	23.3
People's Movement against EC	338 953	4	18.9
Liberal Democrats	297 565	3	16.6
Conservative People's Party	238 760	2	13.3
Centre Democrats	142 190	2	8.0
Socialist People's Party	162 902	1	9.1
Progress Party	93 985	–	5.3
Others	97 964	–	5.5
Turnout 46.2%	1 789 935	16	100.0
Federal Republic of Germany			
Christian Democratic Union (CDU)	8 334 433	25	29.6
Christian Social Union (CSU)	2 324 655	7	8.2
Social Democrat Party (SPD)	10 524 859	31	37.3
Greens	2 381 278	8	8.4
Republicans	2 005 555	6	7.1
Free Democrats	1 576 280	4	5.6
Others	1 056 206	–	3.8
Turnout 62.4%	28 203 266	81	100.0
France			
Union UDF/RPR	5 241 354	26	28.9
(Giscard d'Estaing list)			
Centre Party	1 528 931	7	8.4
(Simone Veil list)			
Socialist Party (PS)	4 284 734	22	23.6
National Front (FN)	2 128 589	10	11.7
Green Party (Verts)	1 922 353	9	10.6
Communist Party (PCF)	1 399 939	7	7.7
Others	1 639 688	–	9.1
Turnout 48.7%	18 145 588	81	100.0
Greece			
New Democracy (ND)	2 647 215	10	40.4
Socialist (PASOK)	2 352 271	9	35.9
Communist Alliance (SAP)	936 175	4	14.3
Centre/Right Alliance	89 469	1	1.4
Extreme Right Wing (EPEN)	75 877	–	1.2
Others	443 662	–	6.8
Turnout 79.9%	6 544 669	24	100.0
Ireland			
Fianna Fail (FF)	514 537	6	31.5
Fine Gael (FC)	353 094	4	21.6
Progressive Democrats (PD)	194 059	1	11.9
Independents (Ind)	193 823	2	11.9
Labour Party (Lab)	155 782	1	9.5
Workers' Party (WP)	123 265	1	7.5

* Socialist People's Party had second seat when Greenland left EC on 1 Jan 1985.

	Votes per party	Seats	% of votes
Green Alliance	61 041	–	3.8
Sinn Fein	37 127	–	2.3
Turnout 68.3%	1 632 728	15	100.0

Italy

Christian Democracy (DC)	11 460 702	26	32.9
Communist (PCI)	9 602 618	22	27.6
Socialist (PSI)	5 154 515	12	14.8
Green Alliance (Verdi/Arco)	2 148 723	5	6.2
Centre Parties (PRI/PLI)	1 533 053	4	4.4
Social Movement (MSI)	1 922 761	4	5.5
Social Democrat (PSDI)	946 856	2	2.7
Lombardy Regional	636 546	2	1.8
Proletarian Democracy (DP)	450 058	1	1.3
Others	973 296	3	2.8
Turnout 81.0%	34 829 128	81	100.0

Luxembourg

Christian Social People's (PCS)	346 621	3	34.9
Socialist Workers (POSL)	252 920	2	25.5
Democratic (PD)	198 254	1	19.9
Others	196 951	–	19.7
Turnout 87.4%	993 951	6	100.0

Netherlands

Christian Democrats (CDA)	1 813 935	10	34.6
Labour (PvdA)	1 609 408	8	30.7
Freedom and Democracy (VVD)	715 721	3	13.6
Green Progressive Alliance	365 527	2	7.0
Coalition of Protestants	309 059	1	5.9
Dem '66	311 973	1	5.9
Others	117 260	–	2.3
Turnout 47.2%	5 241 883	25	100.0

Portugal

Social Democrats (PSD)	1 349 996	9	32.7
Socialist (PS)	1 175 671	8	28.5
Social Democratic Centre (CDS)	584 602	3	14.2
United Democratic Alliance (Communist/Green)	594 771	4	14.4
Others	423 644	–	10.2
Turnout 51.3%	4 128 684	24	100.0

Spain

Socialists (PSOE)	6 258 749	27	39.6
Popular Party (PP)	3 389 341	15	21.4
Centre Party (CDS)	1 129 599	5	7.1
Communists and Allies (IU)	959 270	4	6.1
Catalan Party (CiU)	662 757	2	4.2
José Maria Ruiz – Mateos (JMRM)	609 171	2	3.9
Others	2 612 200	5	17.7
Turnout 54.8%	15 621 087	60	100.0

	Votes per party	Seats	% of votes
United Kingdom			
Labour	6 153 640	45	40.0
Conservative	5 331 077	32	34.6
Green	2 292 705	–	14.9
SLD	986 292	–	6.4
Scot Nat	406 686	1	2.6
Plaid Cymru	115 062	–	0.7
SDP	75 886	–	0.5
Others	41 295	–	0.3
Turnout 35.9%	15 402 643	78	100.0

DIRECT ELECTIONS, 1994*

Belgium

	Seats	% of votes
Socialist (SP-Flanders)	3	10.8
Socialist (PS-Wallonia)	3	11.3
Christian People's (CVP-Flanders)	4	17.0
Social Christian (Wallonia)	2	6.9
Liberal Democratic Party (Flanders)	3	11.4
Liberal Democratic Party (Wallonia)	3	9.0
People's Union (Flanders)	1	4.4
Vlaams Blok (Far Right)	2	7.8
National Front (Far Right)	1	2.9
Agalev, Flanders (Green)	1	6.7
Ecologists (Wallonia)	1	4.8
Others	1	7.1

Denmark

Social Democrats	3	15.8
Radical Liberals	2	8.5
Conservatives	3	17.7
Centre Democrats	0	0.9
Socialist People's Party	1	8.6
June Movement	2	15.2
Anti-EC Movement	2	10.3
Christian Party	0	1.1
Liberal Party	4	18.9
Progress Party (far right)	0	2.9

France

UDF/RPR (Centre Right)	28	25.6
Socialist Party (Europe Solidaire)	15	14.5
L'Autre Europe (de Villiers list)	13	12.3
Energie Radicale (Tapie list)	13	12.0
National Front (FN)	11	10.5

*Source: *Times Guide to the European Parliament* (1995); *The Times* 14 Jun 1994. For the direct elections to Austria, Finland and Sweden on their accession to the EU, see pp. 197–8.

	Seats	% of votes
Communist Party (PCF)	7	6.9
Union of Ecologists	–	2.9
Other Greens	–	2.0
Regional Lists	–	0.4
Others	–	12.8

Germany

	Seats	% of votes
Social Democrat Party	40	32.2
Christian Democratic Union	39	30.2
Christian Social Union	8	6.8
Greens	12	10.1
Republicans (Far Right)	–	3.9
Free Democrats (Liberals)	–	4.1
Others	–	11.0

Greece

	Seats	% of votes
PASOK (Socialists)	10	37.6
New Democracy	8	32.7
Political Spring	3	8.7
Left Coalition	2	6.3
KKE (Communists)	2	6.3
Others	–	8.5

Ireland

	Seats	% of votes
Fianna Fail	7	35.0
Fine Gael	4	24.3
Labour Party	1	11.0
Green Party	2	7.9
Independents	1	6.9
Progressive Democrats	–	6.5
Democratic Left	–	3.5
Others	–	4.9

Italy

	Seats	% of votes
Forza Italia	27	30.6
Democratic Left	16	19.1
National Alliance	11	12.5
Popular Party	8	10.0
Northern League	6	6.6
Refounded Communists	5	6.1
Segni Pact (Christian Democrats)	3	3.3
Greens	3	3.2
Radical Party	2	2.1
Socialist Party	2	1.8
La Rete	1	1.1
Others	3	3.6

Luxembourg

	Seats	% of votes
Christian Social People's Party	2	31.4
Socialist Workers' Party	2	24.8
Democratic Party	1	18.9

	Seats	% of votes
Green Party	1	10.9
Others	–	14.0

Netherlands

	Seats	% of votes
CDA (Christian Democrat)	10	30.8
PvdA (Labour Party)	8	22.9
VVD (Right-wing Lib)	6	17.9
Democrats 66 (centre-left)	4	11.7
SGP-GPV-RPF (right-wing, religious)	2	7.8
Groen-Links (ecologists/left)	1	3.7
Others	–	5.2

Portugal

	Seats	% of votes
Socialist	10	34.8
Social Democrat	9	34.4
Central Democratic and Social Party	3	12.5
United Democratic Coalition	3	11.2
(Communist/Green) Democratic Renewal	–	0.2
Others (incl. invalid votes)	–	7.0

Spain

	Seats	% of votes
Popular Party	28	40.2
Socialist	22	30.7
United Left	9	13.5
Catalan Party	3	4.7
Nationalist Coalition (Regional Parties)	2	2.8
Others	–	8.3

United Kingdom

	Seats	% of votes
Labour	62	44.2
Conservative	18	27.8
Liberal Democrats	2	16.7
Scot Nationalists	2	3.2
Green	–	3.2
Plaid Cymru	–	1.1
Others	–	3.7

Note: Following the enlargement of the European Union with the accession of Austria, Finland and Sweden, elections took place during 1996 to the European Parliament in each of these three countries.

Austria

The first European elections since Austrian accession to the EU took place in Oct 1996.

ÖVP (Austrian Peoples Party)	29.6	7
SPÖ (Social Democrats)	29.1	6
FPÖ (Freedom Party of Austria)	27.6	6
Greens	6.7	1
Liberals	4.2	1

Finland

The first Finnish elections to the European Parliament were held on 20 Oct 1996. Seats won were as follows:

	Seats	% of votes
Centre Party	4	24.4
Social Democrats	4	21.5
Conservatives	4	19.9
Left-Wing Alliance	2	10.5
Green League	1	7.6
Others	1	16.1

Sweden

In the first Swedish elections to the European Parliament, the outcome was:

	Seats	% of votes
Social Democrats	7	28.1
Centre Party	2	7.2
Ecology Party	4	17.2
Left Party (ex-communist)	3	12.9
Moderate Unity Party	5	23.1
Peoples Party	1	4.8

FEDERAL REPUBLIC OF GERMANY

From 1949, direct elections for 60% of the seats in the Bundestag, the others filled by election from lists. From 1953, each voter votes (1) for a candidate in his constituency and (2) for a party list. Seats are distributed proportionally to the second vote. Suffrage since 1949 is for men and women over 21. For elections prior to 1949, see p. 206.

		Votes per party	Seats	% of votes
1949	CDU/CSU	7 359 100	139	31.0
	SPD	6 935 000	131	29.2
	FDP	2 829 900	52	11.9
1953	CDU/CSU	12 444 000	244	45.2
	SPD	7 994 900	151	28.8
	FDP	2 629 200	48	9.5
1957	CDU/CSU	15 008 400	270	50.2
	SPD	9 495 600	169	31.8
	FDP	2 307 100	41	7.7
1961	CDU/CSU	14 298 400	242	45.4
	SPD	11 427 400	190	36.2
	FDP	4 028 800	67	12.8
1965	CDU/CSU	15 524 100	245	47.6
	SPD	12 813 200	202	39.3
	FDP	3 096 800	49	9.5

	Votes per party		Seats	% of votes
1969	CDU/CSU	15 195 187	242	46.1
	SPD	14 065 716	224	42.7
	FDP	1 903 422	30	5.8
1972	CDU/CSU	16 806 020	225	44.9
	SPD	17 175 169	230	45.8
	FDP	3 129 982	41	7.6
1976	SPD	16 099 019	214	42.6
	CDU	14 367 302	190	38.0
	CSU	4 027 403	53	10.6
	FDP	2 995 085	39	7.9
	NPD	122 428	–	0.3
	DKP	118 488	–	0.3
	Others	92 571	–	0.4
1980	CDU	12 992 334	174	34.2
	CSU	3 908 036	52	10.3
	SPD	16 262 096	218	42.9
	FDP	4 030 608	53	10.6
	Die Grünen	568 265	–	1.5
	Others	181 713	–	0.4
1983	SPD	14 866 210	193	38.2
	CDU	14 856 835	191	38.2
	CSU	4 140 351	53	10.6
	FDP	2 705 795	34	6.9
	Die Grünen	2 164 988	27	5.6
	Others	203 391	–	0.4
1987	SPD	14 025 763	186	37.0
	CDU	13 045 745	174	34.5
	CSU	3 715 827	49	9.8
	FDP	3 440 911	46	9.1
	Die Grünen	3 126 256	42	8.3
	NPD	227 054	–	0.6
	Others	285 763	–	0.7

Following German reunification in Oct 1990, the first elections for the all-German parliament were held on 2 Dec 1990. The outcome was:

Votes per party		Seats	% of votes
CDU	17 051 128	268	36.7
CSU*	3 301 239	51	7.1
FDP	5 123 936	79	11.0
(Coalition		401	54.8)
SPD	15 539 977	239	33.5
PDS	1 129 290	17	2.4
Alliance 90/Greens	558 552	8	1.2
Die Grünen	1 788 214	–	3.9
Republicans	985 557	–	2.1
Others**	966 165	–	2.1

	Votes per party	*Seats*	*% of votes*
	Turnout 77.8% (West Germany, 78.5%, East Germany, 74.5%)	636	

* DSU in Germany.
** 16 parties in all.

		Votes*	*Seats*	*% of votes*
1994 (16 Oct)	SPD	17 141 000	252	36.4
	CDU	16 089 000	244	34.2
	CSU	3 427 000	50	7.3
	Alliance 90/The Greens	3 423 000	49	7.3
	FDP	3 258 000	47	6.9
	PDS	2 067 000	30	4.4
	Republican Party	875 000	–	1.9
	Others	823 000	–	1.7
			672	100.0

* rounded to nearest '000.

FINLAND

Voting procedures. Direct proportional elections from multi-member constituencies. Suffrage for all adults over 24 until 1945, and then over 21. In 1919, part of the population disenfranchised by the civil war.

		Votes per party	*Seats*	*% of votes*
1919	SSP	365 046	80	38.0
	MI	189 297	42	19.7
	KK	151 018	28	15.7
	KE	123 090	26	12.8
	RK	116 582	22	12.1
1922	SSP	216 861	53	25.1
	MI	175 401	45	20.3
	KK	157 116	35	18.1
	RK	107 414	25	12.4
	KE	79 676	15	9.2
1924	SSP	255 068	60	29.0
	MI	177 982	44	20.3
	KK	166 880	38	19.0
	RK	105 733	23	12.0
	KE	79 937	17	9.0
1927	SSP	257 572	60	28.3
	MI	205 313	52	22.5
	KK	161 450	34	17.7
	RK	111 005	24	12.2
	KE	61 613	10	6.8

	Votes per party		*Seats*	*% of votes*
1929	SSP	260 254	59	27.4
	MI	248 762	60	26.1
	KK	138 008	28	14.5
	RK	108 886	23	11.4
	KE	53 301	7	5.6
1930	SSP	386 026	66	34.2
	MI	308 280	59	27.3
	KK	203 958	42	18.1
	RK	113 318	20	10.0
	KE	65 830	11	5.8
1933	SSP	413 551	78	37.3
	MI	249 758	53	22.6
	RK	131 440	21	11.2
	KK	121 619	20	10.4
	IK	97 891	14	8.3
1939	SSP	515 980	85	39.8
	MI	296 529	56	22.9
	KK	176 215	25	13.6
	RK	124 720	18	9.6
1945	SSP	425 948	50	25.1
	SKDI	398 618	49	23.5
	MI	362 662	49	21.3
	KK	255 394	28	15.0
1948	MI	455 635	56	24.2
	SSP	494 719	54	26.3
	SKDI	375 820	38	20.0
	KK	320 366	33	17.1
1951	SSP	480 754	53	26.5
	MI	421 613	51	23.2
	SKDI	391 362	43	21.6
	KK	264 044	28	14.6
1954	SSP	527 094	54	26.2
	MI	483 958	53	24.1
	SKDI	433 528	43	21.6
	KK	257 025	24	12.8
1958	SKDI	450 506	50	23.2
	SSP	450 212	48	23.2
	MI	448 364	48	23.1
	KK	297 094	29	15.3
1962	MI	528 409	53	23.0
	SKDI	507 124	47	22.0
	SSP	448 930	38	19.5
	KK	346 638	32	15.0
1966	MI	503 047	49	21.2
	SKDI	502 635	41	21.2
	SSP	645 339	55	27.2
	KK	326 928	26	13.8

		Votes per party	Seats	% of votes
1970	MI	434 150	37	17.1
	SKDI	420 556	36	16.6
	SSP	594 185	51	23.4
	KK	457 582	37	18.0
1972	MI	423 039	35	16.4
	SKDI	438 757	37	17.0
	SSP	664 724	55	25.8
	KK	453 434	34	17.6
1975	SSDP	695 394	54	24.9
	SKDL	528 026	40	18.9
	KP	488 930	39	17.5
	KK	512 213	35	18.4
	SFP	141 381	10	5.0
	LKP	121 722	9	4.4
	SKL	92 108	9	3.3
	Others	214 364	4	7.6
1979	SSDP	691 256	52	23.9
	KK	626 108	47	21.7
	KP	501 012	36	21.0
	SKDL	516 276	35	17.9
	SFP	122 450	10	4.6
	LKP	106 609	4	4.2
	SKL	137 850	9	4.8
	Others	180 744	7	1.7
1983	SSDP	795–813	57	26.7
	KK	658 975	44	22.1
	KP	525 091	38	17.6
	SKDL	400 483	26	13.5
	SMP	288 435	17	9.7
	SFP	137 189	10	4.6
	SKL	90 374	3	3.0
	Others	79 506	5	2.7
1987	SSDP	694 666	56	24.1
	KK	665 477	53	23.1
	KP	507 384	40	17.6
	SKDL	269 678	16	9.4
	SFP	153 141	12	5.3
	SMP	181 557	9	6.3
	SKL	74 011	5	2.6
	Others	331 606	9	11.4
1991	SSDP		48	22.1
	Centre Party (KESK)		55	24.8
	National Coalition Party (KK)		40	19.3
	Left-Wing Alliance (VL)		19	10.1
	Swedish People's Party (SFP)		12	5.5
	Greens		10	6.8
	Finnish Christian Union		8	3.1
	Rural Party (SMP)		7	4.8
	Others		1	3.5
1995	SSDP		63	28.3
	Centre Party		44	19.8

Votes per party	Seats	% of votes
National Coalition Party	39	17.9
Left-Wing Alliance	22	11.2
Swedish People's Party	12	5.1
Greens	9	6.5
Finnish Christian League	7	3.0
Progressive Finnish Party	2	2.8
Minor Parties and Others	2	5.3

FRANCE

Voting procedures. From 1919–27, mixed proportional and majority representation. From 1927–45 the system was as in 1852. In 1945 proportional representation was restored as the sole system; this lasted until 1951 when mixed representation returned. Universal male suffrage until 1945, when women received the vote.

	Votes per party		Seats	% of votes
1902	Left Rep.	2 501 000	180	29.7
	Cons.	2 383 000	147	28.3
	Ind. Rad.	1 414 000	123	16.8
	Rad. Soc.	853 000	75	10.1
1906	Rad. Soc.	2 515 000	241	28.5
	Cons.	2 572 000	109	29.2
	Lib. Popular Action	1 238 000	69	14.0
	Soc.	877 000	53	10.0
1910	Rad. Soc.	1 727 000	121	20.4
	Cons.	1 602 000	112	19.0
	Rep. U.	1 472 000	103	7.4
	Soc.	1 111 000	78	13.1
1914	Rad. Soc.	1 530 000	140	18.1
	Soc.	1 413 000	103	16.8
	Rep. U.	1 588 000	96	18.8
	Ind. Rad.	1 400 000	96	16.6
1919	Rep. U.	1 820 000	201	22.3
	Rad. Soc.	1 420 000	106	17.4
	Rep. (left)	889 000	79	10.9
	Soc.	1 615 000	67	20.1
1924	Rep. U.	3 191 000	204	35.5
	Rad. Soc.	1 613 000	162	17.9
	Soc.	1 814 000	104	20.2
1928	Rep. U.	2 082 000	182	22.0
	Rad. Ind. } Rep. (left)	2 196 000	126	23.2
	Soc.	1 709 000	99	18.0
1932	Rad. Soc.	1 837 000	157	19.2

	Votes per party		*Seats*	*% of votes*
	Soc.	1 964 000	129	20.5
	Rep. U.	1 233 000	76	12.9
	Rep. (left)	1 300 000	72	13.6
	Rad. Ind.	956 000	62	10.0
1936	Centre party	2 536 000 ⎫	222	25.8
	Right-wing	1 666 000 ⎭		16.9
	Soc.	1 955 000	149	19.9
	Rad. Soc.	1 423 000	109	14.5
	Communist	1 502 000	72	15.3
1945	Communist ⎫ Progressive ⎭	5 005 000	148	26.1
	Soc.	4 561 000	134	23.8
	Chr. Dem.	4 780 000	141	24.9
1946(1)	Chr. Dem.	5 589 000	160	28.1
	Communist ⎫ Progressive ⎭	5 119 000	146	25.7
	Soc.	4 188 000	115	21.1
1946(2)	Communist ⎫ Progressive ⎭	5 489 000	166	28.6
	Chr. Dem.	5 058 000	158	26.3
	Soc.	3 432 000	90	17.9
	Moderates	2 566 000	70	13.4
1951	Gaulliste	4 125 000	107	21.6
	Com. and Prog.	5 057 000	97	26.4
	Soc.	2 745 000	94	14.3
	Moderates	2 657 000	87	13.9
	Chr. Dem.	2 370 000	82	12.4
1956	Com. and Prog.	5 514 000	147	25.8
	Moderates	3 258 000	95	15.2
	Soc.	3 247 000	88	15.2
	Rep. Front Radicals ⎫	1 996 000 ⎫		9.3
	Right ⎬ Centre	⎬	73	
	Radicals ⎭	838 000 ⎭		3.9
	Chr. Dem.	2 366 000	71	11.1
1958	Gaulliste	4 165 000	198	20.4
	Moderates	4 502 000	133	22.1
	Chr. Dem.	2 273 000	57	11.1
	Soc.	3 194 000	44	15.7
	Com. and Prog.	3 908 000	10	19.2
1962	Gaulliste	5 847 000	234	31.9
	Soc.	2 320 000	64	12.6
	Com. and Prog.	3 992 000	41	21.7
	Moderates	1 743 000	37	9.6
	Chr. Dem.	1 635 000	37	8.9
1967	Gaulliste	8 454 000	232	37.7
	Dem. Soc. Fed.	4 207 000	116	18.8
	Com. and Prog.	5 030 000	72	22.4

	Votes per party		Seats	% of votes
1968	Gaulliste	10 201 024	349	46.1
	Communist	4 435 357	33	20.0
	F.G.D.S.	3 654 003	57	16.5
	Moderates	2 700 864	31	12.2
1973	Communists	4 438 834	73	20.6
	PSU, extreme left	85 678	102	0.3
	Socialists	4 722 886		21.9
	Other Left	823 084		3.8
	Reformers	1 325 058	34	6.1
	URP UDR	6 730 147	183	31.3
	Ind Rep.	1 658 060	55	7.7
	CDP	841 576	30	3.9
	Various	706 942		3.2
	Others	139 236	13	0.6
1977	RPR	6 651 756	154	26.1
	UDF	5 907 603	124	23.2
	Communists	4 744 868	86	18.6
	Socialists	7 212 916 ⎱	103	28.3
	Left Radicals	595 478 ⎰		2.3
	Other Parties (inc	357 418 ⎱	14	1.2
	Presidential Majority	305 763 ⎰		1.2
1981	Socialists + Left Radicals	9 198 332	285	
	RPR	4 191 482	85	
	UDF	3 481 849	65	
	Communists	1 303 587	44	
	Other Right-wing	408 861	8	
	Other Left-wing	112 481	4	
	Extreme Left	3 517	–	
1986	Communists	2 740 972	35	9.8
	Socialists	8 702 137	206	31.0
	RPR	3 142 373	76	11.2
	UDF	2 330 072	53	8.3
	UDF/RPR joint	6 017 207	147	21.5
	Various Right	1 094 336	14	3.9
	National Front	2 705 838	35	9.6
	Others	1 304 245	9	4.7

		Seats	% votes 1st ballot	% votes 2nd ballot
1988	Socialists (rallies)	276	37.5	48.7
	UDF* ⎱	129	18.5	21.2
	RPR* ⎰	127	19.2	23.1
	Communists (PCF)	27	11.3	3.4
	Various Right-Wing	16	2.9	2.6
	National Front	1	9.7	1.1
	Others	–	0.9	–

* Contested elections jointly as URC (Union du Rassemblement et du Centre).

		Seats	% votes 1st ballot	% votes 2nd ballot
1993	RPR (Gaullists)	247	20.4	28.3
	UDF (allied to RPR)	213	19.1	25.8
	Socialist Party	70	17.6	28.2
	National Front	–	12.4	5.7
	PCF (Communists)	23	9.2	4.6
	Greens	–	4.0	–
	Ecology	–	3.6	–
	Right-wing parties	24	4.7	–

GEORGIA

For elections 1918–21, see note on p. 269. After the declaration of independence in 1991, direct elections to the presidency were held on 26 May. These were won by Zviad Gamsakhurdia with 86.5% of the votes cast. Presidential as well as parliamentary elections were subsequently held on 5 Nov 1995. Eduard Shevardnadze was elected president with 1 589 909 votes (74.9% of the 2 121 510 votes cast). The parliamentary elections were dominated by the Citizen's Union of Georgia (107 seats), followed by the National Democratic Party of Georgia (34 seats) and the All-Georgian Union of Revival (31 seats).

GERMANY

Between 1900 and 1914 elections were held on three occasions in the German Empire (1903, 1907 and 1912). The Centre Party won most seats in 1903 and 1907, but the steadily growing Social Democrats emerged as the largest party in 1912. The figures below are for the top four parties in each of these elections.

		Votes per party	Seats	% of votes
1903	Centre Party	1 875 300	100	19.8
	Social Democrats	3 010 800	81	31.7
	German Conservatives	948 500	54	10.0
	National Liberals	1 317 400	51	13.9
1907	Centre Party	2 179 800	105	19.4
	German Conservatives	1 060 200	60	9.4
	National Liberals	1 630 600	54	14.5
	Social Democrats	3 259 000	43	29.0
1912	Social Democrats	4 250 400	110	34.8
	Centre Party	1 996 800	91	16.4
	National Liberals	1 662 700	45	13.6
	German Conservatives	1 126 300	43	9.2

From 1918–1933, direct proportional elections by list system with a uniform quota of 60 000 votes for one representative. Suffrage for all men and women over 20. From 1933 to 1945 there were three elections, but these are not recognized as free elections and no figures are given.

		Votes per party	*Seats*	*% of votes*
1919	SPD	11 509 100	163	37.9
	BVP	5 980 200	91	19.7
	DDP	5 641 800	75	18.6
	DNVP	3 121 500	44	10.3
1920	SPD	6 104 400	102	21.6
	BVP	5 083 600	85	17.8
	USPD	5 046 800	84	18.0
	DVP	3 929 400	65	14.0
1924	SPD	6 008 900	100	20.5
	DNVP	5 696 500	95	19.5
	BVP	4 861 100	81	16.6
	KPD	3 693 300	62	12.6
1924	SPD	7 881 000	131	26.0
	DNVP	6 205 800	103	20.5
	BVP	5 252 900	88	17.3
	DVP	3 049 100	51	10.7
1928	SPD	9 153 000	153	29.8
	BVP	4 657 800	78	15.2
	DNVP	4 381 600	73	14.2
	KPD	3 264 800	54	10.6
1930	SPD	8 577 700	143	24.5
	NSDAP	6 409 600	107	18.3
	BVP	5 187 000	87	14.8
	KPD	4 592 100	77	13.1
1932	NSDAP	13 745 800	230	37.4
	SPD	7 959 700	133	21.6
	BVP	5 782 000	97	15.7
	KPD	5 282 600	89	14.6
1932	NSDAP	11 737 000	196	33.1
	SPD	7 248 000	121	20.4
	KPD	5 980 200	100	16.9
	BVP	5 325 200	90	15.0
	DNVP	2 959 000	52	8.8
1933	NSDAP	17 277 200	288	43.9
	SPD	7 181 600	120	18.3
	BVP	5 498 500	92	13.9
	KPD	4 848 100	81	12.3
	DNVP	3 136 800	52	8.0

GERMAN DEMOCRATIC REPUBLIC

Electors voted at 18 and could be candidates at 21. Elections to the People's Chamber (*Volkskammer*) were 'universal, equal, direct and secret' and were held every four years. East Berlin had its own Assembly (*Ostberliner Abgeordenetenhaus*) of 200 and did not elect to the *Volkskammer*. However, it nominated 66 representatives thereto without voting rights.

There were 434 seats in the *Volkskammer* (500 in all when the East Berlin nominees were added). The parties were represented in pre-arranged proportions. Since 1967 more candidates were allowed to stand than there were seats. All candidates who received more than 50% of the votes were considered elected; those in excess of the number of seats were placed on a reserve list in order of votes gained. As well as to parties, seats were allotted to social and cultural organizations, *e.g.* to trade unions.

The *Volkskammer* evolved through a series of People's Congresses dominated by the USSR and East German Communists which claimed to speak for all Germany. At the *Länder* elections of Oct 1946 the SED failed to gain 50% of the vote and elections thereafter were conducted on the Soviet single-list model.

	Electorate	Valid votes	Seats	
1949	13 533 071	12 887 234	SED	90
			CDU	45
			LDPD	45
			NDPD	15
			DBP	15
			others	130

These elections resulted in the 3rd People's Congress of 1525 delegates, which elected from among its members a German People's Council of 330 on 3 May 1949. On 7 Oct 1949 the formation of a go-it-alone German Democratic Republic was announced and the People's Council became the Provisional *Volkskammer* of 400 representatives. West Germany declared the GDR illegal in that it was not founded upon free elections.

An upper chamber of representatives of provinces (*Länderkammer*) was formed in 1949 but abolished in 1958. The term 'Provisional' was dropped from the title of the *Volkskammer* after that Chamber had been confirmed by the 1950 elections.

	Electorate	Valid votes	Seats	
1950	12 331 905	12 139 932	SED	100
			CDU	60

208

	Electorate	Valid votes	Seats	
			LDPD	60
			NDPD	30
			others	150
1954	12 085 380	11 892 849	SED	102
			CDU	47
			LDPD	46
			NDPD	45
			DBD	45
			others	115
1958	11 839 217	11 707 715	SED	102
			CDU	47
			LDPD	46
			NDPD	45
			DBD	45
			others	115

At the 1963 elections the electorate was 11 621 158 (valid votes, 11 533 859); 1967, 11 341 729 (11 208 816); 1971, 11 401 090 (11 227 535). The distribution of seats in all 3 elections was the same: SED, 128; CDU, 52; LDPD, 52; NDPD, 52; DBP, 52; others 164.

In elections held on 17 Oct 1976, of the total electorate of 11 425 194 some 11 262 948 (98.58%) cast their vote. Of the valid votes, 99.85% were cast for the National Front list.

In elections held on 14 Jun 1981, of the total electorate of 12 356 263 some 12 255 006 (99.21%) cast their vote. Of the valid votes, 99.86% were cast for the National Front list.

In the elections of 8 Jun 1986, 99.94% of those eligible to vote duly voted for the National Front, once again the only party allowed to contest the elections.

After the fall of the Honecker regime and the end of the Communist era, the first free elections in East Germany were held in Mar 1990. The outcome was:

Party	Seats	% of votes
Alliance for Germany	193	48.1
⎰ Christian Democrats	164	40.9
⎱ Social Union	25	6.3
Democratic Awakening	4	0.9
Social Democrats	87	21.8
Party of Democratic Socialism*	65	16.3
Alliance of Free Democrats	21	5.3
Alliance '90 (inc. New Forum)	12	2.9
Democratic Farmers	9	2.2
Greens/Ind. Women	8	1.9
Others	5	1.5

Of the eligible electorate of 12.1 million, 93.2% voted.
* Formerly the Communists.

For the results of the first all-German elections of 2 Dec 1990, *see* under Federal Republic of Germany, p. 199.

GREECE

Voting procedures. Party list system in electoral departments. Direct election, majority vote. Universal male suffrage. From 1926, proportional representation until 1928, and then again for the election of Sep 1932 and the elections of Jan 1936, Mar 1946, Mar 1950, Sep 1951 and May 1958 onwards. Vote extended to women in 1955.

	Votes per party		*Seats*	% of votes
1926	Liberals	303 140	102	31.6
	Populists	194 243	60	20.3
	Freedom Party	151 044	51	15.8
1928	Liberals	477 502	178	46.9
	Pro-Liberals	74 976	25	2.5
	Workers and Agrarian	68 278	20	6.7
	Populists	243 543	19	23.9
1932	Liberals	391 521	98	33.4
	Populists	395 974	95	33.8
	Progressive	97 836	15	8.4
1933	Populists	434 550	118	38.1
	Liberals	379 968	80	33.3
1935	Populists ⎱ Nat. Radical ⎰	669 434	287	65.0
	Royalists	152 285	7	14.8
1936	Liberals	474 651	126	37.3
	Populists	281 597	72	22.1
	Populists and Rad.	253 384	60	19.9
1946	Nationalist (union of Populists, Nat. Lib., Reformist and others)	610 995	206	55.1
	Nat. Pol. Union (Venizelos Liberals, Soc. Dem., Nat. United Party and others)	213 721	68	19.3
	Liberals	159 525	48	14.4
1950	Populists	317 512	62	18.8
	Liberals	291 083	56	17.2
	Nat. Prog. Union	277 739	45	16.4
	Papandreou Party (ex-Soc. Dem.)	180 185	35	10.7
1951	Hellene Party	624 316	114	36.5

	Votes per party		*Seats*	*% of votes*
	Nat. Prog. Union	401 379	74	23.5
	Liberals	325 390	57	19.0
1952	Hellenes	783 541	247	49.2
	Nat. Prog. Union $\}$ Liberals	544 834	51	34.2
1956	Nat. Rad. Union	1 594 112	165	47.4
	Dem. Union (Populists, Liberals, Nat. Prog. Union, Agrarians and Centre)	1 620 007	132	48.2
1958	Nat. Rad. Union	1 583 885	171	41.2
	United Democratic Left	939 902	79	24.4
	Liberals	795 445	36	20.7
1961	Nat. Rad. Union	2 347 824	176	50.8
	Centre Union $\}$ Progressives	1 555 442	100	33.7
	Un. Dem. Left (under title Pandemocratic Agrarian Front)	675 867	24	14.6
1963	Centre Union	1 962 079	138	42.0
	Nat. Rad. Union	1 837 377	132	39.4
	Un. Dem. Left	669 267	28	14.3
1964	Centre Union	2 424 477	171	52.7
	Nat. Rad. Union $\}$ Progressives	1 621 546	108	35.3
	Un. Dem. Left	542 865	21	11.8

Note: On 21 Apr 1967 dictatorial power was seized by right-wing army colonels, aiming to forestall the expected electoral victory of the Centre Union under George Papandreou. Democracy was restored in 1974 when Constantine Karamanlis returned from exile in Paris to head a government of National Unity.

	Votes per party		*Seats*	*% of votes*
1974	New Democracy	2 670 804	220	54.4
	Panhellenic Socialist Union	666 806	12	13.6
	Centre Union	1 002 908	60	20.4
	Communists/United Left	464 331	8	9.4
	National Democratic Union	54 162	–	1.1
	Others	53 345	–	1.1
1977	New Democracy	2 146 687	172	41.8
	Panhellenic Socialist Movement	1 299 196	93	25.3
	Democratic Centre Union	613 113	15	11.9
	Communist Party (KKE)	480 188	11	9.4
	Left-Wing and Progressive Alliance	139 762	2	2.7
	Others	405 411	7	7.9

	Votes per party		Seats	% of votes
1981	Panhellenic Socialist			
	Movement	2 725 395	172	48.1
	New Democracy	2 033 774	115	35.9
	Communists (KKE			
	exterior)	619 296	13	10.9
	Progressive Party	95 697	–	1.7
	KKE (interior)	77 465	–	1.4
	Others	119 314	–	2.0
1985	PASOK	2 916 450	161	45.8
	New Democracy	2 599 949	126	40.9
	KKE – Exterior	629 578	12	9.9
	KKE – Interior	117 050	1	1.8
	Others	102 072		1.6
1989 (June)	New Democracy		145	44.3
	PASOK		125	39.2
	Left Coalition		28	13.1
	Inds & Others		2	3.5
1989 (Nov)	New Democracy		148	46.2
	PASOK		128	40.7
	Left Coalition		21	11.0
	Ecologists		1	0.6
	Others*		2	1.5
1990 (Apr)	New Democracy		150	46.9
	PASOK		123	38.6
	Left Coalition		19	10.2
	Ecologists		1	0.8
	Others		7	3.5
1993 (Oct)	PASOK		170	46.9
	New Democracy		111	39.3
	Political Spring		10	4.9
	Communist Party		9	4.5
	Others		–	3.1

HUNGARY

Before its extensive territorial reduction in 1918 the kingdom of Hungary formed part of the Austro-Hungarian empire. It had no codified written constitution. There was a bicameral parliament (*Országház*), but only 6% of the population possessed the vote.

Towards the close of the war M. Károlyi's Party of Independence emerged on the political scene, standing for independence from Austria and unilateral withdrawal from hostilities. At a time of popular unrest Károlyi was appointed prime minister on 31 Oct 1918, leading a coalition government of Party of Independence, Radicals and Social Democrats. On 13 Nov 1918 King Charles IV renounced participation in affairs of state, and on 16 Nov 1918 Hungary was proclaimed a Republic with

Károlyi as provisional President (he became President on 11 Jan 1919). Parliament was dissolved and replaced by a provisional unicameral National Assembly.

This government resigned on 22 May 1919 in protest at Allied territorial demands, and was succeeded by a Soviet republic of Communists and Social Democrats led by Béla Kun. Elections to the Soviets were held on 17 Apr 1919. The Communist régime was short-lived and harassed by hostilities with foreign invaders and native anti-Communist forces. Kun resigned on 1 Aug 1919, and Romania occupied Budapest until M. Horthy entered on 16 Nov 1919 at the head of an anti-Communist army.

At Allied insistence an election with universal secret suffrage was held on 25 Jan 1920. The Christian Nationalists (government party) gained 77 seats, the Smallholders 49. The Social Democrats refused to take part.

This government annulled all Károlyi's and Kun's legislation and re-established the former constitution. The link with Austria was dissolved. On 23 Mar 1920 Hungary was proclaimed a kingdom again; Horthy had been chosen as regent on 1 Mar 1920.

This government decreed a new electoral system. The upper house (House of Magnates) was re-established. Secret ballot was abolished except in towns (20% of constituencies were urban). Some 1.5m. lost the vote. Educational, property and residence qualifications were introduced. Men voted at 24, women at 30. Candidates had to be nominated by 10 000 electors. The National Assembly was to consist of 245 deputies.

On 7 Mar and 29 Oct 1921 Charles IV made unsuccessful attempts to regain the throne.

At the elections of 28 May and 2 Jun 1922 Smallholders and Christian Nationalists combined to form the Party of National Unity, which gained 143 seats. The opposition parties gained 78 (including 25 Social Democrats).

An electoral law of 11 Nov 1926 gave definitive form to the House of Magnates, which was to consist of nominated members of the nobility and upper middle class, and other dignitaries. A small proportion of members were elected for ten-year terms.

1926   Party of National Unity, 171; Christian Social Union, 35; Social Democrats, 14; others, 25.
1931   Party of National Unity, 155; Christian Social Union, 32; Social Democrats, 14; Independent Smallholders, 11; Independents, 21; others, 12.
1935   Party of National Unity, 170; Independent Smallholders, 23; Christian Social Union, 14; Social Democrats, 11.

By an electoral law of Dec 1938 residential and educational qualifications were made stricter, and male voting age raised from 24 to 26. In order to vote, women over 30 had to be self-supporting or the wives of electors. The number of deputies was raised to 260. 135 single-member constituencies were formed, election requirement being a simple majority over 40%. Multi-member constituencies elected the remainder on a proportional representation scheme.

Secret ballot was introduced in May 1939, and many Jews were disenfranchised.

1939   Party of Hungarian Life (formerly Party of National Unity) in alliance, 186; Christian Union, 3; Arrow Cross (fascists), 29; Independent Smallholders, 14; National Social Front Union, 5; Citizens' Freedom Party, 5; Social Democrats, 5; Racialists, 4; National Front, 3; Christian National Social Front, 3; People's Will, 1; Independents, 2.

During the war an Independence Front began to take shape of Social Democrats, crypto-Communists, Smallholders, National Peasants and Legitimists.

With the Soviet invasion a provisional government was set up at Debrecen on 21 Dec 1944, which ultimately consisted of 127 Communists, 123 Smallholders, 94 Social Democrats, 63 Trade Unionists, 39 National Peasants, 22 Democrats and 30 independents.

By an electoral law of 19 Sep 1945 universal secret suffrage at 20 was introduced.

		Votes	Seats
1945	Smallholders	2 688 161	245
	Social Democrats	821 566	69
	Communists	800 257	70
	National Peasants	322 988	23
	Democrats	78 522	2
			409

1947 Electorate: 5 407 893. Voted: 4 996 100 (93%). Seats 411.

Government bloc	Votes	Seats
Communists	1 082 497	100
Smallholders	757 821	68
Social Democrats	732 178	67
National Peasants	435 170	36
	3 007 027	271

Opposition	Votes	Seats
Popular Democrats	805 450	60
Hungarian Independence Party	718 193	49
Independent Democrats	256 396	18
Radicals	93 270	6
Christian Women's Union	67 792	4
Citizen Democrats	48 055	3
	1 989 156	140

During the next two years the opposition parties were eliminated or amalgamated into the People's Front. The Social Democrats merged into the Communists in Jun 1948. At the election of 15 May 1949 candidates were presented on a single list, the People's Front. Electorate: 6 053 972. Voted: 5 730 519 (94.6%). For the People's Front. 5 478 515 (95.6%).

A new constitution of Soviet type was promulgated on 18 Aug 1949. Hungary was proclaimed a 'People's Republic'. Voting age was lowered to 18. The National Assembly was to be elected every four years by universal secret suffrage.

At the election of 17 May 1953 there was a single list of People's Front. Electorate: 6 501 869. Voted: 6 370 519 (98%). Votes for People's Front: 6 256 653 (98.2%).

On 27 Oct 1956 there was a major reorganization of the government in response to armed insurrection: independent Smallholders and National Peasants were co-opted in. Revolutionary councils sprang up demanding a free general election. On 30 Oct 1956 I. Nagy proclaimed the restoration of multi-party government. On 3 Nov 1956 the government was reorganized as a coalition of Communists, Smallholders, National Peasants and Social Democrats.

This government was overthrown by armed Soviet intervention and a 'Revolutionary Worker-Peasant government' set up under J. Kádár.

At the election of 16 Nov 1958, 6 493 680 voted (98.4% of electorate). For People's Patriotic Front: 6 431 832 (99.6%). There were 338 candidates for 338 seats.

At the election of 24 Feb 1963 the electorate was 7 114 855. Voted: 6 915 644 (97.2%). Voted for the single list of People's Patriotic Front 6 813 058 (98.9%). 340 deputies elected.

On 11 Nov 1966 an electoral law brought an end to the strict rigidity of the one seat-one candidate system by replacing the 20 multi-seat mega-constituencies by 349 single-member constituencies. All candidates remained nominees of the People's Patriotic Front, but it became possible for more than one candidate to contest a single seat.

In the election of 19 Mar 1967 this happened in nine constituencies. None of the nine challengers was elected. 7 131 151 votes were cast (99.7% of the electorate) and 98.8% of these were for the People's Patriotic Front candidates.

In Oct 1970 another electoral law liberalized the position further by introducing the participation of the ordinary citizenry in the nomination of candidates. In the election of 25 Apr 1970, 49 seats were contested by more than one candidate. Electorate: 7 432 420. Voted: 7 334 918 (98.7%). Voted for the People's Patriotic Front: 7 258 121 (98.9%). 352 deputies were elected.

In elections held on 15 Jun 1975, 7 527 169 votes were cast (97.6% of a total electorate of 7 760 464). Of these, 99.6% of votes were cast for official candidates.

In elections held on Jun 1980, only 15 of the 352 seats were contested by more than one candidate. Of the 7.7 million who voted, 99.3% of votes cast were for the official People's Patriotic Front.

In elections held in Jun 1985, 873 candidates were put forward for the 352 seats elected on a territorial basis (35 additional members were elected unopposed on a national list). The electorate was 7.7 m., of whom 93.9% voted in the first round and 83% in the second round. Of the candidates, 795 were proposed by the Patriotic People's Front, 78 direct from the floor of nomination meetings (of these 78, 43 were elected). A total of 244 members were elected for the first time.

The first free elections in Hungary since the fall of the Communist regime were held on 25 Mar and 8 Apr 1990. The results of the elections for the 386 elected deputies were:

	No. of seats	% of votes
Hungarian Democratic Forum	165	42.74
Alliance of Free Democrats	92	23.83
Independent Smallholders' Party	43	11.13
Hungarian Socialist Party	33	8.54
Federation of Young Democrats	21	5.44
Christian Democratic People's Party	21	5.44
Independents	6	1.55
Joint candidates	4	1.03
Agrarian Alliance	1	0.25

Parliamentary elections were held in two rounds on 8 and 29 May 1994.

	No. of seats	% of votes
Hungarian Socialist Party	209	54.1

	No. of seats	% of votes
Alliance of Free Democrats	70	18.1
Hungarian Democratic Forum	37	9.6
Independent Smallholders' Party	26	6.7
Christian Democratic People's Party	22	5.7
Federation of Young Democrats	20	5.2
Agrarian Alliance	1	0.3
Liberal Bloc	1	0.3
	386	

ICELAND

Voting procedures. From 1915–1920, the Althing had 40 members directly elected, 6 proportionally and 34 by majority. Majority elections were in 25 constituencies, 9 of them two-member, the rest single. Suffrage for the election of 34 members, all men and women property-holders over 25; for the 6, all those over 35. From 1920 onwards the Althing had additional members, including some elected by direct proportional election in Reykjavik. From 1934, suffrage extended to all men and women over 21 'in charge of their own finances and properties'.

	Votes per party		Seats	% of votes
1916	Home Rule Party	5 333	12	40.0
	Hardline Independence	2 097	7	15.7
	Farmers Party	1 173	5	8.8
	Others	4 745	10	36.5
1923	Citizens Party	16 272	21	53.6
	Progressives	8 062	13	26.6
	Soc. Dem.	4 912	1	16.2
1927	Progressives	9 532	17	29.8
	Liberals Conservatives }	15 474	13	42.0
	Soc. Dem.	6 097	4	19.1
1931	Progressives	13 844	12	35.9
	Independence	16 891	21	43.8
1933	Independence	17 131	17	48.0
	Progressives	8 530	14	23.9
1934	Independence	21 974	20	42.3
	Progressives	11 377	15	21.9
	Soc. Dem.	11 269	10	21.7
1937	Progressives	14 556	19	24.9
	Independence	24 132	17	41.3
	Soc. Dem.	11 084	8	19.0

	Votes per party		*Seats*	*% of votes*
1942(1)	Progressives	16 033	20	27.6
	Independence	22 975	17	39.5
	United Soc.	11 059	10	18.5
1942(2)	Independence	23 001	20	38.5
	Progressives	15 869	15	26.6
	United Soc.	11 059	10	18.5
1946	Independence	26 428	20	39.4
	Progressives	15 429	13	23.1
	United Soc.	13 049	10	19.5
	Soc. Dem.	11 914	9	17.8
1949	Independence	28 546	19	39.5
	Progressives	17 659	17	24.5
	United Soc.	14 077	9	19.5
1953	Independence	28 738	21	37.1
	Progressives	16 959	16	21.9
	United Soc.	12 422	7	16.1
1956	Independence	35 027	19	42.4
	Progressives	12 925	17	15.6
	People's Un.	15 859	8	19.2
	Soc. Dem.	15 153	8	18.3
1959(1)	Independence	36 029	20	42.5
	Progressives	23 061	19	27.2
	People's Un.	12 929	7	15.3
1959(2)	Independence	33 800	24	39.7
	Progressives	21 882	17	25.7
	People's Un.	13 621	10	16.0
	Soc. Dem.	12 909	9	15.2
1963	Independence	37 021	24	41.4
	Progressives	25 217	19	28.2
	People's Un.	14 274	9	16.0
1967	Independence	36 036	23	37.5
	Progressives	27 029	18	28.1
	People's Un.	13 403	9	13.9
	Soc. Dem.	15 059	9	15.7
1971	Independence	38 170	22	36.2
	Progressives	26 645	17	25.3
	People's Un.	18 055	10	17.1
	Soc. Dem.	11 020	6	10.5
1974	Independence	48 758	25	42.8
	People's Alliance	20 922	11	18.3
	Soc. Dem.	10 321	5	9.1
	Progressives	28 388	17	24.9
	Liberal and Leftist Union	5 244	2	4.6
1978	Independence	39 973	20	32.7
	People's Alliance	27 962	14	22.9
	Soc. Dem.	26 912	14	22.0
	Progressives	20 561	12	16.9
	Liberal and Leftist Union	na	0	3.5

	Votes per party		Seats	% of votes
1979	Independence	42 957	21	33.6
	People's Alliance	24 390	11	19.1
	Soc. Dem.	27 078	10	21.2
	Progressives	30 871	17	24.2
	Others	2 433	1	1.9
1983	Independence	50 251	23	38.7
	Progressives	24 095	14	18.5
	People's Alliance	22 490	10	17.3
	Soc. Dem.	15 214	6	11.7
	Soc. Dem. Alliance	9 489	4	7.3
	Others	8 423	3	6.5
1987	Independence		18	27.2
	Progressives		13	18.9
	Soc. Dem.		10	15.2
	People's Alliance		8	13.3
	Citizens' Party		7	10.9
	Women's Alliance		6	10.1
	Others		1	4.4
1991	Independence Party		26	38.6
	Progressive Party		13	18.9
	Social Democratic Party		10	15.5
	People's Alliance		9	14.4
	Women's Alliance		5	8.3
	Others		–	4.3
1995	Independence Party		25	37.1
	Progressive Party		15	23.3
	People's Alliance		9	14.3
	Social Democratic Party		7	11.4
	Awakening of the Nation		4	7.2
	Women's Alliance		3	4.9

IRELAND

Voting procedures. From 1918–1921, single-member constituencies, spot voting and plurality counting. From 1921, multi-member constituencies with preferential voting and quota counting. Suffrage for men of 21 and over, and women of 30 and over, until 1923 when the age limit for both was 21. From 1918–1923, University graduates and owners of businesses had extra votes.

	Electorate	Valid votes	Votes per party		Seats	% of electorate	% of votes
1918	1 936 673	1 046 541	Sinn Fein	496 961	73	–	47.5
			Unionists	298 726	26	–	28.5
			Nationalists	233 690	6		22.3
1921	–	–	Sinn Fein	–	124		–
			Unionists	–	4		

	Electorate	Valid votes	Votes per party		Seats	% of electorate	% of votes

(*Note*: This was not a normal election; no poll took place; all borough and county seats were taken by Sinn Fein and the Unionists were returned for Dublin University.)

	Electorate	Valid votes	Votes per party		Seats	% of electorate	% of votes
1922	1 026 289	627 623	Pro-Treaty	245 336	58	–	39.1
		(first preference)	Anti-Treaty	134 801	36	–	21.5
			Labour	132 511	17		21.1

(*Note*: Pro- and Anti-Treaty parties were the result of the division of Sinn Fein.)

	Electorate	Valid votes	Votes per party		Seats	% of electorate	% of votes
1923	1 785 436	1 052 495	Fine Gael	409 184	63	22.9	38.9
			Fianna Fail	291 191	44	16.3	27.7
			Labour	130 659	16	7.3	12.4
1927(1)	1 730 426	1 146 460	Fine Gael	314 711	46	18.2	27.5
			Fianna Fail	299 476	44	17.3	26.1
			Labour	159 046	23	9.2	13.9
1927(2)	1 728 340	1 170 856	Fine Gael	453 013	61	26.2	38.7
			Fianna Fail	411 833	57	23.8	35.2
			Labour	111 287	13	6.4	9.5
1932	1 601 933	1 274 026	Fianna Fail	566 498	72	33.5	44.5
			Fine Gael	449 506	56	26.6	35.3
			Independence	106 466	12	6.3	8.4
			Labour	114 163	9	6.7	9.0
1933	1 724 420	1 386 558	Fianna Fail	689 054	76	40.0	49.7
			Fine Gael	422 495	48	24.5	30.5
			Labour	88 347	9	5.1	6.4
1937	1 775 055	1 324 449	Fianna Fail	599 040	68	33.7	45.2
			Fine Gael	461 171	48	26.0	34.8
			Labour	147 728	15	8.3	11.2
1938	1 697 323	1 286 259	Fianna Fail	667 996	76	39.4	51.9
			Fine Gael	428 633	45	25.3	33.3
			Labour	140 099	9	8.3	10.9
1943	1 816 142	1 331 709	Fianna Fail	557 525	66	30.7	41.9
			Fine Gael	307 499	32	16.9	23.1
			Labour	214 743	17	11.8	16.1
1944	1 776 850	1 217 349	Fianna Fail	595 259	75	33.5	48.9
			Fine Gael	249 329	30	14.0	20.5
			Labour	140 245	12	7.9	11.5
1948	1 800 210	1 323 443	Fianna Fail	553 914	67	30.8	41.9
			Fine Gael	262 393	31	14.6	19.8
			Labour	150 229	19	8.3	11.4
1951	1 785 144	1 331 573	Fianna Fail	161 212	68	34.5	46.3
			Fine Gael	342 922	40	19.2	25.8
			Labour	151 828	16	8.5	11.4
1954	1 763 209	1 335 202	Fianna Fail	578 960	65	32.8	43.4
			Fine Gael	427 031	50	24.2	32.0
			Labour	163 982	18	9.3	12.3

	Electorate	Valid votes	Votes per party		Seats	% of electorate	% of votes
1957	1 738 278	1 227 019	Fianna Fail	592 994	78	34.1	48.3
			Fine Gael	326 699	40	18.8	26.6
			Labour	111 747	11	6.4	9.1
1961	1 670 860	1 168 404	Fianna Fail	512 073	70	30.6	43.8
			Fine Gael	374 099	47	22.4	32.0
			Labour	139 822	16	8.4	12.0
1965	1 683 019	1 253 122	Fianna Fail	597 414	72	35.4	47.7
			Fine Gael	427 081	47	25.4	34.1
			Labour	192 740	22	11.5	15.4
1969	1 735 388	1 318 953	Fianna Fail	602 234	75	34.7	45.7
			Fine Gael	449 749	50	25.9	34.1
			Labour	224 498	18	12.9	17.0

In the five elections of 1973–1982, the seats won were as follows:

Party	1973	1977	1981	1982 (Feb)	1982 (Nov)
Fianna Fail	69	34	78	81	75
Fine Gael	54	43	65	66	70
Labour	19	17	15	15	16
Independents / Others	2	4	8	7	5

In the elections of 1987, 1989 and 1992 the seats won were as follows:

Party	1987	% of votes**	1989	% of votes	1992	% of votes
Fianna Fail	81	44.1	77	43.7	68	39.1
Fine Gael	51	27.1	55	29.6	45	245
Labour Party	12	6.5	15	8.0	33	19.3
Workers' Party***	4	3.8	7	5.6	4	2.8
Progressive Democrats	14	11.9	6	5.0	10	4.7
Others*	4	6.6	6	8.2	6	9.6

* Including in 1989 the first Green Party elected member.
** First preference votes.
*** Democratic Left in 1992

ITALY

The elections of 1919 and 1921 were fought on adult male suffrage and the *d'Hondt* system of proportional representation. The election of 1924 was not a free election because of Fascist intimidation. After 1945, the new constitution provided for a bicameral Parliament, with a minimum voting age of 21. Deputies are chosen by proportional representation using the *Imperiali* system. Proportional representation was introduced into the lower house in 1994.

	Votes per party		Seats	% of votes

From 1900 to 1914, four elections were held (in 1900, 1904, 1909 and 1913). Each election was dominated by the combined Ministerial and Opposition Liberals (412 out of 508 seats in 1900, 415 in 1904, 382 in 1909 and 310 in 1913). The Socialist vote rose from 13% (33 seats) in 1900 to 17.6% (52 seats) in 1913. The best Republican performance was 6.2% in 1900, the best Radical Party 11.7% in 1913.

Year	Party	Votes	Seats	% of votes
1919	Socialist	1 834 792	156	32.3
	Popular	1 167 354	100	20.5
	Centre coalition	904 195	96	15.9
	Democrats	622 310	60	10.9
1921	Socialist	1 631 435	123	24.7
	Popular	1 377 008	108	20.4
	Nat. Bloc.	1 260 007	105	19.1
	Lib. Dem.	684 855	68	10.4
1924	Fascist	4 671 550	375	65.3
	Popular	645 789	39	9.0
1946	Chris. Dem.	8 101 004	207	35.2
	Socialist	4 758 129	115	20.7
	Communist	4 356 686	104	18.9
1948	Chris. Dem.	12 741 299	305	48.5
	Communist[1] Socialist }	8 137 047	183	31.0
1953	Chris. Dem.	10 864 282	263	40.1
	Communist	6 121 922	143	22.6
	Socialist	3 441 305	75	12.7
	Monarchist	1 855 843	30	6.9
1958	Chris. Dem.	12 520 556	273	42.4
	Communist	6 704 763	140	22.7
	Socialist	4 206 777	84	14.2
1963	Chris. Dem.	11 763 418	260	38.3
	Communist	7 763 854	166	25.3
	Socialist	4 251 966	87	13.8
1968	Chris. Dem.	12 441 553	266	39.1
	Communist	8 557 404	177	26.9
	Socialist	4 605 832	91	14.5
1972	Chris. Dem.	12 943 675	267	38.8
	Communist	9 085 927	179	27.2
	Socialist	4 925 700	89	14.7
1976	Chris. Dem.	14 211 005	262	38.7
	Communists	12 620 509	228	34.4
	Socialists	3 541 383	57	9.6
	Social Democrats	1 237 483	15	3.4
	Republicans	1 134 648	14	3.1
	Liberals	478 157	5	1.3
	Italian Social Movement	2 243 849	35	6.1
	Others	1 248 543	14	3.4

[1] Under the name Democratic Popular Front

	Votes per party		*Seats*	% of *votes*
1979	Chris. Dem.	14 007 594	262	38.3
	Communists	11 107 883	201	30.4
	Socialists	3 586 256	62	9.8
	Italian Social Movement	1 924 251	30	5.3
	Social Democrats	1 403 873	20	3.8
	Republicans	1 106 766	16	3.0
	Liberals and Radicals	1 967 384	27	5.3
	Others	1 462 578	12	4.1
1983	Chris. Dem.	12 145 800	225	32.9
	Communists	11 028 158	198	29.9
	Socialists	4 222 487	73	11.4
	Italian Social Movement	2 511 722	42	6.8
	Republicans	1 872 536	29	5.1
	Social Democrats	1 507 431	23	4.1
	Liberals and Radicals	1 875 505	27	5.1
	Others	1 726 642	13	4.7
1987	Chris. Dem.	13 231 960	234	34.3
	Communists	10 249 690	177	26.6
	Socialists	5 501 980	94	14.3
	Italian Social Movement	2 282 212	35	5.9
	Republicans	1 428 358	21	3.7
	Social Democrats	1 140 086	17	3.0
	Liberals and Radicals	1 798 636	24	4.7
	Greens	969 534	13	2.5
	Others	1 970 598	15	5.0
1992	Christian Democrats		206	29.7
	Democratic Party of the Left		107	16.1
	Socialists (PSI)		92	13.6
	Italian Social Movement (MSI)		34	5.4
	Republicans (PRI)		27	4.4
	Social Democrats (PSDI)		16	2.7
	Liberals (PLI)		17	2.8
	Northern League		55	8.7
	Communists		35	5.6
	Greens		16	2.8
	La Rete		12	1.9
	Others		13	6.3
1994 (27–28 Mar)	Freedom Alliance		366	42.9
	Forze Italia			(21.0)
	National Alliance			(13.5)
	Northern League			(8.4)
	Progressive Alliance		213	34.4
	Democratic Party of the Left			(20.4)
	PRC (Refounded Communists)			(6.0)
	Greens			(2.7)
	Socialists, La Rete, AD			(5.3)
	Centre (Popular Party, Segni Pact)		46	15.7
	Others		5	7.0
1996 (21 Apr)	Olive Tree Alliance		284	41.2
	Freedom Alliance		246	37.3
	Northern League		59	
	Refounded Communists		35	8.6
	Minor Parties		6	

LATVIA

A Constituent Assembly in May 1920 established a parliament (*Saeima*) of 100 deputies to be elected every three years. Elections were held in 1922, 1925, 1928 and 1931. The system favoured a proliferation of parties: 22 in 1922; 27 in 1925; 25 in 1928 and 24 in 1931. The more numerous parties were, from right to left: Farmers' Union; Catholics; Democratic Centre; New Settlers; Right-wing Socialists; Social Democrats. The Communist Party was illegal, but ran as the Workers' Bloc in 1931, gaining seven seats. The Social Democrats had 30 deputies in each government, except that of 1931, when they had 22. There were Jewish, Polish, Russian and German national minority parties, and a fascist party, Thunder Cross (*Perkonkrusts*).

On 15 May 1932 Ulmanis assumed dictatorial powers by dismissing the *Saeima* and prohibiting all party political activity.

The country was occupied by Soviet troops on 16 Jun 1940 and an election was held on 14 and 15 Jul 1940. The resultant People's *Saeima* voted unanimously for incorporation into the USSR.

Elections in newly-independent Latvia took place on 5 and 6 Jun 1993, with 874 candidates from 23 parties.

	Seats	% of votes
Latvian Way	36	32.4
Latvian National Independence Movement[1]	15	13.3
Harmony for Latvia – Revival of the Economy	13	12.0
Latvian Farmers' Union	12	10.6
Equal Rights Movement	7	5.8
Fatherland and Freedom Union	6	5.4
Christian Democratic Union of Latvia	6	5.0
Democratic Centre Party[2]	5	4.8
Others	0	10.7
Total	100	

[1] Now renamed the Latvian National Conservative Party
[2] Now taken name Democratic Party

LITHUANIA

On 22 Sep 1917 a congress of 214 Lithuanian delegates elected a 20-strong council (*Taryba*) which proclaimed independence and organized elections for a Constituent Assembly. These were held by universal suffrage on the proportional representation system on 15 May 1920. One representative stood for 15 000 inhabitants. There were 112 seats in the Constituent Assembly, distributed as follows: Christian Democrats, 59; Social Populist Democrats, 29; Social Democrats, 13; Jews, 6; Poles, 3; Independents, 2.

224

This enacted that a parliament (*Semias*) of 80 was to be elected every three years by universal suffrage on the proportional representation system, one deputy representing 25 000 electors.

At the elections of 10 Oct 1922 the results were: Christian Democrats (including the Farmers' Union and the Workers' Federation), 38; Social Populist Democrats, 19; Social Democrats, 11; Workers' Party, 5; Jews, 3; Poles, 2. A Stulginskis was elected President.

A further election was held on 5 Jun 1923: Christian Democrats, 40; Social Populist Democrats, 16; Social Democrats, 8; Jews, 5; Poles, 5; Germans, 2; Russians, 2.

Elections 8 and 10 May 1926: Christian Democrats, 30; Social Populist Democrats, 22; Social Democrats, 15; Poles, 4; Jews, 3; Germans, 1; and from Memel (Klaipeda) Agrarians, 3; People's Party, 2.

By a *coup d'état* of 17 Dec 1926, A. Smetona assumed dictatorial powers as President, and parliamentary government lapsed.

Elections in newly-independent Lithuania took place on 25 Oct 1993 (with run-offs in 51 constituencies on 10 Nov). The former Communists (now the Lithuanian Democratic Labour Party) dominated the results.

	Seats
Democratic Labour Party	73
Sajudis	30
Christian Democratic Party	16
Social Democratic Party	8
Union of Poles	4
Independents and Others	10
	141

In elections in Oct and Nov 1996 the result was:

Homeland Union (party of Vytautas Landsbergis)	70
Democratic Labour Party (ex-communists)	12
Christian Democratic Party	16
Social Democratic Party	12
Others	27
Total	137

MACEDONIA

The first general election in independent Macedonia took place on 16 and 30 Oct 1994. The presidential election, easily won by Kiro Gligorov, was also held on 16 Oct. The general election was dominated by the three-party Alliance for Macedonia (comprising the Social Democratic Alliance of Macedonia (58 seats), the Liberal Party (29 seats) and the Socialist Party of Macedonia (8 seats)). Of the remaining 25 seats in the 120-seat Assembly, the Party for Democratic Prosperity had 10 and the National Democratic Party 4.

MALTA

In the first election held after independence (held in 1966), the Nationalists under Dr Borg Olivier won 28 seats, the Labour Party won 22. Thereafter the results were as follows:

		Votes per party	Seats	% of votes
1971	Malta Labour Party	85 448	28	50.8
	Nationalist Party	80 753	27	48.1
	Others	1 756	–	–
1976	Malta Labour Party	105 854	34	51.5
	Nationalist Party	99 551	31	48.5
	Independent	35	–	–
1981	Malta Labour Party	109 990	34	49.1
	Nationalist Party	114 132	31	50.9
1987	Nationalist Party	119 721	35	50.9
	Malta Labour Party	114 937	34	48.9
	Others	511	–	0.2
1992	Nationalist Party	127 932	34	51.8
	Malta Labour Party	114 911	31	46.5
	Others	4 296	–	1.7
1996	Malta Labour Party	132 497	31*	50.7
	Nationalist Party	124 864	34	47.8
	Others	3 863	–	1.5

* Eventual seat allocation to Labour was 35.

MOLDOVA

The first elections in independent Moldova were held on 27 Feb 1994. The outcome was a victory for the Agrarian Democratic Party.

	Seats	% of votes
Agrarian Democratic Party	56	43.2
Socialist Unity	28	22.0
Bloc of Peasants and Intellectuals	11	9.2

	Seats	% of votes
Popular Front Alliance	9	7.5
Others (including Social Democrats, Democratic Labour and Reform)	–	18.1

THE NETHERLANDS

Voting procedures. Direct proportional elections on the party list system. Elections to 100 seats, the rest allocated according to the greatest remainder vote. Suffrage for men over 25, until 1922 when it was extended to women the same age. In 1946, extended to all citizens 23 and over and in 1967 all citizens over 21.

Between 1900 and 1914, elections were held on four occasions (1901, 1905, 1909 and 1913). The period saw a steady rise in the Social Democratic Workers vote (from 9.5% in 1901 to 18.5% in 1913). The largest party in 1901 and 1905 was the Free Liberal League. The Catholic Party and the Anti-Revolutionary Party each won 25 seats in 1909. The Catholic Party won 25 seats again in 1913 with the Liberal Union taking 22.

	Votes per party		Seats	% of votes
1918	RKS	402 908	30	30.0
	SDAP	296 145	22	22.0
	PvV	202 972	15	15.1
	ARP	179 523	13	13.4
1922	RKS	874 745	32	29.9
	SDAP	567 769	20	19.4
	ARP	402 277	16	13.7
1925	RKS	883 333	30	28.6
	SDAP	706 689	24	22.9
	ARP	377 426	13	12.2
1929	RKS	1 001 589	30	29.6
	SDAP	804 714	24	23.9
	ARP	391 832	12	11.6
	CHU	354 548	11	10.5
1933	RKS	1 037 364	28	27.9
	SDAP	798 632	22	21.5
	ARP	499 892	14	13.4
1937	RKS	1 170 431	31	28.8
	SDAP	890 661	23	22.0
	ARP	665 501	17	16.4
1946	KV	1 466 582	32	30.8
	PvA	1 347 940	29	28.3
	ARP	614 201	13	12.9
1948	KV	1 531 154	32	31.0
	PvA	1 263 058	27	25.6
	ARP	651 612	13	13.2

		Votes per party	Seats	% of votes
1952	KV	1 529 508	30	28.7
	PvA	1 545 867	30	29.0
	ARP	603 329	12	11.3
1956	PvA	1 872 209	50	32.7
	KV	1 529 508	49	31.7
	ARP	567 535	15	9.9
1959	KV	1 895 914	49	31.6
	PvA	1 821 825	48	30.3
	VVD	732 658	19	12.2
	ARP	563 091	14	9.4
1963	KV	1 993 352	50	31.9
	PvA	1 753 084	43	28.0
	VVD	643 839	16	10.3
	ARP	545 836	13	8.7
	CHU	536 801	13	8.6
1967	KV	1 822 904	42	26.5
	PvA	1 620 112	37	23.5
	VVD	738 202	17	10.7
	ARP	681 060	15	9.9
1971	KV	1 379 672	35	21.8
	PvA	1 554 280	39	24.6
	VVD	653 370	16	10.3
	ARP	542 742	13	8.6
1972	KV	1 305 401	27	17.7
	PvA	2 021 454	43	27.3
	VVD	1 068 375	22	14.4
	ARP	653 609	14	8.8
1977	CDA	2 652 278	49	31.9
	PvdA	2 813 793	53	33.8
	VVD	1 492 689	28	17.9
	D-66	452 423	8	5.4
	PSP	77 972	1	0.9
	CPN	143 481	2	1.7
	Others	684 976	9	8.2
1981	CDA	2 676 525	48	30.8
	PvdA	2 455 424	44	28.3
	VVD	1 504 293	26	17.3
	D-66	959 661	17	11.0
	PSP	184 039	3	2.1
	CPN	178 147	3	2.0
	Others	728 298	9	8.5
1982	PvdA	2 499 562	47	30.4
	CDA	2 141 176	45	29.3
	VVD	1 897 986	36	23.0
	D-66	355 830	6	4.3
	PSP	187 150	3	2.3
	SGP	156 782	3	1.9
	CPN	147 510	3	1.8
	PPR	136 095	2	1.6
	RPF	124 018	2	1.5
	Others	313 711	3	3.8

	Votes per party		Seats	% of votes
1986	CDA	3 170 081	54	34.6
	PvdA	3 012 268	52	33.3
	VVD	1 595 377	27	17.4
	D-66	561 865	9	6.1
	SGP	159 897	3	1.8
	PPR	115 009	2	1.3
	PSP	110 331	1	1.2
	GPV	88 006	1	1.0
	Others	314 501	1	3.3
1989	CDA	3 140 502	54	35.3
	PvdA	2 835 251	49	31.9
	VVD	1 295 402	22	14.6
	D-66	701 934	12	7.9
	Greens	362 304	6	4.1
	SGP	166 082	3	1.9
	GPV	109 637	2	1.2
	Others	166 658	2	3.1
1994	PvdA		37	24.0
	CDA		34	22.2
	VVD		31	19.9
	D-66		24	15.5
	SGP		7	4.8
	AOV (Third Age)		6	3.6
	Green Links		5	3.5
	Extreme Right		3	2.5
	Extreme Left		2	1.3
	Others		1	2.7

NORWAY

Voting procedures. Direct proportional elections in multi-member constituencies. Suffrage for men and women over 23 until 1949, when it was extended to men and women over 21.

	Votes per party	Seats	% of votes

Prior to 1918, elections were held in 1900, 1903, 1906, 1909, 1912 and 1915. The elections were dominated by the battle between Liberals and Conservatives (the Conservatives won only in 1903 and 1909). A major trend was the rise of Labour (from 3% of the vote and no seats in 1900 to 32% of the vote and 19 seats in 1915).

	Votes per party		Seats	% of votes
1918	Left	187 657	51	28.3
	Right	201 325	50	30.4
	Labour	209 560	18	31.6
1921	Right	301 372	57	33.3
	Left	181 989	37	20.1
	Labour	192 616	29	21.3
	Agrarian	18 657	17	13.1

	Votes per party		Seats	% of votes
1924	Right	316 846	54	32.5
	Left	180 979	34	18.6
	Labour	179 567	24	18.4
	Agrarian	131 706	22	13.5
1927	Labour	388 106	59	36.8
	Conservative	240 091	30	24.0
	Liberal	172 568	30	17.3
	Agrarian	149 026	26	14.9
1930	Labour	374 854	47	31.4
	Conservative	327 731	41	21.1
	Liberal	241 355	33	20.2
	Agrarian	190 220	25	15.9
1933	Labour	500 526	69	40.1
	Conservative	252 506	30	20.2
	Liberal	213 153	24	17.1
	Agrarian	173 634	23	13.9
1936	Labour	618 616	70	42.5
	Conservative	310 324	36	21.3
	Liberal	232 784	23	16.0
	Agrarian	168 038	18	11.6
1945	Labour	609 348	76	41.0
	Conservative	252 608	25	27.0
	Liberal	204 852	20	13.8
1949	Labour	803 471	85	45.7
	Conservative	311 819	23	17.7
	Liberal	235 876	21	13.4
1953	Labour	830 448	77	46.7
	Conservative	344 067	27	18.8
	Liberal	177 662	15	10.0
	Chr. People's	186 627	14	10.5
	Agrarian	160 583	14	9.0
1957	Labour	865 675	78	48.3
	Conservative	338 651	29	18.9
	Liberal	173 525	15	9.7
	Agrarian	166 757	15	9.3
1961	Labour	860 526	74	46.8
	Conservative	368 340	29	20.0
	Agrarian	170 645	16	9.3
	Chr. People's	176 896	15	9.6
1965	Labour	883 320	68	43.1
	Conservative	432 025	31	21.1
	Liberal	211 853	18	10.4
	Agrarian	202 396	18	9.9
1969	Labour	1 000 348	74	46.5
	Conservative	406 209	13	18.8
	Liberal	202 553	13	9.4
	Agrarian	194 128	20	9.0

	Votes per party		Seats	% of votes
1973	Labour	759 482	62	35.3
	Conservative	375 782	29	17.5
	Centre (Agrarian)	237 073	21	11.0
	Christian Democrats	261 869	20	12.2
	Left Socialists	241 816	16	11.2
	Liberals	76 155	2	3.5
	Others	200 966	5	9.3
1977	Labour	962 728	76	42.4
	Conservative	560 025	41	24.7
	Centre (Agrarian)	196 005	12	8.6
	Christian Democrats	274 516	22	12.1
	Left Socialists	102 371	2	4.5
	Liberals	73 371	2	3.2
	Others	80 929	–	3.6
1981	Labour	896 796	66	37.6
	Conservative	746 614	53	31.3
	Centre	220 827	10	9.3
	Christian Democrats	160 224	16	6.7
	Left Socialists	116 637	4	4.9
	Progress Party	107 971	4	4.5
	Liberals	92 266	2	3.9
	Others	40 860	–	1.7
1985	Labour	1 033 650	71	41.2
	Conservative	755 159	50	30.1
	Christian People's	208 315	16	8.3
	Centre Party	169 223	12	6.7
	Left Socialists	135 191	6	5.4
	Progressives	92 635	2	3.7
	Liberals	77 919	–	3.1
	Others	39 637	–	1.6
1989	Labour	907 393	63	34.3
	Conservative	588 682	37	22.2
	Progressives	345 185	22	13.0
	Left Socialists	266 782	17	10.1
	Christian People's	224 852	14	8.5
	Centre Party	171 269	11	6.5
	Liberals	84 740	–	3.2
	Others	59 701	1	2.2
1993	Labour	908 724	67	36.9
	Centre Party	412 187	32	16.7
	Conservatives	419 373	28	17.0
	Left Socialists	194 633	13	7.9
	Christian People's	193 885	13	7.9
	Progress	154 497	10	6.3
	Liberals	88 985	1	3.6
	Others	89 665	1	3.7

POLAND

J. Piłsudski proclaimed independence on 10 Nov 1918 and appointed governments on 18 Nov 1918 and 16 Jan 1919.

Elections to the Sejm (parliament) were held in non-occupied Poland on 26 Jan 1919 and supplemented by by-elections in Nov. There were 394 deputies from 14 parties including:

National Democrats and allies (dubbed 'Endecja' from the initials)	140	(of these 116 were National Democrats, *i.e.* 37% of all deputies)
Polish Peasant Party 'Liberation' (*i.e.* left-wing)	71	
Polish Peasant Party 'Piast' (*i.e.* right-wing)	46	
Polish Socialist Party	35	
National Workers' Party	32	
National minority parties	13	

A constitution was promulgated on 17 Mar 1921 by which a bicameral parliament was set up, to be elected by universal suffrage every five years by proportional representation, consisting of a Senate of 111 senators and the Sejm of 444 deputies.

At the elections of 5 and 12 Nov 1922 the electorate was 13 109 793 of whom 8 760 195 (67%) voted. Representatives of 15 parties were elected to the Sejm, including:

Party	Votes	Seats	% of Votes
Christian League of National Union	2 551 000	169	29.1
Polish Peasant Party 'Piast'	1 150 000	70	13.1
Polish Peasant Party 'Liberation'	963 000	49	11
Polish Socialist Party	906 000	41	10.3
National Workers' Party	474 000	18	5.4
Polish Centre	260 000	6	3
Communist Party	121 000	2	1.4
National minority parties	1 963 000	86	22.4

On 14 May 1926 Piłsudski staged a *coup d'état* and issued a constitution in June which restricted the powers of the Sejm.

At the elections of 4 Mar 1928 the electorate was 15m. and 11 408 218 voted.

Party	Votes	Seats	% of Votes
Non-party pro-Piłsudski Bloc (BBWR)	2 399 032		130
Polish Peasant Party 'Liberation'			66
Polish Socialist Party	1 148 279		63
People's Party (SN; formerly National Democrats)	925 744		37
Polish Peasant Party 'Piast'			21
Christian Democratic Party			19
National Workers' Party			14
Communist Party (illegal, but running under the name 'Union of Town and Country Proletariat')	940 000		8
National minority parties			86

This Sejm was dissolved on 30 Aug 1930.

During the campaign before the elections of 16 and 23 Nov 1930 opposition politicians were imprisoned.

The electorate was 15 520 342, of whom 13 078 682 voted. 372 deputies were elected to the Sejm, and the number was made up to 444 by allotments according to proportional representation:

Non-party pro-Piłsudski Bloc (BBWR)	5 292 725	247
People's Party (SN)	1 455 399	62
6-Party Centre-Left coalition	1 907 380	
Polish Peasant Party 'Liberation'		33
Polish Socialist Party		24
Christian Democrats		15
Polish Peasant Party 'Piast'		15
National Workers' Party		10
Communist Party		5
National minority parties		33

A new constitution was promulgated on 23 Apr 1935. The Sejm was reduced to 208 deputies, elected by universal suffrage at 24 years. The Senate was reduced to 96, of whom one-third were appointed by the President and the remainder elected by a college of 300 000. Methods of election were not changed but district electoral assemblies acquired a decisive role in the designation of candidates.

All political parties boycotted the elections of 8 and 15 Sep 1935. The electorate was 16 332 100, of whom according to the government's own figures only 45.9% voted (7 512 102). 153 BBWR members were returned to the Sejm and 22 members of national minority groups.

President Móscicki dissolved Sejm and Senate on 22 Sep 1935.

All political parties abstained from the elections of 6 and 13 Nov 1938. The turn-out was 67.4%. 161 members of the non-party Camp of National Unity (OZN) were returned to the Sejm.

The liberation of part of Poland from German occupation by Soviet forces enabled the Polish Committee of National Liberation (PKWN) to be set up on 21 Jul 1944, proclaiming itself the sole legal Polish executive power. It was composed of Communists, left-wing socialists, left-wing peasants and Democratic Party representatives. It became the provisional government on 31 Dec 1944. At the Yalta conference (Feb 1945), it was agreed that a Provisional Government of National Unity should be formed based on this government, and this was done on 28 Jun 1945. It contained Communists (PPR, *i.e.* Polish Workers' Party) and representatives of the Polish Socialist Party (PPS), and the Polish Peasant (PSL), Democratic (SD) and Christian Democratic Labour (SP) parties.

A referendum was held on 30 Jun 1946, at which the electorate were asked to approve (1) the abolition of the Senate, (2) basic nationalization and land reform, (3) the fixing of Poland's borders on the Baltic and the Oder–Neisse line. The turn-out was 80.8% (11 530 551), and affirmative answers were recorded as follows: (1) 68%, (2) 77.2%, (3) 91.4%.

An electoral law of Sep 1946 disfranchised collaborators: approximately 1m. people lost their vote in this way.

During the elections of 19 Jan 1947 some 12.7m. votes were cast, of which 11 244 873 were valid (89.19% of electorate voted). The Communists together with the Polish Socialist, Peasant and Democratic parties stood as the Democratic Bloc, polling 9m. votes (80.1% of the vote) and gaining 392 seats in the Sejm. Other parties:

Party	Seats	% of Votes
Polish Peasant Party	27	10.3
Christian Labour Party (SP)	15	4.7
Peasant Party 'Liberation'	7	
Catholic independents	3	

On 19 Feb 1947 the Sejm passed an interim constitution, which became known as the 'Little Constitution'. A permanent constitution was passed on 22 Jul 1952. This gave the ground plan of the electoral provisions later extant, although these were liberalized by later amendments. The Sejm was elected every four years by all citizens over 18. Citizens could stand as candidates at 21. There was one deputy per 60 000 inhabitants. Only political and social organizations (trade unions, youth and

cultural organizations) could nominate candidates, who had to be on the single list of the National Unity Front (FJN), which grouped three parties: Communist (PZPR), United Peasant (ZSL) and Democratic (SD).

The office of President was abolished. The Chairman of the Council of State would henceforth be head of state.

At the elections of 26 Oct 1952 the number of candidates was the same as the number of seats. The electorate was 16 305 891: votes cast, 15 495 815. The single list of National Front candidates gained 99.8% of valid votes and took up seats in the Sejm:

Party	Seats
Communist Party (PZPR)	273
United Peasant Party (ZSL)	90
Democratic Party (SD)	25
Independents	37
	425

By an electoral law of 24 Oct 1956 the single list of candidates was allowed to include up to two-thirds more candidates than seats. All electors were to make their vote behind curtains. Negative votes were to be recorded by crossing out the candidates' names.

At the elections of 20 Jan 1957 there were 717 candidates (51% of whom were Communists) for 459 seats. Turn-out was 94.14% (16 892 213 votes were cast from an electorate of 17 944 081). 280 002 votes (1.6% of votes) were made against National Front candidates. Seats:

Communists (PZPR)	239
United Peasant Party (ZSL)	118
Democratic Party (SD)	39
Independents (including 12 Catholics, 9 of whom from the Znak group)	63
	459

An electoral law of 22 Dec 1960 reduced the ratio of candidates to seats.

At the elections of 16 Apr 1961 there were 616 candidates for 460 seats. The turn-out was 94.83%. There were 292 009 votes against the National Front list (1.57% of votes).

Party	Seats
Communists (PZPR)	256
United Peasant Party (ZSL)	117

Party	Seats
Democratic Party (SD)	39
Independents (including 5 Catholics of the Znak group)	48
	460

After the elections of 30 May 1965, 1 Jun 1969 and 19 Mar 1972 the parties' positions were the same.

Communists (PZPR)	255
United Peasant Party (ZSL)	117
Democratic Party (SD)	39
Independents (including 14 Catholics)	49
	460

	1965	1969	1972
Electorate	19 645 893	21 148 879	21 854 481
Turn-out	96.62%	97.61%	97.94%
Votes against	226 324	161 569	–
National Front List	(1.15% of votes)	(0.78% of votes)	–

In elections held on 21 Mar 1976, 631 candidates contested the 460 seats. Of the 24 069 579 registered voters, 23 652 256 (98.27%) cast their votes. Some 99.43% voted for the official candidates of the National Unity Front.

In elections held on 23 Mar 1980, 646 candidates contested the 460 seats. Official figures stated that 98.87% of the 25 098 816 total electorate voted. Of these 99.52% voted for the list of National Unity Front candidates.

In elections for the Sejm held on 4 and 18 Jun 1989, it had been agreed at talks between government and opposition earlier in the year that Solidarity and other opposition groups would contest only 35% of the seats. The outcome was:

Party	Seats
Polish United Workers' Party (PZPR)*	173
Solidarity	161
Catholics allied to PZPR	23
Others	103
	460

* Dissolved in Jan 1990 to become part of a social democratic grouping.

The first free presidential elections in Poland since the end of Communist rule were held on 25 Nov and 9 Dec 1990. The outcome of the second round was: Walesa, 74.25%, Tyminski, 25.75%. Mazowiecki was eliminated on the first ballot.

The following general elections have been held since 1990:

		Seats	% of votes
1991 (27 Oct)	Democratic Union	62	12.3
	Democratic Left Alliance (DLA)	60	12.0
	Catholic Action	49	8.7
	Polish Peasant Party (PPP)	48	8.7
	Confederation for an Independent Poland	46	7.5
	Centre Citizens' Alliance	44	8.7
	Liberal Democratic Congress	37	7.5
	Peasant Alliance	28	5.5
	Solidarity	27	5.0
	Polish Beer Lovers' Party	16	3.3
	Others	43	20.8
	Total	460	100.0
1993 (19 Sep)	Democratic Left Alliance (DLA)	171	20.4
	Polish Peasant Party (PPP)	132	15.4
	Democratic Union	74	10.6
	Union of Labour	41	7.3
	Confederation for an Independent Poland	22	5.8
	Non-Party Bloc for Reform	16	5.4
	Others	4*	–

* Other parties to contest the election and poll over 4% included the Catholic Electoral Committee ('Homeland'), Solidarity, the Centre Alliance and the Liberal Democratic Congress.

DANZIG

Danzig was created a Free City by the Versailles Treaty of 28 June 1919, under a League of Nations High Commissioner and in customs union with Poland. It was incorporated into Germany during World War II, and into Poland (as Gdańsk) after it.

The constitution provided for a Senate of 20 plus a President and Vice-President elected by the People's Assembly for four years. The President was head of state: 1918, H. Sahm; 1931, E. Ziehm; 1933, H. Rauschning; 1934, A. Greiser. The Assembly (*Volkstag*) of 120 (reduced to 72 in 1930) was elected by universal secret suffrage at 20 for four-year terms on a proportional representational system.

Election 16 May 1920. Social Democrats, 37 seats; German Nationalists, 34, Centre (Catholics), 17; German Democrats, 10; Poles, 7; Populists, 6; National Liberals, 3; German Liberals, 3; Communists, 3.

Election 9 Nov 1923. Social Democrats, 30; German Nationalists, 26; Centre (Catholics), 15; Communists, 11; German Social Party, 7 (10 301 votes; the first appearance of a racialist party); Populists, 6; German

Democrats, 5; German Liberals, 5; Poles, 5; National Liberals, 4; Middle-class Federation, 2; Independents, 4.

Election 13 Nov 1927. Social Democrats, 42; German Nationalists, 25; Centre (Catholics), 18; Communists, 8; Populists, 5; National Liberals, 5; German Liberals, 4; Middle-class Federation, 3; Poles, 3; German Social Party, 1 (2130 votes); Nazis, 1 (1483 votes).

ELECTIONS

	16 Nov 1930		28 May 1933		7 Apr 1935	
	Votes	*Seats*	*Votes*	*Seats*	*Votes*	*Seats*
Social Democrats	49 965	19	38 703	13	37 804	14
Nazis	32 457	12	107 335	38	128 619	40
Centre (Catholics)	30 232	11	31 339	10	31 576	11
German Nationalists	25 938	10	13 595	4	9 822	3
Communists	20 194	7	44 766	5	7 935	2
Poles	6 377	2	6 738	2	8 311	2
Others		11				

The 1935 election was fought for a two-thirds majority to enable the Nazis to ask the League of Nations to revise the constitution. The Polish government and the opposition parties alleged terror and unlawful practices by the Nazis. The Danzig Court discovered some illegality, and reduced the Nazi vote and number of seats as first officially proclaimed. The final figures are given above.

By dissolutions and amalgamations the Nazis became supreme in the Assembly by 1939, except for the two Polish deputies. On 22 Mar 1939 it was declared that the elections then due were 'unnecessary' and would not be held.

PORTUGAL

On 19 Mar 1933, the *Estado Novo* constitution (providing for an authoritarian Republic on a corporative basis) was voted upon and adopted. This constitution provided for a President, to be elected for seven years by direct suffrage by male Portuguese citizens, of age or emancipated, able to read or write, and those unable to read or write, being taxpayers to the state or administrative corporations for direct taxes, and Portuguese citizens, females, of age or emancipated, with a special, secondary school, or university diploma; and for a National Assembly (one chamber) of 90 deputies elected for four years by direct suffrage. In the two elections for the National Assembly (1934 and 1938) the only lists presented were those organized by the National Union, an association legally recognized, but without the character of a party, whose aim was to defend the principles contained in the constitution. The electoral law permitted, however, the presentation of more than one list of the deputies to be elected.

At the elections of 8 Nov 1953 the União Nacional (National Union) obtained all 120 seats; the 28 opposition candidates were defeated. At subsequent elections only government candidates stood for re-election.

On 25 Apr 1974, an almost bloodless *coup* took place in Portugal. The new military government promised a return of normal political life. After a troubled period, the first elections to a Constituent Assembly were held in Apr 1975.

The outcome was

	Votes per party	*Seats*	*% of votes*
Portuguese Socialist Party (PSP)	2 145 392	115	37.9
Portuguese Democratic Party (PDP)	1 494 575	80	26.4
Portuguese Communist Party (PCP)	709 639	30	12.5
Social Democratic Centre (CDS)	433 153	16	7.6
Portuguese Democratic Movement (MDP)	233 362	5	4.1
Portuguese Socialist Front (FSP)	66 161	–	1.2
Movement of the Socialist Left (MES)	57 682	–	1.0
Others	132 579	1	2.3

Elections for a legislative assembly were subsequently held in Apr 1976, the Socialists again emerging as the largest party.

Portuguese Socialist Party (PSP)	1 887 180	107	35.0
Portuguese Democratic Party (PPD)	1 296 432	73	24.0
Social Democratic Centre (CDS)	858 783	42	15.9
Portuguese Communist Party (PCP)	785 620	40	14.6
Popular Democratic Union (UDP)	91 383	1	1.7
Popular Socialist Front (FSP)	41 954	0	0.8

After a succession of political crises, Parliament was dissolved prematurely and elections took place on 2 Dec 1979.

Democratic Alliance	2 497 019	118	42.2
Socialists	1 621 950	73	27.4
Communists	1 121 224	47	19.0
Others	503 933	8	8.6

Under the new constitution, elections had still to be held in Oct 1980.

239

	Seats	% of votes
Democratic Alliance		47.1%
PSD	82 ⎫	
CDS	46 ⎬ = 134	
PPM	6 ⎭	
Republican and Socialist Front		28.0
PSP	66 ⎫	
UEDS	4 ⎬ = 74	
ASDI	4 ⎭	
United People's Alliance		16.9
PCP	39 ⎫ = 41	
MDP	2 ⎭	
Popular Democratic Union	1	1.4

Elections were next held in 1983. The results were:

PSP	101	36.3
PSD	75	27.0
PCP	44	18.2
CDS	30	12.4
PPM	–	0.5
Pop. Dem. Un.	–	0.5
Others	–	5.1

The results of elections held in Portugal in Oct 1985 were:

	Seats	% of votes
PSD	88	29.9
PSP	57	20.8
PRD	45	18.0
APU	38	15.4
CDS	22	9.8
Others	–	6.1

The results of the Jul 1987 elections were:

PSD	148	50.2
PS	60	22.2
CDU	31	12.1
PRD	7	4.9

	Seats	*% of votes*
CDS	4	4.5
Others	–	6.1

The results of the Oct 1991 elections were:

	Seats	*% of votes*
PSD	135	50.6
PS	72	29.1
CDU	17	8.8
CDS	5	4.4
PSN	1	1.7
Others	–	5.4

The results of the Oct 1995 elections were:

	Seats	*% of votes*
PS	112	42.9
PSD	88	34.0
CDS	15	5.1
CDU	15	8.6
Others	–	9.4

ROMANIA

1919	Chamber of Deputies: 568 of which:	
	National Party of Transylvania	199
	Peasants	130
	National Liberals	120
	Nationalists and Democrats	27
	Conservative Democrats	16

In 1920 the number of deputies was reduced to 369 and conducted under proportional representation.

1920	People's Party	224
	Peasants	40
	National Party of Transylvania	30
	Socialists	19
	National Liberals	17
	Germans	8

241

	Seats	% of votes
1922 National Liberals		227
Peasants and National Party of Transylvania		62
People's Party		11
Conservative Democrats		8
Germans		8
Social Democrats		1
Jews		1

Opposition parties challenged validity of this election and withdrew.

A new constitution of 23 Mar 1923 reorganized the Senate to consist of 249 seats elected on a more restricted suffrage (over 40-year-olds and members of the ruling élite). The Chamber of Deputies was to be elected by universal secret suffrage at 21 years of age on a constituency basis.

By an electoral law of 1926 that party which obtained 40% of the vote was awarded 50% of the seats plus a proportionate share of the seats remaining.

Party	Number of votes	Seats gained	% of votes
1926 Electorate: 3 496 814, of which 75% voted.			
National Liberals	192 309	16	7
National Peasants	727 202	69	28
People's Party	1 306 100	292	52
Christian League of National Defence	124 778	10	5
1927 The electorate was 3 586 806, of which 77% voted.			
National Liberals ⎱ Peasants ⎰	1 704 435	⎰ 298 ⎱ 22	62
National Peasants	610 149	54	22
Hungarians	173 517	15	6
1928 The electorate was 3 671 352, of which 77.4% voted.			
National Peasants	2 228 922	348	78
National Liberals	185 939	13	7
People's Party	70 490	5	2
Peasants	70 506	5	2
Hungarians	172 699	16	6

Party	Number of votes	Seats gained	% of votes

1931   The electorate was 4 038 464, of which 72.5% voted.

Party	Number of votes	Seats gained	% of votes
National Union	1 389 901	289	48
National Peasants	438 747	30	15
National Liberals (G. Brătianu)	173 586	12	6
People's Party	141 141	10	5
Hungarians	139 003	10	5
Christian League of National Defence	113 863	8	4
Peasant Party	100 682	7	3
Social Democrats	94 957	6	3
Peasant Democrats Union in alliance with League against Usury	80 570	6	3
Labour and Peasant Group	73 716	5	3
Jews	64 193	4	2

1932   The electorate was 4 220 731, of which 70.8% voted.

Party	Number of votes	Seats gained	% of votes
National Peasants	1 203 700	274	41
National Liberals (Duca)	407 023	28	14
National Liberals (Brătianu)	195 048	14	7
Peasants	170 860	12	6
Christian League of National Defence	159 071	11	5
Hungarians	141 894	14	5
National Agrarians	108 857	8	4
Social Democrats	101 068	7	3
Iron Guard	70 674	5	2
National Union	68 116	5	2
Jews	67 582	5	2
People's Party	64 525	4	2

1933   The electorate was 4 380 354, of which 68% voted.

Party	Number of votes	Seats gained	% of votes
National Liberals	1 518 864	300	51
National Peasants	414 685	29	14
Peasants	152 167	11	5
National Liberals (Brătianu)	147 665	10	5
Christian League of National Defence	133 205	9	5
National Agrarians	121 748	9	4
Hungarians	119 562	8	4
Radical Peasants	82 930	6	3
Agrarian Union	73 208	5	2

Party	Number of votes	Seats gained	% of votes
1937	66% of the electorate voted.		
Government Party (National Liberals, etc.)	1 103 323	152	36
National Peasants	626 642	86	20
'All-for-Country' (*i.e.* Iron Guard)	478 378	66	16
Christian League of National Defence	281 167	39	9
Hungarians	136 139	19	4
National Liberals (Brătianu)	119 361	16	4
Radical Peasants	69 208	9	2

The government failed to get its necessary 40% of the votes. King Carol II picked on the Christian League of National Defence to form a government. He dismissed this government on 10 Feb 1938 and instituted a royal dictatorship, called the Government of National Concentration.

A new constitution of 20 Feb 1938 reduced the electorate to some 2m. (voting was universal and secret at age 30) and established a Senate. Political parties were banned except for the royalist monolithic National Renaissance Front. A plebiscite of 24 Feb 1938, conducted by open voting, confirmed the new constitution by 4 283 395 to 5413 votes. Turn-out (compulsory): 92%. A corporatist parliament was returned at the election of 2 Jun 1939: 86 representatives of agrarian and labour interests, 86 of commerce and industry, 86 intelligentsia and 88 senators. Turn-out was 85%. There were twice as many candidates as seats.

An electoral law of 14 Jul 1946 abolished the Senate, enfranchised all at 21 and provided for a unicameral Assembly elected for four-year terms.

At the election of 19 Nov 1946 the government bloc (National Democratic Front) obtained 71% of the votes cast and 347 seats. The National Peasants gained 33, the National Liberals 3. The validity of the results has been challenged.

1947	Electorate: 7 859 212. Voted: 6 934 563 (88.9%).	
National Democratic Front	(348)	(4 766 630)
National Liberals	75	
Social Democrats	75	
Communists	73	
Ploughmen's Front	70	
National People's Party	26	
Dissident National Peasants	20	
Jews	2	
Independents	7	

244

Party	Number of votes	Seats gained
Opposition parties	(1 361 536)	(66)
National Peasants	879 927	32
National Liberals	259 306	3
Democratic Peasants	156 775	2
Hungarian People's Union	569 651	29

The opposition parties protested at the falsification and terror used in these elections.

In Dec 1947 King Michael abdicated, and a People's Republic was proclaimed on the 30th. On 28 Mar 1948, an election was held for a new National Assembly to pass a new constitution.

The remnants of the Social Democrats were merged with the Communists to form the Workers' Party, which ran for election in the single-list monolithic National Democratic Front comprising also the Ploughmen's Front, the National Peasants and the Hungarian People's Union. Electorate 8 417 467. Voted: 7 663 675 (91% turn-out). Voted for National Democratic Front: 6 958 531 (90.8%). The Front gained 405 of the 414 Assembly seats, the Liberals 7, the Democratic Peasants 1 with 1 Independent.

On 13 Apr 1948 a new constitution, of the Soviet type, was promulgated: vote at 18, stand at 23, universal secret suffrage.

A further constitution was instituted on 24 Sep 1949, in general outline the same as that of 1948. Deputies to the Grand National Assembly (*Marea Adunare Naţională*) were to represent 40 000 electors for four-year terms.

1952   Electorate: 10.5m. Voted: 97%. For National Democratic Front: 98%.
1957   Electorate: 11.7m. Voted: 99.15%. For National Democratic Front: 99.88%.

At the elections of 5 Mar 1961, 7 Mar 1965 and 2 Mar 1969 a single list of candidates was presented, the number of candidates equalling the number of seats. At least 99% of the voters turned out, at least 99% of these voted for the National Democratic Front (Socialist Unity Front since 19 Nov 1968).

In elections held on 9 Mar 1975 for the first time 139 of the 349 seats were contested by more than one candidate (although all belonged to the Socialist Unity Front). According to official figures, 99.96% of the 14 900 000 registered voters went to the polls.

In elections held on 9 Mar 1980, officially some 15 629 098 voters (99.99%) of the total electorate voted. Of these, 98.52% voted for official candidates.

In elections held on 17 Mar 1985, officially some 15 732 095 voters (99.99%) of the total electorate voted. Of these 97.7% voted for official candidates.

Following the revolution of Dec 1989 and the overthrow of the Ceauçescu regime, during the first half of 1990 Presidential elections were held and elections to the National Assembly.

Presidential Election

	Votes	% of votes
Ion Iliescu (Nat. Salv. Front)	12 232 498	85.1
Radu Campeanu (NLP)	1 529 188	10.2
Ion Ratiu (CDNPP)	617 007	4.3

Electorate, 17 200 722
Turnout 86.2%

National Assembly Elections May 1990

	Votes	Seats	% of votes
National Salvation Front	9 090 000	263	66.3
Hungarian Democratic Union of Romania	992 000	29	7.2
National Liberal Party	879 000	29	6.4
Ecological Movement	359 000	12	2.6
CDNPP (Christian Democrat National Peasants' Party)	351 000	12	2.6
Unity Alliance	300 000	9	2.2
Others	1 080 000	33	12.7

At the general election of Sep 1992 the outcome was:

	Seats	% of votes
Democratic National Salvation Front (DNSF)[1]	117	27.7
Democratic Convention of Romania Alliance	82	20.0
National Salvation Front	43	10.2
Romanian National Unity Party	30	7.7
Hungarian Democratic Union of Romania	27	7.5
Greater Romania Party	16	3.9
Socialist Labour Party (ex-communists)	13	3.0
Ethnic Minorities (reserved seats)	13	na
Others	0	
Total	341	

[1] Became Party of Social Democracy of Romania in Jul 1993.

The presidential elections of Nov 1996 marked a watershed in the history of the country with the victory of the right-wing candidate Emil Constantinescu over the incumbent, former communist Ion Iliescu. Constantinescu took 54.4% of the votes cast on a turn-out of 75.9%.

RUSSIA

No reliable statistics of voting in Tsarist Russia can be obtained. Various estimates have been made, however, of the relative strengths of different groups in the four Dumas. These are given below:

THE FIRST DUMA

The predominance of the large landowners and upper middle class was made certain by the electoral law of 11 Dec 1905. The actual elections (in Feb–Mar 1906) took place in an atmosphere of active police repression. The Bolsheviks boycotted the election (with obvious success in St Petersburg, Poland and the Baltic). The Kadets (Constitutional Democrats) easily emerged as the largest single party.

Composition of the First Duma

The Right (Monarchists, Octobrists, Industrialists, etc.)	44
The Autonomists (Polish League, Lithuanian Circle, Ukrainian Democrats, etc.)	44
Party for Democratic Reform	6
Kadets	179
Labour Group	94
Social Democratic Group	18
Cossack Group	1
Non-party	100

Composition of the Second Duma

The Reactionary Right	10
Octobrists	42
Polish League	46
Muslim Group	30
Party for Democratic Reform	1
Kadets	98
Labour Group	104
Popular Socialists	16
Socialist Revolutionaries	37
Social Democrats	65

Cossack Group	17
Non-party	50
	516

Composition of the Third Duma (First Session)

The Reactionary Right	49
Moderate Right Wing	69
Russian National Group	26
Alliance of 17 October	148
Polish/Lithuanian Group	7
Polish League	11
Progressives	25
Muslim Group	8
Kadets	53
Labour Group	14
Social Democrats	20
Non-party	16
	446

Composition of the Fourth Duma (First Session)

The Reactionary Right	64
Moderate Right	88
Centre Party	32
Alliance of 17 October	99
Polish/Lithuanian Group	6
Polish League	9
Progressives	47
Muslim Group	6
Kadets	58
Labour Group	10
Social Democrats	14
Non-party	5
	438

After the elections to the Fourth Duma, no further elections occurred until after the fall of the Tsarist régime. During 1917, the Provisional Government had been organizing elections to establish a Constituent Assembly. The Bolsheviks allowed these elections to take place on 25 Nov 1917. With universal suffrage, the electorate numbered 41 700 000. No reliable figures exist for the results, but the following table gives approximate figures.

Party	Votes cast	Delegates returned
	17 100 000 (Total)	429 (Total)
Bolsheviks	9 600 000	168
Mensheviks	1 400 000	18
Kadets	2 000 000	17
Monarchists	300 000	–
National Minorities	1 700 000	–

At the end of 1917, the Kadets were proscribed. The Constituent Assembly met on 18 Jan 1918. It was dissolved by the Bolsheviks a day later after rejecting (237 votes to 136) a Bolshevik motion to recognize the Congress of Soviets as the supreme government authority. For the position in the Soviet Union, see p. 266.

Following the collapse of the Soviet Union, the first free presidential elections in the history of Russia were held on 12 Jun 1991. The result was:

	Vote	% of votes
Boris Yeltsin	45 552 041	57.3
Nikolai Ryzhkov	13 395 335	16.9
Vladimir Zhirinovsky	6 211 007	7.8
Others (3)	8 148 357	10.3

The nationwide elections for Russia's Parliament were held on 12 December 1993. Duma seats gained (including, where blocs surpassed the 5% threshold for proportional representation votes, seats thus gained with percentage votes cast) were as follows:

	Seats (total)	% of votes
Liberal Democrats (extreme Right)	59 (70)	22.8
Russia's Choice (Pro-Government)	40 (96)	15.4
Communists	32 (65)	12.4
Agrarian	21 (47)	7.9
Women's Party of Russia	21 (25)	8.1
Yavlinsky bloc (free market)	20 (33)	7.8
Democratic Party	14 (21)	5.5
Others	18 (30)	19.0
Independents	(30)	

Presidential elections were again held in Russia in Jun 1996, with Boris Yeltsin decisively emerging as the victor in the second-round of voting on 3 Jul. The second-round voting figures were Yeltsin (40 100 000; 53.8%). Zyuganov (the communist candidate, 30 110 000; 40.3%). Turnout was 68%, with 3 600 000 voting against both candidates.

SLOVAKIA

The first elections following independence on 1 Jan 1993 were held on 30 Sep and 1 Oct 1994. Approximately 76% of the electorate of 3 900 000 voted in an election dominated by HZDS (Movement for a Democratic Slovakia) which won 61 of the 150 seats. Results were: the HZDS (61 with 35% of the vote), the Common Choice Coalition (a left-wing grouping), 18 with 10.4%; the Hungarian Coalition, 17 with 10.2%; the Christian Democratic Movement, 17 with 10.1%; the Democratic Union, 15 with 8.6%; the Union of Slovak Workers (ZRS), 13 with 7.3%; the Slovak National Party (SNS), 9 with 5.4%.

SLOVENIA

Following Independence in 1991, presidential and general elections were held on 6 Dec 1992. In the presidential election, Milan Kučan was the easy victor with 63.9% of the vote. The general election result was:

	Seats	% of votes
Liberal Democratic Party	22	23.3
Christian Democratic Party	15	14.5
Associated List (Left-Wing Coalition including former Communists)	14	13.6
National Party	12	9.9
People's Party	10	8.8
Democratic Party	6	5.0
Greens	5	3.7
Social Democratic Party	4	3.3
Others	–	–

A further election was held in November 1996:

Liberal Democracy of Slovenia*	25	27.0
Slovene People's Party	19	19.4
Social Democratic Party	16	16.1
Christian Democrats of Slovenia	10	9.6
United List of Social Democrats	9	9.0
Democratic Party of Pensioners	5	4.3
Others	4	14.6

* Formed in Mar 1994 out of the Liberal Democratic Party, the Democratic Party and the Greens

250

SPAIN

Elections held in Feb 1918 were followed by a long period of political stability.

On 12 Sep 1923 Primo de Rivera took over the country in a *coup d'état*. In Sep 1927 the National Assembly met, members having been nominated by Primo de Rivera.

In Feb 1931 elections were announced but postponed because of a government crisis and elections under a provisional government were held for the constituent *Cortes*. Franchise minimum voting age reduced from 25 to 23 years. Eligibility for *Cortes* membership extended to women and priests. Electoral divisions revised to give one deputy for every 50 000 inhabitants to a *Cortes* which was a single chamber elected by direct popular vote.

		Party	*Seats*
Feb 1931		Socialists	116
		Radical Socialists	60
		Azana's Republican Action Party	30
		Radicals (following Lerroux)	90
		Progressives (following Zamona)	22
		Catalan Esquerra	43
		Casares Quirozaś Gallegan Nationalists	16
		Parties of the right of which only 19 were members of the Monarchist Party	60
Nov 1933	*Parties of the left centre*	Acción Republicana	8
		Socialists	58
		Remainder of pro-government parties	33
		Radicals (following Lerroux)	167
		Parties to the right	207
Feb 1936		Parties of the left	278
		Centre parties	55
		Parties of the right	134

Traditionally designated as the *Cortes* (courts), the Spanish parliament was revived by General Franco in 1942 as a unicameral body with very limited powers under the official name of Spanish Legislative Assembly (*Las Cortes Españolas*). Until 1967 it had no directly elected members but was made up of appointed and *ex officio* dignitaries, representatives of syndical (trade-union) and professional and business associations, and 108 indirectly elected representatives from the 53 Spanish and African provinces and the two North African *presidios*. Under the Organic Law of 1967, its membership was expanded by the addition of 108 'family representatives' to be directly elected for a four-year term by heads of families, married women and widows. The first elections of family representatives were held 10 Oct 1967.

In 1969, the membership of the *Cortes* was made up of the categories and approximate numbers listed below; however, since some members sat in more than one capacity, the total membership was somewhat less than the indicated 563. The succession law of 22 Jul 1969 was adopted by a vote of 491 in favour, 19 opposed, 9 abstaining, and 15 absent, making a total of 534.

High Officials		23
Appointed		25
Members of the National Council of the Movement		102
Representatives of cultural bodies		18
Representatives of professional associations		22
Syndical representatives		150
Municipal and provincial representatives		115
Family representatives		108
		563

	Party	Seats
1977	UCD	165
	PSOE	118
	PCE	20
	CD	16
	CU	11
	PNV	8
	Others	12
1979	UCD	168
	PSOE	121
	PCE	23
	CD	9
	CU	8
	PNV	7
	PSA	5
	Others	9

		Votes per party	Seats	% of votes
1982	PSOE/PSC-PSOE	10 127 392	202	48.7
	APAP-PDP	5 543 107	106	26.6
	UCD	1 425 093	12	6.8
	CU	772 726	12	3.7
	PNV	395 656	8	1.9
	PCE-PSUC	844 976	4	4.1
	CDS	600 842	2	2.9
	HB	210 601	2	1.0

		Votes per party	Seats	% of votes
	ERC	138 116	1	0.7
	EE	100 326	1	0.5
	Others	648 346		3.1
1986	PSOE	8 887 345	184	44.3
	CP	5 245 396	105	26.2
	CDS	1 862 856	19	9.3
	CiU	1 012 054	18	5.0
	IU	930 223	7	4.6
	PNV	308 991	6	1.5
	HB	231 558	5	1.2
	EE	106 937	2	0.5
	Others	1 472 380	4	7.4
1989	PSOE		175	39.6
	PP		106	25.8
	IU		18	9.1
	CDS		14	7.9
	CiU		18	5.0
	PNV		5	1.2
	HB		4	1.1
	PA		2	1.0
	Others		9	9.3
1993	PSOE		159	38.8
	PP		141	34.8
	United Left		18	9.6
	CiU		17	4.9
	PNV (Basques)		5	1.2
	Others		10	4.7
			350	
1996	PP		156	38.9
	PSOE		141	37.5
	United Left		21	10.6
	CiU		16	4.6
	PNV (Basques)		5	1.3
	Others		11	7.1
			350	

SWEDEN

Voting procedures. Election to the First Chamber indirect through electoral colleges. Direct election to the Second Chamber. Proportional representation. Suffrage – for the First Chamber, universal suffrage extended at age 27; for the Second, suffrage for men at 24. In 1927, the First Chamber suffrage extended to age 23, and to age 21 in 1941. In 1945 suffrage for the Second Chamber altered to universal suffrage at 21.

		Votes per party	Seats	% of electorate
1902	Social Democrats	6 000	4	3.5
	Liberals	93 000	107	51.2
	Conservatives	82 000	119	45.3
1905	Social Democrats	21 000	13	9.5
	Liberals	98 000	109	45.2
	Conservatives	98 000	108	45.3
1908	Social Democrats	45 000	34	14.6
	Liberals	144 000	105	46.8
	Conservatives	119 000	91	38.5
1911	Conservatives	189 000	65	31.2
	Liberals	243 000	101	40.2
	Social Democrats	172 000	64	28.5
1914 (Mar)	Conservatives	286 000	86	37.7
	Liberals	245 000	71	32.2
	Social Democrats	229 000	73	30.1
1914 (Sep)	Conservatives	267 000	86	36.5
	Liberals	196 000	57	26.9
	Social Democrats	266 000	87	36.4
1917	Högern (Con.)	181 333	59	16.1
	Agrarians/Centre	62 658	12	5.6
	Liberaler (Lib.)	202 936	62	18.0
	Social Dem.	288 020	97	25.6
	Others	1 037	0	0.1
1920	Högern (Con.)	183 019	70	15.3
	Agrarians/Centre	92 941	30	7.8
	Liberaler (Lib.)	144 946	48	12.2
	Social Dem.	237 177	82	19.9
	Others	100	0	0.0
1921	Högern (Con.)	449 302	62	13.9
	Agrarians/Centre	192 269	21	6.0
	Liberaler (Lib.)	332 765	41	10.3
	Social Dem.	687 096	99	21.3
	Soc. and Comm.	80 355	7	2.5
	Others	165	0	0.0
1924	Högern (Con.)	461 257	65	13.8
	Agrarians/Centre	190 396	23	5.7
	Liberaler (Lib.)	69 627	5	2.0
	Frisinnade (Lib.)	228 913	28	6.9
	Social Dem.	725 407	104	21.7
	Soc. and Comm.	89 902	5	2.7
	Others	84	0	0.0
1928	Högern (Con.)	692 434	73	19.8
	Agrarians/Centre	263 501	27	7.5
	Liberaler (Lib.)	70 820	4	2.1
	Frisinnade (Lib.)	303 995	28	8.7
	Social Dem.	873 931	90	25.0
	Soc. and Comm.	151 567	8	4.4
	Others	2 563	0	0.1

		Votes per party	Seats	% of electorate
1932	Högern (Con.)	585 248	58	15.8
	Agrarians/Centre	351 215	36	9.5
	Liberaler (Lib.)	48 722	4	1.3
	Frisinnade (Lib.)	244 577	20	6.6
	Social Dem.	1 040 689	104	28.0
	Socialist	132 564	6	3.6
	Communist	74 245	2	2.0
	Others	17 846	0	0.5
1936	Högern (Con.)	512 781	44	13.0
	Agrarians/Centre	418 840	36	10.7
	Folkpartiet (Lib.)	376 161	27	9.6
	Social Dem.	1 338 120	112	34.0
	Socialist	127 832	6	3.3
	Communist	96 519	5	2.5
	Others	47 500	0	1.2
1940	Högern (Con.)	518 346	42	12.6
	Agrarians/Centre	344 345	28	8.4
	Folkpartiet (Lib.)	344 113	23	8.4
	Social Dem.	1 546 804	134	37.6
	Socialist	18 430	0	0.4
	Communist	101 424	3	2.5
1944	Högern (Con.)	488 921	39	11.3
	Agrarians/Centre	421 094	35	9.8
	Folkpartiet (Lib.)	398 293	26	9.2
	Social Dem.	1 436 571	115	33.3
	Socialist	5 279	0	0.1
	Communist	318 466	15	7.6
	Others	17 680	0	0.4
1948	Högern (Con.)	478 786	23	10.2
	Agrarians/Centre	480 421	30	10.2
	Folkpartiet (Lib.)	882 437	57	18.7
	Social Dem.	1 789 459	112	38.0
	Communist	244 826	8	5.2
	Others	3 062	0	0.0
1952	Högern (Con.)	543 825	31	11.3
	Agrarians/Centre	406 183	26	8.5
	Folkpartiet (Lib.)	924 819	58	19.2
	Social Dem.	1 742 284	110	36.3
	Communist	164 194	5	3.4
	Others	2 402	0	0.0
1956	Högern (Con.)	663 693	42	13.6
	Agrarians/Centre	366 612	19	7.5
	Folkpartiet (Lib.)	923 564	58	18.9
	Social Dem.	1 729 463	106	35.4
	Communist	194 016	6	4.0
	Others	1 982	0	0.0
1958	Högern (Con.)	750 332	45	15.0
	Agrarians/Centre	486 760	32	9.7
	Folkpartiet (Lib.)	700 019	38	14.0
	Social Dem.	1 776 667	111	35.6

		Votes per party	Seats	% of electorate
	Communist	129 319	5	2.6
	Others	1 155	0	0.0
1960	Högern (Con.)	704 365	39	14.2
	Agrarians/Centre	579 007	34	11.6
	Folkpartiet (Lib.)	744 142	40	15.0
	Social Dem.	2 033 016	114	40.9
	Communist	190 560	5	3.8
1964	Högern (Con.)	582 609	33	11.4
	Agrarians/Centre	559 632	36	11.0
	Folkpartiet (Lib.)	720 733	43	14.1
	Social Dem.	2 006 923	113	39.4
	Communist	221 746	8	4.4
	Others	154 137	0	3.0
1968	Högern (Con.)	621 031	29	12.9
	Agrarians/Centre	757 215	37	15.7
	Folkpartiet (Lib.)	688 456	32	14.3
	Social Dem.	2 420 277	125	50.1
	Communist	145 172	3	3.0
	Others	197 228	7	4.1
1970	Högern (Con.)	573 812	41	11.5
	Agrarians/Centre	991 208	71	19.9
	Folkpartiet (Lib.)	806 667	58	16.2
	Social Dem.	2 256 369	163	45.3
	Communist	236 659	17	4.8
	Others	111 481	0	2.3
1973	Social Democrats	2 247 727	156	43.6
	Communist Left	274 929	19	5.3
	Centre Party	737 584	51	14.3
	Moderates	1 295 246	90	25.1
	Liberals	486 028	34	9.4
	Minor Parties	117 325	–	2.3
1976	Social Democrats	2 320 818	152	42.9
	Communist Left	257 967	17	4.7
	Centre Party	845 580	55	15.6
	Moderates	1 307 927	86	24.1
	Liberals	600 249	39	11.0
	Minor Parties	90 790	–	1.7
1979	Social Democrats	2 356 234	154	43.5
	Communist Left	305 420	20	5.6
	Moderates	1 108 406	73	20.5
	Centre Party	984 589	64	18.2
	Liberals	577 063	38	10.6
	Minor Parties	86 855	–	1.6
1982	Social Democrats	2 533 250	166	45.6
	Communist Left	308 899	20	5.6
	Moderates	1 313 337	86	23.6
	Centre Party	859 618	56	15.5
	Liberals	327 770	21	5.9
	Minor Parties	211 670	0	3.8

		Votes per party	Seats	% of votes
1985	Social Democrats	2 487 551	159	44.7
	Communist Left	298 419	19	5.4
	Moderates	1 187 335	76	21.3
	Liberals	792 268	51	14.2
	Centre Party/KDS	691 258	44	12.4
	Others	110 191	–	2.0
1988	Social Democrats		156	43.6
	Communist Left		21	5.9
	Moderates		66	18.4
	Liberals		44	12.2
	Centre Party		42	11.4
	Greens		20	5.5
	Others		–	3.0
1991	Social Democratic Labour		138	37.6
	Moderates		80	21.9
	Liberals		33	9.1
	Centre party		31	8.5
	Christian Democrats		26	7.1
	New Democracy		25	6.7
	Left Party		16	4.6
	Green Party		–	3.4
	Others		–	1.2
			349	100.0
1994	Social Democratic Labour		161	45.3
	Moderates		80	22.4
	Centre Party		27	7.7
	Liberals		26	7.2
	Left Party		22	6.2
	Green Party		18	5.0
	Christian Democrats		15	4.1
	New Democracy			1.2
	Others		–	1.1
	Total		349	100.0

SWITZERLAND

A general election takes place by ballot every four years. Every citizen of the Republic who has entered on his 20th year is entitled to vote, and any voter, not a clergyman, may be elected as a deputy. Laws passed by both chambers may be submitted to direct popular vote, when 30 000 citizens or eight cantons demand it; the vote can be only 'Yes' or 'No'. This principle, called the referendum, is frequently acted on.

Women's suffrage, although advocated by the Federal Council and the Federal Assembly, was repeatedly rejected but at a referendum held on 7 Feb 1971 women's suffrage was carried.

The elections between 1900 and 1918 were dominated by the Radical Democrats. Seats won were as follows:

	1902	1905	1908	1911	1914	1917
Catholic Conservatives	34	34	34	38	38	42
Democrats	3	5	4	5	3	4
Liberal Conservatives	19	18	16	13	14	12
Radical Democrats	99	104	104	114	111	105
Social Democrats	7	2	7	17	19	22
Others	5	4	2	2	4	4
	167	167	167	189	189	189

		Votes per party	Seats	% of votes
1919	Liberal Democratic	28 497	9	3.8
	Peasant and Middle Class	114 537	31	15.3
	Catholic Conservative	156 702	41	21.0
	Radical	215 566	58	28.8
	Socialist	175 292	41	23.5
	Others	59 360	9	7.6
1922	Liberal Democratic	19 041	10	4.0
	Peasant and Middle Class	118 382	35	16.1
	Catholic Conservative	153 836	44	20.9
	Radical	208 144	58	28.3
	Socialist	170 974	43	23.3
	Communist	13 441	2	1.8
	Others	43 605	6	5.6
1925	Liberal Democratic	30 523	7	4.1
	Peasant and Middle Class	113 512	31	15.3
	Catholic Conservative	155 467	42	20.9
	Radical	206 485	59	27.8
	Socialist	192 208	49	25.8
	Communist	14 837	3	2.0
	Others	34 106	7	4.1
1928	Liberal Democratic	23 752	6	2.9
	Peasant and Middle Class	126 961	31	15.8
	Catholic Conservative	172 516	46	21.4
	Radical	220 135	58	27.4
	Socialist	220 141	50	27.4
	Communist	14 818	2	1.8
	Others	29 149	5	3.3
1931	Liberal Democratic	24 573	6	2.8
	Peasant and Middle Class	131 809	30	15.3
	Catholic Conservative	184 602	44	21.4
	Radical	232 562	52	26.9
	Socialist	247 946	49	28.7
	Communist	12 778	2	1.5
	Others	32 305	4	3.4
1935	Independent	37 861	7	4.2
	Liberal Democratic	30 476	7	3.3
	Peasant and Middle Class	100 300	21	11.0
	Catholic Conservative	185 052	42	20.3
	Radical	216 664	48	23.7
	Socialist	255 843	50	28.0
	Communist	12 569	2	1.4
	Others	78 810	10	8.1

		Votes per party	*Seats*	*% of electorate*
1939	Independent	43 735	9	7.1
	Liberal Democratic	10 241	6	1.6
	Peasant and Middle Class	91 182	22	14.7
	Catholic Conservative	105 018	43	17.0
	Radical	128 163	51	20.8
	Socialist	160 377	45	25.9
	Communist	15 962	4	2.6
	Others	69 062	7	10.3
1943	Independent	48 557	7	5.5
	Liberal Democratic	28 434	8	3.2
	Peasant and Middle Class	101 998	22	11.6
	Catholic Conservative	182 916	43	20.8
	Radical	197 746	43	22.5
	Socialist	251 576	56	28.6
	Others	76 449	11	7.8
1947	Independent	42 428	9	4.4
	Liberal Democratic	30 492	7	3.2
	Peasant and Middle Class	115 976	21	12.1
	Catholic Conservative	203 202	44	21.2
	Radical	220 486	52	23.0
	Socialist	251 625	48	26.2
	Communist	49 353	7	5.1
	Others	53 118	6	4.8
1951	Independent	49 100	10	5.1
	Liberal Democratic	24 813	5	2.6
	Peasant and Middle Class	120 819	23	12.6
	Catholic Conservative	216 616	48	22.5
	Radical	230 687	51	24.0
	Socialist	249 857	49	26.0
	Communist	25 659	5	2.7
	Others	50 438	5	4.5
1955	Independent	53 450	10	5.5
	Liberal Democratic	21 688	5	2.2
	Peasant and Middle Class	117 847	22	12.1
	Catholic Conservative	226 122	47	23.2
	Radical	227 370	50	23.3
	Socialist	263 664	53	27.0
	Communist	25 060	4	2.6
	Others	46 819	5	3.4
1959	Independent	54 049	10	5.5
	Liberal Democratic	22 934	5	2.3
	Peasant and Middle Class	113 611	23	11.6
	Catholic Conservative	229 088	47	23.3
	Radical	232 557	51	23.7
	Socialist	259 139	51	26.3
	Communist	26 346	3	2.7
	Others	51 281	6	4.1
1963	Independent	48 224	10	5.0
	Liberal Democratic	21 501	6	2.2
	Peasant and Middle Class	109 202	22	11.4
	Catholic Conservative	225 160	48	23.4

259

		Votes per party	Seats	% of electorate
	Radical	230 200	51	24.0
	Socialist	256 063	53	26.6
	Communist	21 088	4	2.2
	Others	49 693	6	4.2
1967	Independent	89 950	16	9.1
	Liberal Democratic	23 208	6	2.3
	Peasant and Middle Class	109 621	21	11.0
	Catholic Conservative	219 184	45	22.1
	Radical	230 095	49	23.2
	Socialist	233 873	51	23.5
	Communist	28 723	5	2.9
	Others	59 194	7	3.6
1971	Independent	150 684	13	7.6
	Liberal Democratic	43 338	6	2.2
	Peasant and Middle Class	217 909	23	11.0
	Catholic Conservative	402 528	44	20.4
	Radical	431 364	49	21.8
	Socialist	452 194	46	22.9
	Communist	50 834	5	2.6
	Republican Movement	88 327	7	4.5
	Others	138 417	7	5.3
1975	Social Democrats		55	25.4
	Radical Democrats		47	22.2
	Christian Democrats		46	20.6
	Swiss People's Party		21	10.1
	Independent Party		11	6.2
	Liberal Democrats		6	2.3
	Republican Movement		4	3.0
	Party of Labour (Communists)		4	2.2
	Others		6	8.0
1979	Social Democrats		51	24.4
	Radical Democrats		51	24.1
	Christian Democrats		44	21.5
	Swiss People's Party		23	11.6
	Independents Party		8	4.1
	Liberal Democrats		8	2.8
	Republican Movement		1	1.9
	Party of Labour (Communist)		3	1.7
	Others		11	7.9
1983	Radical Democrats		54	23.4
	Social Democrats		47	22.8
	Christian Democrats		42	20.2
	Swiss People's Party		23	11.1
	Independents Party		8	4.0
	Liberal Party		8	2.8
	Others		18	11.5
1987	Radical Democratic Party		51	22.9
	Christian Democratic People's Party		42	20.0
	Social Democrats		41	18.4
	Swiss People's Party		25	11.0
	Greens		9	4.8

		Seats	% of votes
	Liberal Party	9	2.7
	Independent Alliance	8	4.2
	Minor Parties	15	15.9
1991	Radical Democratic Party	44	
	Social Democratic Party	43	
	Christian-Democratic People's Party	37	
	Swiss People's Party	25	
	Greens	14	
	Liberals	10	
	Independent Alliance	9	
	Automobile Party	8	
	Minor Parties	10	
		200	
1995 (Oct)	Radical Democratic Party	45	
	Christian Democratic Party	34	
	Swiss Social Democratic Party	54	
	Swiss People's Party/Democratic Centre Union	29	
	Others	38	
		200	

TURKEY

No meaningful figures are available for the elections held in the old Ottoman Empire in 1908 and 1912. The first Turkish Grand National Assembly met in Ankara on 23 Apr 1920. In these circumstances, only indirect elections proved possible, every province putting forward five delegates. The Assembly consisted of 337 members, 232 of whom had been newly elected. Under the constitution of 20 Jan 1921, which the Assembly adopted and which legalized the organization it had set up, the deputies' term of office was set at two years.

In the 1920 elections Kemalists held 197 seats; Opposition, 118; Non-aligned, 122. In 1923, Grand National Assembly Party n.a.; Progressive Republican Party n.a.; Republican People's Party, 304.

The first Assembly was prorogued on 1 Apr 1923 after deciding that new elections should be held. On 19 Oct 1923, the Republic was proclaimed and the 1924 constitution extended the franchise to all men aged 18 or over. Candidates had to be at least 30 years old, and the deputies' term of office was lengthened to four years. A constitutional amendment adopted on 5 Jan 1934 extended the franchise to women, but raised the minimum voting age to 22. Elections continued to be indirect: voters chose an electoral college which then elected the Assembly.

This practice was continued until 1946. The membership of the Assembly increased constantly until the adoption of the 1961 constitution, since it had been laid down that there should be one deputy per 40 000 citizens.

The first effective political party in the history of the Turkish Republic, the People's Party, was formed in Oct 1923; in Nov 1924 its name was changed to Republican People's Party. This party remained in power until 1950. The Free Republican Party, formed in 1930, had a brief existence. Then between 1930 and 1945 Turkey had a single-party regime. On 5 Jun 1945 the authorities allowed the formation of political parties without a preliminary permit, and as a consequence the elections held on 21 Jul 1946 were for the first time contested by more than one party. Voting was direct and public, electors were allowed to divide their votes between party lists of candidates (producing 'mixed' lists), but votes were counted in secret. To win, candidates needed to obtain the simple majority of the votes cast. Two changes were introduced in the elections held on 14 May 1950: voting became secret, and the counting of votes open. In 1957 mixed lists were banned, but electors were allowed to delete the names of individual candidates from the party lists of their choice. After 27 May 1960, the National Unity Committee first assumed all the powers vested in the Grand National Assembly under the 1924 constitution. This transfer of power, legalized by the provisional constitution of 12 Jun 1960, was followed on 13 Dec of the same year by a law setting up a Constituent Assembly, which was opened on 6 Jan 1961. The constitution which this Assembly drew up governed the elections held on 15 Oct 1961 which produced a new Turkish Grand National Assembly. Article 55 of the constitution required voting to be free, direct, universal and secret, and the counting of votes to be open. However, the constitution did not define the system of representation which was to be used, and this was regulated by electoral laws. Proportional representation was introduced for the first time in the elections of 15 Oct 1961 and has been retained since, although the basic d'Hondt formula has been varied: first candidates had to obtain a minimum number of votes (known as the 'barrage') to qualify for consideration: then the country-wide pooling and redistribution of wasted votes ('the national residue') was introduced in time for the elections of 12 Oct 1965, but dropped together with the 'barrage' requirement before the 1969 elections.

		Votes per party	Seats
1950	Democratic Party	4 242 831	396
	Republican People's Party	3 165 096	68

		Votes per party	*Seats*
	Nation Party	240 209	1
	Independents	258 698	7
1954	Republican People's Party	3 161 696	31
	Republican Nation Party	434 085	5
	Democratic Party	5 151 550	505
	Peasant Party	57 011	–
	Independents	137 318	1
1957	Republican People's Party	3 753 136	178
	Republican Nation Party	652 064	4
	Democratic Party	4 372 621	424
	Freedom Party	350 497	4
	Independents	4 944	–
1961	Justice Party	3 527 435	158
	Republican People's Party	3 724 752	173
	Republican Peasants and Nation Party, renamed Nationalist Action Party	1 415 390	54
	New Turkey Party	1 391 934	65
	Independents	81 732	–
1965	Justice Party	4 921 235	240
	Republican People's Party	2 675 785	134
	Republican Peasants and Nation Party, renamed Nationalist Action Party	208 696	11
	Nation Party	582 704	31
	Turkish Workers' Party	276 101	14
	New Turkey Party	346 514	19
	Independents	296 528	1
1969	Justice Party	4 219 712	256
	Republican People's Party	2 487 006	143
	Republican Peasants and Nation Party, renamed Nationalist Action Party	275 091	1
	Nation Party	292 961	6
	Turkish Workers' Party	243 631	2
	New Turkey Party	197 929	6
	Independents	511 023	13
	Unity Party	254 695	8
	Reliance Party, renamed National Reliance Party in 1971	597 818	15

Senators are elected for six years, but one-third of the membership is reelected every other year. Voting is free, equal, universal, direct and secret, and counting open. The Senate was first set up in 1961. That year and in 1964, a simple majority sufficed for the election of a senator; in 1966 and 1968 proportional representation (with 'national residue') was introduced.

		Votes per party	*Seats*
1961	Justice Party	3 560 675	71
	Republican People's Party	3 734 285	76
	Republican Peasants and Nation Party	1 350 892	16
	New Turkey Party	1 401 636	27
	Independents	39 558	–
1964	Justice Party	1 385 655	31
	Republican People's Party	1 125 783	19
	Republican Peasants and Nation Party	88 400	–
	New Turkey Party	96 427	–
	Independents	64 498	1
1966	Justice Party	1 688 316	35
	Republican People's Party	877 066	13
	Republican Peasants and Nation Party	57 367	1
	Nation Party	157 115	1
	Turkish Workers' Party	116 375	1
	New Turkey Party	70 043	1
	Independents	980	–
1968	Justice Party	1 656 802	38
	Republican People's Party	899 444	13
	Republican Peasants and Nation Party	66 232	–
	Reliance Party, renamed	284 234	1
	National Reliance Party		
	Nation Party	200 737	1
	Turkish Workers' Party	157 062	–
	Independents	58 317	–

After a period of disguised military rule, Parliament reasserted its influence in 1973. In the elections of Oct 1973 there was a shock rebuff for Mr Demirel with major gains by Ecevit (much more in the Social

Democrat mould).

	Votes per party		Seats	% of votes
1973	Republican People's Party	3 570 583	185	33.3
	Justice Party	3 179 897	149	29.8
	National Salvation Party	1 265 771	48	11.8
	National Action Party	362 208	3	3.4
	Democratic Party	1 275 502	45	11.9
	Republican Reliance Party	564 343	13	5.3
	Turkish Unity Party	121 759	1	1.1
	Others	365 595	6	3.4
1977	Republican People's Party	6 117 280	213	41.4
	Justice Party	5 457 649	189	36.9
	National Salvation Party	1 271 620	24	8.6
	National Action Party	942 606	16	6.4
	Republican Reliance Party	277 059	3	1.9
	Democratic Party	273 426	1	1.8
	Turkish Unity Party	58 319	–	0.4
	Others	387 855	4	2.6

On 10 Sep 1980, for the third time in 20 years, the military took control of Turkey. A general election took place on 6 Nov 1983. The result was

Motherland Party	7 823 827	212	45.7
Populist Party	5 277 698	117	30.8
Nationalist Democracy Party	4 032 046	71	23.5

Recent election results have been as follows:

	Votes per party		Seats	% of votes
1987	Motherland Party	8 704 335	292	36.3
	Social Democratic Populist	5 931 000	99	24.7
	True Path	4 587 062	59	19.1
	Democratic Left	2 044 576	–	8.5
	Welfare Party	1 717 425	–	7.2
	Others*	987 231	–	4.1

* All polling less than 5% of the votes each.

1991 (Oct)	True Path Party		178	27.0
	Motherland Party		115	27.0

Votes per party	Seats	% of votes
Social Democratic Populist	88	na
Welfare Party (Refah)	62	16.9
Democratic Left Party	7	10.8
Total	450	
1995 (Dec) Welfare Party (Refah)	158	21.4
True Path Party	135	19.2
Motherland Party	132	19.7
Democratic Left	76	14.6
Republican Populist Party	49	10.7
Others	0	14.4
Total	550	

UKRAINE

The first presidential elections in independent Ukraine, following the collapse of the Soviet Union, were on 1 Dec 1991. The easy victor was Leonid Kravchuk with 19 643 000 votes (61.6%). His nearest rival was Vyacheslav Chornovil with 7 420 000 (23.3%). The first general election, held in Mar/Apr 1994, resulted in 112 of the 450 seats left unfilled. Of the 338 seats, the Communist Party of the Ukraine had 86 seats followed by Rukh with 20 and the Peasants' Party with 18. No less than 170 Independents were returned.

USSR

In 1917 the Provisional Government had been organizing elections to establish a Constituent Assembly, and these the Bolsheviks allowed to take place on 25 Nov 1917. Suffrage was universal, and the electorate numbered 41.7m. Figures are uncertain and contradictory. See p. 249 for some reputable estimates.

The Kadets were proscribed at the end of 1917. The Constituent Assembly met on 18 Jan 1918, just over half the delegates being present.

It was dissolved by the Bolsheviks the following day after rejecting by 237 votes to 136 a Bolshevik motion which would have recognized the Congress of Soviets to be the supreme government authority.

The Congress of Soviets was therefore the supreme organ of state power until it was replaced by the Supreme Soviet in 1937. There were altogether ten All-Russian Congresses until the formation of the USSR (30 Dec 1922) and eight All-Union Congresses thereafter.

Elections were indirect, from amongst the deputies in the hierarchy of soviets throughout the country. The latter were elected on a franchise restricted to workers, peasants and the armed forces. Deputies to town soviets were elected on a basis of 1 per 25 000 electors; to rural soviets on a basis of 1 per 125 000.

By 1922 all public opposition to the Communist Party had been brought to an end. Party allegiance in the early Congresses of Soviets (for the first two see above):

> 3rd (Jan 18) Bolsheviks 61%
> 4th (Extraordinary (Mar 18) Bolsheviks 66%
> 5th (Jul 18) Bolsheviks (now called Communists) 66%
> 6th (Nov 18) Communists 90%
> 7th (Dec 18) Communists 95%
> 8th (Dec 20) Communists 95%

The 'Stalin' Constitution of 1936 replaced the Congresses of Soviets with the Supreme Soviet (*Verkhovnyi Sovet*). This had two chambers: the Soviet of the Union (*Sovet Soyuza*) and the Soviet of Nationalities (*Sovet Natsionalnostei*). Elections were held every four years. Suffrage universal at 18 years; candidates could stand at 23. The Soviet of the Union was elected on a basis of 1 deputy per 300 000 electors. Deputies to the Soviet of Nationalities were elected in the following proportions: 32 from each federative republic, 11 from each Autonomous Republic, 5 from each Autonomous Oblast (Province) and 1 from each National District.

Although it was constitutionally the supreme legislative body, the Supreme Soviet had no significance in the realm of policy-making: *de facto* supreme power was in the hands of the Communist Party. Candidates for election could be nominated only by recognized organizations: the Communist Party, trade unions, industrial co-operatives, agricultural collectives, youth organizations and cultural organizations. Candidates need not belong to the party, but they had to support its programme. On the average, some 75% of deputies were party members.

More than one candidate could be nominated, and there was no constitutional bar to more than one standing for election, but the practice was that one only of the nominees was selected to stand by local party officials, and the elector's choice was thus limited to voting for or against him.

The ballot was secret but so arranged that only a contrary vote actually required entry into the polling booth.

Elections were held in Dec 1937, Feb 1946, Mar 1950, Mar 1954, Mar 1958, Mar 1962, Jun 1966, Jun 1970, Jun 1974 and Mar 1979. In 1937, 91 113 153 votes were cast out of an electorate of 93 139 478, and subsequently the turn-out had always exceeded 99%. Less than 1% of votes cast had been against candidates, and no candidate ever failed to be elected.

For elections in Russia following the collapse of the Soviet Union, See p. 249.

INDEPENDENT TERRITORIES (1918–1921)

Armenia, Azerbaijan and Georgia proclaimed independence jointly as the Transcaucasian Federative Republic on 22 Apr 1918; reconquered respectively 29 Nov 1920, 27 Apr 1920 and 18 Mar 1921.

The Transcaucasian Federative Republic was governed by a *Seim* of delegates based upon the elections to the Russian Constituent Assembly (dissolved on 18 Jan 1918): Mensheviks, 33; Musavat (Moslem Nationalists), 30; Dashnaktsutiun (Armenian Nationalists), 27; Moslem Socialists, 7; Socialist revolutionaries, 5; others 10.

The Federation collapsed upon the secession of Georgia on 26 May 1918, and each republic became separately independent.

Armenia set up a National Council (*Khorhurd*) on 1 Aug 1918, the party composition of which was: Dashnaktsutiun, 18; Populist, 6; Moslems, 6; Mensheviks, 5; independents, 2; Bolsheviks, 1; Yezidis, 1; Russians, 1.

Azerbaijan set up a National Council composed as follows: Musavat (Moslem Nationalists) and Neutral Democratic Group (Sunni Moslems), 30; Socialists, 11; Moslem Union, 3. In Jun 1918 the Council was reformed under the insistence of the Turkish military commander to exclude socialists and give predominance to the conservative Moslem Union.

In turn the British military commander after the surrender of the Turks objected to the Council as unrepresentative. A new Council was created in Dec 1918: Musavat, 38; Neutral Democratic Group, 7; Unity Party, 13; Socialists, 11; Dashnaktsutiun (Armenian Nationalists), 7; other Armenian parties, 4; Bolsheviks, 1; others, 15.

Georgia. In Feb 1919 the National Council held elections for a Constituent Assembly. Suffrage was universal and by proportional representation. 15 parties presented candidates for election. 505 477 votes were cast (some 60% of the electorate). The Assembly had 130 deputies, distributed as follows:

	Votes cast	*Deputies in the Assembly*
Mensheviks	409 766	109
National Democrats	30 154	8
Social-Federalists	33 721	8
Social-Revolutionaries	21 453	5

UNITED KINGDOM

In 1911 the maximum duration of a parliament, which since 1715 had been seven years, was reduced to five years.

By 1918 virtually all men were enfranchised together with all women over 30 years of age who were householders or the wives of householders. Voting in more than two constituencies was prohibited. General elections which had hitherto been spread over two weeks and more were concentrated on a single day. Candidates were required to provide a deposit of £150 to be forfeit if they failed to secure one-eighth of the votes cast in their constituency. Seats were redistributed, for the first time on the basis of approximately equal electorates, and the House of Commons was increased to 707 members (this fell to 615 in 1922, with the independence of Southern Ireland).

The age of women voting was lowered to 21 in 1928 and they were given the vote on exactly the same basis as men.

In 1948 university seats and all plural voting were abolished. Machinery was set up for Permanent Boundary Commissions to redraw constituencies once in the life of every normal five-year parliament, but because the first routine distribution of seats in 1954–5 (which increased the House to 630 members) had caused so much annoyance and difficulty, an Act was passed in 1958 to reduce the frequency of redistribution to between 10 and 15 years.

		Votes	% share of total vote	Members
1900	Conservatives	1 767 958	50.3	402
	Liberals	1 572 323	45.0	184
	Irish Nationalist	91 055	2.6	82
	Labour	62 698	1.3	2
	Others	29 448	0.8	–
				670
1906	Conservatives	2 422 071	43.4	157
	Liberals	2 751 057	49.4	400
	Irish Nationalist	35 031	0.7	83
	Labour	321 663	4.8	29
	Others	96 269	1.7	1
				670
1910 (Jan)	Conservatives	3 104 407	46.8	273
	Liberals	2 866 157	43.5	275
	Irish Nationalist	126 647	1.9	82
	Labour	505 657	7.0	40
	Others	64 532	0.8	–
				670
1910 (Dec)	Conservatives	2 420 169	46.6	273
	Liberals	2 293 869	44.2	271
	Irish Nationalist	131 720	2.5	84
	Labour	371 802	6.4	42
	Others	17 678	0.3	–
				670
1918	Electors:	21 392 322	Turnout: 58.9%	
	Total votes cast	10 766 583	100.0	707
	Coalition Unionist	3 504 198	32.6	335
	Coalition Liberal	1 455 640	13.5	133
	Coalition Labour	161 521	1.5	10
	(Coalition)	(5 121 259)	(47.6)	(478)
	Conservative	370 375	3.4	23
	Irish Unionist	292 722	2.7	25
	Liberal	1 298 808	12.1	28
	Labour	2 385 472	22.2	63
	Irish Nationalist	238 477	2.2	7
	Sinn Fein	486 867	4.5	73
	Other	572 503	5.3	10
1922	Electors:	21 127 663	Turnout: 71.3%	
	Total votes cast	14 393 632	100.0	615
	Conservative	5 500 382	38.2	345
	National Liberal	1 673 240	11.6	62
	Liberal	2 516 187	17.5	54
	Labour	4 241 383	29.5	142

270

		Votes	% share of total vote	Members
	Other	462 340	3.2	12
1923	Electors:	21 281 232	Turnout: 70.8%	
	Total votes cast	14 548 521	100.0	615
	Conservative	5 538 824	38.1	258
	Liberal	4 311 147	29.6	159
	Labour	4 438 508	30.5	191
	Other	260 042	1.8	7
1924	Electors:	21 731 320	Turnout: 76.6%	
	Total votes cast	16 640 279	100.0	615
	Conservative	8 039 598	48.3	419
	Liberal	2 928 747	17.6	40
	Labour	5 489 077	33.0	151
	Communist	55 346	0.3	1
	Other	126 511	0.8	4
1929	Electors:	28 850 870	Turnout: 76.1%	
	Total votes cast	22 648 375	100.0	615
	Conservative	8 656 473	38.2	260
	Liberal	5 308 510	23.4	59
	Labour	8 389 512	37.1	288
	Communist	50 614	0.3	–
	Other	243 266	1.0	8
1931	Electors:	29 960 071	Turnout: 76.3%	
	Total votes cast	21 656 373	100.0	615
	Conservative	11 978 745	55.2	473
	National Liberal	341 370	1.6	13
	Liberal National	809 302	3.7	35
	Liberal	1 403 102	6.5	33
	(National government)	(14 532 519)	(67.0)	(554)
	Independent Liberal	106 106	0.5	4
	Labour	6 649 630	30.6	52
	Communist	74 824	0.3	–
	New Party	36 377	0.2	–
	Other	256 917	1.2	5
1935	Electors:	31 379 050	Turnout: 71.2%	
	Total votes cast	21 997 054	100.0	615
	Conservative	11 810 158	53.7	432
	Liberal	1 422 116	6.4	20
	Labour	8 325 491	37.9	154
	Independent Labour Party	139 577	0.7	4
	Communist	27 117	0.1	1
	Other	272 595	1.2	4
1945	Electors:	33 240 391	Turnout: 72.7%	
	Total votes cast	25 085 978	100.0	640
	Conservative	9 988 306	39.8	213
	Liberal	2 248 226	9.0	12
	Labour	11 995 152	47.8	393
	Communist	102 780	0.4	2
	Common Wealth	110 634	0.4	1
	Other	640 880	2.0	19

271

		Votes	% share of total vote	Members
1950	Electors:	33 269 770	Turnout: 84.0%	
	Total votes cast	28 772 671	100.0	625
	Conservative	12 502 567	43.5	298
	Liberal	2 621 548	9.1	9
	Labour	13 266 592	46.1	315
	Communist	91 746	0.3	–
	Other	290 218	1.0	3
1951	Electors:	34 645 573	Turnout: 82.5%	
	Total votes cast	28 595 668	100.0	625
	Conservative	13 717 538	48.0	321
	Liberal	730 556	2.5	6
	Labour	13 948 605	48.8	295
	Communist	21 640	0.1	–
	Other	177 329	0.6	3
1955	Electors:	34 858 263	Turnout: 76.7%	
	Total votes cast	26 760 493	100.0	630
	Conservative	13 286 569	49.7	344
	Liberal	722 405	2.7	6
	Labour	12 404 970	46.4	277
	Communist	33 144	0.1	–
	Other	313 410	1.1	3
1959	Electors:	35 397 080	Turnout: 78.8%	
	Total votes cast	27 859 241	100.0	630
	Conservative	13 749 830	49.4	365
	Liberal	1 638 571	5.9	6
	Labour	12 215 528	43.8	258
	Communist	30 897	0.1	–
	Other	224 405	0.8	1
1964	Electors:	35 892 572	Turnout: 77.1%	
	Total votes cast	27 655 374	100.0	630
	Conservative	12 001 396	43.4	304
	Liberal	3 092 878	11.2	9
	Labour	12 205 814	44.1	317
	Communist	45 932	0.2	–
	Other	302 982	1.1	–
1966	Electors:	35 964 684	Turnout: 75.8%	
	Total votes cast	27 263 606	100.0	630
	Conservative	11 418 433	41.9	253
	Liberal	2 327 533	8.6	12
	Labour	13 064 951	47.9	363
	Communist	62 040	0.2	–
	Other	390 649	1.4	2
1970	Electors:	39 384 364	Turnout: 72%	
	Total votes cast	28 344 807	100.0	630
	Conservative	13 144 692	46.4	330
	Liberal	2 117 638	7.5	6
	Labour	12 179 166	42.9	287
	Communist	38 431	0.1	–
	Other	864 880	3.1	7
1974 (Feb)	Electors:	39 798 899	Turnout: 78.7%	
	Total votes cast	31 333 226	100.0	635

		Votes	% share of total vote	Members
	Conservative	11 868 906	37.9	297
	Liberal	6 063 470	19.3	14
	Labour	11 639 243	37.1	301
	Communist	32 741	0.1	–
	Plaid Cymru	171 364	0.6	2
	SNP	632 032	2.0	7
	National Front	76 865	0.3	–
	Others (G.B.)	131 059	0.4	2
	Others (N.I.)	717 986	2.3	12
1974 (Oct)	Electors:	40 072 971	100.0	Turnout: 72.8%
	Conservative	10 464 817	35.8	277
	Liberal	5 346 754	18.3	13
	Labour	11 457 079	39.2	319
	Communist	17 426	0.1	–
	Plaid Cymru	166 321	0.6	3
	SNP	839 617	2.9	11
	National Front	113 843	0.4	–
	Others (G.B.)	81 227	0.3	–
	Others (N.I.)	702 094	2.4	12
1979	Electors:	41 093 264	100.0	Turnout: 76.0%
	Conservative	13 697 690	43.9	339
	Liberal	4 313 811	13.8	11
	Labour	11 532 148	36.9	269
	Communist	15 938	0.1	–
	Plaid Cymru	132 544	0.4	2
	SNP	504 259	1.6	2
	National Front	190 747	0.6	–
	Ecology	38 116	0.1	–
	WRP	13 535	0.1	–
	Others (G.B.)	85 338	0.3	–
	Others (N.I.)	695 889	2.2	12
1983	Conservatives	13 012 602	42.4	397
	Liberal/SDP Alliance	7 780 577	25.4	23*
	Labour	8 457 124	27.6	209
	Plaid Cymru	125 309	0.4	2
	SNP	331 975	1.1	2
	Others (G.B.)	289 033	1.0	–
	Others (N.I.)	674 275	2.1	17

* SDP 6, Liberals 17

		Votes	% share of total vote	Members
1987	Conservative	13 763 747	42.2	375
	Labour	10 029 270	30.8	229
	Liberal/SDP	7 341 275	22.6	22
	Plaid Cymru	123 589	0.3	3
	SNP	416 873	1.4	3
	Others (N. Ireland)	730 152	2.3	17
	Others	151 517	0.4	1* (Speaker)
1992	Conservative	14 092 891	41.9	336
	Labour	11 559 735	34.4	271
	Lib. Dems.	5 999 384	17.8	20

		Votes	% share of total vote	Members
	Plaid Cymru	154 439	0.5	4
	SNP	629 552	1.9	3
	Others (N.I.)	740 485	2.4	17
	Others	436 107	1.4	–
1997	Labour	13 517 911	43.2	418
	Conservative	9 600 940	30.7	165
	Lib. Dems.	5 243 440	16.8	46
	Plaid Cymru	161 030	0.5	4
	SNP	622 260	2.0	6
	Others (N.I.)	780 920	2.5	18
	Others	1 361 701	4.3	2

YUGOSLAVIA

The 1920 elections were held on proportional principles by universal male suffrage. 65% of electorate voted.

	Party	Seats	% of votes
1920	Democrats (a combination of S. Pribičevič's Habsburg Serbs and the Independent Radicals	92	19.9
	Radicals	91	17
	Communists (became illegal 1921)	58	12.4
	Croat Peasants	50	14.3
	Serbian Agrarians	39	
	Moslems	32	
	Slovene Catholic People's Party	27	
	Social Democrats	10	
	Others	19	

The proportional system was modified in the 1923 election. 73% of the electorate voted.

1923	Radicals	108	25.8
	Croat Peasants	70	21.8
	Democrats	51	
	Slovene Catholic People's Party	22	
	Moslems of Bosnia	18	
	Moslems of Macedonia	14	
	Serbian Agrarians	10	
	Germans	8	

Party	Seats
Social Democrats	2
Others	9

At the 1925 elections 76.9% of the electorate voted.

1925	Radicals	142
	Independent Democrats	22
	Croat Peasants	67
	Slovene Catholic People's Party	20
	Moslems	15
	Serbian Agrarians	5
	Germans	5
	Montenegrans	3
	Others	34

At the 1927 elections 68% of the electorate voted.

1927	Radicals	112
	Croat Peasants	61
	Democrats	59
	Independent Democrats	22
	Slovene Catholic People's Party	21
	Moslems	18
	Serbian Agrarians	9
	Germans	6
	Social Democrats	1
	Others	6

The *Vidovdan* constitution and the *Skupština* were abolished on 6 Jan 1929 by King Alexander, who set up a royal dictatorship which found permanent expression in the constitution of 3 Jun 1931. This instituted a bicameral legislature: a National Assembly elected every four years publicly by all males over 21, each deputy representing 50 000 inhabitants; and a Senate half appointed and half elected by regional colleges of electors. The powers of the *Skupština* were reduced. In an attempt to eliminate regionalism all parties centred about ethnic or religious particularities were declared illegal. The name of the kingdom was changed to Yugoslavia in a similar gesture against separatism. Proportional representation was abolished: any party which won a majority of votes would henceforth be allotted two-thirds of the seats in the *Skupština*.

At the elections of 8 Nov 1931 only the government list was presented. 65% of the electorate voted.

In 1933 this electoral law was relaxed. The winning party was to receive three-fifths of the seats; and conditions for establishing countrywide lists of candidates were made easier.

On 9 Oct 1934 King Alexander was assassinated, and Prince Paul became Regent.

The elections of 25 May 1935 were public. The opposition parties (Croat Peasant, Independent Democrats, Democrats, Serbian Agrarians and Moslems) formed a united bloc. 73.7% of the electorate voted.

	Votes	Seats
The Government	1 746 982	303
The Opposition	1 076 345	67

At the elections of 11 Dec 1938, 74.5% of the electorate voted.

The Government (Yugoslav Radical Union)	1 643 783	306
The Opposition	1 364 524	67

All opposition parties abstained from the elections to the Constituent Assembly of 11 Nov 1945 leaving only a single Popular Front list. 88% of the electorate voted, 90% for the Popular Front.

In 1950 an electoral law abolished the single list system, and candidates were nominated individually. In the election of 26 Mar 1950 the number of candidates was still the same as the number of seats: there was no contest. Popular Front candidates polled 93.25% of the votes cast.

At the elections of 22 Nov 1953 the electorate for the Federal Council was 10 580 648.527 candidates stood for 484 seats (Federal Council, 282; Council of Producers, 202, of whom 135 were industrial and 67 were agricultural). 89.4% of the electorate voted.

At the elections of 23–26 Mar 1958, 307 candidates stood for the 301 seats of the Federal Council. The electorate was 11 331 727: 94% of the electorate voted. 216 representatives were elected to the Council of Producers: 168 industrial, 48 agricultural.

By the constitution of 7 Apr 1963 Yugoslavia became a 'Socialist' instead of a 'People's' Republic. This constitution did away almost entirely with direct elections, replacing these by an electoral filtering system. The electoral emphasis moved from the formal act of voting to the nominating process in which citizens participated through their local government wards and workers through their workplace. The Council of Producers was abolished and replaced by four specialized councils (Administration; Culture; Economy; Welfare). The Federal Assembly of 670 was to be elected for four-year terms. Every second year one-half of each council was renewed.

Elections were held on 25 May and 16 Jun 1963. The number of candidates was the same as the number of seats. 95.5% of the electorate voted. Half the seats came up for renewal on 19 Mar and 19 Apr 1965, when a few constituencies had more than one candidate. 93.6% of the electorate voted.

By a constitutional amendment in 1968 the Federal Council was abolished and divided into its two political components: (1) Social and Political Council, elected by citizens in local government wards: (2) Council of Nations, representing the republican legislatures.

At the elections of 12 Apr and 10 May 1969 for the Social and Political Council there were 179 candidates for the 120 seats. 87% of the electorate voted. There were 624 candidates for the 360 seats of the four specialized councils.

The first elections to be held on the 'delegate' principle, as outlined in the new Constitution, took place between Mar and May 1974. In early May elections were held to the two Chambers of the new Assembly of the Federation. At subsequent elections, until 1990, all candidates were either chosen or screened by the Socialist Alliance of the Working People of Yugoslavia, the official Communist organization.

During 1990, against a background of growing separatism and the collapse of Communism elsewhere in Eastern Europe, multi-party elections took place in the constituent republics of Yugoslavia. In Apr and May 1990, elections were held in Slovenia and Croatia. In Slovenia, the greatest number of seats in the Assembly was won by the Democratic Opposition of Slovenia (DEMOS), a centre-right coalition. In Croatia, an absolute majority was won by the Croatian Democratic Union (CDU), a nationalist movement. Elsewhere Communists retained power and in Serbia in Dec 1990 won 194 of the 250 seats (fighting under the new name of the Socialist Party).

Elections were held in 'rump' Yugoslavia (comprising Serbia and Montenegro) in Dec 1992, when the Socialist Party of Serbia won 47 seats (31.4%), the Serbian Radical Party 34 seats (22.4%) and the Democratic Movement of Serbia 20 seats (17.2%) out of the 138 seats in the Chamber of Citizens. The most recent elections, in Nov 1996, were again dominated by the Socialist Coalition led by Slobodan Milosevic (with 50% of the vote). The Zajedno ('Together') opposition alliance (including the Serbian Renewal Party) took 23% and the Radical Party 18%.

6 POLITICAL PARTIES

ALBANIA

During the Communist era, the ruling party was the Albanian Party of Labour (originally founded in 1941). It was the only recognized party in the state. Following anti-government demonstrations in Dec 1990, the ruling Party of Labour announced its abandonment of Stalinism, the legalization of political parties, and free elections to the People's Assembly. The following main parties have emerged:

DEMOCRATIC PARTY OF ALBANIA (DPA)

Formed in Dec 1990, the DPA advocates free-market economics within a parliamentary democratic system. The party took 62% of the vote for the People's Assembly in the Mar 1992 elections.

SOCIALIST PARTY OF ALBANIA

Formerly the Albanian Party of Labour, the party took the name Socialist Party of Albania in 1991 and is committed to democratic socialism and a free-market economy. The SPA won 26% of the vote in the Mar 1992 People's Assembly elections.

SOCIAL DEMOCRATIC PARTY (SDA)

The SDA was formed in 1990 and has a platform of gradual economic reform. The party took 4% of the vote in the Mar 1992 general election.

UNION FOR HUMAN RIGHTS

Formed in 1992, the Union for Human Rights won 3% of the vote for the People's Assembly in Mar 1992.

ALBANIAN REPUBLICAN PARTY (ARP)

The ARP, which was formed in 1991, took 3% of the vote in the March 1992 general election.

Among a profusion of other parties are the Albanian Green Party, the Albanian Liberal Party, the People's Party, the Independent Party, the Democratic Union of the Greek Minority, and the Albanian Women's Federation, all of which were formed in 1991.

ARMENIA

Political parties in Armenia have had a chequered history. During the first brief period of independence, 1918–20, the Armenian Revolutionary Federation (ARF), founded in 1891, was the ruling party. Banned under Soviet rule, it has operated legally again since 1991. In the Soviet era, the ruling party was the Communist Party of Armenia (which dissolved itself in Sep 1991). Its current successor is the Democratic Party of Armenia, founded 1993. The Armenian Pan-National Movement (APM), founded in 1989, emphasizes Armenian culture and sovereignty.

AUSTRIA

Up to the 1880s, political parties in the Habsburg Monarchy were really only informal groupings of parliamentary notables. There was virtually no constituency organization. The Liberals tended to represent the German-speaking urban middle class, whilst the Conservatives spoke for the nobility, the interests of agriculture and the non-German minorities. The main developments prior to 1918 were:

1882 Foundation of Georg von Schonerer's Pan-German League. Extremely anti-clerical and racialist, with a more militant defence of German-speaking interests. Essentially a dissident Liberal Party.
1887 Formation of the Catholic Social Union. Anti-Liberal (and anti-Semitic) with support from lower middle class in Vienna.
1889 Foundation of the Social Democratic Party.
1896 German People's Party founded.
1903 German Radical Party founded.
1905 German Agrarian Party founded.
1910 Union of the Liberal-National parties into the *Deutscher National-verband*.

SOCIAL DEMOCRATIC PARTY 1889

Socialist social and economic aims, supported political union with Germany. After World War II, changed its name to the *Austrian Socialist Party (SPÖ)*, no longer pan-German. The SPÖ obtained an absolute majority in parliament in 1970 under the leadership of Bruno Kreisky and remained in power for 13 years before losing its majority and forming a 'small coalition' with the FPÖ (*q.v.*). Its support is disproportionately concentrated in Vienna. It took the name Social Democratic Party in 1991.

279

CHRISTIAN SOCIALIST PARTY 1892

Conservative with strong clerical Roman Catholic influence. Politically divided with one section monarchist and the other pan-German. In 1945 it was reformed as the *Austrian People's Party (ÖVP)* with a conservative Christian-Democrat programme. The core of its support comes from the urban middle classes and farmers.

ALL-GERMANY PARTY 1917

Developed out of the German National Club and some sections of the old National Democratic Party. Politically centre, committed to union with Germany. Dissolved by World War II.

COMMUNIST PARTY (KPÖ) 1918

Communist programme included committal to strict neutrality. Major strength was in the trade unions.

AUSTRIAN LIBERAL PARTY (FPÖ) 1955

Partially succeeds the previous Independent League dissolved in 1956. Programme of moderate social reform and inter-Europe co-operation. It is structured on a federal basis, and regional parties enjoy a great deal of autonomy. The party first came to power in 1983 as the junior coalition partner of the SPÖ.

DEMOCRATIC PROGRESSIVE PARTY (DPF) 1965

UNITED GREENS OF AUSTRIA (VGÖ)/THE ALTERNATIVE LIST OF AUSTRIA (1982)

A more conservative and middle-class party than its German counterpart. First entered parliament in 1986 with 9 members.

LIBERAL FORUM (1993)

Founded by former members of the FPÖ. Currently led by Heide Schmidt.

NATIONAL DEMOCRATIC PARTY (NDP)

A right-wing extremist party.

BELARUS

Since independence the number and position of political parties has constantly changed. Among those dominating the 1995 elections were the Communist Party of Belarus (which had been suspended in 1991, re-legalized in 1993 and subsequently merged with the Party of Communists of Belarus) and the Agrarian Party. The centrist United Civic Party of Belarus (f. 1990) came third. The Party of People's Accord won 8 seats. No other party (of the 25 or so groupings) won more than two seats.

BELGIUM

Before the advent of the Belgian Labour Party, party politics were dominated by two parties: the Liberals, who formed a national party organization in 1846, and the Conservatives, whose national organization, dating from the 1860s, remained weak until 1921, when the Catholic Union (*Union Catholique Belge*) was established.

The Liberals lost ground after 1884 with the rise of the Belgian Labour Party and the extension of the franchise.

The Belgian Labour Party (*Parti Ouvrier Belge*) was founded in 1885 by César de Paepe, rapidly making progress in such cities as Brussels, Ghent, the Liège country and Hainaut province. The Daensists (*Christene Volkspartis*) were formed in 1894 by the Abbé Daens.

CATHOLIC PARTY

This, with the Liberal Party, was one of the main parties of the nineteenth century. It was divided on the French-Flemish language question, and had clearly defined left and right wings but was mainly conservative and clerical. It survived until 1945, when it was reformed as the *Christian Socialist Party (PSC)* which is now undenominational and has a Christian-Democrat moderate reform programme.

LIBERAL PARTY

The other main party of the nineteenth century, less influential since. It had a moderate social and religious policy. In 1961 it was succeeded by the *Party for Liberty and Progress (PLP)*. This is anti-federalist and concerned specially with farmers and industrial workers.

BELGIAN SOCIALIST PARTY (PSB) 1885

Founded as *Parti Ouvrier Belge*. Orthodox socialist programme. Split from the Flemish wing in 1979.

FRONT PARTY 1918

Founded to divide Belgium by setting up a separate Flemish state. Modern counterpart is the *People's Union* (see below).

FRONT DEMOCRATIQUE DES FRANCOPHONES

Front composed of several small Walloon parties.

FLEMISH PARTY

The Vlaamske Blok was founded in 1979.

PEOPLE'S UNION (VOLKSUNIE)

Flemish Nationalist Party, founded in 1954, aiming at a Federal structure for the country.

ECOLOGIST PARTY

There are two Ecologist parties. *Agalev* is the Dutch-speaking environmental party, founded 1982; *Ecolo* is the environmental party for the French-speaking community.

NATIONAL FRONT 1988

An extreme right-wing nationalist party.

WALLOON PARTY (PW) 1985

An amalgamation of previous Walloon groupings. PW is a left-wing socialist party which advocates an independent Walloon state.

Other parties include the Feminist Humanist Party, which adopted this name in 1990 from the former United Feminist Party. ROSSEM (f.1991) is the ultra-liberal party advocating privatization of social security, abolition of the monarchy etc.

BOSNIA–HERCEGOVINA

In the very confused political situation of independent Bosnia, the following three major parties represent the main ethnic groupings:

PARTY OF DEMOCRATIC ACTION (PDA)

The leading Muslim nationalist party, led by Dr Alija Izetbegovič.

CROATIAN DEMOCRATIC UNION OF BOSNIA AND HERCEGOVINA (f.1990)

The Croat nationalist party, affiliated to the CDU in Croatia.

SERBIAN DEMOCRATIC PARTY OF BOSNIA AND HERCEGOVINA (f.1990)

The Serb nationalist party, allied to the SDP in Serbia.

Other parties include the Socialist Democratic Party (the former ruling League of Communists) and the secular Muslim Liberal Bosniak Organization (created in 1992 from a merger of the Liberal Party of Bosnia and the Muslim Bosniak Organization).

BULGARIA

After independence, Bulgarian politics was dominated by the political groupings around Stambulov, Radoslavov and Tontchev. Among other groups active prior to 1914 were:

(1) *The Social Democratic Party* (founded 9 Aug 1891). By 1899, its membership was 800. In 1901, this total had risen to 2180 and by 1902 to 2507. An orthodox evolutionary party, its extremist left broke away in 1903, eventually forming the Communist Party in 1918.
(2) *The Democratic Party* was founded in 1895 by P. Karavelov. The governing party from Jan 1908 to Mar 1911.
(3) *The Radical Party*. Founded in 1906 by N. Tsanov, who broke away from the Democratic Party. It advocated radical tax reforms and protection of co-operative societies.
(4) *The Agrarians' Union*. Founded in 1899, and ably led by Stamboulisky. Secured a major increase in influence during the Balkan Wars. Its programme was heavily in favour of the protection of agriculture and allied industries. In 1919 a breakaway group, led by D. Dragyhev, organized a rival, more moderate faction.

From 1918 to 1945 the major parties were:

COMMUNIST PARTY 1918

Dominant party of the Fatherland Front organization which claimed 800 000 members. Founded from a splinter group of the moderate left *Social Democratic Party* (1893). Renamed Bulgarian Socialist Party (1989).

AGRARIANS' UNION 1899

Founded to protect farming and related industries. Main body continued as Stamboulinsky's party when Draghyev's party broke away in 1919 as a more moderate group, defending parliamentary methods in politics.

DEMOCRATIC PARTY 1895

Founded as a group to reconcile differing parties with a centre policy. In 1906 the *Radical Party* split off, in support of co-operatives, radical tax reforms and a federation of Balkan states.

NATIONAL LIBERAL PARTY 1920

United three small parties to rebuild post-war Bulgaria and gain a revision of the peace treaty. Stambulov's *National Liberal Party* broke away in 1925.

PARTY OF THE DEMOCRATIC ENTENTE 1923

Moderate reform party committed to peace and strengthening of the law and the economy.

After 1945 Bulgaria was effectively a one-party state until 1989. The Fatherland Front, which included the Bulgarian Communist Party and the Bulgarian Agrarian Party, attracted more than 99% of the vote. Anti-government demonstrations in 1989 forced the Fatherland Front to relinquish sole governing power and to allow the formation of other parties. The first free elections in 58 years were held on 10 and 17 Jun 1990.

BULGARIAN AGRARIAN PARTY (BAP)

The BAP was founded in 1899 as a mass peasant party. Some members refused to cooperate with the Communists in the Fatherland Front of 1944 and formed an independent agrarian party, which effectively ceased to exist after the establishment of Communist rule in 1947.

BULGARIAN COMMUNIST PARTY (BCP)

Formed in 1891 as the Bulgarian Social Democratic Party, from which it split in 1919, it formed part of the broad-based Fatherland Front, which took power in 1946 with the backing of the USSR, and subsequently came to dominate the organization. In 1989, it changed its name to Bulgarian Socialist Party (see below).

BULGARIAN SOCIALIST PARTY (BSP)

The former Bulgarian Communist Party changed its name following anti-government demonstrations that led to constitutional reforms in 1989.

284

In the Jun 1990 Assembly elections the BSP won 211 of the 400 seats.

UNION OF DEMOCRATIC FORCES (UDF)

The main opposition grouping, an alliance of 16 parties formed in 1989, the UDF includes the Ecoglasnost Independent Association, Citizens' Initiative Movement and Bulgarian Workers' Social Democratic Party (United) among its component organizations. The UDF won 144 National Assembly seats in the 1990 elections.

Among other parties in what remains a fluid situation are the Agrarian Party (which had been absorbed in the Fatherland Front in 1946) and the Movement for Rights and Freedom (MRF), an ethnic Turkish minority party that took 23 seats in the 1990 elections. Over 80 political parties (some very small) exist.

CROATIA

Since independence, political life has been dominated by the Croatian Democratic Union. In addition to the parties listed below, over 30 smaller groupings exist.

CROATIAN DEMOCRATIC UNION (CDU) (f.1989)

Nationalist party led by Franjo Tudjman. It dominated the presidential election of Aug 1992 and the 1995 general election.

CROATIAN SOCIAL-LIBERAL PARTY (CSLP) (f.1989)

Second strongest party, led by Dražen Budisa. Part of the 1995 opposition electoral alliance.

SERBIAN PEOPLE'S PARTY (SPP)

The party of the ethnic Serbs in Croatia.

SOCIAL DEMOCRATIC PARTY – PARTY OF DEMOCRATIC REFORM OF CROATIA

The former ruling League of Communists; adopted present name in 1991.

CROATIAN PARTY OF RIGHTS

Right-wing, nationalist.

CYPRUS

Since the division of the island, political parties have polarized as follows:

GREEK

These include AKEL (Progressive Party of the Working People, successor to the Communist Party), the Democratic Party (f.1976, supports UN policy on Cyprus), the Democratic Rally (f.1976, opposition party) and the socialist EDEK (f.1969). The Liberal Party (f.1986) advocates solving the Cyprus problem by adhering to United Nations resolutions. ADISOK, formed 1990, also supports a settlement of the Cyprus problem based on UN resolutions.

TURKISH

These include the socialist Republican Turkish Party (f.1970), the social democratic Democratic People's Party (f.1979), the Populist Party (f.1976) and the government National Unity Party (f.1976). The Social Democratic Party (f.1982) advocates a two-community Cyprus federation. The Northern Cyprus Socialist Party (f.1985) stands for complete independence for the Turkish area. There is also a right-wing New Dawn Party (f.1984).

The Democratic Struggle Party was an opposition alliance to contest the 1990 general election.

CZECHOSLOVAKIA

Note: From the communist takeover until 1989 Czechoslovakia was effectively a one-party state. Free elections took place in 1990. On 31 Dec 1992 Czechoslovakia ceased to exist.

COMMUNIST PARTY OF CZECHOSLOVAKIA 1921

Incorporated extreme left elements of the former Czech Social Democratic Labour Party, a working-class and mainly anti-communist socialist party, and the Slovak Labour Party.

CZECH CATHOLIC PEOPLE'S PARTY 1918

Founded from three smaller Catholic parties, with mainly peasant support. The *Slovak Catholic People's Party* seceded from it in 1921.

CZECH NATIONAL DEMOCRATIC PARTY 1917

Developed from the Young Czech Party (liberals), the Radical Party (right-wing), the Moravian Progressive Party and the Realist Party. The bulk of membership of the last two seceded in 1925 to form the National Party of Labour. The party represented big industrial and banking interests and the anti-Socialist bourgeoisie.

NATIONAL PARTY OF LABOUR 1925

Liberal intellectual support. Programme of moderate social reform, its socialist tendencies evolutionary and not revolutionary.

CZECH PEOPLE'S PARTY 1919

Christian party which supported the National Front government.

SLOVAK RECONSTRUCTION PARTY 1948

Developed from the former Slovak Democratic Party. Supported the National Front government.

CIVIC FORUM 1989

Party advocating a return to parliamentary democracy formed by human rights and opposition groups. In February 1991 the party split into two, with moderate and radical supporters.

PUBLIC AGAINST VIOLENCE 1989

The sister-party to Civic Forum in Slovakia.

CHRISTIAN DEMOCRATIC UNION 1989

Conservative coalition formed by the Czech and Slovak *Christian Democrats* and the *People's Party*.

CZECH REPUBLIC

Among the political parties in the newly-independent Czech Republic are:

CIVIC DEMOCRATIC PARTY (f. 1991)

Liberal-Conservative Party, formed following a split in Civic Forum.

BOHEMIAN-MORAVIAN UNION OF THE CENTRE

Renamed in 1994 following merger of the Liberal Social Union and the Agrarian Party.

CZECH SOCIAL DEMOCRATIC PARTY

Originally founded 1878. Banned in 1948, and re-founded 1989.

Other significant parties include the Christian Democratic Union, the extreme right-wing Association for the Republic (f.1989), the Free Democrats, the Liberal National Social Party, the reorganized Communist Party of Bohemia and Moravia, and the Green Party.

DENMARK

The Liberal Party (*Venstre*) exercised a dominant control of the Folketing prior to the First World War, despite repeated secession to both right and left. Founded in 1870, it was split and reunited on several occasions. A traditional Liberal Party, its aims were free trade and a minimum of state control.

The historic opponents of the Liberals were the Right (*Hojre*). From 1875 to 1894, under the leadership of Estrup the main planks in the Conservative programme were the elevation of the Landsting (upper house) to equal authority with the Folketing and the strengthening of national defences. In 1915 the Right was formally constituted as the Conservative People's Party (*Konservative Folkeparti*). The period prior to 1914 also saw the emergence of the Social Democratic Party (see below).

LIBERAL-DEMOCRATIC PARTY 1870

Support mainly from farmers, and its main aim the dominance of the Folkesting (second chamber) over Landsting (first chamber). Name changed to *Venstre*, a moderate liberal party with support no longer confined to farmers. Programme of free trade and a minimum of state interference.

SOCIAL DEMOCRATIC PARTY 1871

Non-communist socialist party supported mainly by industrial and farm workers.

CONSERVATIVE PEOPLE'S PARTY 1916

Originally supported by propertied class and concerned to support the authority of the Landsting over the Folkesting. Developed as a party of free initiative, maintaining private property, restricting state action to necessary economic and social intervention.

RADICAL LIBERAL PARTY 1905

The party was founded in 1905 as a result of a split in the Liberal Party. Its chief adherents were the small landed proprietors and certain intellectuals. It held office from 1909 to 1910, and again, with Zahle as Prime Minister, from 1913 to 1920. The main planks of its programme were social reform, reduction of armaments, and the establishment of small-holdings.

Other parties included the Retsforbund (Single Tax Party), founded 1919, the Communist Party (f.1919), the Left Socialists (f.1967), the Christian People's Party (f.1970), the left-wing Socialist People's Party (f.1959), the Progress Party (f.1972), the European Centre-Democrats (f.1974), and the Green Environmentalists' Party (f.1983).

ESTONIA

During the first period of independence (1918–1940) the two main parties were:

CHRISTIAN PEOPLE'S PARTY 1918

Formed mainly to introduce religious teaching into the elementary and secondary schools. A centre party, slightly to the right.

REFORMIST LABOUR PARTY 1917

Left of centre, formed from the old Radical Socialist Party.

PEOPLE'S PARTY

Right of centre, developed from the old Democratic and Radical-Democratic parties.

ESTONIAN COMMUNIST PARTY 1920

The party declared its independence from the Communist Party of the Soviet Union in Mar 1990.

Since 1988, the following parties have emerged:

POPULAR FRONT OF ESTONIA 1988

Advocated an independent Estonian republic and a multi-party parliamentary system.

ESTONIAN NATIONAL INDEPENDENCE PARTY (ESRP) 1988

Supported complete Estonian independence from the USSR.

There are also, among many other parties, the *Estonian Christian Democratic Party* (f.1988), the *Estonian Democratic Labour Party* (f.1989), the *Estonian Green Party* (f.1989), the *Estonian Coalition Party* (f.1991), three rural parties, a royalist party and in 1994 three parties representing the Russian-speaking minority.

FINLAND

In the late nineteenth century, the main political party in Finland was the Finnish Nationalist Party. This later split into the Old Finns and the Young Finns. Other developments were:

1899 Foundation of the Finnish Social Democratic (i.e. Labour) Party.
1903 Finnish Labour Party renamed Social Democratic Party.
1906 Formation of the Swedish People's Party representing the Swedish minority.

Other parties contesting elections prior to 1918 were the Christian Labour Union and the Agrarian Union. The following parties flourished in the modern period:

SOCIAL DEMOCRATIC PARTY 1899

Constitutional socialist.

CENTRE PARTY 1906

Formed as the Agrarian Union, name changed in 1965. Centre with tendencies to the left, aims to support the interests of smallholders and small farmers.

FINNISH PEOPLE'S DEMOCRATIC LEAGUE 1944

Union of Communists and left-wing socialists, including the old Socialist Union Party. Advocated broad left platform. Declined in 1970s. Merged to form Left-Wing Alliance in 1990.

COMMUNIST PARTY 1918

Established in Moscow in 1917 before becoming active in Finland. It did not become legal in Finland until 1944.

NATIONAL COALITION PARTY 1918

Conservative, supporting private enterprise.

SWEDISH PEOPLE'S PARTY 1906

To protect the interests of the Swedish minority; divided politically, but mainly liberal.

FINNISH RURAL PARTY 1959

An anti-socialist party appealing to smaller farmers and owners of small businesses.

Among many other parties are the Finnish Pensioners' Party (formed in 1986, the Green Association (formed in 1988); the Communist Workers Party (formed in 1989); and the Constitutional Party of the Right (formed in 1973).

FRANCE

Despite the many upheavals in French politics, the development of clear-cut political parties in France was a slow process. Inside the parliament, deputies often belonged to more than one group whilst constituency organization at local level was hardly developed. By 1900, in addition to the Conservative Right and a variety of socialists, other parties contesting elections included *Action Française* (see below). Key events between 1900 and 1914 were the foundation of the Radical Socialist Party (1901), the foundation of the Socialist Party in 1905 (see p. 292) and the involvement of the Republican Union in the 1910 elections.

ACTION FRANÇAISE 1898

Right-wing, nationalist, monarchist, anti-democratic and originally anti-semitic. Supported considerable autonomy for the provinces and a government of ministers responsible only to a king.

ACTION NATIONALE 1918

A combination of the former Action Liberale Populaire (Catholic), the Federation of Democratic Republicans and the Republican Federation. A centre party supporting indirect taxation, the free play of economic laws, decentralized administration and free enterprise.

DEMOCRATIC AND SOCIAL REPUBLICAN PARTY 1901

Founded as Republican Democratic Alliance. Favoured direct taxation, diplomatic relations with the Vatican, but a careful balance between clerical and anti-clerical influences and the separation of church and state.

GAUCHE RADICALE

Moderate socialist party, most active following 1918. Conciliatory in foreign policy.

FEDERATION OF RADICALS AND RADICAL SOCIALISTS POST-1918

Socialist reform party supporting state monopolies, the League of Nations and the full implementation of the Treaty of Versailles.

SOCIALIST PARTY 1905

Amalgamation of the Socialist Party of France (revolutionary) and the French Socialist Party (moderate evolutionary). The union split in 1920 and the resulting party was anti-communist, collectivist in theory but moderate in practice. Moved towards the eventual abolition of private property.

UNION OF DEMOCRATS FOR THE REPUBLIC

Development through several former parties with successive titles:
  Democratic Labour Union,
  Union for the New Republic,
  Democratic Union for the Fifth Republic,
  Union for the Defence of the Republic, and
the Gaullist Party, which actively supported continuation of Gaullist policy and a more independent role for France in the Western Alliance.

NATIONAL FEDERATION OF INDEPENDENT REPUBLICANS 1962

Liberal policy.

REPUBLICAN RADICAL AND RADICAL-SOCIALIST PARTY

Traditional centre party of the Third Republic. Extreme left-wing dissidents broke away in 1956, the remaining body continued with a liberal economic policy, support for NATO and European unity.

UNITED SOCIALIST PARTY 1960

Developed from the Independent Socialist Party, the Union of the Left Socialist Party and the Tribune of Communism dissident section.

DEMOCRATIC CENTRE

Formed from former sections of the Independent and Republican Movement parties. Centre left policy, supported a united Europe and NATO.
Of the parties active in the post-de Gaulle years, there have been:

SOCIALIST PARTY (PS) 1971

Proposed planned economy, nationalization of key industries.
Subscribed to the United Left programme with the Communists until 1977.

COMMUNIST PARTY (PCF) 1920

Advocates democratic path to socialism.
Subscribed to United Left programme with Socialists until 1977.

RASSEMBLEMENT POUR LA REPUBLIQUE (RPR) 1976

A successor of the Gaullist UDR (Union of Democrats for the Republic) following the resignation of Jacques Chirac. Campaigned with UDF in 1988.

UNION POUR LA DEMOCRATIE FRANÇAISE (UDF) 1978

Formed to unite the non-Gaullist 'majority' candidates.

REPUBLICAN PARTY 1977

Part of the UDF (see above).

RADICAL PARTY 1901

Forms part of the UDF (see above).

NATIONAL FRONT (FN) 1972

An extreme right-wing party led by Jean-Marie Le Pen. Virulently anti-immigrant.

THE GREENS 1972

Formerly the Ecologists, this environmental party was renamed in 1984.

MOUVEMENT GAULLISTE POPULAIRE 1982

GERMANY

In the German Empire, the electoral stage was dominated up to 1900 by three main groups: the Centre Party (*Deutsche Zentrums-partei*), the National Liberals (the *Nationalliberale*) and a small but rapidly-growing Social Democratic Party, formed in 1871. In 1877, the National Liberals split, with the Liberal Union (*Liberale Vereinigung*) breaking away over the tariff question. In addition there were some right-wing German national parties (e.g. the *Deutsche Reichs partei* and the *Deutsche-Konservative*) and the national minority parties of Poles, Danes and Alsatians, these latter first fighting elections after 1874. Prior to 1914 other developments included:

1884   Elections contested by the Free Thinking Party (*Freisinnige Partei*), a merger of the Progressive Party and the Liberal Union.
1892   The Free Thinking Party split in this year to form the Free Thinking People's Party (*Freisinnige Volks Partei*) and the Free Thinking Union (*Freisinnige Vereinigung*).
1898   Two farmers parties, the Bavarian Farmers League (*Bayerische Bauernbund*) and the Farmers League (*Bund der Landwirte*) contested the elections.
1907   The Economic Union (*Wirtschafts Vereinigung*) formed.
1912   Progressive People's Party formed from a merger of the Free Thinking Union, the Free Thinking Peoples Party and the German People's Party.

During the period 1918 to 1945 the following parties were active:

GERMAN NATIONAL PEOPLE'S PARTY (DNVP) 1918

Conservative, formed from a union of the Free Conservative Party, the Economic Union, the Conservative Party and the Christian Socialists. Aimed at a restoration of German sovereignty and a revision of the Treaty of Versailles. Protection for home industries, anti-Communist, pro-Christian.

NATIONAL PARTY OF GERMAN MODERATES (RDM) 1920

Supported by and concerned for the industrial and commercial middle classes. Anti-Socialist and against state controls.

SOCIAL DEMOCRATIC PARTY OF GERMANY 1871

Republican, democratic. Unqualified support for peace and reconciliation after 1918. Repudiated nationalism, aimed at socialization of large-scale production.

GERMAN DEMOCRATIC PARTY 1918

Formed from the former Progressive People's Party of 1910 and the left-wing of the National Liberal Party. Republican and moderate reformist.

GERMAN COMMUNIST PARTY 1919

Revolutionary communist.

GERMAN CENTRE PARTY 1870

Catholic centre party committed to fulfilling Versailles treaty obligations with a view to reconciliation. Supported the Weimar constitution.

GERMAN PEOPLE'S PARTY 1918

Formed from the right-wing of the former National Liberal Party, Protectionist in trade, nationalist and monarchist in politics.

NATIONAL SOCIALIST GERMAN WORKERS' PARTY 1925

Seceded from the German People's Party. Nationalist, supporting rearmament. Anti-Semitic. Protectionist in trade policy. Committed to social and educational reform, expansion of German sovereignty in Europe.

FEDERAL REPUBLIC OF GERMANY

{ CHRISTIAN-DEMOCRATIC UNION (CDU) 1945

{ CHRISTIAN SOCIAL UNION (CSU) – EQUIVALENT BAVARIAN PARTY 1945

United Catholic-Protestant action on Christian principles, supporting maintenance of private property and individual freedom. Moderate conservative. The dominant party in recent years under Helmut Kohl.

SOCIAL DEMOCRATIC PARTY OF GERMANY (SPD) 1945

Orthodox social-democrat policies, supporting a competitive economy, moderate social policy.

FREE DEMOCRATIC PARTY (FDP)

Liberal social policies. Long-time junior partner of the Christian Democrats.

NATIONAL DEMOCRATIC PARTY OF GERMANY (NPD) 1964

Right-wing, nationalist.

DIE GRÜNEN (THE GREENS)

Founded 1980. A left-wing party concentrating on ecological issues, it was anti-NATO, anti-Warsaw Pact and favoured smaller economic units. Merged in 1993 with Bundnis 90 (f.1990) to form new Green Alliance (Alliance 90/The Greens).

REPUBLICAN PARTY 1983

Right-wing nationalist party.

PARTY OF DEMOCRATIC SOCIALISM (PDS) 1989

The successor party to the collapsed Communist Party.

GERMAN DEMOCRATIC REPUBLIC

SOCIALIST UNITY PARTY OF GERMANY 1946

Founded as a union of the Social Democratic Party and the Communist Party. Communist policy. The party collapsed in 1989, becoming the Party of Democratic Socialism (see above).

CHRISTIAN DEMOCRAT UNION OF GERMANY 1945

These and six others belonged to a National Front and issued a joint manifesto before elections.

CHRISTIAN DEMOCRATIC UNION (CDU) 1989

Sister-party of the West German conservative CDU.

GERMAN SOCIAL UNION (DSU) 1989

Formed by twelve centre-right and opposition groups as the sister-party of the Bavarian Christian Social Union.

DEMOCRATIC AWAKENING (DA) 1989

A Christian party.

SOCIAL DEMOCRATIC PARTY (SPD) (1989)

Sister-party of the West German SPD, reconstituted in 1989 following the collapse of the Socialist Unity Party in which it had been forcibly united with the Communists.

GREECE

POPULAR PARTY 1920

Parliamentary methods, moderate socialist policies.

LIBERAL-CONSERVATIVE PARTY 1920s

Republican. Aimed at government through a state council.

REPUBLICAN UNION 1920s

Formerly the extreme left of the Liberal Party. Committed to increased industrial production and the welfare of industrial workers. Supported proportional representation.

COMMUNIST PARTY

Supported proportional representation, women's suffrage, confiscation of large properties. Anti-armament.

NATIONAL RADICAL UNION 1956

Concerned with stimulating production and economic stability. Moderate.

These and other parties were suspended in 1967 when all political parties ceased to function. Other parties recently formed and then suspended:

> Union of Democratic Left – extreme left-wing.
> Progressive Agrarian Democratic Union – moderate.
> Union of Populist Parties – right-wing, monarchist.
> Centre Union – liberal and progressive coalition.
> Liberal Democratic Centre Party – breakaway group from the CU.

Since the restoration of democracy in Greece, the following major parties have emerged:

PANHELLENIC SOCIALIST MOVEMENT (PASOK) 1974

Left-wing, incorporating Democratic Defence and Panhellenic Liberation Movement resistance organizations. Led until his death by Andreas Papandreou, it favoured socialization of the means of production.

DEMOCRATIC CENTRE UNION (EDIK) 1974

A democratic socialist party which combined the Centre Union (f.1961) and the New Political Forces (f.1974).

COMMUNIST PARTY OF GREECE (KKE) 1918

The orthodox Moscow-dominated party. It was banned in 1947 and reappeared in 1974. It became part of the Left Coalition in 1989.

GREEK COMMUNIST PARTY (KKE-INTERIOR) 1968

A Marxist movement, independent of the 'Moscow-line'. It separated from the pro-Moscow Communist Party of Greece in 1968, and joined the Greek Left Party in 1987.

DEMOCRATIC INITIATIVE PARTY 1987

A democratic socialist party supporting a mixed economy and the removal of foreign bases from Greece.

DEMOCRATIC REVIVAL 1985

A populist moderate centre-right party.

POLITICAL SPRING 1993

Formed by former foreign minister Antonis Samatas to 'break the mould' of Greek politics. It won 10 seats in the 1993 election.

LEFT COALITION 1989

Alliance of Greek Left Party (f.1987) and Communist Party of Greece (Exterior).

Other parties include the Democratic Socialist Party (f.Mar 1979 by former EDIK activists), the New Democracy (f.1974), a moderate pragmatic reform party, the right-wing Progressive Party (f.1979), the far-right Golden Dawn, and the Liberal Party (f.1981). There is also an Ecologist Alternative Party.

HUNGARY

PARTY OF NATIONAL UNITY 1921

Developed from the Party of Christian Small Landowners and Citizens. Conservative.

CHRISTIAN ECONOMY PARTY 1923

Formed from the former People's Party, Unionist Party, and Christian Socialists. Conservative and legitimist.

HUNGARIAN SOCIALIST WORKERS' PARTY 1956

The Communist Party and the Social Democratic Party merged to create the Working People's Party. The name was later changed. Moscow-oriented Communist. It became the Hungarian Socialist Party in 1989.

PATRIOTIC PEOPLE'S FRONT 1954

Replaced the former Hungarian Independent People's Front. Represented the mass organizations such as Trade Unions. Independent Communist.
Note: From the Communist takeover after World War II until 1989, Hungary was effectively a one-party state. The Hungarian Socialist Workers' Party dominated the Patriotic People's Front, of which all candidates had to be supporters. Hungary underwent fundamental political and constitutional changes in 1989. Political parties were legalized in Oct 1989. Free elections for the National Assembly were held on 25 Mar 1990, with a second round on 8 Apr 1990.

HUNGARIAN SOCIALIST PARTY 1989

Successor party to the Hungarian Socialist Workers' Party, advocating a mixed economy on Scandinavian lines.

HUNGARIAN DEMOCRATIC FORUM (HDF) 1988

Centre-right party legalized in 1989. It supported economic privatization and a negotiated withdrawal from the Warsaw Pact. Lost support after 1991 over slow pace of reform and disenchantment with the economy.

ALLIANCE OF FREE DEMOCRATS (SzDSz) 1989

Advocates rapid moves towards a market economy and privatization.

INDEPENDENT SMALLHOLDERS' PARTY (FKgP) 1988

Legalized in 1989, the party advocates privatization and the return of land confiscated in 1947 to its former owners.

CHRISTIAN DEMOCRATIC PEOPLE'S PARTY 1989

A centre party.

SOCIAL DEMOCRATIC PARTY 1890, REVIVED 1988

Absorbed by the Communist Party in 1948 to form the Working People's Party, the Social Democrats became a legally organized separate party in 1989.

Other parties include the Agrarian Alliance and the Green Party (f.1989). Representatives of national minorities are guaranteed one seat each in the National Assembly.

ICELAND

INDEPENDENCE PARTY (1929)

Amalgamation of Conservative (1924) and Liberal (1925) parties. Aimed at social reform within a capitalist framework and furtherance of national independence, through renunciation of the Act of Union with Denmark.

PROGRESSIVE PARTY 1916

Supports co-operatives, aims at educational and social reform.

SOCIAL DEMOCRATIC PARTY 1916

Moderate evolutionary socialist.

PEOPLE'S ALLIANCE 1956

Formed from sections of the Social Democrats and the Socialist Unity Party, and reorganized in 1968 as a socialist party.

CITIZENS' PARTY 1987

Shares the Independence Party's ideological position but lays stress on individual rights.

WOMEN'S ALLIANCE 1983

A feminist party emphasizing the rights of women and children, with a rotating parliamentary leadership.

IRELAND

CUMAN-NA-GAEDHEAL

Moderate party accepting partition and the Act of Settlement in 1921. Aimed for economic and social stability within the Empire. Became part of Fine Gael.

FIANNA FAIL 1926

Republican. Successor to those bodies not accepting the Act of Settlement. Neutralist.

FINE GAEL 1933

Formed by amalgamating Cuman-na-Gaedheal, the Centre Party and the National Guard Party. Centre.

LABOUR PARTY 1912

Formed as an organ of the Trades Unions, separated from them in 1930. Socialist.

SINN FEIN 1905

Formed to end British occupation, and then to end partition and achieve a Democratic Socialist Republic of all Ireland.

PROGRESSIVE DEMOCRATS 1985

The party – set up by former Fianna Fail members – advocates constitutional reform, a lessening of church influence in the state, and private enterprise.

GREEN PARTY

Formerly the Ecology Party.

WORKERS PARTY 1905

Formerly Sinn Fein The Workers Party. Seeks an All-Ireland Socialist State.

Among smaller parties are the Irish Republican Socialist Party (f.1974), the Communist Party of Ireland (f.1933), the Democratic Socialist Party (f.1982 out of the earlier Socialist Party), and Republican Sinn Fein (f.1986).

ITALY

In Italy, even by 1900, political parties had been extremely slow to develop. Politics centred around the groups attached to a particular individual. Although after 1870, deputies could usually be identified with the right, (*Destra*) or left (*Sinistra*), such labels often meant little, whilst the deputies from the south could usually be 'bought' by the government. The impetus to the development of political parties came in 1892, with the formation of the Socialist Party (*Partito Socialista Italiano*, PSI). Other developments by 1914 were:

1898   Dissolution of the Italian Republican Party (originally founded in 1880 and reorganized in 1892) by order of Pelloux. It was subsequently reformed.

1904   The Vatican began to allow Catholics to vote for moderate candidates – but no national Catholic party formed until 1919, when the Popular Party (*Partito Popolare Italiano*) came into being.

1913   Splits in the Socialist ranks led to the elections being contested by Independent Socialists and by the Reformist Socialist Party.

ITALIAN LIBERAL PARTY 1848

Founded originally by Cavour as a democratic force in the re-unification of Italy. Liberal.

CHRISTIAN DEMOCRAT PARTY 1943

Successor to the pre-Fascist Popular Party, Anti-Communist, moderate social policy.

ITALIAN COMMUNIST PARTY 1921

The largest in Western Europe. Advocated nationalization and land redistribution. Became the Democratic Party of the Left in February 1991.

ITALIAN SOCIALIST PARTY (PSI) 1966

Founded by a merger of the Italian Socialist Party and the Italian Democratic Socialist Party. The latter broke away in 1969. Centre left, adhering to the Second International.

UNITED SOCIALIST PARTY (PSU) 1969

Democrat splinter from the United Socialists.

ITALIAN SOCIAL MOVEMENT – NATIONAL RIGHT (MSI–DN) 1946

Extreme right, neo-fascist. Now absorbed by Alleanza Nazionale (*q.v.*) A splinter group, National Democracy, broke away in 1977.

UNITED PROLETARIAN ITALIAN SOCIALIST PARTY 1964

Further left than the Italian Socialist Party, from whom it broke away.

NATIONAL FASCIST PARTY 1919

Formed to resist Bolshevism by force. Policies developed as conservative, nationalist, militarist and imperialist. ('Fascismo' = absolute and dictatorial government.) The party of Benito Mussolini.

ITALIAN POPULAR PARTY 1919

Catholic independent party with social-democrat policies.
 (*All non-fascist parties were dissolved in 1926*)

UNITED PARTY 1922

Formed from a section of the old Socialist Party. Revolutionary socialist and reformist.

MASSIMALIST PARTY 1922

Hard-core theoretical socialists remaining after the United Party breakaway.

RADICAL PARTY (PR)

A party which concentrated on civil rights issues.

SOCIAL DEMOCRAT PARTY (PSDI) 1969

A breakaway from the former United Socialist Party, the PSDI stands to the right of the PSI.

GREEN PARTY 1987

Environmental and anti-nuclear party.

During the 1990s political parties in Italy were transformed as old parties (such as the Christian Democrats) became discredited and new alliances were forged. Among the new parties are:

FORZE ITALIA 1994

The right-wing party formed by Berlusconi to fight the 1994 elections.

303

Anti-immigrant, pro-market forces and populist, it gathered much of the old Christian Democrat vote.

NORTHERN LEAGUE

This party represents the populist rising force of northern Italy. The party is anti-Rome, anti-Mafia, anti-immigrant and anti-tax. It is led by Umberto Bossi. Part of the short-lived 1994 Berlusconi alliance.

POPULAR PARTY

The successor to the discredited Christian Democrats. Right-wing, conservative.

DEMOCRATIC PARTY OF THE LEFT

Formed in Feb 1991, this party is the successor to the former Italian Communist Party. Led by Achillo Occhetto, it is seeking to find a new identity after the collapse of Communism in the Eastern bloc.

COMMUNIST REFOUNDATION

The hard-line core of the old Communist Party that refused to join the PDS when it abandoned Marxism in 1991.

LA RETE

The Anti-Mafia Party founded originally in 1991 to contest regional elections in Sicily.

OLIVE TREE ALLIANCE

The Centre-Left Alliance which won power in the 1996 elections. Led by Romano Prodi.

ALLEANZA NAZIONALE (NATIONAL ALLIANCE)

The extreme right party formed in 1994 which absorbed the old neo-fascist Italian Social Movement in 1995. Led by Gianfranco Fini.

LATVIA

SOCIAL DEMOCRATIC PARTY

Allied with the Jewish Bund. Moderate.

DEMOCRATIC CENTRE PARTY

Middle-class support, policy left of centre.

FARMERS' UNION

Left-of-centre party to support rural interests.

INDEPENDENT NATIONALISTS

Right-wing, support from the commercial and industrial class.

Following the ending of the Communist Party's monopoly of power in 1990 (and the subsequent ban on the Communist Party in August 1991) political parties have proliferated. The first elections (see p. 224) were dominated by Latvian Way. Latvian Way (f. 1993) advocates a democratic state with a free market economy, private ownership of land, and closer links with the other Baltic states.

Other parties include the Latvian National Independence Movement (f.1988), the National Harmony Party (f.1993) and the rural centrist Latvian Farmer's Union. Following a split in the Communist Party of Latvia, the Democratic Labour Party of Latvia was formed in 1990. The Latvian Social Democratic Workers' Party, originally founded in 1904, was re-established in 1989.

LIECHTENSTEIN

PROGRESSIVE CITIZENS' PARTY

PATRIOTIC UNION 1936

Evolved from the Peoples Party.

CHRISTIAN-SOCIALIST PARTY 1962

FREE LIST (FL) 1985

An environmental party supporting social progress.

LITHUANIA

Christian Democrats	
Farmers' Union	Extreme right.
Labour Federation	
Populist Party	
Nationalist Party	Liberal.
Social Democrats	Left of centre.

SAJUDIS (LITHUANIAN REFORM MOVEMENT) 1988

Advocated complete secession from the USSR.

COMMUNIST PARTY OF LITHUANIA 1919

Declared itself independent of the Communist Party of the Soviet Union in 1989.

LITHUANIAN DEMOCRATIC PARTY 1989

Supported a demilitarized neutral Lithuania.

COMMUNIST PARTY LEAGUE OF LITHUANIA 1990

The pro-CPSU remnant of the Communist Party of Lithuania.

The period immediately prior to independence was dominated by Sajudis, the main nationalist movement (founded in 1988 as the Lithuanian Movement for Reconstruction). The period saw the refounding of many old parties (the Christian Democratic Party, originally founded in 1905, the Lithuanian Democratic Party founded 1902 and the Lithuanian Social Democratic Party, founded 1896). The 1993 elections, however, were dominated by the former communists (now the Lithuanian Democratic Labour Party).

LUXEMBOURG

From 1868, when the first directly-elected parliament was introduced, the Liberals were the dominant party. They formed every administration until 1915. Major dates in the evolution of national party organizations were:

1896 Formation of the Socialist Party (*Parti Sociale Démocrate*).
1904 The *Ligue Liberale* formed, first national organization of the Liberals.
1914 Right-wing (*Parti de la Droite*) established rival national organization.

LUXEMBOURG SOCIALIST WORKERS' PARTY 1902

Orthodox socialist policies.

COMMUNIST PARTY 1921

CHRISTIAN SOCIALIST PARTY 1914

Dominant party in government since its foundation.

306

GREEN ALTERNATIVE PARTY 1983

An environmental party supporting decentralization of power and increased aid to developing states.

MACEDONIA

Among the parties to have emerged since independence are:

INTERNAL MACEDONIAN REVOLUTIONARY ORGANIZATION – DEMOCRATIC PARTY FOR MACEDONIAN NATIONAL UNITY (IMRO–DPMNU)

The main nationalist party, led by Ljučo Georgievski.

PARTY OF DEMOCRATIC PROSPERITY 1990

The predominantly ethnic Albanian and Muslim party.

NATIONAL DEMOCRATIC PARTY 1990

Largely Albanian and Muslim.

SOCIAL DEMOCRATIC ALLIANCE OF MACEDONIA

Founded in 1943 as the League of Communists of Macedonia. Part of the 'Alliance for Macedonia' in the 1994 elections.

Many smaller parties have emerged, mainly on ethnic lines, including those representing Turks, Romanies, etc.

MALTA

NATIONALIST PARTY 1880

Supports the European and Catholic tradition in Malta. Democratic conservative. Pro-Western and pro-EU. The party formerly led by Borg Olivier.

MALTA LABOUR PARTY 1920

Socialist. Foreign policy of non-alignment and security through the United Nations. Opposed to membership of EU. The party formerly led by Dom Mintoff.

PROGRESSIVE CONSTITUTIONAL PARTY 1953

Supported association with EU, close relations with Britain and NATO. The party once led by Mabel Strickland.

MALTA DEMOCRATIC PARTY (PDM) 1985

Supports human rights, environmental protection and decentralization of power.

COMMUNIST PARTY (1969)

Neutralist, Marxist Leninist.

DEMOCRATIC ALTERNATIVE (1989)

A recently founded environmentalist and human rights party.

MOLDOVA

The once dominant Communist Party of Moldova was banned in August 1991. In 1991 the National Alliance for Independence was formed, a coalition of 12 pro-independence parties. These included the Moldovan Democratic Movement, the National Christian Party, the Popular Front of Moldova and the Social Democratic Party. Other current parties include the Yedinstvo Movement (founded 1989, representing ethnic minorities in Moldova), the centrist Social Democratic Party of Moldova (f.1990), the centre-right middle-class Reform Party (f.1993). The Christian Democratic Popular Front and also the Congress of Intelligentsia favour union with Romania. The Agrarian Democratic Party is a moderate party favouring economic and agricultural reform. The successor to the Communist Party of Moldova is the Socialist Party.

THE NETHERLANDS

The main political parties began to develop party organization after the establishment of the Anti-Revolutionary Party in 1879. The main groupings were:

(1) *The Catholic State Party* (after 1897, the Catholic Electoral League). The Catholic State Party subscribed to the ruling and tenets of the Roman Catholic Church as expressed, in religious affairs, in the *Quanta Cura* Encyclical and, in social affairs, in the *Rerum Novarum* Encyc-

308

lical. Including, as it did, Conservatives and Democrats, anti-milita-rists and Labour leaders, it was anything but homogeneous, and was repeatedly threatened with schism.

(2) *The Anti-Revolutionary Party* (ARP). Established in 1879 as a politi-cal organization of orthodox neo-Calvinistic Protestants. Strongly opposed to Liberalism and Socialism, it aims at founding a polity 'based on that traditional national character which the Reformation created and which William the Silent moulded'.

(3) *Christian Historical Union* (*Christelijk-Historische Unie*, CHU). Formed in 1908, from a variety of earlier local groupings; these included the Free Anti-Revolutionaries (founded in 1894), the Christian Histori-cal Electoral Union (founded 1896 and became Christian Historical Party in 1903) and the Friesian Christian Historical Party (originally established in 1898) as a result of the secession from the Anti-Rev-olutionary Party of its anti-democratic elements. The Christian Historicals constituted the more conservative Protestants, approxi-mating on politico-religious questions to the Anti-Revolutionaries and on economic questions to the Liberals. The Union leaned towards Nationalism and Orangism, advocated a strong army and navy, and upheld the rights of the Dutch Reformed Church as the national church.

(4) *The Liberal Union* (Liberale Unie).

(5) *The Radicals*. Merged in 1901 as the Liberal Democratic League (*Urijzinnig-Democratische Bond*).

(6) *The Social Democratic Workers Party*.

(7) *The Free Liberal League* (formed 1891), composed of Conservative dissenters from the Liberal Union.

(8) *The Social Democratic League*.

DEVELOPMENTS AFTER 1900 HAVE INCLUDED:

CATHOLIC PEOPLE'S PARTY (KVP) 1945

Democratic section seceding from the above. Present-day membership open to Protestants.

CHRISTIAN HISTORICAL UNION (CHU) 1908 (see above)

RADICAL POLITICAL PARTY (PPR) 1968

Progressive, pro-environmental, anti-nuclear party. Co-operates with socialist groups.

PEOPLE'S PARTY FOR FREEDOM AND DEMOCRACY (VVD) 1948

Non-denominational. Liberal. Free enterprise and social security within one system.

SOCIAL DEMOCRATIC WORKERS' PARTY

Developed from the previous Socialist Party which it saw as anarchical and non-parliamentary. Moderate left. In 1946 the most active section broke away and formed the Labour Party (*q.v.*).

LABOUR PARTY (PvDA) 1946

A democratic socialist party, it took many members from the Social Democratic Workers Party.

CHRISTIAN DEMOCRATIC APPEAL (CDA) 1980

Formed by the merger of the Anti-Revolutionary Party, the Christian Historical Union, and the Catholic People's Party.

EVANGELICAL POLITICAL FEDERATION (RPF) 1975

A Calvinist party with support from other Christians.

Among recent smaller parties are the Socialist Workers Party (Trotskyist, f.1974), the General Union of the Elderly (AOV), the Liberal Democratic Party (founded 1994 out of Democrats '66), the extreme right-wing Nederlands Blok, founded 1992), the Green Party (f.1983) and the Green Left (f.1991, arising from a merger of the Old Communist Party, the Radical Party etc).

NORWAY

In the second half of the nineteenth century, the main party division lay between the left (the *Venstre*, or Liberals) and the conservative right (the *Höyre*). Generally, the left had the support of the radicals and the peasantry. From 1903 to 1913, the Conservatives fought under the title of *Samlingspartei* (Unionist Party). From 1894, the Norwegian Labour Party (*Norske Arbeiderpartei*) began to capture the working-class vote. By 1912, it was polling over 26% of all votes cast.

Other parties to contest elections were the Free-Thinking Left (*Frisinnide Venstre*) after 1909, the Worker Democrats (after 1906) and the Agrarian League (formed in 1915).

Parties since 1918 have included:

HØYRE 1884 (see above)

Conservative. Aimed at a property-owning democracy, private enterprise.

CENTRE PARTY 1920

Moderate democratic party. Formed as Farmers' Party, name changed in 1959.

CHRISTIAN DEMOCRATIC PARTY 1933

Traditional Christian Democrat Party.

LIBERAL PARTY (VENSTRE) 1884 (see above)

Moderate reform party.

WORKERS' PARTY (ARBEIDERPARTIET) 1887 (see above)

Orthodox evolutionary socialist.

SOCIALIST PEOPLE'S PARTY 1961

Broke away from Workers' Party, being farther to the left. Opposed nuclear weapons and the Atlantic alliance. Neutralist. Merged into the Socialist Left Party in 1975.

SOCIALIST LEFT PARTY 1975

A union of the group which had formed the Socialist Electoral League in 1973 *e.g.* the Socialist People's Party, the Democratic Socialists etc.

PROGRESS PARTY (FP) 1978

Advocates reducing the welfare state, tax and immigration and increasing privatization.

GREEN ENVIRONMENTAL PARTY 1988

An ecological grouping.

Other recent developments include the transformation of the Communist Party which merged with the Red Electoral Alliance in 1989 to become Local Candidates for the Environment and Solidarity.

POLAND

Prior to the communist takeover, the main parties included:

Polish People's Party ⎫
National Christian Club ⎬ The right wing, Catholic, alliance of Church
Christian Democrats ⎭ and State, nationalist, anti-Communist and
anti-Socialist.

PEASANTS' UNION 1924

Aimed for the abolition of the senate and universal franchise for all.

UNION OF POLISH PEASANT PARTIES 1923

Radical, concerned for small farmers and labourers. Aimed for peasant proprietorship.

RADICAL PEASANTS' PARTY 1918

Bolshevik.

NATIONAL LABOUR PARTY 1905

Workers' reform party, nationalist.

POLISH SOCIALIST PARTY 1892

Orthodox socialist, evolutionary reform party.

The main parties under communism were:

POLISH UNITED WORKERS' PARTY 1948

Formed by merging the former Socialist Party and Workers' Party. Communist.

UNITED PEASANTS' PARTY 1949

Formed from merging the Peasant Party and the Polish Peasant Party. Communist, concerned for small farmers and rural workers.

The parties that helped the fall of communism were:

SOLIDARITY CITIZENS' COMMITTEE 1989

The political wing of the Solidarity trade union movement formed to contest elections.

POLISH PEASANT PARTY – SOLIDARITY 1989

The political wing of Solidarity in rural areas, formed to contest elections.

With the collapse of communism, a bewildering number of political parties have emerged (135 had registered by mid-1992). Lech Walesa's supporters were gathered round the Centre Alliance, a christian democratic party. The Polish Peasant Party replaced the United Peasants Party, whilst Social Democracy of the Republic of Poland replaced the Polish United Workers' Party. The power of the former communists was reflected in the success of Aleksander Kwaśniewski in the 1995 presidential elections.

PORTUGAL

MONARCHIST PARTY

Formed to support the claims of former King Manuel or Prince Duarte Nuno.

CATHOLIC PARTY

Conservative.

NATIONALIST PARTY   pre-Salazar

Consevative policy, republican.

REPUBLICAN PARTY

Democratic policy, republican.

POPULAR NATIONAL ACTION

Formerly National Union, the ruling conservative party under the Salazar régime until the revolution.

After the military *coup* of 25 Apr 1974, the following main parties emerged in Portugal.

SOCIAL DEMOCRATIC PARTY (PSD) 1974

Policies similar to major European Social Democratic parties. A partner in the Democratic Alliance.

PORTUGUESE COMMUNIST PARTY (PCP) LEGALIZED 1974

Marxist-Leninist. Ultimate goal of a Socialist Portugal.
Led for many years by Secretary-General Alvaro Cunhal. A partner in the United People's Alliance (*q.v.*).

DEMOCRATIC ALLIANCE (AD) 1979

An alliance of the Social Democratic Party (*q.v.*) and the Centre Democratic Party (*q.v.*) to fight the 1979 elections.

CENTRE DEMOCRATIC PARTY (CDS) 1974

Centrist Party, in Christian Democrat tradition. The party of Professor Freitas Do Amaral. Partner in the Democratic Alliance.

UNITED PEOPLE'S ALLIANCE (APU) 1979

An electoral alliance of two main groupings: the People's Democratic Movement (*q.v.*) and the Portuguese Communist Party (*q.v.*).

PEOPLE'S DEMOCRATIC MOVEMENT

A partner in the United People's Alliance led by Jose Tengarrinha.

SOCIALIST PARTY (PS) 1973

Democratic socialist. Affiliated to Socialist International. A successor to the earlier Portuguese Socialist Action. Led for many years by Dr Mario Soares.

PEOPLE'S MONARCHIST PARTY (PPM) 1974

An anti-nuclear environmentalist party which supports restoration of the monarchy.

DEMOCRATIC RENEWAL PARTY (PRD) 1985

A centre-left party.

An ecological party (The Greens, *Os Verdes*) has had little success. The elderly are represented by the National Solidarity Party (f.1991).

ROMANIA

For political parties and groupings contesting elections prior to 1939, see p. 241. The Romanian Nazis, the Iron Guard, polled well after 1935.

After the Second World War, until the revolution of 1989, Romania was effectively a one-party state dominated by the Romanian Communist Party, technically part of the Socialist Unity Front. Founded in 1921, the party campaigned with others in a People's Democratic Front (PDF) after 1944. Following its union with the Social Democratic Party in 1947, it changed its name to the Romanian Workers' Party. Unsympathetic social democrats and other non-Communists were subsequently excluded from the PDF. The party was led by Nicolae Ceauçescu from 1965 to 1989. The Socialist Labour Party now claims the mantle of the former Communists.

Following the 1989 revolution, provisional power was taken by a 145-strong National Salvation Front which ruled by decree. Political parties were legalized, and in February 1990 the NSF offered to share power with other parties. Presidential and legislative elections were held in May 1990.

Parties since 1989 include:

NATIONAL SALVATION FRONT (NSF) (1989)

The party is a centre-left grouping founded to advance political democratization. The NSF formed a provisional government until the May 1990 elections, in which its presidential candidate, Ion Iliescu, was elected with 85.0% of the vote. The NSF won 263 out of the 387 National Assembly seats.

NATIONAL LIBERAL PARTY (NLP) (1869)

Originally founded in 1869, banned in 1947 and revived in 1989. It advocates privatization of the economy and parliamentary democracy. The NLP won 29 National Assembly seats with 6.4% of the popular vote in the 1990 elections. Its presidential candidate was the runner-up with 10% of the vote.

HUNGARIAN DEMOCRATIC UNION OF ROMANIA (HDUR) (1989)

The party represents the interests of Romania's Hungarian minority population. The HDUR was elected to 29 seats with 7.2% of the vote in the 1990 elections.

SOCIALIST LABOUR PARTY (see above)

CHRISTIAN DEMOCRATIC NATIONAL PEASANTS PARTY (CDNPP) (1990)

Formed in 1990 by a merger of the previously banned National Peasant Party and the Christian Democratic Party. It is a centre-right party supporting parliamentary democracy and a market economy. It took 2.6% of the vote and 12 seats in the 1990 National Assembly elections.

Among other parties are the Romanian Ecological Movement, the Romanian Unity Alliance, the Agrarian Democratic Party (f.1990), the Romanian Ecological Party, and the Socialist Democratic Party of Romania. A monarchist party was formed in 1990. Over 80 political parties have registered to contest elections.

RUSSIA

For the emergence of political parties in Russia prior to the 1917 revolution, see section on elections (pp. 247–8).

During the era of the Soviet Union, from 1917 to 1991, the ruling party was the Communist Party of the Soviet Union (see p. 325). As the decline of the Soviet Union gathered momentum, a large number of non-communist parties emerged in 1988–1991 (the most prominent of which was Democratic Russia) and more were formed following the collapse of Soviet communism in 1991. The early parties included:

DEMOCRATIC PARTY IN RUSSIA

Formed in 1990 by members of the Democratic Platform wing of the CPSU and the Moscow Society of Electors, the party was moderately conservative and advocated a united Russia.

PEOPLE'S PARTY OF FREE RUSSIA

Formed in 1990 as the Democratic Party of Communists of Russia as part of the former CPSU.

PEOPLE'S PARTY OF RUSSIA

A liberal democratic party formed in 1991.

REPUBLICAN PARTY OF THE RUSSIAN FEDERATION

Formed in 1990 from members of the Democratic Platform grouping in the CPSU, the party was committed to a mixed economy and the unity of Russia.

RUSSIAN CHRISTIAN-DEMOCRATIC MOVEMENT

Formed in 1990, the movement advocated the restoration of the monarchy and parliamentary democracy.

Among the many parties formed to contest the 1993 elections, or emerging since, have been the following (of 65 registered parties by 1995):

RUSSIAN COMMUNIST PARTY

A Russian Communist Party was formed in Jun 1990 but was outlawed following the coup. The party was re-legalized in November 1992. It is a left-wing party advocating a change to economic reforms, including more state protection for industry and slower privatization. Led by Gennadi Zyuganov.

RUSSIA'S CHOICE

The main former pro-government, pro-Yeltsin party led by Yegor Gaidar, the architect of the Yeltsin economic reforms. It was committed to reduce state involvement in economic management. Liberal reformist.

MOVEMENT FOR DEMOCRATIC REFORM

Reformist party, led by Mayor of St Petersburg, Anatoly Sobchak.

OUR HOME IS RUSSIA

Centre-right bloc created with President Yeltsin's blessing. Led by Viktor Chernomyrdin. Deeply unpopular.

PARTY OF UNITY AND ACCORD

Reformist. Led by Sergei Shakrai. It would give greater power to the regions.

YABLOKO (APPLE) BLOC

The Yavlinsky-led bloc emphasizes continuation of slower, more considered reforms. Led by Grigori Yavlinsky.

LIBERAL DEMOCRATIC PARTY

Extreme-right, nationalist and anti-Semite. Led by Vladimir Zhirinovsky. Polled well in 1993 elections.

AGRARIAN PARTY

Left-wing and anti-reform. Favours collective and state farms and wants strict controls on private land ownership. Support in rural areas.

CONGRESS OF RUSSIAN COMMUNITIES

Nationalist group which has emerged under popular General Aleksandr Lebed and Yuri Skokov. Lebed went on to form the Russian Popular Republican Party (see next page).

WOMEN OF RUSSIA

Centre-left women's group formed mainly by former Communists. It supports moderate reforms. Led by Alevtina Fedulova.

DERZHAVA

Nationalist party with name meaning Great Power. Led by Aleksandr Rutskoi.

COMMUNISTS OF WORKING RUSSIA

Extreme left Stalinist Party

RUSSIAN POPULAR REPUBLICAN PARTY (f.1996)

Formed in late December 1996 by Aleksandr Lebed as a 'third way' alternative to communism and 'the current democratic elite'.

Centre parties include the Civic Union, the Democratic Party of Russia and the 'Future of Russia'. The green movement is represented by Kedr (Cedar) (the Constructive Ecological Movement). The Russian Christian Democratic Movement (f.1990) favours the restoration of the Monarchy.

SLOVAKIA

Since the independence of Slovakia, political parties have begun to take a distinct shape. The old Communist Party of Slovakia was replaced in 1991 by the Party of the Democratic Left. The Social Democratic Party of Slovakia was re-established in 1990. The Democratic Union of Slovakia was formed in 1994 by members of the Movement for a Democratic Slovakia (f.1991) and in 1995 it absorbed the National Democratic Party – New Alternative. Separate parties represent ethnic Hungarian interests (such as Coexistence, Hungarian Christian Democratic Movement, etc.).

SLOVENIA

Political parties in independent Slovenia have been subject to rapid change. The former League of Communists of Slovenia changed its name to become the Party of Democratic Reform in 1990. The Socialist Party of Slovenia is the successor to the former communist Socialist Alliance of Slovenia. The Liberal Democratic Party, a centre-left group, emerged from the former Union of Socialist Youth. Until its dissolution in December 1991 the Democratic Opposition of Slovenia (DEMOS) was an electoral alliance which included the Democratic Party of Slovenia (the first opposition party to the communists), the Greens of Slovenia, the Liberal Party, Christian Democrats, etc. The Associated List of Social Democrats became a single party in 1993. Liberal Democracy of Slovenia emerged in 1994.

SPAIN

Prior to the Franco régime, the historic parties included:

CONSTITUTIONAL LIBERAL PARTY 1875

Advocated religious toleration, a bicameral system of government, a constitutional monarchy and universal suffrage. Split into left and right factions in 1903.

REFORMIST PARTY 1913

Sovereignty to be vested in the people. Foreign policy of friendship with neighbouring states.

PATRIOTIC UNIONISTS 1924

'Religion, country, monarchy' – party formed and inspired by the Military Directory.

In the Franco régime, there was only one political party, the National Movement. Its adherents were better known as Falangists.

In the post-Franco era, a large number of political parties, both national and regional, emerged. By the mid-1990s over 1000 political parties were registered. They include:

POPULAR ALLIANCE (AP) 1976

Centrist party. Part of the Democratic Coalition (CD).

COMMUNIST PARTY OF SPAIN (PCE) 1922

A Euro-Communist party. Absorbed PCOE in 1986.

SOCIALIST PARTY (PSOE) 1879

Democratic Socialist. Affiliated to the Socialist International. A splinter group formed Democracia Socialista in 1989.

CENTRE DEMOCRATIC UNION (UCD) 1977

A coalition of several centre parties to fight elections.

DEMOCRATIC AND SOCIAL CENTRE (CDS) 1982

A centre-left party.

NATIONAL FRONT (FN) 1986

Extreme right-wing party.

POPULAR PARTY (PP) 1989

Formerly the Popular Alliance (AP).

GREEN PARTY (1984)

Los Verdes is anti-military, anti nuclear energy.

SWEDEN

In the late nineteenth century, the main party divisions in Sweden re-volved round the tariff question – the Free Traders, (*Frihardelssinade*) against the Protectionist Right (*Protektionistiska Hôgermân*). The Swed-ish Social Democratic Party was originally formed in 1880 . By 1914, it had secured 36% of all votes cast. During the First World War, other parties to begin contesting elections were the Agrarian Party, (*Bonde-fôrbundet*), the Farmers Union and the Left Socialists. The Left Socialists provided the core of the Swedish Communist Party (established in 1921).

SOCIAL DEMOCRATIC LABOUR PARTY 1880 (SEE ABOVE)

Socialist party, economical reform policy, supports United Nations. Except for 1976–1982, it has been in office or in coalition almost continuously.

PEOPLE'S PARTY 1902

Liberal. Advocates traditional liberal policies and a free-market economy.

MODERATE UNION PARTY 1904

Conservative, free enterprise and private property.

LEFT PARTY 1990

Formed as the Left Social Democratic Party of Sweden in 1917, renamed the Communist Party in 1921. Changed its name to the Communist Party of the Left in 1967. Current name, Left Party (Vänsterpartiet), adopted in 1990.

CENTRE PARTY 1922

Formed from a coalition of two smaller moderate parties. Developed more progressive social policies. Strongly opposed to nuclear power.

CHRISTIAN DEMOCRATIC UNION 1964

Orthodox Christian-Democrat policies.

SWEDISH WORKERS' COMMUNIST PARTY 1977

A breakaway group from the Communist Left Group (VPK), which it regarded as too Euro-Communist.

GREEN ECOLOGY PARTY (MpG) 1981

An environmental party. Relatively small membership (8000).

NEW DEMOCRACY 1991

A right-wing populist party.

SWITZERLAND

In the last decade of the nineteenth century, the present divisions in Swiss party politics began to appear. Hitherto, Swiss parties had been almost exclusively cantonal affairs.

The first organized group was the Social Democratic Party (founded in 1888). The old left wing formed the Radical Democratic Party in 1894, whilst the right came together the same year as the Popular Catholic Party.

RADICAL DEMOCRATIC PARTY 1894

Led the movement towards the confederation of 1848. Liberal policies, supports strong central, federal power.

CHRISTIAN DEMOCRATIC PEOPLE'S PARTY OF SWITZERLAND 1912

Formed by parties which had opposed centralization since 1848. Joined also by the Kulturkampf of the Radical Majority Party. Non-sectarian Christian; the most numerous parliamentary group in the Council of States.

SOCIAL DEMOCRATIC PARTY OF SWITZERLAND 1888

Socialist. Its influence dates mainly from the first proportional representation in 1919.

FARMERS', ARTISANS' AND CITIZENS' PARTY 1919

Seceded from the Radical Democrats. Mainly agrarian concerns, liberal social policies. Merged into Swiss People's Party, 1971.

LABOUR PARTY 1944

Communist and left-wing socialist; aims to co-ordinate all left-wing influences.

SWISS PEOPLE'S PARTY 1971

A union of the Democratic Party and the Farmers', Artisans' and Citizens' Party.

REPUBLICAN MOVEMENT 1917

Founded to maintain Swiss independence. Opposed to UN or EU entry.

INDEPENDENT PARTY 1936

An opposition party, liberal in social policies.

LIBERAL PARTY 1977

A party which opposes moves towards centralization.

GREEN PARTY OF SWITZERLAND 1983

An environmental party.

AUTOMOBILE PARTY 1985

Founded to support motorists rights.

TURKEY

Political parties were late to develop in Turkey and have always had a precarious, shifting existence. No political parties had emerged in time to contest the elections of 1876 or 1877. Under the despotism of Abdul Hamid, a number of illegal opposition groups were formed. Easily the most important was the Committee of Union and Progress. This party dominated the parliaments of the second constitutional period (1908–1920). Only one other party, the Liberals (Ahrar) contested the 1908 elections. The Liberals stood only in Istanbul; all were defeated. After 1913, the Committee of Union and Progress established a virtual dictatorship. In the May 1914 elections, the Committee was the only party to fight. It remained the only party until the 1918 armistice. It dissolved itself at its last party Congress on 14–19 Oct 1918.

Prior to 1980 (when the National Security Council banned all political parties), some of the more important parties had been:

REPUBLICAN PEOPLE'S PARTY 1923

Founded by Kemal Atatürk. Left of centre, favoured a combination of state and private enterprise. The party once led by Bulent Ecevit.

PROGRESSIVE REPUBLICANS 1924

Liberal policies, free trade programmes. Dissolved for 'being in league with reactionary groups'.

JUSTICE PARTY 1961

Private enterprise party. The party once led by Süleyman Demirel.

NATIONAL SALVATION PARTY 1972

Right-wing Islamic. The replacement party for the National Order Party (*q.v.*).

RELIANCE PARTY 1967

Broke away from the Republican People's Party. Belief in political democracy. Policies left of centre. Merged 1973 with the Republican Party.

NATIONAL ORDER PARTY 1969

Extreme right-wing, aimed for the abolition of the Senate. Dissolved 1971, but resurrected 1979.

TURKISH SOCIALIST WORKERS' PARTY 1974

Left-wing socialist. Supported nationalization, withdrawal from NATO.

Note: Political parties were allowed to reform from May 1983. They have included:

MOTHERLAND PARTY (ANAP) 1983

Advocated a market economy, support for the European Union and closer relations with the Islamic world. Merged in 1986 with the Free Democratic Party.

TRUE PATH PARTY (DYP) 1983

A centre-right party which replaced the Justice Party (*q.v..*) The party of Tansu Çiller.

SOCIAL DEMOCRATIC POPULIST PARTY (SDP) 1985

A centre-left party formed by the merger of the Populist Party and the Social Democratic Party. Merged with Republican People's Party in 1995.

DEMOCRATIC LEFT PARTY (DSP) 1985

Centre-left party supported by former members of the Republican People's Party.

REPUBLICAN PEOPLE'S PARTY (CHP)

The old CHP, dissolved in 1981, was reorganized in 1992. Merged with Social Democratic Populist Party in 1995.

NATIONALIST MOVEMENT PARTY (MCP)

Founded in 1983 from the old Conservative Party.

REFAH (WELFARE PARTY)

The Islamic fundamentalist party founded in 1983. Supports closer Islamic ties with its neighbours, opposed to EU entry. Gained electoral successes in mid-1990s.

NEW DEMOCRACY MOVEMENT (YDH)

Founded 1994 to support a political solution to Kurdish conflict and greater emphasis on human rights.

UKRAINE

During the period prior to the collapse of the Soviet Union, the only legal political party was the Communist Party of the Ukraine. Its monopoly of power was abolished in 1990 and it was banned after the August

1991 coup attempt. Earlier, the nationalist movement Rukh (the People's Movement for Restructuring) was formed in 1988 and in 1993 it became a fully-fledged political party (People's Movement of Ukraine). Over 30 other political parties have registered, from the far-right National Fascist Party to the extreme left socialist Party of Ukraine. The old Communist Party was allowed to contest the 1994 elections and went on to dominate the polls, with the Rukh second but a long way behind.

USSR

From 1917 to 1991 the ruling party was the Communist Party of the Soviet Union. The Russian Social Democratic Labour Party was founded in 1898. Lenin's Bolsheviks broke away in 1903 becoming a separate party in 1912. The Bolsheviks seized power during the Oct 1917 Revolution. The Bolsheviks became the Russian Communist Party in 1917, the All-Union Communist Party of Bolsheviks in 1925 and the Communist Party of the Soviet Union in 1952. The CPSU's last general secretary, Mikhael Gorbachev, resigned from the party following the abortive August 1991 coup mounted by party conservatives. See also p. 316.

UNITED KINGDOM

Prior to 1900, British politics was dominated by two parties: Conservative and Liberal. The Labour Party emerged after 1900. A strong Irish Nationalist Party was influential at Westminster.

CONSERVATIVE AND UNIONIST PARTY 1886

Formed by merger of the original Tory Party, renamed Conservative, with Liberals who did not accept Home Rule for Ireland. Policy imperialist and protectionist. Current policy free enterprise, EU membership, and strongly for privatization. Increasingly right-wing and Euro-sceptic.

LABOUR PARTY 1900

Formed as a federation of trades unions and similar organizations. Socialist economic and social policies, support for UN in foreign relations, formerly opposed EC membership. Modernization began under leadership of Neil Kinnock and John Smith. Currently (under Tony Blair) has become a centrist party, distancing itself from trade unions and socialism.

LIBERAL PARTY 1832

Formed from amalgamation of the old Whig Party, the Radical Party and the Reformers. Originally aimed at free trade, Home Rule for Ireland, reform of the House of Lords and moderate social reform and land reform. Supported the League of Nations and later the United Nations. Supported entry into EC. Fought 1983 election in alliance with Social Democratic Party (*q.v.*). Now the Social and Liberal Democratic Party.

SOCIAL DEMOCRATIC PARTY 1981

Launched 26 Mar 1981 by Labour moderates opposed to left-wing movement in the Labour Party. Its four leading figures were Roy Jenkins, David Owen, William Rodgers and Shirley Williams. It merged in 1988 with the Liberal Party to form the Social and Liberal Democrats (*q.v.*).

CO-OPERATIVE PARTY 1917

Sponsored Labour and Co-operative candidates through a formal agreement of 1926, in which Co-operative parties became eligible for affiliation to Labour parties, and a further agreement of 1946 whereby Co-operative candidates were to run as Co-operative and Labour candidates.

INDEPENDENT LABOUR PARTY 1893

Originally affiliated to the Labour Party until policy differences grew and the parties split in 1932. Its members gradually returned to the Labour Party after 1946.

WELSH NATIONALIST PARTY (PLAID CYMRU) 1925

Campaigns for greater independence for Wales.

SCOTTISH NATIONAL PARTY 1928

Formed as the National Party of Scotland. Merged with the Scottish Party in 1933. Campaigns for independence for Scotland.

COMMUNIST PARTY OF GREAT BRITAIN 1920

Not represented in Parliament since 1950. After adjusting to the fall of communism in Eastern Europe has become Democratic Left.

ECOLOGY PARTY 1973

The environmentalist party. Now the Green Party (since 1985) (*q.v.*).

326

NATIONAL FRONT 1974

A nationalist, anti-immigration extreme right grouping.

SOCIAL AND LIBERAL DEMOCRATS (LIBERAL DEMOCRATS) 1988

Formed by the merger of the Liberal Party and the Social Democratic Party.

GREEN PARTY 1985

Formerly the Ecology Party. It has no representation in Parliament, but secured more votes than the Liberal Democrats in the 1989 European Elections, but its membership and influence has since declined.

REFERENDUM PARTY

Campaigned on single issue of a referendum on the EU. Led by Sir James Goldsmith.

SOCIALIST LABOUR PARTY 1996

Left-wing socialist party led by Arthur Scargill.

UK INDEPENDENCE PARTY

An anti federalist anti-EU grouping led by an LSE academic, Alan Sked.

YUGOSLAVIA

National Radical Party	– monarchist, centralist and nationalist	
Slovenian People's Party	– anti-centralist, demanding autonomy for different groups	
National Democratic Party	– split from the Radicals, centralists but ready to grant autonomy as a concession in some cases	pre-1945
Peasants' Party	– originally republican, by 1925 veering towards monarchy: supported co-operatives and agrarian reform	

LEAGUE OF COMMUNISTS OF YUGOSLAVIA

The only effective party until 1989.

After 1989, over 250 parties emerged. Among early groups were:

ASSOCIATION FOR A YUGOSLAV DEMOCRATIC INITIATIVE 1989

Formed as a national opposition party to the League of Communists of Yugoslavia.

RADICAL PARTY 1881, RE-ESTABLISHED 1990

Advocated retaining federal control over the economy, defence, foreign policy and security.

SOCIAL DEMOCRATIC ALLIANCE OF YUGOSLAVIA 1990

Supported preserving the Yugoslav federation with greater equality.

WORKERS' PARTY OF YUGOSLAVIA 1990

Advocated retaining the federal system, but stressed Serbian interests.

YUGOSLAV DEMOCRATIC PARTY 1990

Supported the federal system, but with election of a single national president in free elections.

YUGOSLAV GREEN PARTY 1990

An environmental party which was open to all nationalities and creeds in the state.

With the disintegration of Yugoslavia, 'rump' Yugoslavia (*i.e.* Serbia and Montenegro) has seen the former dominant League of Communists become the Socialist Party of Serbia. The People's Assembly Party (f.1992 as the Democratic Movement of Serbia) is a multi-party coalition. The Democratic Party is a nationalist party, the Serbian Radical party is an extreme nationalist party advocating a 'Greater Serbia'.

7 JUSTICE

ALBANIA

Prior to 1992, under the Communist regime, there was a revised Penal Code in Oct 1977 followed by a Labour Code and a Code of Penal Procedure in 1980, a Civil Code with a Code of Civil Procedure in 1982 and a Family Code in 1982. Justice was administered by the People's Courts and minor crimes were tried by tribunals. Judges of the Supreme Court were elected by the People's Assembly for 4-year terms.

In 1992 a Constitutional Court, a High Court of Appeal and Regional Courts of Justice were instituted and a new Criminal Code and Code of Procedure in 1995. The administration of justice is presided over by the Council of Justice, chaired by the President of the Republic. An Investigator's Office was established in 1983 separate from the Ministry of the Interior and was answerable to the People's Assembly and is now (1996) an independent body. A Ministry of Justice was re-established in 1990 and a Bar Council set up. In Nov 1993 the number of capital offences was reduced from 13 to 6 and the death penalty for women was abolished.

ANDORRA

Judicial power is exercised in civil matters in the first instance, according to the plaintiff's choice, by either the *Bayle Français* or the *Bayle Episcopal*, nominated by the respective co-princes. The judge of appeal is nominated alternately for 5 years by each co-prince; the third instance is the Supreme Court at Perpignan or the supreme court of the Bishop at Urgel.

Criminal justice is administered by the *Corts* consisting of the judge of appeal, 2 *rahonadors* elected by the General Council of the Valleys, a general attorney and an attorney nominated for 5 years alternately by each of the co-princes. Under the new democratic constitution of 1993 the co-princes are made a single constitutional monarch, and Andorra has the right to establish an independent judicial system.

AUSTRIA

The Austrian legal system provides for 3 supreme courts, all of them located in Vienna: the Constitutional Court (*Verfassungsgerichtshof*), the Administrative Court (*Verwaltungsgerichtshof*) and the Supreme Court (*Oberster Gerichtshof*), the latter being the highest court for all judicial matters.

At the next level below the Supreme Court 4 High State Courts (*Oberlandesgerichte*) are instituted which have merely appellate competence. Beneath them 16 State Courts of Justice (*Landes- und Kreisgerichte*) are competent for civil and criminal justice both in first instance for major cases and as courts of appeal for those petty matters for which, at the lowest level, 187 District Courts (*Bezirksgerichte*) are installed as courts of first instance, again in civil and penal matters. With the exception of the District Courts, all courts of justice with competence for penal matters have an office of the public prosecution at their side.

AUSTRIA-HUNGARY

In Austria the ordinary judicial authorities were: (i) The Supreme Court of Justice and Court of Cassation (*Oberste Gerichts-und Kassationshof*) in Vienna. (ii) The higher provincial courts (*Oberlandesgerichte*). (iii) The provincial and district courts (*Landes-und Kreisgerichte*), and, in connection with these, the jury courts (*Geschworenengerichte*). (iv) The county courts (*Bezirksgerichte*). Of these, the third and fourth groups were courts of first instance; the second group consisted of courts of second instance. Courts of first instance acted as courts of inquiry and had summary jurisdiction. Courts of second instance were courts of appeal from the lower courts, and had the supervision of the criminal courts in their jurisdiction. The jury courts tried certain cases where severe penalties were involved, political offences, and press offences. The county courts exercised criminal jurisdiction in the counties and co-operated in preliminary proceedings regarding crime. There existed also special courts for commercial, revenue, military, shipping and other matters.

In case of conflict between different authorities the Imperial Court (*Reichsgerichte*) in Vienna had power to decide. Private persons could in certain cases appeal against the decisions of magistrates to the High Court for Administrative Affairs.

For Hungary with Fiume the judicial authorities were: [The Royal] Court (*Kuria*) in Budapest, and the Supreme Court of Justice in Zagreb, of the highest instance in all civil and criminal matters.

BELGIUM

Judges are appointed for life. There is a court of cassation, 5 courts of appeal, and assize courts for political and criminal cases. There are 27 judicial districts, each with a court of first instance. In each of the 222 cantons is a justice and judge of the peace. There are, besides, various special tribunals. There is trial by jury in assize courts. The death penalty, which had been in abeyance for 45 years, was formally abolished in 1991. The Gendarmerie ceased to be part of the army in Jan 1992.

BULGARIA

The Constitution of 1947 provided for the election (and recall) of the judges by the people and, for the Supreme Court, by the National Assembly, but in 1982 this was amended so that all judges are elected and recalled by the National Assembly. The lower courts include laymen ('assessors') as well as jurists. There are a Supreme Court, 28 provincial (including Sofia) courts and 105 (formerly 103) people's courts.

In Jun 1961, 'Comrades' Courts' were set up for the trial of minor offenders by their fellow-workers. The maximum term of imprisonment is 20 (formerly 15) years. 'Exceptionally dangerous crimes' carry the death penalty.

From 1992 the Prosecutor-General is elected by the Supreme Judicial Council.

CYPRUS

The administration of justice is exercised by a separate and independent judiciary. There is a Supreme Court of the Republic, the Assize Courts and the District Courts.

The Supreme Court is composed of 13 judges, one of whom is the President of the Court. The Supreme Court adjudicates exclusively and finally (a) on all constitutional and administrative law matters, including any recourses that any law or decision of the House of Representatives, or the budget, is discriminatory against either of the two communities; (b) on any conflict of competence between state organs in the republic; (c) questions of the unconstitutionality of any law, or on any question of interpretation of the constitution in case of ambiguity; and (d) on recourses for annulment of administrative acts, decisions or omissions.

All judicial power in civil and criminal matters is also exercised by the Supreme Court and its subordinate Courts. The Supreme Court is the highest appellate Court in the republic and has jurisdiction to hear and determine all appeals from any Court.

There are six Assize Courts and six District Courts, one for each district. The Assize Courts have unlimited criminal jurisdiction and power to order compensation up to £C3000. The District Courts exercise original civil and criminal jurisdiction, the extent of which varies with the composition of the Bench.

There is a Supreme Council of Judicature, consisting of the President and Judges of the Supreme Court entrusted with the appointment, promotion, transfers, termination of appointment and disciplinary control over all judicial officers, other than Judges of the Supreme Court.

The Attorney-General is head of the independent Law Office and legal adviser to the President and his Ministers.

CZECHOSLOVAKIA

The criminal and criminal procedure codes dated from 1 Jan 1962, as amended in Apr 1973. There was a Federal Supreme Court and federal military courts, with judges elected by the Federal Assembly. Both republics had Supreme Courts and a network of regional and district courts whose professional judges were elected by the republican National Councils. Lay judges were elected by regional or district local authorities. Local authorities and social organizations could participate in the decision-making of the courts.

CZECH REPUBLIC

The post-Communist judicial system became law in Jul 1991. This provides for 4 types of courts: civil, criminal, commercial and administrative. Commercial courts arbitrate in disputes arising from business activities. Administrative courts examine the legality of the decisions of state institutions when appealed by citizens. In addition, there are military courts which operate under the jurisdiction of the Ministry of Defence. There is a Supreme Court, and a hierarchy of courts under the Ministry of Justice at republic, region, and district level. District courts are courts of first instance. Cases are usually decided by senates comprising a judge and 2 associate judges, though occasionally by a single judge. (Associate judges are citizens in good standing over the age of 25 who are elected for 4-year terms.) Regional courts are courts of first instance in more serious cases and also courts of appeal for district courts. Cases are usually decided by a senate of 2 judges and 3 associate judges, although again occasionally by a single judge. There is also a Supreme Administrative Court. The Supreme Court interprets law as a guide to other courts and functions also as a court of appeal.

Judges are appointed for life by the National Council. The death penalty has been abolished.

DENMARK

The lowest courts of justice are organized in 82 tribunals (*byretter*), where minor cases are dealt with by a single judge. The tribunals at Copenhagen have 40 judges and Aarhus 15 and the other tribunals have 1 to 10. Cases of greater consequence are dealt with by the 2 superior courts (*Landsretterne*); these courts are also courts of appeal for the above-named minor cases. Of superior courts there are two: *Østre Landsret* in Copenhagen with 48 judges. *Vestre Landsret* in Viborg with 32 judges. From these an appeal lies to the Supreme Court (*Højesteret*) in Copenhagen, composed of 17 judges. Judges under 65 years of age can be removed only by judicial sentence.

ESTONIA

A post-Communist criminal code was introduced in 1992. The death penalty is retained for murder and terrorism. There is a 3-tier court system with the State Court and both city and district courts. The latter act as courts of appeal. The State Court is the final court of appeal, and also functions as a constitutional court. There are also administrative courts for petty offences. Judges are appointed for life. City and district judges are appointed by the President; State Court judges are elected by Parliament.

EUROPEAN UNION

The Court of Justice comprises 15 judges assisted by 9 advocates-general. A Court of First Instance also comprising 15 judges was set up in 1989. The members of these Courts, which sit in Luxembourg, are appointed for 6 years by agreement between the governments of the Member States. Their independence is guaranteed.

The Court's role is to ensure that the European Treaties are interpreted and applied in accordance with the law. The Court can find that a Member State has failed to fulfil an obligation under the Treaties. If the Member State does not comply with the judgment, the Court may impose a lump-sum or penalty payment on it. The Court reviews the legality of measures taken by the institutions in actions brought to have such measures set aside, and it has power to judge that they are in breach of the Treaties for failing to act.

The Court also gives preliminary rulings, on application by a national court, on the interpretation or validity of points of Community law. If a legal action produces a disputed point of this kind, a national court may seek a ruling from the European Court; it *must* do so if there is no higher court of appeal in the Member State concerned, in which case the judgment of the Court is binding.

The Court of First Instance deals with actions brought by individuals and businesses; appeals on points of law are only dealt with by the Court of Justice.

Between 1952 and 1994 more than 8600 actions were brought before the Court, including 2900 references for preliminary rulings.

FINLAND

The lowest court of justice is the District Court. In most civil cases a District Court has a quorum with 3 legally-qualified members present. In criminal cases as well as in some cases related to family law the District Court has a quorum with a chair and 3 lay judges present. In the preliminary preparation of a civil case and in a criminal case concerning a minor offence a District Court is composed of the chair only. From the District Court an appeal lies to the courts of appeal (*Hovioikeus*) in Turku, Vaasa, Kuopio, Helsinki, Kouvola and Rovaniemi. The Supreme Court (*Korkein oikeus*) sits in Helsinki. Appeals from the decisions of administrative authorities are in the final instance decided by the Supreme Administrative Court (*Korkein hallintooikeus*), also in Helsinki. Judges can be removed only by judicial sentence.

Two functionaries, the *Oikeuskansleri* or Chancellor of Justice, and the *Oikeusasiamies* (ombudsman), or Solicitor-General, exercise control over the administration of justice. The former acts also as counsel and public prosecutor for the Government; while the latter, who is appointed by the Parliament, exerts a general control over all courts of law and public administration.

FRANCE

The system of justice is divided into 2 jurisdictions: the judicial, and the administrative.

334

Within the judicial jurisdiction are common law courts including 473 lower courts (*tribunaux d'instance*, including 11 in overseas departments), 186 higher courts (*tribunaux de grande instance*, including 5 *tribunaux de première instance* in the overseas territories), 454 police courts (*tribunaux de police*, including 11 in overseas departments).

The *tribunaux d'instance* are presided over by a single judge. The *tribunaux de grande instance* usually have a collegiate composition, although they may be presided over by a single judge in some civil cases. The police courts, presided over by a judge on duty in the *tribunal d'instance*, deal with petty offences (*contraventions*); correctional chambers (*chambres correctionelles*, of which there is at least one in each *tribunal de grande instance*) deal with graver offences (*délits*), including cases involving imprisonment up to 5 years. Correctional chambers consist of 3 judges of a *tribunal de grande instance* (a single judge in some cases). Sometimes in cases of *délit*, and in all cases of more serious *crimes*, a preliminary inquiry is made in secrecy by one of 569 examining magistrates (*juges d'instruction*), who either dismisses the case or sends it for trial before a public prosecutor.

Still within the judicial jurisdiction are various specialized courts, including 227 commercial courts (*tribunaux de commerce*), composed of tradesmen and manufacturers elected for 2 years initially and then for 4 years; 271 conciliation boards (*conseils de prud'hommes*), composed of an equal number of employers and employees elected for 5 years to deal with labour disputes; 437 courts for settling rural landholding disputes (*tribunaux paritaires des baux ruraux,* including 11 in overseas departments); and 110 social security courts (*tribunaux des affaires de sécurité sociale*).

When the decisions of any of these courts are susceptible of appeal, the case goes to one of the 35 courts of appeal (*cours d'appel*) each composed of a president and a variable number of members. There are 102 courts of assize (*cours d'assises*), each composed of a president who is a member of the court of appeal, and 2 other magistrates, and assisted by a lay jury of 9 members. These try crimes involving imprisonment of over 5 years. The decisions of the courts of appeal and the courts of assize are final. However, the Court of Cassation (*Cour de cassation*) has discretion to verify if the law has been correctly interpreted and if the rules of procedure have been followed exactly. The Court of Cassation may annul any judgment, following which the cases must be retried by a court of appeal or a court of assizes.

The administrative jurisdiction exists to resolve conflicts arising between citizens and central and local government authorities. It consists of 33 administrative courts (*tribunaux administratifs*, including 7 in overseas departments and territories) and 7 administrative courts of appeal (*cours administratives d'appel*). The Council of State is the final court of appeal in administrative cases, though it may also act as a court of first instance.

Cases of doubt as to whether the judicial or administrative jurisdiction is competent in any case are resolved by a *Tribunal de conflits* composed in equal measure of members of the Court of Cassation and the Council of State.

On 24 Jan 1973 the first Ombudsman (*médiateur*) was appointed for a 6-year period.

Capital punishment was abolished in Aug 1981, and a revised penal code came into force on 1 Mar 1994, replacing the *Code Napoléon* of 1810.

Penal institutions consist of: (1) *maisons d'arrêt*, where persons awaiting trial as well as those condemned to short periods of imprisonment are kept; (2) punishment institutions – (a) central prisons (*maisons centrales*) for those sentenced to long imprisonment, and (b) detention centres for offenders showing promise of rehabilitation; (3) hospitals for the sick. Special attention is being paid to classified treatment and the rehabilitation and vocational re-education of prisoners including work in open-air and semi-free establishments. There are 3 penal institutions for women.

Juvenile delinquents go before special judges in 137 (11 in overseas departments and territories) juvenile courts (*tribunaux pour enfants*); they are sent to public or private institutions of supervision and re-education.

GERMANY

A uniform system of law courts existed throughout Germany, though, with the exception of the *Reichsgericht*, all courts were directly subject to the State in which they exercised jurisdiction, and not to the central Government.

After Apr 1935 all courts became organs of central Government. The Nazi concept of justice was defined as 'Right is that which is useful to the nation.'

The lowest courts of first instance were the *Amtsgerichte*, competent to try petty civil and criminal cases, with the exception of capital cases which fell within the jurisdiction of the Court of Assizes, or the *Reichsgericht*. Cases relating to property in which the amount involved did not exceed 500 marks were usually tried by a single judge. In the trial of more serious criminal cases the judge was assisted by two assessors (laymen), to whom on the request of the public prosecutor a professional magistrate might further be added (*Schoffengericht*). The

Amtsgerichte dealt also with guardianships, estates and official records. The *Landgerichte* contained both civil and criminal chambers. The former, consisting of three judges, were competent to deal in first instance with all civil cases in as far as they had not been referred to the *Amtsgerichte*, especially with divorces, and also exercised a revisory jurisdiction over the *Amtsgerichte*. For trying commercial cases there were further commercial chambers, consisting of one judge and two laymen. The criminal chamber heard appeals from the *Amtsgerichte* in criminal cases; if the appeal was from the decision of a single magistrate it was heard by one judge with two lay assessors (small chamber); if from a decision of the *Schoffengericht*, by three judges and two laymen (large chamber). For the trial of capital cases, the *Landgerichte* were transformed into *Schwurgerichte*, consisting of three judges and six laymen. The *Amtsgerichte* and *Landgerichte* had as superior court the *Oberlandesgerichte*. There were twenty-seven such courts in Germany. The *Oberlandesgerichte* contained criminal and civil senates consisting of three judges. They exercised appellate jurisdiction over the *Landgerichte* in civil cases, and over the 'small chambers' (and in some cases over the 'large chambers') in criminal cases. The supreme court was the *Reichsgericht*, which sat at Leipzig. This court exercised an appellate jurisdiction over all inferior courts, and also an original and final jurisdiction in cases of treason.

A law promulgated in Jul 1935 established the novel principle in criminal law that the courts should punish offences not punishable under the Criminal Code if they were deserving of punishment 'according to the underlying idea of a penal code or according to healthy public sentiment'.

Special courts existed for all civil disputes arising from the relationship between employers and employed. Qualified judges were appointed to these judicial bodies and they were attended by representatives of employers and employed.

There were 206 Sterilization Courts, composed of 1 judge and 2 medical men, in 1934, and 56 344 persons were sterilized.

FEDERAL REPUBLIC OF GERMANY

Justice is administered by the Federal Courts and by the courts of the Länder. In criminal procedures, civil cases and procedures of non-contentious jurisdiction the courts on the Land level are the local courts (*Amtsgerichte*), the regional courts (*Landgerichte*) and the courts of appeal (*Oberlandesgerichte*). On the Federal level decisions regarding these matters are taken by the Federal Constitutional Court (*Bundesverfassungsgericht*) elected by the Bundestag and Bundesrat. The Länder also have constitutional courts. In labour law disputes the courts of the first and second instance are the labour courts and the Land labour courts and in the third instance, the Federal Labour Court (*Bundesarbeitgericht*). Disputes about public law in matters of social security, unemployment insurance, maintenance of war victims and similar cases are dealt with in the first and second instances by the social courts and the Land social courts and in the third instance by the Federal Social Court (*Bundessozialgericht*). In most tax matters the finance courts of the Länder are competent and in the second instance, the Federal Finance Court (*Bundesfinanzhof*). Other controversies of public law in non-constitutional matters are decided in the first and second instance by the administrative and the higher administrative courts (*Oberverwaltungsgerichte*) of the Länder, and in the third instance by the Federal Administrative Court (*Bundesverwaltungsgericht*).

For inquiry into maritime accidents the admiralty courts (*Seeämter*) are competent on the Land level and in the second instance the Federal Admiralty Court (*Bundesoberseeamt*).

The death sentence has been abolished.

Under the Unification Treaty signed 31 Aug 1990, the Basic Law of the Federal Republic of Germany was applied to the 5 new Länder of Brandenburg, Mecklenburg-Western Pomerania, Saxony, Saxony-Anhalt and Thuringia.

GERMAN DEMOCRATIC REPUBLIC

The judicial system of the German Democratic Republic was instituted following World War II. The principles on which the judicial system functioned were embodied in the constitution. Judges were elected by the people's representative bodies or by the citizens directly. State Prosecuting Counsels were nominated by the Prosecutor-General. Jurisdiction was exercised by the Supreme Court, by the *Bezirke* Courts and by the *Kreis* Courts. All courts decided on the appointment of one presiding and two assistant magistrates. The Assistant Magistrates in the First instance were jurors (lay magistrates from all classes of society); the Labour Law Tribunal of the Supreme Court appointed two official judges and three lay magistrates.

Judges were independent and subject only to the constitution and the Legislature. A Judge could be recalled only if he had committed a breach of the law, grossly neglected his duties or been convicted by a court.

Lay magistrates were elected for a period of four years after nomination by the democratic parties and organizations. Magistrates of the *Kreis* Courts were directly elected by the people; Magistrates of the *Bezirke* Courts, by the *Bezirkstag*; Magistrates of the Labour Law Tribunal of the Supreme Court, by the *Volkshammer*. All were equally authorized Judges.

Attached to the *Volkshammer* was a Constitutional and Legislature Commission in which all parties were represented according to their numbers. In addition there were on the Commission three members of the Supreme Court as well as three State Law Teachers who might not be members of the *Volkshammer*. All members of the Constitutional and Legislature Commission were appointed by the *Volkshammer*.

On 14 Jan 1968 the whole judicial and penal system was reformed; the most important reform being the introduction of a new criminal code to replace the German Criminal Code of 1871.

GIBRALTAR

The judicial system is based on the English system. There is a Court of Appeal, a Supreme Court presided over by the Chief Justice, a court of first instance, a magistrates' court, a coroner's court and a juvenile court.

GREECE

Under the 1975 Constitution, judges are appointed for life by the President of the Republic, after consultation with the judicial council. Judges enjoy personal and functional independence. There are three divisions of the courts – administrative, civil and criminal – and they must not give decisions which are contrary to the Constitution. Final jurisdiction lies with a Special Supreme Tribunal. Some laws, passed before the 1975 Constitution came into force, and which are not contrary to it, remain in force.

HUNGARY

The administration of justice is the responsibility of the Procurator-General, who is elected by parliament for a term of six years. There were (1996) 105 local courts, 20 labour law courts, 20 county courts, 6 district courts and a Supreme Court. Criminal proceedings are dealt with by district courts through three-member councils and by county courts and the Supreme Court in five-member councils. A new Civil Code was adopted in 1978 and a new Criminal Code in 1979.

Regional courts act only as courts of first instance; county courts as either courts of first instance or of appeal. The Supreme Court acts normally as an appeal court, but may act as a court of first instance in cases submitted to it by the Public Prosecutor. All courts, when acting as courts of first instance, consist of one professional judge and two lay assessors, and, as courts of appeal, of three professional judges. Local government Executive Committees may try petty offences.

Regional or county judges and assessors are elected by the district or county councils, all members of the Supreme Court by Parliament. There are also military courts of the first instance. Military cases of the second instance go before the Supreme Court.

Judges are appointed for life, subject to removal for disciplinary reasons.

The death penalty was abolished in 1990.

The office of Ombudsman was established in 1993, elected by parliament for a six-year term, renewable once.

ICELAND

The courts consist of courts of first instance, exercising jurisdiction on a district level, and the Supreme Court, a national court of appeal. There were 33 judicial districts in 1990. Each had one court of ordinary jurisdiction for civil cases and another for criminal cases, as well as a Sheriff's Court, a Probate Court and a Court of Auctions. However, one district, being divided for purposes of criminal law and law enforcement, had an additional Criminal Court and Sheriff's Court, making 34 in all. The urban districts also had a Maritime and Commercial Court. Other special courts are of less importance.

There are no intermediate courts of appeal, but these existed on a regional level prior to 1920, at which time the Supreme Court was established in its current form.

Appeal to the Supreme Court could be made from all other courts except the High Court of State, the decisions of which were not subject to judicial review. The Labour Court and the Ecclesiastical Court also constituted an exception. As to the Labour Court, only questions of procedure could be appealed to the Supreme Court. As regards the Ecclesiastical Court, its decisions were subject to appeal to the Synodal Court, which thus replaced the Supreme Court as the court of last resort.

Generally, unanimity of opinion in a court of more than one judge was not required for a valid decision, the issue being conclusively decided by a majority of votes. Dissenting opinions would be recorded and published in the same manner as the majority opinion. Juries are not used within the judicial system.

New laws were enacted in 1992 on practically all aspects of legal procedure. Traditionally Icelandic procedural law has been similar to that of Denmark and Norway, but in some respects Icelandic legal procedure now has no exact correlation in the Nordic countries.

There are two judicial instances, the lower instance being formed by the 8 district courts, and the Supreme Court being the superior instance and the only appeal court, thus transferring jurisdiction from the provincial magistrates to the district courts and separating the judiciary from the prosecution. The principle that a case may pass through these two instances is, however, subject to three exceptions. Firstly, certain cases concerning labour disputes and the interpretation of collective labour agreements are subject to the jurisdiction of the Labour Court. Secondly the special Court of Impeachment, whose judgments are not subject to appeal, has jurisdiction in cases concerning criminal violations committed in public office by ministers of the government. Thirdly in cases of damages claimed on account of tortious acts in judicial office the Supreme Court is the first and only instance.

IRELAND

The Constitution provides that justice shall be administered in public in Courts established by law by judges appointed by the President on the advice of the Government.The jurisdiction and organization of the Courts are dealt with in the Courts (Establishment and Constitution) Act, 1961 and the Courts (Supplemental Provisions) Acts, 1961–1991. The Courts consist of Courts of First Instance and a Court of Final Appeal, called the Supreme Court. The Courts of First Instance are the High Court with full original jurisdiction and the Circuit and the District Courts with local and limited jurisdiction. A judge may not be removed from office except for stated misbehaviour or incapacity and then only on resolutions passed by both Houses of the *Oireachtas*. Judges of the Supreme, High and Circuit Courts are appointed from among practising barristers. Judges of the District Court (called District Justices) may be appointed from among practising barristers or practising solicitors.

The Supreme Court, which consists of the Chief Justice (who is *ex officio* an additional judge of the High Court) and 4 ordinary judges, has appellate jurisdiction from all decisions of the High Court. The President may, after consultation with the Council of State, refer a Bill, which has been passed by both Houses of the *Oireachtas* (other than a money bill and certain other bills), to the Supreme Court for a decision on the question as to whether such Bill or any provision thereof is repugnant to the Constitution.

The High Court, which consists of a President (who is *ex officio* an additional Judge of the Supreme Court) and 16 ordinary judges, has full original jurisdiction in and power to determine all matters and questions, whether of law or fact, civil or criminal. In all cases in which questions arise concerning the validity of any law having regard to the provisions of the Constitution, the High Court alone exercises original jurisdiction. The High Court on Circuit acts as an appeal court from the Circuit Court.

The Court of Criminal Appeal consists of the Chief Justice or an ordinary judge of the Supreme Court, together with either 2 ordinary judges of the High Court or the President and one ordinary judge of the High Court. It deals with appeals by persons convicted on indictment where the appellant obtains a certificate from the trial judge that the case is a fit one for appeal, or, in case such certificate is refused, where the court itself, on appeal from such refusal, grants leave to appeal. The decision of the Court of Criminal Appeal is final, unless that court or the Director of Public Prosecutions certifies that the decision involves a point of law of exceptional public importance, in which case an appeal is taken to the Supreme Court.

The High Court exercising criminal jurisdiction is known as the Central Criminal Court. It consists of a judge or judges of the High Court, nominated by the President of the High Court. The Court sits in Dublin and tries criminal cases which are outside the jurisdiction of the Circuit Court or which may be sent forward to it for trial from the Circuit Court on the application of the Director of Public Prosecutions.

The Offences against the State Act, 1939 provides for the establishment of Special Criminal Courts. A Special Criminal Court sits without a jury. The rules of evidence that apply in proceedings before a Special Criminal Court are the same as those applicable in trials in the Central Criminal Court.

The Circuit Court consists of a President (who is *ex officio* an additional judge of the High Court) and 17 ordinary judges. The country is divided into 8 circuits for the purposes of the Circuit Court. The Circuit Court acts as an appeal court from the District Court.

The District Court, which consists of a President and 45 ordinary judges, has summary jurisdiction in a large number of criminal cases where the offence is not of a serious nature.

All criminal cases, except those of a minor nature, and those tried in the Special Criminal Court, are tried by a judge and a jury of 12. A majority vote of the jury (10 must agree) is necessary to determine a verdict.

ITALY

Italy has 1 court of cassation, in Rome, and is divided for the administration of justice into 26 appeal court districts, subdivided into 161 tribunal districts, and these again in *mandamenti* each with its own magistracy

(*Pretura*), 628 in all. There are also 90 first degree assize courts and 26 assize courts of appeal. For civil business, besides the magistracy above mentioned, *Conciliatori* have jurisdiction in petty plaints.

LATVIA

The criminal code is inherited from the former USSR. Judges are appointed for life. There are a Supreme Court, regional and district courts and administrative courts. The death penalty is retained.

LIECHTENSTEIN

The principality has its own civil and penal codes. The lowest court is the county court, *Landgericht*, presided over by one judge, which decides minor civil cases and summary criminal offences. The criminal court, *Kriminalgericht*, with a bench of 5 judges is for major crimes. Another court of mixed jurisdiction is the court of assizes (with 3 judges) for misdemeanours. Juvenile cases are treated in the Juvenile Court (with a bench of 3 judges). The superior court, *Obergericht*, and Supreme Court, *Oberster Gerichtshof*, are courts of appeal for civil and criminal cases (both with benches of 5 judges). An administrative court of appeal from government actions and the State Court determines the constitutionality of laws.

The death penalty was abolished in 1989.

LITHUANIA

Trial by jury has been introduced for capital offences. The death penalty is retained for premeditated murder.

LUXEMBOURG

The courts are entrusted by the Constitution with the exercise of judicial power. The Constitution applies to them the principle of the separation of powers by making them independent in performing their functions, restricting their sphere of activity, defining their limits of jurisdiction and providing for a number of procedural guarantees.

The courts of the Justices of the Peace are the lowest; they are at Luxembourg City, Esch-sur-Alzette and Diekirch. They deal with minor civil, commercial and criminal cases. There are two judicial districts of Luxembourg and Diekirch. The district courts deal with civil, commercial and criminal cases. The Superior Court of Justice includes both a court of appeal, hearing decisions made by district courts, and a *Cour de Cassation*. The Court of Assizes, which fell within the jurisdiction of the Superior Court, heard criminal cases, but was abolished in 1987. There is no jury system. A defendant is acquitted if fewer than four of the six judges finds them guilty.

The High Court of Justice sits in Luxembourg. It consists of a Supreme Court of Appeal and a Court of Appeal. The Court of Appeal is subdivided in six chambers each sitting with three magistrates. The Court of Appeal deals with judgments passed in the first instance by district courts. The Supreme Court of Appeal consists of one chamber which sits with five magistrates *i.e.* the President of the Court, two councillors from the Appeal Court and two judges chosen among councillors who never dealt with the case at any time previously. It deals primarily with decisions made by the Court of Appeal, the Military Court and with judgments passed without appeal by district courts or by Justices of the Peace. No decision or judgment may be brought before the Supreme Court of Appeal except for violations of the law, action ultra vires or procedural offences, either substantial or barred under pain of being declared void. Matters of social administration such as social insurance are dealt with by special tribunals. The administration of the judiciary and the supervision of judicial police investigations is the responsibility of the *Procureur général*.

Judges are appointed for life by the Grand Ducal order, and are not removable except by judicial sentence.

Capital punishment was abolished in 1979.

MACEDONIA
Former Yugoslavia

Courts are autonomous and independent. Judges are tenured and elected for life on the proposal of the *Judicial Council*, whose members are themselves elected for renewable 6-year terms. The highest court is the Supreme Court. There are 28 courts of first instance and 3 higher courts.

MALTA

Civil law has generally evolved from Roman law. Public law and some commercial and maritime affairs are influenced by English law.

There is a Constitutional Court, a Court of Appeal and a Criminal Court of Appeal, together with a Civil Court, a Criminal Court, a Commercial Court and from 1990 a three-tier system of Magistrates' Courts.

MONACO

There are the following courts, *Juge de Paix*, Tribunal of the First Instance, a Court of Appeal, *Cour de Révision* and a Supreme Tribunal.

There is no death penalty.

THE NETHERLANDS

Justice is administered by the High Court of the Netherlands (Court of Cassation), by 5 courts of justice (Courts of Appeal), by 19 district courts and by 63 cantonal courts; trial by jury is unknown. The Cantonal Court, which deals with minor offences, comprising a single judge; more serious cases are tried by the district courts, formed as a rule by three judges (in some cases one judge is sufficient); the courts of appeal are constituted of three and the High Court of five judges. All judges are appointed for life by the Sovereign (the judges of the High Court from a list prepared by the Second Chamber of the States-General). They can be removed only by a decision of the High Court.

Juvenile courts were set up in 1922. The juvenile court is formed by a single judge especially appointed to try children's civil cases, at the same time charged with the administration of justice for criminal actions committed by young persons who are between 12 and 18 (in special cases up to 21) years old, unless imprisonment of 6 months or more ought to be inflicted; such cases are tried by three judges.

NORWAY

The judicature is common to civil and criminal cases; the same professional judges preside over both cases. These judges are as such state officials. The participation of lay judges and jurors, both summoned for the individual case, varies according to the kind of court and kind of case.

The ordinary Court of First Instance, the District or City Courts (*Herredsrett* and *Byrett*) is in criminal cases composed of one professional judge and two lay judges, chosen by ballot from a panel elected by the district council. In civil cases two lay judges may participate. The ordinary

Court of First Instance is in general competent in all kinds of cases, with the exception of criminal cases where the maximum penalty prescribed in the Criminal Code for the offence in question exceeds six years' imprisonment. Altogether there are 96 District and City Courts.

In every community there is a Conciliation Board (*Forliksråd*) composed of three lay persons elected by the district council. A civil lawsuit usually begins with mediation in the council which can also pronounce judgement in certain cases.

The ordinary Courts of Second Instance, High Courts (*Lagmannsrett*), of which there are five, are composed of three professional judges. Additionally, in civil cases two or four lay judges may be summoned. In serious criminal cases which are being brought before the High Court in the first instance, a jury of ten lay persons is summoned to determine whether the defendant is guilty according to the charge. In other criminal cases the court is composed of two professional judges and three lay judges (*Meddomsrett*). In civil cases, the Court of Second Instance is an ordinary court of appeal. In criminal cases in which the lower court does not have judicial authority, it is itself the court of first instance. In other criminal cases it is an appeal court as far as the appeal is based on an attack against the lower court's assessment of the facts when determining the guilt of the defendant. An appeal based on any other alleged mistakes is brought directly before the Supreme Court.

The Supreme Court (*Høyesterett*) is the court of last resort. There are eighteen Supreme Court judges. Each individual case is heard by five judges. Some major cases are determined in plenary session. The Supreme Court may in general examine every aspect of the case and the handling of it by the lower courts. However, in criminal cases the Court may not overrule the lower court's assessment of the facts as far as the guilt of the defendant is concerned.

The Court of Impeachment (*Riksretten*) is composed of five judges of the Supreme Court and ten members of parliament.

All serious offences are prosecuted by the state. The public prosecution authority (*påtalemyndigheten*) consists of the Director-General of Public Prosecutions, eighteen district attorneys (*statsadvokater*) and legally qualified officers of the ordinary police force. Counsel for the defence is in general provided for by the state.

POLAND

The legal system was reorganized in 1950. A new penal code was adopted in 1969. Espionage and treason carry the severest penalties. For minor crimes there is more provision for probation sentences and fines. Previous jurisprudence was based on a penal code of 1932 supplemented by the Concise Penal Code of 1946.

In 1955 the death penalty was suspended for 5 years. No executions have taken place since 1988.

There exist the following courts: Supreme Courts, voivodship courts, district courts and family consultative centres. Judges and lay assessors are elected. The State Council elects the judges of the Supreme Court for a term of five years and appoints the Prosecutor-General. The office of the Prosecutor-General is separate from the judiciary. An ombudsman's office was established in 1987.

Family courts (now consultative centres) were established in 1977 for cases involving divorce and domestic relations, but divorce suits were transferred to ordinary courts in 1990.

PORTUGAL

Portuguese law distinguishes civil (including commercial) and penal, labour, administrative and fiscal law, each branch having its lower courts, courts of appeal and the Supreme Court.

There are four judicial districts (Lisbon, Porto, Coimbra and Evora) divided into 47 circuits. In 1993 there were 346 common courts, including 300 of the first instance (63 specialized). There were also 29 administration and fiscal courts. There are 4 courts of appeal (*Tribunal de Relação*) at Lisbon, Coimbra, Evora and Porto, and a Supreme Court in Lisbon (*Supremo Tribunal de Justiça*).

Capital punishment was totally abolished under the 1976 Constitution. It was abolished for political crimes in 1852, common law crimes in 1867 and common law crimes in overseas territories in 1870.

ROMANIA

Justice is administered by the Supreme Court, the 41 county courts, 81 courts of first instance and 15 courts of appeal. Lay assessors (elected for 4 years) participate in most court trials, collaborating with the judges. In 1991 there were 1547 judges. The Procurator-General exercises 'supreme supervisory power to ensure the observance of the law' by all authorities, central and local, and all citizens. The Procurator's Office and its organs are independent of any organs of justice or administration, and only responsible to the Grand National Assembly (which appoints the Procurator-General for 4 years) and between its sessions, to the State Council. The Ministry of the Interior is responsible for ordinary police work. State security is the responsibility of the State Security Council. The death penalty was abolished in Jan 1990 and is forbidden by the 1991 constitution.

RUSSIA

The Supreme Court is the highest judicial body on civil, criminal and administrative law. The Supreme Arbitration Court deals with economic cases. The KGB, and the Federal Security Bureau which succeeded it, were replaced in Dec 1992 by the Federal Counter-Intelligence Service.

A new civil code was introduced in 1993 to replace the former Soviet code. It guarantees the inviolability of private property and includes provisions for the freedom of movement of capital and goods. Twelve-member juries were introduced in a number of courts after Nov 1993.

SAN MARINO

Judges are appointed permanently by the Great and General Council; they may not be San Marino citizens. Petty civil cases are dealt with by a justice of the peace; legal commissioners deal with more serious civil cases and all criminal cases and appeals lie to them from the justice of the peace. Appeals against the legal commissioners lie to an appeals judge, and the Council of the Twelve functions as a court of third instance.

SERBIA

The judges were appointed by the King, but according to the constitution could not be removed against their will; however, when the constitution was suspended on 9 May 1894, their irremovability ceased. There were (1892) 22 courts of first instance, a court of appeal, a court of cassation, and a tribunal of commerce.

SLOVAKIA

The post-Communist judicial system was established by a federal law of Jul 1991. This provided for a unified system of 4 types of court: civil, criminal, commercial and administrative. Commercial courts arbitrate in disputes arising from business activities. Administrative courts examine the legality of the decisions of state institutions when appealed by citizens. In addition, there are military courts which operate under the jurisdiction of the Ministry of Defence. There is a Supreme Court, and a hierarchy of courts under the Ministry of Justice at republic, region and district level. District courts are courts of first instance. Cases are usually decided by senates comprising a judge and 2 associate judges, though occasionally by a single judge. (Associate judges are citizens in good standing over the age of 25 who are elected for 4-year terms).

Regional courts are courts of first instance in more serious cases and also courts of appeal for district courts. Cases are usually decided by a senate of 2 judges and 3 associate judges, although again occasionally by a single judge. The Supreme Court interprets law as a guide to other courts and functions also as a court of appeal. Decisions are made by senates of 3 judges. The judges of the Supreme Court are nominated by the President; other judges are appointed by the National Council.

SLOVENIA

There are 8 courts of first instance, 4 higher courts and a supreme court.

SPAIN

Justice is administered by *Tribunales* and *Juzgados* (Tribunals and Courts), which conjointly form the *Poder Judicial* (Judicial Power). Judges and magistrates cannot be removed, suspended or transferred except as set forth by law. The constitution of 1978 has established a new organ, the *Consejo General del Poder Judicial* (General Council of the Judicial Power), formed by one president and 20 magistrates, judges, attorneys and lawyers, governing the Judicial Power in full independence from the other two powers of the State, the Legislative (Cortes) and the Executive (President of the Government and his Cabinet). Its President is that of the *Tribunal Supremo*.

The Judicature is composed of the *Tribunal Supremo* (Supreme High Court; 17 *Audiencias Territoriales* (Division High Courts); 52 *Audiencias Provinciales* (Provincial High Courts); *Juzgados de Primera Instancia* (Courts of First Instance), *Juzgados de Distrito* (District Courts) and *Juzgados Municipales y de paz* (Municipal and Peace Courts, Courts of Lowest Jurisdiction held by Justices of the Peace).

The *Tribunal Supremo* consists of a President (appointed by the monarch, on proposal from the *Consejo General de Poder Judicial*) and various judges distributed among seven chambers; one for trying civil matters, three for administrative purposes, one for criminal trials, one for social

349

matters and one for military cases. The *Tribunal Supremo* has disciplinary faculties; is court of cassation in all criminal trials; for administrative purposes decides in first and second instance disputes arising between private individuals and the State, and in social matters makes final decisions.

The jury system consisting of 9 members became operative in Nov 1995 in criminal cases.

The death penalty was abolished in 1978 by the Constitution (Art. 15). Divorce was allowed from Jul 1981 and abortion since Aug 1985. A new penal code came in force in May 1996 replacing the code of 1848. It provides for a maximum of 30 years imprisonment in specified exceptional cases, with a normal maximum of 20 years. New offences include money laundering, misleading publicity, sexual harassment, damage to the environment, defamation in the press, sexual, racial, political or religious discrimination and incitement to genocide.

A new juvenile criminal law of 1995 lays emphasis on rehabilitation.

SWEDEN

The administration of justice is independent. The Attorney-General (appointed by the Government) and 3 Ombudsmen exercise a check on judicial affairs administration.

There is a 3-tier hierarchy of courts: The Supreme Court, 6 intermediate courts of appeal, and 97 district courts. Of the district courts 27 also serve as real estate courts and 6 as water rights courts.

District courts are courts of first instance and deal with both civil and criminal cases. Petty cases are tried by 1 judge. Civil and criminal cases are tried as a rule by 3 to 4 judges or in minor cases by 1 judge. Disputes of greater consequence relating to the Marriage Code or the Code relating to Parenthood and Guardianship are tried by a judge and a jury of 3–4 lay assessors. More serious criminal cases are tried by a judge and jury of 5 members (lay assessors) in felony cases, and 3 members in misdemeanour cases. The cases in courts of appeal are generally tried by 4 or 5 judges, but the same cases, which are tried with a judge and jury in the first instance, are tried by 3 or 4 judges and a jury of 2–3 members.

Those with low incomes can receive free legal aid out of public funds. In criminal cases a suspected person has the right to a defence counsel, paid out of public funds.

The Attorney-General and the Judicial Commissioner for the Judiciary and Civil Administration supervise the application in the public sector of acts of Parliament and regulations. The Attorney-General is the government's legal adviser and also the Public Prosecutor.

SWITZERLAND

The Federal Tribunal (*Bundes-Gericht*), which sits at Lausanne consists of 30 judges, with 15 supplementary judges, and 15 temporary supplementary judges elected by the Federal Assembly for six years and eligible for re-election; the president and vice-president serve for two years and cannot be re-elected. The Tribunal has original and final jurisdiction in suits between the Confederation and cantons; between cantons and cantons; between the Confederation or cantons and corporations or individuals; between parties who refer their cases to it in such suits as the constitution or legislation of cantons places within its authority; and in many classes of railway suits. It is a court of appeal against decisions of other federal authorities, and of cantonal authorities applying federal laws. The Tribunal comprises 2 courts of public law, 2 civil courts, a chamber of bankruptcy, a chamber of prosecution, a court of criminal appeal, a court of extraordinary appeal, a federal criminal court and a criminal chamber for cases of treason (sitting very rarely).

On 3 Jul 1938 the Swiss electorate accepted a new federal penal code, to take the place of the separate cantonal penal codes. The new code, which abolished capital punishment, came into force on 1 Jan 1942.

A Federal Insurance Court sits at Lucerne and its judges are elected for 6 years by the Federal Assembly.

By federal law of 5 Oct 1950 several articles of the penal code concerning crimes against the independence of the state have been amended with a view to reinforcing the security of the state.

TURKEY

The unified legal system consists of: (1) justices of the peace (single judges with limited but summary penal and civil jurisdiction); (2) courts of first instance (single judges, dealing with cases outside the jurisdiction of (3) and (4); (3) central criminal courts (a president and two judges, dealing with cases where the crime is punishable by imprisonment over five years); (4) commercial courts (three judges); and (5) state security courts (a president and four judges, two of the latter being military).

The Council of State is the highest administration tribunal; it consists of five chambers. Its 31 judges are nominated from among high-ranking personalities in politics, economy, law, the army, etc. The Military Court of Cassation in Ankara is the highest military tribunal.

The Civil Code and the Code of Obligations have been adapted from the corresponding Swiss codes. The Penal Code is largely based upon the Italian Penal Code, and the Code of Civil Procedure closely resembles that of the Canton of Neuchâtel, Switzerland. The Commercial Code is based on the German.

UNION OF SOVIET SOCIALIST REPUBLICS (USSR)

The basis of the judiciary system was the same throughout the Soviet Union, but the constituent republics had the right to introduce modifications and to make their own rules for the application of the code of laws. The Supreme Court of the USSR was the chief court and supervising organ for all constituent republics and was elected by the Supreme Soviet of the USSR for five years. Supreme Courts of the Union and Autonomous Republics were elected by the Supreme Soviets of these republics, and Territorial, Regional and Area Courts by the respective Soviets, each for a term of five years. At the lowest level were the People's Courts, which were elected directly by the population.

Court proceedings were conducted in the local language with full interpreting facilities as required. All cases were heard in public, unless otherwise provided for by law, and the accused was guaranteed the right of defence.

Laws establishing common principles of criminal legislation, criminal responsibility for state and military crimes, judicial and criminal procedure and military tribunals were adopted by the Supreme Soviet on 25 Dec 1958 for the courts both of the USSR and the constituent Republics.

The Law Courts were divided into People's Courts and higher courts. The People's Courts consisted of the People's Judges and two Assessors, and their function was to examine, as the first instance, most of the civil and criminal cases, except the more important ones, some of which were tried at the Regional Court, and those of the highest importance at the Supreme Court. People's Judges and rota-lists of assessors were elected directly by the citizens of each constituency: judges for five years, assessors for two and a half; they had to be over 25 years of age.

The Procurator-General of the USSR was appointed for five years by the Supreme Soviet. All procurators of the republics, autonomous republics and autonomous regions were appointed by the Procurator-General of the USSR for a term of five years. The procurators supervised the correct application of the law by all state organs, and had special responsibility for the observance of the law in places of detention. The procurators of the Union republics were subordinate to the Procurator-General of the USSR, whose duty was to see that acts of all institutions of the USSR were legal, that the law was correctly interpreted and uniformly applied.

Capital punishment was abolished on 26 May 1947, but was restored on 12 Jan 1950 for treason, espionage and sabotage; on 7 May 1954 for certain categories of murder; in Dec 1958 for terrorism and banditry; on 7 May 1961 for embezzlement of public property, counterfeiting and attacks on prison warders and, in particular circumstances, for attacks on the police and public order volunteers and for rape (15 Feb 1962), and for accepting bribes (20 Feb 1962). However, females and men who had reached 60 by the time of sentence were exempt.

In view of criminal abuses extending over many years, discovered in the security system, the powers of administrative trial and exile previously vested in the security authorities (MVD) were abolished in 1953; accelerated procedures for trial on charges of high treason, espionage, wrecking, etc., by the Supreme Court were abolished in 1955; and extensive powers of protection of persons under arrest or serving prison terms were vested in the Procurator-General's Office (1955). Supervisory commissions, composed of representatives of trade unions, youth organizations and local authorities, were set up in 1956 to inspect places of detention.

Further reforms of the civil and criminal codes were decreed on 25 Dec 1958. Thereby the age of criminal responsibility was raised from 14 to 16 years; deportation, banishment and deprivation of citizenship were abolished; a presumption of innocence was not accepted, but the burden of proof of guilt had been placed upon the prosecutor; secret trials and the charge of 'enemy of the people' have been abolished. Articles 70 and 100 of the Criminal Code, which dealt with 'anti-Soviet agitation and propaganda' and 'crimes against the system of administration' respectively, were, however, widely used against political dissidents but were abolished by 1990.

UNITED KINGDOM

Although the United Kingdom is a unitary state, it does not have a single body of law applicable universally within its limits. Scotland has its own distinctive legal system and law courts, and although a single Parliament exists for Great Britain since 1707, common opinions on broader issues, and a common final court of appeal in civil cases have resulted in substantial identity on many points, differences in legal procedure and practice remain. In Northern Ireland on the other hand, the structure of the courts and legal procedure and practice have closely resembled those of England and Wales for centuries but, as Northern Ireland had its own parliament with defined powers (as well as being represented in the parliament at Westminster), its enacted law derives in certain spheres from a different source and may differ in substance from that which operates in England and Wales. However, a large volume of modern legislation, particularly in the social field, applies throughout the United Kingdom. A feature common to all systems of law in the United Kingdom (which differentiates them from some continental systems) is that there is no complete code, although the Law Commission is working on the codification of certain branches of law. The sources of law in all the systems include legislation and unwritten or 'common' law.

Legislation includes some 3000 Acts of Parliament and delegated or subordinate legislation made by ministers and others under powers conferred by parliament, Acts of Parliament being absolutely binding on all courts of the United Kingdom, and taking precedence over any other source of law. The common law of England originated in the customs of the realm and was built up by decisions of the courts. A supplementary system of law, known as 'equity', came into being during the Middle Ages to provide and enforce more effective protection for existing legal rights. It was administered by a separate court and later became a separate body of legal rules. In 1875 the courts of equity were fused with the courts of common law, so that all courts now apply both systems but, where they conflict, equity prevails. In Scotland the basis of common law, which largely depends on the canon law of Rome, helped by continental commentators, is embodied in the writings of certain seventeenth-, eighteenth- and early nineteenth-century lawyers who, between them, described systematically almost the whole field of private and criminal law as existing in their times. Broadly speaking, the principles enunciated by these lawyers, together with the many judicial decisions which have followed and developed from those principles, form the body of Scots non-statutory law. Scotland has never had a separate system of equity – equitable principles having always permeated the ordinary rules of law. A feature common to the legal systems of the United Kingdom is the distinction made between the criminal law and the civil law. Criminal law is concerned with wrongs against the community as a whole; civil law is concerned with the rights, duties and obligations of individual members of the community between themselves.

YUGOSLAVIA

In the Socialist Federal Republic of Yugoslavia there were county tribunals, district courts, the Supreme Court of the Autonomous Province of Vojvodina, Supreme Courts of the constituent republics and the Supreme Court of the Socialist Federal Republic of Yugoslavia. In county tribunals and district courts the judicial functions were exercised by professional judges and by law assessors constituted into collegia. There were no assessors at the supreme courts.

All judges were elected by the social-political communities in their jurisdiction. The judges exercised their functions in accordance with the legal provisions enacted since the liberation of the country.

The constituent republics enacted their own criminal legislation, but offences concerning state security and the administration were dealt with at federal level.

FORMER YUGOSLAVIA
Serbia and Montenegro

The Federal Republic of Yugoslavia (Serbia and Montenegro) had (1994) 2 supreme courts, 32 district courts and 153 communal courts, with 2242 judges and 9601 lay assessors. There were 19 economic courts with 263 judges.

8   DEFENCE AND TREATIES

PRINCIPAL EUROPEAN ARMED CONFLICTS
1900–1996

Note From 1900–1914, apart from the Italo-Turkish War and the two Balkan Wars, Europe was at peace.

WORLD WAR I (EUROPE). *July 1914 – November 1918*

On 28 Jul 1914 Austria-Hungary declared war on Serbia. Austria was supported by her ally Germany, but they were faced by the 'Entente' powers, Russia, France and Britain. In late 1914 the Germans failed to capture Paris and the war settled into the deadlock of trench warfare. In 1915 the Entente tried to break the deadlock by expeditions to the Dardanelles and Salonika in south-east Europe, and by inducing Italy to attack Austria. In 1917 both sides were given hope – the Germans by the Russian Revolution (which eventually removed Russia from the war) and the Allies by the USA's entry into the war. The next year proved decisive. Germany agreed to an armistice in November. Her allies, Austria and the Ottoman Empire, had already given up the fight.

RUSSIAN CIVIL WAR. *June 1918–November 1920*

Civil War between Soviet Communists and White Russian forces, with intervention by outside powers on behalf of the anti-Communists. The first landing of British forces took place at Murmansk in Jun 1918, and further French and British troops landed at Archangel in Aug 1918; Japan and the United States also sent troops. The Civil War effectively ended when White Russian forces under General Wrangel evacuated the Crimea in Nov 1920.

RUSSO-POLISH WAR. *April 1919–October 1920*

Invasion by Polish forces of territory occupied by the Soviet Union as the German army withdrew at the end of World War I, in the hope of establishing a Soviet-Polish frontier which would give Poland possession of all the areas it traditionally claimed. After a Soviet counter-attack had been defeated, an armistice was signed on 12 Oct 1920, and a settlement was reached in the treaty of Riga (18 Mar 1921).

GRECO-TURKISH WAR. *January 1921–October 1922*

Greek invasion of Asian Turkey (Anatolia). This was repelled by the Turkish republican forces, and the Armistice of Mudanya (11 Oct 1922) ended the fighting. By the Treaty of Lausanne (24 Jul 1923), Greece renounced any claim to territory in Asia Minor, whilst Turkey surrendered all claims to territories of the Ottoman empire occupied by non-Turks.

SPANISH CIVIL WAR. *July 1936–March 1939*

A revolt by military leaders in Spanish Morocco against the civilian government led to general civil war. Unofficial military assistance was given by Germany, Italy, Portugal and the USSR; in all, 40 000 foreign volunteers including 2000 British, fought in the International Brigade on the Republican side. The civil war ended when General Franco's Nationalist forces entered Madrid on 28 Mar 1939.

WORLD WAR II (EUROPE). *September 1939–May 1945*

German forces invaded Poland on 1 Sep 1939, which led Britain and France to declare war on Germany on 3 Sep. The Germans invaded the Low Countries on 10 May 1940, and France was compelled to sign an armistice on 22 Jun, the British army being evacuated from Dunkirk. Italy declared war on Britain and France on 10 Jun 1940. Breaking the Nazi-Soviet Pact of Aug 1939, Hitler invaded Russia on 22 Jun 1941. Allied forces drove Italian and German armies out of North Africa and invaded Italy in 1943. The invasion of Normandy was launched on 6 Jun 1944, and Germany was forced to accept unconditional surrender on 7 May 1945.

RUSSO-FINNISH WAR. *November 1939–March 1940*

Soviet forces invaded Finland following Finnish rejection of demands for territorial concessions. The war was ended by the Treaty of Moscow (12 Mar 1940), in which the Finns surrendered to Russia the south-eastern part of the country.

357

GREEK CIVIL WAR. *1946–1949*

Civil war between Communist partisan forces and the civilian government. The likelihood of a Communist victory was reduced by the break between Yugoslavia and the Communist bloc in 1948, which led to the closing of one stretch of Greece's northern frontier to the rebels. The Greek Communist broadcasting station announced the end of open hostilities on 16 Oct 1949.

GERMAN DEMOCRATIC REPUBLIC UPRISING. *June 1953*

Demonstrations in East Berlin and other cities of the German Democratic Republic against Russian domination began on 17 Jun 1953, but were suppressed by Soviet armed forces.

HUNGARIAN UPRISING. *October 1956*

Student demonstrations on 23 Oct 1956 led to a general uprising against the civil government and Soviet occupying power. On 27 Oct Soviet troops were forced to evacuate Budapest, but reinforcements arrived to surround the capital, and after ten days' fighting the uprising was suppressed.

INVASION OF CZECHOSLOVAKIA. *August 1968*

During the night of 20–21 Aug, Soviet troops and Warsaw Pact forces from Poland, Hungary, German Democratic Republic and Bulgaria occupied Prague and other leading cities to reverse the liberalizing reforms of the Czechoslovakian government. Though the Czechoslovakian armed forces were ordered to offer no resistance, there were extensive civilian demonstrations against the occupying forces.

TURKISH INVASION OF CYPRUS. *July–August 1974*

On 15 Jul 1974 a *coup* was staged by men of the Greek ruling junta for the overthrow of President Makarios and fighting between Greek and Turkish Cypriots led to a Turkish invasion of Cyprus on 20 Jul. A cease-fire on 22 Jul was followed by peace talks between Britain, Greece and Turkey at Geneva, but there was renewed fighting 14–16 Aug. Turkey was left in control of the northern two-fifths of the island.

YUGOSLAVIAN CIVIL WAR (SERBO-CROAT WAR). *1991–1995*

Declarations of independence by the former Yugoslav Republics of Slovenia and Croatia led to clashes on Slovenian borders from Jul 1991, followed by heavy fighting on Croatian territory between Croatian militia and Serbian irregulars (chetniks) backed by the Yugoslav Federal Army.

Main centres of fighting were eastern and central Croatia and the Adriatic coast around Dubrovnik. Yugoslavia officially ceased to exist in Jan 1992 and Slovenia and Croatia were recognized as independent states.

On 29 Feb 1992, Muslim leaders in Bosnia-Hercegovina declared independence. Bosnian Serbs and the Serbian leadership in Belgrade rejected this, and war began on 6 Apr with the opening of the siege of the capital Sarajevo, Serbs were accused of 'ethnic cleansing' to secure territorial domination, and a UN trade embargo was imposed on Serbia on 31 May. Peace talks in Geneva, mediated by Lord Owen and Cyrus Vance, began on 26 Aug. On 16 Nov a UN naval blockade was mounted against Serbia and Montenegro. Fighting continued as a further peace conference was held in Geneva on 22–23 Jan 1993. Serbs attacked Muslim enclaves at Srebenica and Goradze. Numerous peace talks collapsed. In 1995 Croatia launched major offensives and an uneasy peace accord was signed at Dayton (Ohio).

RUSSIA–CHECHNYA WAR. *1994–1996*

Russian troops were ordered into Chechnya in Dec 1994 to end the rebel republic's bid for independence. Fighting ensued for 21 months as Russian troops failed to subdue the population. The fighting was the worst on Russian soil since the Second World War, with Grozny, the Chechnya capital, razed to the ground. The Russian army suffered a major loss of face. On 31 Aug 1996 Russia and Chechnya signed a peace deal, freezing the issue of independence for five years.

PRINCIPAL ARMED CONFLICTS (OUTSIDE EUROPE) IN WHICH EUROPEAN POWERS PARTICIPATED 1900–1996

BOXER REBELLION (CHINA). *June 1900–Sept 1901*

The outbreak of rebellion against foreigners in China, provoked by the expansion of European commerce and territorial acquisitions in China by Germany, Russia and Britain. Major Boxer disturbances occurred in Peking and the provinces of Shensi and Manchuria. It was suppressed by forces from the major European powers as well as the United States and Japan.

RUSSO-JAPANESE WAR. *Feb 1904–Sept 1905*

Japan launched a surprise attack on the Russian Far East in Port Arthur on 4 Feb 1904. The Russians suffered major military reverses, culminating at the battle of Mukden. The main Russian fleet was defeated at

Tsushima in May 1905. Although the war was ended by the Treaty of Portsmouth (New Hampshire), the military reverses provided a major catalyst of revolutionary activity in Russia.

ABYSSINIAN WAR. *October 1935–July 1936*

Italy invaded Abyssinia on 3 Oct 1935. Addis Ababa was captured on 5 May 1936, and the Emperor Haile Selassie was forced into exile in Britain. The League of Nations imposed sanctions on Italy, but these proved ineffective; they were lifted in Jul 1936.

WORLD WAR II (ASIA). *December 1941–August 1945*

Japan attacked the American base at Pearl Harbor on 7 Dec 1941, and within six months the Japanese were masters of South-east Asia and Burma. The Allied counter-offensive culminated in the dropping of the first atomic bombs on Hiroshima and Nagasaki in Aug 1945. On 15 Aug 1945 the Emperor of Japan broadcast to the nation to cease fighting. The principal European powers involved in the conflict were Britain and the Netherlands; the Soviet Union also declared war on Japan on 8 Aug 1945.

FIRST VIETNAM WAR. *December 1946–July 1954*

The war between the French colonial government and Communist forces led by Ho Chi Minh began with attacks on French garrisons by Vietminh troops throughout Vietnam on 19 Dec 1946. The French army was defeated at Dien Bien Phu in May 1954, and the war was ended by the Geneva Agreement of 21 Jul 1954, which divided Vietnam into the area north of the 17th parallel and an independent South Vietnam.

MALAYAN EMERGENCY. *July 1948–July 1960*

Insurgency by Communist forces, eventually suppressed by British and Malayan troops. The State of Emergency was ended on 31 Jul 1960. British troops were also involved in the 'confrontation' with Indonesia after the creation of the Malaysia Federation on 16 Sep 1963. An agreement was reached ending confrontation on 1 Jun 1966.

KOREAN WAR. *June 1950–July 1953*

The invasion of South Korea by North Korea on 25 Jun 1950 led to intervention by United Nations forces following an emergency session of the Security Council. The advance of the United Nations forces into North Korea on 1 Oct 1950 led to the entry of the Chinese into the war. An armistice was signed at Panmunjom on 27 Jul 1953. The European powers which contributed to the United Nations force were Britain, France, Turkey, Belgium, Luxembourg, the Netherlands and Greece.

ALGERIAN REVOLUTIONARY WAR. *October 1954–March 1962*

The uprising by the FLN (Front de Libération Nationale) against the French colonial government began during the night of 31 Oct–1 Nov 1954. A cease-fire agreement was signed on 18 Mar 1962, and after a referendum the independence of Algeria was recognized on 3 Jul 1962.

SUEZ WAR. *October–November 1956*

The Israeli army attacked Egypt on 29 Oct 1956. The rejection of a British and French ultimatum by Egypt resulted in a combined British and French attack on Egypt on 31 Oct. Hostilities ended at midnight on 6–7 Nov following the call for a cease-fire by the United Nations.

PORTUGAL'S WARS IN AFRICA. *1961–1975*

The struggle for independence against colonial rule in Portugal's African colonies began with an uprising in Angola in 1961 and spread to Guinea-Bissau and Mozambique. The conflicts put a growing strain on Portugal and by 1974 her forces had suffered some 11 000 dead and 30 000 wounded. Following the overthrow of the Portuguese government by a *coup d'état* in Apr 1974, independence was rapidly granted to Angola (11 Nov 1975), Guinea-Bissau (10 Sep 1974) and Mozambique (25 Jun 1975).

SOVIET INVASION OF AFGHANISTAN. *December 1979*

The instability of the Soviet-backed régime and growing resistance to its reforms led to a full-scale Russian invasion of Afghanistan on 27 Dec 1979. A new government under Babrak Karmal was installed, but a considerable Soviet military presence had to be maintained in the country to combat the Mujaheddin guerrillas. All Soviet troops were withdrawn by 15 Feb 1989.

FALKLANDS CONFLICT. *April–June 1982*

On 2 Apr 1982 Argentinian forces invaded East Falkland to assert Argentina's longstanding claim to sovereignty over the Falkland Islands. The first warships of the British Task Force sailed for the South Atlantic 3 days later. British troops established a beachhead at San Carlos on East Falkland on 21 May and Argentinian forces surrendered on 14 Jun.

THE GULF WAR. *August 1990–February 1991*

On 2 Aug 1990, Kuwait was invaded by Iraqi forces. US naval forces were sent to the Gulf and troops to Saudi Arabia. On 8 Aug 1990 Iraq announced the annexation of Kuwait. Britain joined the Allied forces in Operation 'Desert Storm' to repel the Iraqis from Kuwait. On 26 Feb 1991 Kuwait City was liberated by the Allies but Saddam Hussein retained power in Iraq.

WORLD WAR I
EUROPEAN BELLIGERENTS

	Population (in millions)	Total mobilized (in thousands)	Soldiers killed or died of wounds (in thousands)
Austria-Hungary	47	7800	1 200
Belgium	7	267	14
Britain	41	8904	908
Bulgaria	4	560	87
France	39	8410	1 363
Germany	63	11 000	1 774
Italy	33	5615	560
Romania	7	750	336
Russia	150	12 000	1 700
Serbia	3	707	45
Turkey	26	2850	325

Source: Quincy Wright, *A Study of War*, The University of Chicago Press, 1942: second edition, 1965.

WORLD WAR II
PRINCIPAL EUROPEAN BELLIGERENTS

	Population (in millions)	Total mobilized (in thousands)	Soldiers killed or died of wounds (in thousands)	Civilians killed (in thousands)
Belgium	8	625	8	101
Britain	48	5896	557	61
Bulgaria	7	450	10	..
Czechoslovakia	15	150	10	490
Denmark	4	25	4	..
Finland	4	500	79	..

362

	Population (in millions)	Total mobilized (in thousands)	Soldiers killed or died of wounds (in thousands)	Civilians killed (in thousands)
France	39	5000	202	108
Germany	71	10 200	3250	500
Greece	6	414	73	400
Hungary	9	350	147	..
Italy	44	3100	149	783
Netherlands	9	410	7	242
Norway	3	75	2	2
Poland	35	1000	64	2000
Romania	14	1136	520	–
Soviet Union	175	22 000	7500	7500
Yugoslavia	15	3741	410	1275

Source: Quincy Wright, *A Study of War*, The University of Chicago Press, 1942: second edition, 1965.

PEACE TREATIES ARISING FROM WORLD WAR I 1918–1923

TREATY OF BREST-LITOVSK. *3 March 1918*

The Soviet Union surrendered the Baltic Provinces and Russian Poland to the Central Powers, recognized the independence of Finland and the Ukraine, and ceded to Turkey the districts of Kars, Ardahan and Batum. The Treaty was formally invalidated by the Armistice in the West on 11 Nov 1918.

TREATY OF VERSAILLES. *28 June 1919*

The peace treaty between Germany and the Allied Powers. Germany surrendered territory to Belgium, Denmark, Poland and Czechoslovakia; Alsace-Lorraine was ceded to France. Germany also surrendered all her overseas territories. The Rhineland was declared a demilitarized zone, with Allied occupation for fifteen years from when the Treaty came into effect on 10 Jan 1920. Severe restrictions were placed on the German Armed Forces; the army was limited to 100 000 men. The union of Germany and Austria was forbidden. The Treaty declared Germany's responsibility for causing the war, and made Germany liable for the payment of Reparations. The Treaty also contained the Covenant of the League of Nations.

363

TREATY OF ST GERMAIN. *10 September 1919*

The peace treaty between the Austrian Republic and the Allied Powers. By the settlement Austria lost territory to Italy, Yugoslavia, Czechoslovakia, Poland and Romania. Hungary was recognized as an independent state, and the union of Austria and Germany was forbidden. The Austrian army was limited to 30 000 men, and the Republic was made liable for the payment of Reparations.

TREATY OF NEUILLY. *17 November 1919*

The peace treaty between Bulgaria and the Allied Powers. Bulgaria lost Western Thrace to Greece, and territory to Yugoslavia. The Bulgarian army was limited to 20 000 men, and Bulgaria was made liable for Reparations.

TREATY OF TRIANON. *4 June 1920*

The peace treaty between Hungary and the Allied Powers. Hungary surrendered territory to Romania, Czechoslovakia, Yugoslavia, Poland, Italy and the Austrian Republic, to a total of about two-thirds of its pre-war lands. The Hungarian army was limited to 35 000 and Hungary was made liable for Reparations.

TREATY OF SÈVRES. *10 August 1920*

The peace treaty made with Ottoman Turkey, but never ratified by the Turks.

TREATY OF LAUSANNE. *24 July 1923*

Treaty made necessary by Turkey's refusal to accept the treaty of Sèvres. Turkey surrendered its claims to territories of the Ottoman Empire occupied by non-Turks, whilst retaining Constantinople and Eastern Thrace in Europe. The Greeks surrendered Smyrna, but were confirmed in possession of all the Aegean Islands except Imbros and Tenedos which were returned to Turkey. Turkey recognized the annexation of Cyprus by Britain and of the Dodecanese by Italy. The Bosphorus and the Dardanelles were declared to be demilitarized. (By the Montreux Convention of 20 Jul 1936 Turkey was permitted to re-fortify the Straits.)

TREATIES, AGREEMENTS AND ALLIANCES BETWEEN EUROPEAN COUNTRIES 1900–1996

6 Oct 1900	London	Britain and Germany
20 Dec 1900	Rome	Austria-Hungary and Italy
Dec–Nov 1902	Rome	France and Italy
7 Sep 1901	Peking	Germany, Austria-Hungary, Belgium, Spain, United States, France, Britain, Italy, Japan, the Netherlands, Russia and China
4–17 Apr 1902	Bucharest	Austria-Hungary and Romania (with accession of Germany and Italy)
1 Jun 1902	Berlin	Austria-Hungary and Germany
28 Jun 1902	Berlin	Austria-Hungary, Germany and Italy
31 Mar 1904	Sofia	Bulgaria and Serbia
8 Apr 1904	London	Britain and France
2–15 Oct 1904	St Petersburg	Austria-Hungary and Russia
3 Oct 1904	Paris	France and Spain
7 Apr 1906	Algeciras	Britain, Austria-Hungary, Belgium, France, Germany, Italy, Morocco, Portugal, the Netherlands, Russia, Spain, Sweden and United States
31 Aug 1907	St Petersburg	Britain and Russia
9 Feb 1909	Berlin	France and Germany
30 Nov–15 Dec 1909	Vienna–Rome	Austria-Hungary and Italy
4 Nov 1911	Berlin	France and Germany
29 Feb 1912	Sofia	Bulgaria and Serbia
29 Apr 1912	Varna	Bulgaria and Serbia
16–29 May 1912	Sofia	Bulgaria and Greece
16 Jul 1912	Paris	France and Russia
12 Sep–6 Oct 1912	Lucerne	Serbia and Montenegro
22 Sep 1912	Sofia	Greece and Bulgaria
15 Oct 1912	Ouchy	Italy and Turkey
28 Oct 1912	Paris	France and Italy
5 Dec 1912	Vienna	Austria-Hungary, Germany and Italy
5 Feb 1913	Bucharest	Austria-Hungary and Romania (with accession of Germany and Italy)
22 Apr–5 May 1913	Athens	Greece and Serbia
1–14 May 1913	Salonika	Greece and Serbia
19 May–1 Jun 1913	Salonika	Greece and Serbia
30 May 1913	London	Turkey and Balkan allies
28 Jul 1913– 10 Aug 1913	Bucharest	Bulgaria, Romania, Greece, Montenegro and Serbia
2 Aug 1913	Vienna	Austria-Hungary, Germany and Italy
29 Sept 1913	Constantinople	Turkey and Bulgaria
14 Nov 1913	Athens	Turkey and Greece
15 Jun 1914	London	Britain and Germany
12 Aug 1914	Lisbon	Britain and Portugal
5 Sep 1914	London	Britain, France and Russia (accessions: Japan and Italy)
3 Mar 1918	Treaty of Brest-Litovsk	Russia and the Central Powers
Aug 1919	Franco-Belgian Military Convention	

28 Jun 1919	Treaty of Versailles	Germany and the Allied Powers
10 Sep 1919	Treaty of St Germain	Austrian Republic and the Allied Powers
27 Nov 1919	Treaty of Neuilly	Bulgaria and the Allied Powers
4 Jun 1920	Treaty of Trianon	Hungary and the Allied Powers
10 Aug 1920	Treaty of Sèvres	Turkey and the Allied Powers (not ratified by Turkey)
19 Feb 1921	Franco-Polish Treaty	
3 Mar 1921	Polish-Romanian Treaty	
18 Mar 1921	Treaty of Riga	Poland and the Soviet Union
16 Apr 1922	Treaty of Rapallo	Russia and Germany
31 Aug 1922	Little Entente	Czechoslovakia, Yugoslavia and Romania
24 Jul 1923	Treaty of Lausanne	
1 Dec 1925	Locarno Treaties	France, Belgium, Germany; guaranteed by Britain and Italy
24 Apr 1926	Soviet-German Neutrality Pact	
15 Jul 1932	Polish-Soviet Treaty	
26 Jan 1934	Polish-German Pact	
2 May 1935	Franco-Russian Alliance	
20 Jul 1936	Montreux Convention	Turkey permitted to re-fortify the Straits
25 Nov 1936	Anti-Comintern Pact	Germany and Japan; signed by Italy 6 Nov 1937
2 Jan 1937	Anglo-Italian Gentleman's Agreement	
29 Sep 1938	Munich Agreement	Britain, France, Germany, Italy
22 May 1939	Pact of Steel	Germany and Italy
23 Aug 1939	Nazi-Soviet Pact	
25 Aug 1939	Polish-British Treaty	
19 Oct 1939	British-French-Turkish Agreement	
12 Mar 1940	Treaty of Moscow	Ended war between Finland and Soviet Union
27 Sep 1940	Tripartite Pact	Germany, Italy, Japan
26 May 1942	Anglo-Soviet Treaty	
12 Dec 1943	Soviet-Czech Pact	
10 Dec 1944	Franco-Soviet Treaty	
21 Apr 1945	Soviet-Polish Pact	
4 Mar 1947	Dunkirk Treaty	Britain and France
10 Mar 1947	Polish-Czech Pact	
16 Dec 1947	Bulgarian-Albanian Pact	
16 Jan 1948	Bulgarian-Romanian Pact	
24 Jan 1948	Hungarian-Romanian Pact	
4 Feb 1948	Soviet-Romanian Pact	
18 Feb 1948	Soviet-Hungarian Pact	
17 Mar 1948	Brussels Treaty	Britain, France, Benelux
18 Mar 1948	Soviet-Bulgarian Pact	
5 Apr 1948	Soviet-Finnish Pact	
23 Apr 1948	Bulgarian-Czech Pact	
9 Jun 1948	Polish-Hungarian Pact	
18 Jun 1948	Bulgarian-Hungarian Pact	
21 Jul 1948	Romanian-Czech Pact	
21 Jan 1949	Polish-Romanian Pact	
4 Apr 1949	North Atlantic Treaty	

16 Apr 1949	Hungarian-Czech Pact	
9 Aug 1954	Balkan Pact	Greece, Turkey, Yugoslavia
24 Feb 1955	Baghdad Pact	Turkey and Iraq; Britain 5 Apr 1955; Pakistan 23 Sep 1955
5 May 1955	London and Paris Agreements	
13 May 1955	Warsaw Pact	
15 May 1955	Austrian State Treaty	
22 Jan 1963	Franco-Federal German Treaty	
27 Nov 1963	Soviet-Czech Pact	
12 Jun 1964	Soviet-Democratic German Pact	
8 Apr 1965	Soviet-Polish Pact	
1 Mar 1967	Polish-Czech Treaty	
15 Mar 1967	Polish-Democratic German Treaty	
17 Mar 1967	Democratic German-Czech Treaty	
13 May 1967	Soviet-Bulgarian Pact	
18 May 1967	Hungarian-Democratic German Pact	
6 Apr 1967	Polish-Bulgarian Pact	
7 Sep 1967	Soviet-Hungarian Pact	
7 Sep 1967	Bulgarian-Democratic German Pact	
26 Apr 1968	Bulgarian-Czech Pact	
16 May 1968	Polish-Hungarian Pact	
10 Jul 1969	Bulgarian-Hungarian Pact	
20 Mar 1970	Soviet-Czech Pact	
7 July 1970	Soviet-Romanian Pact	
12 Aug 1970	Soviet-Federal German Treaty	
12 Nov 1970	Polish-Romanian Treaty	
7 Dec 1970	Polish-Federal German Treaty	
26 Mar 1972	British-Maltese Agreement	Seven-year agreement on bases
21 Dec 1972	Federal German-Democratic German Treaty	Normalization of relations
11 Dec 1973	Czech-Federal German Treaty	
14 Jun 1975	Portuguese-Romanian Treaty	
7 Oct 1975	Soviet-Democratic German Treaty	
10 Nov 1975	Treaty of Osimo	
24 Mar 1977	Democratic German-Hungarian Treaty	
28 May 1977	Democratic German-Polish Treaty	
14 Sep 1977	Democratic German-Bulgarian Treaty	
3 Oct 1977	Democratic German-Czech Treaty	
20 Jun 1983	Soviet-Finnish Treaty	Renewed for 20 years.
12 Jun 1985	Portugal, Spain, EC	Treaty of Accession

15 Nov 1985	Anglo-Irish Agreement	
1 Feb 1986	Single European Act	Creation of Single European Market in EU
14 Apr 1988	USSR-Afghanistan	Geneva Accord ending war
2 Dec 1989	USSR-Vatican	Re-establish diplomatic relations
Feb 1990	Hungary-Vatican	Re-establish diplomatic relations
27 Feb 1990	USSR-Czechoslovakia	Agreement on troop withdrawal
10 Mar 1990	USSR-Hungary	Agreement on troop withdrawal
19 Jun 1990	Schengen Agreement	Abolition of borders within EC states
12 Sep 1990	German Final Settlement Treaty	Union of two Germanies, end of allied role in Germany
19 Nov 1990	Conventional Forces in Europe Treaty	
6 Sep 1991	USSR-Baltic States	Independence of Estonia, Latvia and Lithuania recognized
18 Oct 1991	USSR-Israel	Diplomatic relations established
11 Dec 1991	Treaty of Maastricht	Agreement on future development of European Union (ratified later by individual countries)
7 Feb 1992	Russia-France	Treaty of Solidarity
21 Jul 1992	Russia-Moldova	Settlement of Transdniestra question
3 Aug 1992	Russia-Ukraine	Division of Black Sea fleet
Sep 1992	Russia-Lithuania	Agreement on troop withdrawals
Apr 1993	Russia-Latvia	Agreement on troop withdrawals
21 Nov 1995	Dayton Accord	Warring parties agreements to end war in Bosnia-Hercegovina (Bosnia, Croatia, Yugoslavia)
16 Mar 1996	Hungary-Slovakia	Bilateral agreement on outstanding issues (followed by Hungarian-Romanian agreement)
Dec 1996	Russia-China	Troop reductions along 2700-mile frontier

OUTLINE OF PRINCIPAL EUROPEAN DEFENCE TREATIES AND AGREEMENTS 1900–1996

FRANCO-BELGIAN MILITARY CONVENTION. *August 1920*

The abrogation of treaties for the neutralization of Belgium was confirmed in a treaty signed by Britain, France and Belgium on 22 May 1926. Belgium announced its return to neutrality in Oct 1936 after the remilitarization of the Rhineland (7 Mar 1936), thereby preventing the vital co-ordination of strategic planning with France prior to World War II.

FRANCO-POLISH TREATY. *19 February 1921.*

Provided for mutual defence against unprovoked aggression. Poland concluded a similar treaty with Romania on 3 Mar 1921.

TREATY OF RAPALLO. *16 April 1922*

Germany and Soviet Russia re-established diplomatic relations, renounced financial claims on either side, and pledged economic co-operation. The Treaty was reaffirmed by the German-Soviet Neutrality Pact of 24 Apr 1926.

THE LITTLE ENTENTE. *31 August 1922*

Bilateral agreements between Yugoslavia, Czechoslovakia and Romania were consolidated into a single treaty in Aug 1922, and further strengthened in May 1929. The object of the Little Entente was the maintenance of the *status quo* in Central Europe.

LOCARNO TREATIES. *1 December 1925*

The signatories, France, Germany and Belgium, recognized the inviolability of the Franco-German and Belgo-German frontier, and the existence of the demilitarized zone of the Rhineland; this was guaranteed by Britain and Italy. Franco-Polish and Franco-Czech Treaties of Mutual Guarantee were also signed, and action under these treaties was not to be regarded as aggression against Germany. The treaty was violated on 7 Mar 1936 when Hitler sent troops into the Rhineland.

POLISH-SOVIET TREATY. *25 July 1923*

A non-aggression treaty, valid for five years. It was prolonged for ten years in Dec 1934 after the signing of a Polish-German Treaty.

POLISH-GERMAN TREATY. *26 January 1934*

A non-aggression treaty, valid for ten years; repudiated by Hitler on 28 Apr 1939.

FRANCO-RUSSIAN ALLIANCE. *2 May 1935*

Provided for mutual aid in the event of unprovoked aggression.

ANGLO-GERMAN NAVAL AGREEMENT. *18 June 1935*

Limited the German navy to 35% of the British, with submarines at 45% or equality in the event of danger from Russia.

ANTI-COMINTERN PACT. *25 November 1936*

Signed by Germany and Japan to oppose the spread of communism. Italy joined the Pact on 6 Nov 1937.

369

ANGLO-ITALIAN 'GENTLEMAN'S AGREEMENT'. *2 January 1937*

An agreement to maintain the *status quo* in the Mediterranean.

MUNICH AGREEMENT. *29 September 1938*

An agreement reached by Britain, France, Italy and Germany, by which territorial concessions were to be made to Germany, Poland and Hungary at the expense of Czechoslovakia. The rump of Czechoslovakia was to be guaranteed against unprovoked aggression, but German control was extended to the rest of Czechoslovakia in Mar 1939.

THE PACT OF STEEL. *22 May 1939*

The formal treaty of alliance between Italy and Germany. Prior to this Mussolini had announced the existence of the 'Rome-Berlin Axis' in a speech at Milan on 1 Nov 1936.

NAZI-SOVIET PACT. *23 August 1939*

The Soviet Union agreed to remain neutral if Germany was involved in a war. The Pact was broken when Hitler invaded Russia on 22 Jun 1941.

BRITISH-POLISH TREATY. *25 August 1939*

A mutual assistance treaty, subsequent to the Franco-British guarantee against aggression given to Poland on 31 Mar 1939.

BRITISH-FRENCH-TURKISH AGREEMENT. *19 October 1939*

A mutual assistance treaty. Turkey, however, remained neutral until 1 Mar 1945, and signed a treaty of non-aggression with Germany in Jun 1941.

TRIPARTITE PACT. *27 September 1940*

Germany, Italy and Japan undertook to assist each other if one of them was attacked by a power not already in the war. The Pact was signed by Hungary, Romania, Slovakia, Bulgaria and Yugoslavia 1940–1.

ANGLO-SOVIET TREATY. *26 May 1942*

A treaty of alliance and mutual assistance, valid for twenty years. The treaty was abrogated by the Soviet Union on 7 May 1955 as a result of the ratification of the London and Paris Agreements by the British government.

FRANCO-SOVIET TREATY. *10 December 1944*

A treaty of alliance and mutual assistance, valid for twenty years. The treaty was abrogated by the Soviet Union on 7 May 1955 as a result of the ratification of the London and Paris Agreements by the French government.

DUNKIRK TREATY. *4 March 1947*

Treaty of alliance between Britain and France, valid for fifty years.

BRUSSELS TREATY. *17 March 1948*

An agreement signed by France, Britain and the Benelux countries for mutual aid in military, economic and social matters.

NORTH ATLANTIC TREATY. *4 April 1949*

Collective Security treaty signed by Belgium, Britain, Canada, Denmark, France, Iceland, Italy, Luxembourg, the Netherlands, Norway, Portugal, and the United States. Greece and Turkey joined NATO in Feb 1952, and the Federal Republic of Germany joined in May 1955.

BALKAN PACT. *9 August 1954*

A treaty of alliance, political co-operation and mutual assistance signed by Greece, Turkey and Yugoslavia, and valid for twenty years.

BAGHDAD PACT. *24 February 1955*

A mutual assistance treaty signed by Turkey and Iraq. Britain joined the Pact on 5 Apr 1955, and Pakistan on 23 Sep 1955.

LONDON AND PARIS AGREEMENTS. *5 May 1955*

The occupation régime in West Germany was ended, and the German Federal Republic attained full sovereignty and independence. The Federal Republic became a member of NATO, and of the Western European Union, the expanded Brussels Treaty Organization which came into being on 5 May.

WARSAW PACT. *13 May 1955*

A treaty of friendship, co-operation and mutual assistance signed by the Soviet Union, Poland, Czechoslovakia, German Democratic Republic, Hungary, Romania, Bulgaria and Albania. The treaty also provided for the creation of a unified command for all the countries.

AUSTRIAN STATE TREATY. *15 May 1955*

Signed by the Soviet Union, Britain, France and the United States, the treaty re-established Austria as a sovereign, independent and neutral state.

FRANCO-WEST GERMAN TREATY. *22 January 1963*

Treaty of co-operation, providing for co-ordination of the two countries' policies in foreign affairs, defence, information and cultural affairs.

SOVIET-FEDERAL GERMANY TREATY. *12 August 1970*

A treaty renouncing the use of force.

POLISH-FEDERAL GERMAN TREATY. *7 December 1970*

An agreement that the existing boundary line on the Oder and the West Neisse constitutes the western frontier of Poland, and renouncing the use of force for the settlement of disputes.

TREATY OF OSIMO. *10 November 1975*

A treaty between Italy and Yugoslavia in which the two countries accepted border changes around Trieste slightly in favour of Italy, that national minorities were to be protected and there was to be greater economic co-operation.

CONVENTIONAL FORCES IN EUROPE TREATY. *19 November 1990*

A non-aggression treaty which aimed to reduce conventional weapons in Europe by almost a third, signed in Paris by 16 NATO members (Belgium, Canada, Denmark, France, the Federal Republic of Germany, Greece, Iceland, Italy, Luxembourg, Netherlands, Norway, Portugal, Spain, Turkey, UK and USA) and 6 Warsaw Pact members (Bulgaria, Czech and Slovak Federal Republic, Hungary, Poland, Romania and USSR).

TREATY OF MAASTRICHT. *11 December 1991*

The agreement on the future development of the European Union. It was ratified later by individual countries (after considerable opposition in such countries as Britain).

9 DEPENDENCIES

BELGIUM

Congo, formerly Belgian Congo, then Congo (Kinshasa) and then Zaïre. Until the middle of the nineteenth century the territory drained by the Congo River was practically unknown. When Stanley reached the mouth of the Congo in 1877, King Leopold II of the Belgians recognized the immense possibilities of the Congo Basin and took the lead in exploring and exploiting it. The Berlin Conference of 1884–1885 recognized King Leopold II as the sovereign head of the Congo Free State.

The annexation of the state to Belgium was provided for by treaty of 28 Nov 1907, which was approved by the chambers of the Belgian Legislature in Aug and Sep and by the King on 18 Oct 1908. The law of 18 Oct 1908, called the Colonial Charter (last amended in 1959), provided for the government of the Belgian Congo, until the country became independent on 30 Jun 1960.

The departure of the Belgian administrators, teachers, doctors, etc., on the day of independence left a vacuum which speedily resulted in complete chaos. Neither Joseph Kasavubu, the leader of the Abako Party, who on 24 Jun 1960 had been elected head of state, nor Patrice Lumumba, leader of the Congo National Movement, who was the prime minister of an all-party coalition government, could establish his authority. Personal, tribal and regional rivalries led to the breakaway of Katanga province under premier Moïse Tshombe. Lumumba found his main support in the Oriental and Kivu provinces. Early in July the *Force Publique* mutinied and removed all Belgian officers. Lumumba called for intervention by the UN as well as the USSR. The Secretary-General dispatched a military force of about 20 000, composed of contingents of African and Asian countries. Lumumba was kidnapped by Katanga tribesmen and, in early Feb 1961, murdered; his place was taken by Antoine Gizenga, who set up a government in Stanleyville.

On 15 Aug 1961 the UN recognized the government of Cyrille Adoula as the central government. UN forces, chiefly Irish and Ethiopians, in mid-Sep invaded Katanga.

On 15 Jan 1962 the forces of Gizenga in Stanleyville surrendered to those of the central government, and on 16 Jan Adoula dismissed Gizenga. UN forces, chiefly Ethiopians and Indians, again invaded Katanga in Dec 1962 and by the end of Jan 1963 had occupied all key towns; Tshombe left the country. The UN troops left the Congo by 30 Jun 1964.

The Gizenga faction started a fresh rebellion and after the capture of Albertville (19 Jun) and Stanleyville (5 Aug) proclaimed a People's Republic on 7 Sep 1964. Government troops, Belgian paratroopers and a mercenary contingent captured Stanleyville on 24 Nov after the rebels had massacred thousands of black and white civilians. The last rebel strongholds were captured at the end of Apr 1965.

DENMARK

The Faroe Islands (Faerøerne). The islands were first colonized in the ninth century and were Norwegian possessions until 1380 and subsequently belonged to Denmark. They were occupied by British troops in World War II. In Sep 1946 they voted for independence from Denmark but now return two members to the *Folketing.* Home rule was granted in 1948.

Greenland (Grønland). From 1261 to 1953 Greenland was a Danish colony. On 5 Jun 1953 Greenland became an integral part of the Danish Realm with the same rights as other counties in Denmark, returning two members to the *Folketing*, and with a democratically elected council (*landsråd*). A Danish–American agreement for the common defence of Greenland was signed on 27 Apr 1951.

Iceland (Island). The first settlers came to Iceland in 874. Between 930 and 1264 Iceland was an independent republic, but by the 'Old Treaty' of 1263 the country recognized the rule of the King of Norway. In 1381 Iceland, together with Norway, came under the rule of the Danish kings, but when Norway was separated from Denmark in 1814, Iceland remained under the rule of Denmark. Since 1 Dec 1918 it has been acknowledged as a sovereign state. It was united with Denmark only through the common sovereign until it was proclaimed an independent republic on 17 Jun 1944.

FRANCE

The French Community (La Communauté). The constitution of the Fifth Republic, promulgated on 6 Oct 1958, 'offers to the overseas territories which manifest their will to adhere to it new institutions based on the common ideal of liberty, equality and fraternity and conceived with a view to their democratic evolution'. The territories were offered three solutions: they could keep their status; they could become overseas *départements*; they could become, singly or in groups, member states of the Community (Art. 76).

According to the amendment of the constitution adopted on 4 Jun 1960, member-states of the Community could become independent and sovereign republics without ceasing to belong to the Community. The 12 African and Malagasy members availed themselves of this *loi constitutionnelle* and became independent by the transfer of 'common powers' (*compétences communes*).

The territorial structure of the Community and affiliated states was as follows:

I. FRENCH REPUBLIC

   A. Metropolitan Departments.

   B. Overseas Departments:
   (i) Martinique; (ii) Guadeloupe; (iii) Réunion; (iv) Guiana.

   C. Overseas Territories:
   (i) French Polynesia; (ii) New Caledonia; (iii) French Territory of the Afars and the Issas; (iv) Comoro Archipelago; (v) Saint-Pierre and Miquelon; (vi) Southern and Antarctic Territories; (vii) Wallis and Futuna Islands.

II. MEMBER STATES

   1. French Republic; 2. Central African Republic; 3. Republic of Congo; 4. Republic of Gabon; 5. Madagascar; 6. Republic of Senegal; 7. Republic of Chad.

These countries concluded formal 'Community participation agreements'.

III. 'Special relations' or 'special links' were established by agreements between France and the other Franc zone countries and the following states:
1. Republic of Ivory Coast; 2. Republic of Dahomey; 3. Republic of Upper Volta; 4. Islamic Republic of Mauritania; 5. Republic of Niger; 6. Federal Republic of Cameroun.

IV. Co-operation in certain fields was established by special agreements between France and the Republic of Mali.

V. Co-operation was established between France and the Togo Republic by a convention signed on 10 Jul 1963.

VI. The states listed under II, 2–7, III, 1–3, 5 and 6, and V are the members of the Organization *Commune Africaine et Malgache*.

VII. Other regional organizations:

1. The Customs and Economic Union of Central Africa, comprising the Central African Republic, Congo, Gabon, Chad and Cameroun; the common external tariff, effective from 1 Jul 1962, did not apply to the countries listed under II and III;

2. The entente of Ivory Coast, Dahomey, Upper Volta, Niger;

3. The customs union of Senegal, Mali, Ivory Coast, Dahomey, Upper Volta, Niger and Mauritania;

4. The West African monetary union of Senegal, Mauritania, Ivory Coast, Upper Volta, Niger, Dahomey and Togo.

VIII. Relations between France and Algeria (comprising the former Algerian and Sahara Departments) are governed by the Évian agreements of 19 Mar 1962 and subsequent agreements.

 IX. The Anglo-French Condominium of the New Hebrides is administered according to the London Protocol of 6 Aug 1914.

Guinea opted out of the Community in 1958.

Algeria. Algeria was annexed by France in 1885 and became a department of France. French policy was to integrate Algeria completely into France itself but this was not acceptable to the French settlers, *colons*.

On 1 Nov 1954 the National Liberation Front (FLN), founded 5 Aug 1951, went over to open warfare against the French administration and armed forces. In Sep 1958 a free Algerian government was formed in Cairo with Ferhat Abbas as provisional president.

A referendum was held in Metropolitan France and Algeria on 6–8 Jan 1961 to decide on Algerian self-determination as proposed by President de Gaulle. His proposals were approved by 15 200 073 against 4 996 474 votes in Metropolitan France, and by 1 749 969 against 767 546 votes in Algeria. In Metropolitan France 20.2m. out of 27.2m. registered voters went to the polls; in Algeria 2.5m. out of 4.5m. registered voters.

Long delayed by the terrorism, in Metropolitan France as well as Algeria, of a secret organization (OAS) led by anti-Gaullist officers, a ceasefire agreement was concluded between the French government and the representatives of the Algerian Nationalists on 18 Mar 1962; but OAS terror acts continued for some months. On 7 Apr a provisional executive of 12 members was set up, under the chairmanship of Abderrhaman Farès.

On 8 Apr 1962 a referendum in Metropolitan France approved the Algerian settlement with 17 505 473 (90.7%), against 1 794 553 (9.3%) and 1 102 477 invalid votes; 6 580 772 voters abstained. On 1 Jul 1962, 5 975 581 Algerians voted in favour of, 16 534 against, the settlement.

Morocco. From 1912 to 1956 Morocco was divided into a French protectorate (established by the Treaty of Fez concluded between France and the Sultan on 30 Mar 1912), a Spanish protectorate (established by the Franco-Spanish convention of 27 Nov 1912) and the international zone of Tangier (set up by France, Spain and Britain on 18 Dec 1923).

On 2 Mar 1956 France and the Sultan terminated the Treaty of Fez; on 7 Apr 1956 Spain relinquished her protectorate, and on 29 Oct 1956 France, Spain, Britain, Italy, USA, Belgium, the Netherlands, Sweden and Portugal abolished the international status of the Tangier Zone.

Indo-China (Cambodia). Attacked on either side by the Vietnamese and the Thai from the fifteenth century on, Cambodia was saved from annihilation by the establishment of a French protectorate in 1863. Thailand eventually recognized the protectorate and renounced all claims to suzerainty in exchange for Cambodia's north-western provinces of Battambang and Siem Reap, which were, however, returned under a Franco-Thai convention of 1907, confirmed in the Franco-Thai treaty of 1937. In 1904 the province of Stung Treng, formerly administered as part of Laos, was attached to Cambodia.

A nationalist movement began in the 1930s, and anti-French feeling strengthened in 1940–1, when the French submitted to Japanese demands for bases in Cambodia and allowed Thailand to annex Cambodian territory. On 9 Mar 1945 the Japanese suppressed the French administration and the treaties between France and Cambodia were denounced by King Norodom Sihanouk, who proclaimed Cambodia's independence. British troops occupied Phnom Penh in Oct 1945, and the re-establishment of French authority was followed by a Franco-Cambodian *modus vivendi* of 7 Jan 1946, which promised a constitution embodying a constitutional monarchy. Elections for a National Consultative Assembly were held on 1 Sep 1946, and a Franco-Thai agreement of 17 Nov 1946 ensured the return to Cambodia of the provinces annexed by Thailand in 1941.

In 1949 Cambodia was granted independence as an Associate State of the French Union. The transfer of the French military powers to the Cambodian government on 9 Nov 1953 is considered in Cambodia as the attainment of sovereign independence. In Jan 1955 Cambodia became financially and economically independent, both of France and the other two former Associate States of French Indo-China, Vietnam and Laos.

Laos. In 1893 Laos became a French protectorate and in 1907 acquired its present frontiers. In 1945 French authority was suppressed by the Japanese. When the Japanese withdrew in 1945 an independence movement known as *Lao Issara* (Free Laos) set up a government under Prince Phetsarath, the Viceroy of Luang Prabang. This government collapsed with the return of the French in 1946 and the leaders of the movement fled to Thailand.

Under a new constitution of 1947 Laos became a constitutional monarchy under the Luang Prabang dynasty, and in 1949 became an independent sovereign state within the French Union.

Vietnam. French interest in Vietnam started in the late sixteenth century with the arrival of French and Portuguese missionaries. The most notable of these was Alexander of Rhodes, who, in the following century, romanized Vietnamese writing. At the end of the eighteenth century a French bishop and several soldiers of fortune helped to establish the Emperor Gia-Long (with whom Louis XVI had signed a treaty in 1787) as ruler of a unified Vietnam, known then as the Empire of Annam.

An expedition sent by Napoleon III in 1858 to avenge the death of some French missionaries led in 1862 to the cession to France of part of Cochin-China, and thence, by a series of treaties between 1874 and 1884, to the establishment of French protectorates over Tonkin and Annam, and to the formation of the French colony of Cochin-China. By a Sino-French treaty of 1885 the Empire of Annam (including Tonkin) ceased to be a tributary to China. Cambodia had become a French protectorate in 1863, and in 1899, after the extension of French protection to Laos in 1893, the Indo-Chinese Union was proclaimed.

In 1940 Vietnam was occupied by the Japanese and used as a military base for the invasion of Malaya. During the occupation there was considerable underground activity among nationalist, revolutionary and Communist organizations. In 1941 a nominally nationalist coalition of such organizations, known as the Vietminh League, was founded by the Communists.

On 9 Mar 1945 the Japanese interned the French authorities and proclaimed the 'independence' of Indo-China. In Aug 1945 they allowed the Vietminh movement to seize power, dethrone Bao Dai, the Emperor of Annam, and establish a republic known as Vietnam, including Tonkin, Annam and Cochin-China with Hanoi as capital. In Sep 1945 the French re-established themselves in Cochin-China and on 6 Mar 1946, after a cease-fire in the sporadic fighting between the French forces and the Vietminh had been arranged, a preliminary convention was signed in Hanoi between the French High Commissioner and President Ho Chi Minh by which France recognized 'the Democratic Republic of Vietnam' as a 'Free State within the Indo-Chinese Federation'. Subsequent conferences convened in the same year at Dalat and Fontainebleau to draft a definitive agreement broke down chiefly over the question of whether or not Cochin-China should be included in the new republic. On 19 Dec 1946 Vietminh forces made a surprise attack on Hanoi, the signal for hostilities which were to last for nearly eight years.

An agreement signed by the Emperor Bao Dai on behalf of Vietnam on 8 Mar 1949 recognized the independence of Vietnam within the French Union, and certain sovereign powers were forthwith transferred to Vietnam. Others remained partly under French control until Sep 1954. The remainder, connected with services in which Cambodia, France, Laos and Vietnam had a common interest, were regulated by the Pau conventions of Dec 1950. These conventions were abrogated by the Paris agreements of 29 Dec 1954, which completed the transfer of sovereignty to Vietnam. Supreme authority in the military field remained with the French until the departure of the last French C.-in-C. in Apr 1956. Treaties of independence and association were initiated by representatives of the French and Vietnamese governments on 4 Jun 1954.

In 1974 **Mayotte** voted against becoming independent with the rest of the Comoro Archipelago (an Overseas Territory). **Comoros** therefore became an independent state on 6 Jul 1975; Mayotte remained a dependency, and in 1976 was given the status of *collectivité territoriale* – an intermediate status between Overseas Territory and Overseas Department.

In Jul 1976 **Saint-Pierre and Miquelon**, an Overseas Territory, became an Overseas Department and in 1985 became a *collectivité territoriale*.

On 27 Jun 1977 the French Territory of the Afars and Issas, an Overseas Territory, became independent as the Republic of **Djibouti**.

ITALY

Ethiopia (Abyssinia). In 1936 Ethiopia was conquered by the Italians, who were in turn defeated by the Allied forces in 1941 when the Emperor returned.

The former Italian colony of Eritrea, from 1941 under British military administration, was in accordance with a resolution of the General Assembly of the United Nations, dated 2 Dec 1950, handed over to Ethiopia on 15 Sep 1952. Eritrea thereby became an autonomous unit within the federation of Ethiopia and Eritrea, under the Ethiopian Crown. This federation became a unitary state on 14 Nov 1962 when Eritrea was fully integrated with Ethiopia but became an independent sovereign state on 24 May 1993 after a prolonged armed struggle.

Somalia. The Somali Republic came into being on 1 Jul 1960 as a result of the merger of the British Somaliland Protectorate, which became independent on 26 Jun 1960, and the Italian Trusteeship Territory of Somalia.

THE NETHERLANDS

Netherlands Antilles (De Nederlandse Antillen). Since Dec 1954, the Netherlands Antilles have been fully autonomous in internal affairs, and constitutionally equal with the Netherlands and Suriname. The Sovereign of the Kingdom of the Netherlands is head of the Government of the Netherlands Antilles and is represented by a Governor. On 1 Jan 1986 Aruba was constitutionally separated from the Netherlands Antilles and full independence was envisaged after a ten-year period.

Netherlands East Indies. From 1602 the Netherlands East India Company conquered the Netherlands East Indies, and ruled them until the dissolution of the company in 1798. Thereafter the Netherlands government ruled the colony from 1816 to 1945.

Complete and unconditional sovereignty was transferred to the Republic of the United States of Indonesia on 27 Dec 1949, except for the western part of New Guinea, the status of which was to be determined through negotiations between Indonesia and the Netherlands within one year after the transfer of sovereignty. A union was created to regulate the relationship between the two countries. A settlement of the New Guinea (West Irian) question was, however, delayed until 15 Aug 1962, when, through the good offices of the UN, an agreement was concluded for the transfer of the territory to Indonesia on 1 May 1963.

Suriname (Dutch Guiana). At the peace of Breda (1667) between Great Britain and the United Netherlands, Suriname was assigned to the Netherlands in exchange for the colony of New Netherlands in North America, and this was confirmed by the Treaty of Westminster of Feb 1674. Since then Suriname has been twice in British possession, 1799–1802 (when it was restored to the Batavian Republic at the peace of Amiens) and 1804–16, when it was returned to the Kingdom of the Netherlands according to the convention of London of 13 Aug 1814, confirmed at the peace of Paris of 20 Nov 1815. Suriname became fully independent on 25 Nov 1975.

NORWAY

Svalbard. The main islands of the archipelago are Spitsbergen (formerly Vestspitsbergen), Nordaustlandet, Edgeøya, Barentsøya, Prins Karls Forland, Bjørnøya, Hopen, Kong Karls Land, Kvitøya, and many small islands.

The archipelago was probably discovered by Norsemen in 1194 and rediscovered by the Dutch navigator Barents in 1596. In the seventeenth century the very lucrative whale-hunting caused rival Dutch, British and Danish-Norwegian claims to sovereignty and quarrels about the hunting-places. But when in the eighteenth century the whale-hunting ended, the question of the sovereignty of Svalbard lost its actuality; it was again raised in the twentieth century, owing to the discovery and exploitation of coalfields. By a treaty, signed on 9 Feb 1920 in Paris, Norway's sovereignty over the archipelago was recognized. On 14 Aug 1925 the archipelago was officially incorporated in Norway.

Jan Mayen. The island was possibly discovered by Henry Hudson in 1608, and it was first named Hudson's Tutches (Touches). It was again and again rediscovered and renamed. Its present name derives from the Dutch whaling captain Jan Jacobsz May, who indisputably discovered the island in 1614. It was uninhabited, but occasionally visited by seal hunters and trappers, until 1921 when Norway established a radio and meteorological station. On 8 May 1929 Jan Mayen was officially proclaimed as incorporated in the Kingdom of Norway. Its relation to Norway was finally settled by law of 27 Feb 1930.

Bouvet Island, Bouvetøya. This uninhabited island was discovered in 1739 by a French naval officer, Jean Baptiste Lozier Bouvet, but no flag was hoisted until, in 1825, Capt. Norris raised the Union Jack. In 1928 Britain waived its claim to the island in favour of Norway, which in Dec 1927 had occupied it. A law of 27 Feb 1930 declared Bouvetøya a Norwegian dependency.

Peter I Island, Peter I øy. This uninhabited island was sighted in 1821 by the Russian explorer, Admiral von Bellingshausen. The first landing was made in 1929 by a Norwegian expedition which hoisted the Norwegian flag. On 1 May 1931 Peter I Island was placed under Norwegian sovereignty, and on 24 Mar 1933 it was incorporated in Norway as a dependency.

Queen Maud Land, Dronning Maud Land. On 14 Jan 1939 the Norwegian cabinet placed that part of the Antarctic Continent from the border of Falkland Islands dependencies in the west to the border of the Australian Antarctic Dependency in the east (between 20°W. and 45°E.) under Norwegian sovereignty. The territory had been explored only by Norwegians and hitherto been ownerless. Since 1949 expeditions from various countries have explored the area. In 1957 Dronning Maud Land was given the status of a Norwegian dependency.

PORTUGAL

On 11 Jun 1951 the status of the Portuguese overseas possessions was changed from 'colonies' to 'overseas territories'. Each one had a Governor and enjoyed financial and administrative autonomy. Their budgets were under approval of the Minister for the Overseas Territories. They were not allowed to contract public loans in foreign countries. Under the Organic Law for Overseas Territories, of May 1972, the overseas provinces were given greater autonomy 'without affecting the unity of the nation'. Angola and Mozambique were designated States instead of overseas provinces.

On 6 Sep 1961 all Africans were given full Portuguese citizenship, thereby achieving the same status as the inhabitants of Portuguese India and the other provinces.

All customs duties between Portugal and the overseas provinces were abolished with effect from 1 Jan 1964.

Cape Verde Islands. The Cape Verde Islands were discovered in 1460 by Diogo Gomes, the first settlers arriving in 1462. In 1587 its administration was unified under a governor. The territory consists of ten islands and five islets which were administered by a Governor, whose seat was at Praia, the capital. The islands are divided into two groups, named Barlavento (windward) and Sotavento (leeward), the prevailing wind being north-east. The former is constituted by the islands of São Vicente, Santo Antão, São Nicolau, Santa Luzia, Sal and Boa Vista, and the small islands named Branco and Raso. The latter is constituted by the islands of Santiago, Maio, Fogo and Brava, and the small islands named Rei and Rombo. São Vicente was an oiling station which supplied all navigation to South America. The total area is 4033 sq. km. (1557 sq. miles). The islands became independent on 5 Jul 1975 as the Republic of Cape Verde.

Portuguese Guinea. Portuguese Guinea, on the coast of Guinea, was discovered in 1446 by Nuno Tristão. It became a separate colony in 1879. It is bounded by the limits fixed by the convention of 12 May 1886 with France, and is bounded by Senegal in the north and by Guinea in the east and south. It includes the adjacent archipelago of Bijagoz, with the island of Bolama. The capital is, since 1942, Bissau. Area is 36 125 sq. km. (13 948 sq. miles). The dependency became an independent state, as Guinea-Bissau, on 10 Sep 1974.

São Tomé e Principe. The Islands of S. Tomé and Principe, which are about 125 miles off the coast of Africa, in the Gulf of Guinea, were discovered in 1471 by Pedro Escobar and João Gomes, and after 1522 constituted a province under a Governor. The province also included the islands of Pedras Tinhosas and Rolas; the fort of St Jean Baptiste d'Ajudã on the coast was annexed by the Dahomey Republic on 1 Aug 1961. Area of the islands 964 sq. km (372 sq. miles). The islands became independent on 12 Jul 1975.

Angola. Angola, with a coastline of over 1000 miles, is separated from the Congo by the boundaries assigned by the convention of 12 May 1886; from Zaïre by those fixed by the convention of 22 Jul 1927; from Rhodesia in accordance with the convention of 11 Jun 1891, and from South-West Africa in accordance with that of 30 Dec 1886. The Congo region was discovered by the Portuguese in 1482, and the first settlers arrived there in 1491. Luanda was founded in 1575. It was taken by the Dutch in 1641 and occupied by them until 1648. The area is 1 246 700 sq. km. (481 351 sq. miles). By a decree of 20 Oct 1954 it is divided into 13 districts. The important towns are S. Paulo de Luanda (capital), Benguela, Moçâmedes, Lobito, Sá da Bandeira, Malange and Huambo (Novo Lisboa), the future capital. Angola became independent on 11 Nov 1975.

Mozambique. Mozambique was discovered by Vasco da Gama's fleet on 1 Mar 1498, and was first colonized in 1505. The frontier with British Central and South Africa was fixed between Great Britain and Portugal in Jun 1891. The border with Tanganyika, according to agreements of 1886 and 1890, ran from Cape Delgado at 10°40'S. Lat. until it meets the course of the Rovuma, which it follows to the point of its confluence with the 'Msinje, the boundary thence to Lake Nyasa being the parallel of latitude of this point. The Treaty of Versailles, 1919, allotted to Portugal the original Portuguese territory south of the Rovuma, known as the 'Kionga Triangle' (formerly part of German East Africa).

Mozambique, with an area of 784 961 sq. km. (303 070 sq. miles) was administered by the state, since 19 Jul 1942, when the state took over the territory of Manica and Sofala, which was incorporated as a fourth district of the province, with Beira as its capital. Lourenço Marques is the capital of the province. As established by decree of 20 Oct 1954, the province was divided into nine districts: Lourenço Marques, Gazai Inhambane, Manica and Sofala, Tete, Zambézia, Mozambique, Cabo Delgado, Niassa.

There was a government council composed of officials and elected representatives of the commercial, industrial and agricultural classes, and also an executive council. Mozambique became independent on 25 Jul 1975.

Macao. Macao, in China, situated on a peninsula of the same name at the mouth of the Canton River, which came into possession of the Portuguese in 1557, forms with the two small adjacent islands of Taipa and

Colôane a province (1961–74), divided into two wards, each having its own administrator. The boundaries have not yet been definitely agreed upon; at present Portugal holds the territory in virtue of the treaty with China of 1 Dec 1887. The area of the province is 16 sq. km. (6 sq. miles). In 1987, in agreement with China, Macao became a Chinese territory under Portuguese administration. Macao will be returned to China in 1999.

Timor. Portuguese Timor was under Portuguese administration from 1586. It consisted of the eastern portion of the island of that name in the Malay Archipelago, with the territory of Ambeno and the neighbouring islands of Pulo Cambing and Pulo Jako, a total area of 14 925 sq. km. By a treaty of Apr 1859, ratified 18 Aug 1860, the island was divided between Portugal and Holland; by convention of 1 Oct 1904, ratified in 1908, the boundaries were straightened and settled. The territory, formerly administratively joined to Macao, was in 1896 (confirmed in 1926) made an independent province. On 7 Dec 1975, during a civil war, the province was invaded by Indonesian forces. On 17 Jul 1976 it became an Indonesian province and was renamed Loro Sae.

Portuguese India (Estado da India), was under Portuguese rule 1505–1961. It consisted of Goa, containing the capital, Goa, together with the islands of Angediva, São Jorge and Morcegos, on the Malabar coast; Damão, with the territories of Dadrá and Nagar-Haveli, on the Gulf of Cambis; and Diu, with the continental territories of Gogola and Simbor, on the coast of Gujerat.

Indian troops invaded Goa, Damão and Diu without declaration of war on 18–19 Dec 1961 and forcibly incorporated the Portuguese territory in the Indian Union.

SPAIN

In Jan 1958 the territory of 'Spanish West Africa' was divided into the provinces of Ifni and Spanish Sahara; both were under the jurisdiction of the commanding officer of the Canary Islands. The province of Ifni was returned to Morocco on 30 Jun 1969.

The Province of Spanish Sahara consisted of two districts: Sekia El Hamra (82 000 sq. km.). and Rio de Oro (184 000 sq. km.). Area 266 000 sq. km. (102 680 sq. miles). The population consisted of some 10 000 Spanish civilians, about 15 000 Spanish soldiers and perhaps 30 000–50 000 nomadic Saharans. The capital is El Aaiún. The strip between 27°40'N.

and Wad Draa was ceded by Spain to Morocco on 10 Apr 1958. Strong pressure was brought, in 1970, by Morocco, Mauritania and Algeria for a referendum to be conducted by Spain in the province. In 1975, Spain, Morocco and Mauritania reached agreement on the transfer of power over Western Sahara to Morocco and Mauritania. The Spanish province ceased to exist on 31 Dec 1975, and the country was partitioned by Morocco and Mauritania. In Aug 1979 Mauritania withdrew from the territory it took over in 1976 and it was reorganized into a fourth province by Morocco. A Saharan nationalist party, the *Frente Polisario*, claims the independence of the country and has renamed it the Saharan Arab Democratic Republic.

Equatorial Guinea (Territorios Espãnoles del Golfo de Guinea). The territory was ceded to Spain by Portugal in 1777. Spain leased it to Britain in 1827, and began to administer it in 1855, as a colony. In 1959 it was turned into two provinces, comparable to the Spanish metropolitan provinces, and called Fernando Po and Rio Muni. In 1964 a degree of self-government was achieved. Independence followed on 12 Oct 1968 as a federation of two provinces and a unitary state was established on 4 Aug 1973.

UNITED KINGDOM

Until Jul 1925 the affairs of all the British Empire, apart from the United Kingdom and India, were dealt with by the Colonial Office. From that date a new secretaryship of state, for Dominion Affairs, became responsible for the relations between the United Kingdom and all the independent members of the Commonwealth.

In Jul 1947 the designations of the Secretary of State for Dominion Affairs and the Dominions Office were altered to 'Secretary of State for Commonwealth Relations' and 'Commonwealth Relations Office'. The following month, on the independence of India and Pakistan, the India Office ceased to exist and the staff were transferred to the Commonwealth Relations Office, which then became responsible for relations with India and Pakistan.

The Colonial Office was merged with the Commonwealth Relations Office on 1 Aug 1966 to form the Commonwealth Office, and the post of Secretary of State for Commonwealth Relations became Secretary of State for Commonwealth Affairs. The post of Secretary of State for the Colonies was retained until 6 Jan 1967. The Commonwealth Office was merged with the Foreign Office on 17 Oct 1968.

The Secretary of State for Foreign and Commonwealth Affairs is now responsible for relations with the independent members of the Commonwealth, with the Associated States, and for the administration of the

UK dependent territories, in addition to his responsibilities for relations with foreign countries.

On 18 Apr 1949, when the Republic of Ireland Act 1948 came into force, Southern Ireland ceased to be a member of the Commonwealth.

The Inperial Conference of 1926 defined Great Britain and the Dominions, as they were then called, as 'autonomous communities within the British Empire, equal in status, in no way subordinate one to another in any aspect of their domestic or foreign affairs, though united by a common allegiance to the Crown, and freely associated as members of the British Commonwealth of Nations'. On 11 Dec 1931 the Statute of Westminster, which by legal enactment recognized the status of the Dominions as defined in 1926, became law. Each of the Dominions, which then included Canada, Australia, New Zealand, South Africa and Newfoundland (which in 1949 became a Canadian Province) had signified approval of the provisions of the Statute.

India and Pakistan became independent on 15 Aug 1947; Ceylon (now Sri Lanka) on 4 Feb 1948; Ghana (formerly the Gold Coast) on 6 Mar 1957; the Federation of Malaya on 31 Aug 1957 (renamed the Federation of Malaysia on 16 Sep 1963, including from that date North Borneo, Sarawak and Singapore until 9 Aug 1965 when Singapore became a separate independent state); Nigeria on 1 Oct 1960; Cyprus on 16 Aug 1960; Sierra Leone on 27 Apr 1961; Tanganyika on 9 Dec 1961 (renamed United Republic of Tanzania on 26 Apr 1964 when she joined with Zanzibar, which had become independent on 10 Dec 1963); Jamaica on 6 Aug 1962; Trinidad and Tobago on 31 Aug 1962; Uganda on 9 Oct 1962; Western Samoa on 1 Jan 1962; Kenya on 12 Dec 1963; Malawi (formerly Nyasaland) on 6 Jul 1964; Malta on 21 Sep 1964; Zambia (formerly Northern Rhodesia) on 24 Oct 1964; The Gambia on 18 Feb 1965; The Maldives on 26 Jul 1965; Guyana (formerly British Guiana) on 26 May 1966; Botswana (formerly Bechuanaland) on 30 Sep 1966; Lesotho (formerly Basutoland) on 4 Oct 1966; Barbados on 30 Nov 1966; Mauritius on 12 Mar 1968; Swaziland on 6 Sep 1968; Nauru on 31 Jan 1968; Tonga on 4 Jun 1970; Fiji on 10 Oct 1970; Bangladesh on 4 Feb 1972; Bahamas on 10 Jul 1973; Papua New Guinea on 16 Sep 1975; Seychelles on 29 Jun 1976; Solomon Islands on 7 Jul 1978; Tuvalu on 1 Oct 1978; Kiribati on 12 Jul 1979; Zimbabwe on 18 Apr 1980; Vanuatu on 30 Jul 1980; Belize on 21 Sep 1981; Brunei on 31 Dec 1983.

On 4 Jan 1948 Burma became an independent republic outside the Commonwealth.

South Africa withdrew from the Commonwealth on becoming a republic on 31 May 1961, but was re-admitted on 1 Jun 1994.

To cater for the special circumstances of small states (Nauru, Tuvalu, St Vincent and the Grenadines, Maldives) a 'special membership' of the

Commonwealth has been devised in close consultation with their governments. Territories dependent on the United Kingdom comprise dependent territories (properly so-called), a protectorate, a protected state and a Condominium. A dependent territory is a territory belonging by settlement, conquest or annexation to the British Crown. A protectorate is a territory not formally annexed but in which, by treaty, grant and other lawful means the Crown has power and jurisdiction. A protected state is a territory under a ruler which enjoys Her Majesty's protection, over whose foreign affairs she exercises control, but in respect of whose internal affairs she does not exercise jurisdiction.

United Kingdom dependencies administered through the Foreign and Commonwealth Office comprise in the Far East: Hong Kong (dependent territory, until its return to China in 1997); in the Indian Ocean: British Indian Ocean Territory; in the Mediterranean: Gibraltar; in the Atlantic Ocean: Bermuda, Falkland Islands and dependencies, South Georgia and South Sandwich Islands, British Antarctic Territory, St Helena and dependencies of Ascension and Tristan da Cunha; in the Caribbean: Montserrat, British Virgin Islands, Cayman Islands, Turks and Caicos Islands, Anguilla; and in the Western Pacific: Pitcairn.

The islands of Antigua, St Christopher-Nevis-Anguilla, Dominica, Grenada and St Lucia had entered a new form of relationship with Britain in 1967, as associated states. St Vincent became an associated state in 1969. Each had control of its own internal affairs, with the right to amend the constitution and the right to end the associated status if it so wished. Grenada became independent on 7 Feb 1974, Dominica on 3 Nov 1978, St Lucia on 22 Feb 1979, St Vincent and the Grenadines on 27 Oct 1979, Antigua and Barbuda on 1 Nov 1981 and St Christopher-Nevis on 19 Sep 1983. The island of Anguilla, although technically a part of the State of Saint Christopher-Nevis-Anguilla, through the Anguilla Act of 1971 and the Anguilla (Administration) Order 1971, came under the direct administration of the United Kingdom and by the Anguilla Act 1980 *de jure* a separate dependency of the United Kingdom. Provision is thereby made for Her Majesty's Commissioner to administer the island in consultation with the Anguilla council.

While constitutional responsibility to parliament for the government of the dependent territories rests with the Secretary of State for Foreign and Commonwealth Affairs, the administration of the territories is carried out by the governments of the territories themselves.

A protected state is a territory under a ruler which enjoys Her Majesty's protection, over whose foreign affairs she exercises control but in respect of whose internal affairs she does not exercise jurisdiction. Brunei is a protected state. Under the 1959 Agreement, as amended Nov 1971 the UK remains responsible for the external affairs of Brunei, while

Brunei has full responsibility for all internal matters. The two governments would consult together about measures to be taken separately and jointly in the event of any external threat to the State of Brunei. Under a treaty signed 7 Jan 1979 Brunei became a fully sovereign and independent State on 31 Dec 1983.

The following territories were dependencies or protectorates of Britain, and did not become members of the Commonwealth when they became independent:

Aden, held by Britain as a colony since 1939, and its associated territory as a protectorate, became independent on 30 Nov 1967 (as the Southern Yemen People's Republic) and later changed its name to the People's Democratic Republic of Yemen.

Bahrain had been under British protection by treaty since 1882, and became independent on 15 Aug 1971.

British Somaliland had been under British protection since 1887, and became independent on 26 Jun 1960; on 1 Jul 1960 it joined the former Italian Trusteeship Territory of Somalia as the Somali Republic.

Burma was annexed, by provinces, to British India between 1824 and 1886; the Indian Province of Burma was formed in 1852. Burma was separated from India in 1937 and became independent on 4 Jan 1948.

Egypt became a British protectorate in 1914, having been occupied in 1882. The protectorate ended on 28 Feb 1922 and and Egypt became an independent kingdom.

Iraq came under British control in 1916 when it was part of the Ottoman Empire allied with Germany during World War I. It became a kingdom under British mandate in 1921 and an independent state on 3 Oct 1932.

Palestine was administered by Britain under a League of Nations mandate, 1922–48.

Sudan was an Anglo-Egyptian condominium from 1899 until independence on 1 Jan 1956.

Transjordan was administered by Britain under a League of Nations mandate 1922–28, and full independence as a kingdom (Jordan) was achieved on 22 Mar 1946.

10 POPULATION[1]

ALBANIA

	Population	Area	Density
1924	831 877	27 529	30.2
1930	1 003 124	27 529	36.4
1947	1 150 000	28 748	40.0
1960	1 626 315	28 748	56.6
1967	1 964 730	28 748	68.3
1970	2 135 600	28 748	74.2
1980	2 734 000	28 748	95.1
1990	3 262 000	28 748	113.5
1995	3 412 000	28 748	118.7

ANDORRA

	Population	Area	Density
1963	5 000	468	10.7
1977	30 700	468	65.6
1984	41 627	468	88.9
1993	61 599	468	134.4

ARMENIA

	Population	Area	Density
1995	3 548 000	29 300	119.1

AUSTRIA

	Population	Area	Density
1910	7 529 935	101 010	74.5
1920	6 428 336	83 792	76.7
1923	6 534 481	83 835	77.9
1934	6 760 233	83 835	80.6
1951	6 933 905	83 850	82.7
1961	7 073 807	83 850	84.4
1971	7 456 403	83 850	88.9
1981	7 555 338	83 853	90.0
1990	7 623 000	83 857	90.9
1995	8 063 000	83 857	96.2

[1] Area in sq. km.

AUSTRIAN EMPIRE[1]

Population

1900	25 921 671
1910	28 571 934

[1] Exclusive of Bosnia and Hercegovina

BELARUS

	Population	Area	Density
1995	10 332 000	207 595	49.8

BELGIUM

	Population	Area	Density
1900	6 694 000	29 456	227.3
1910	7 423 784	29 456	252.0
1920	7 465 782	30 437	245.3
1930	8 092 004	30 437	265.9
1940	8 294 674	30 497	272.0
1947	8 512 195	30 497	279.1
1961	9 189 741	30 513	301.2
1970	9 690 991	30 513	317.6
1980	9 863 374	30 519	323.2
1990	9 958 000	30 519	326.3
1995	10 064 000	30 528	329.7

BOSNIA–HERCEGOVINA

	Population	Area	Density
1995	3 459 000	51 129	67.6

BULGARIA

	Population	Area	Density
1910	4 337 516	87 146	49.8
1921	4 909 700	103 188	47.6
1926	5 478 741	103 188	53.1
1934	6 077 939	103 146	58.9
1946	7 022 206	110 841	63.3
1956	7 629 254	110 911	68.8

BULGARIA (*continued*)

	Population	Area	Density
1965	8 227 866	110 911	74.2
1970	8 467 300	110 911	76.3
1975	8 727 771	110 911	78.5
1981	8 890 002	110 911	80.2
1990	8 987 400	110 994	81.1
1995	8 351 000	110 994	75.2

CROATIA

	Population	Area	Density
1995	4 495 000	56 691	79.5

CYPRUS

	Population	Area	Density
1931	347 959	9251	37.6
1946	450 114	9251	48.7
1956	528 879	9251	57.2
1960	573 566	9251	62.0
1970	633 000	9251	68.4
1981	637 100	9251	68.9
1990	568 000	5896	96.3
1995	651 000	5896	110.4
1990[1]	171 000	3355	50.9
1995[1]	155 000	3355	46.2

[1] Turkish Republic of Northern Cyprus.

CZECHOSLOVAKIA

	Population	Area	Density
1921	13 613 172	140 490	96.9
1930	14 729 536	140 490	104.8
1947	12 164 661	127 827	95.2
1961	13 745 577	127 870	107.5
1970	14 445 301	127 870	112.9
1980	15 276 799	127 871	119.0
1990	15 664 000	127 899	122.5

CZECH REPUBLIC

	Population	Area	Density
1995	10 345 644	78 864	131.2

DENMARK

	Population	Area	Density
1901	2 450 000	40 357	60.7
1911	2 775 076	40 357	68.8
1921	3 289 195	44 403	74.1
1930	3 550 656	42 931	82.7
1935	3 706 349	42 931	86.3
1950	4 281 275	42 931	99.7
1960	4 585 256	43 069	106.5
1971	4 950 048	43 069	115.0
1981	5 123 989	43 080	119.0
1991	5 146 000	43 093	119.4
1995	5 223 000	43 094	121.2

ESTONIA

	Population	Area	Density
1922	1 110 538	47 549	23.4
1934	1 126 413	47 549	23.7
1939	1 134 000	47 549	23.8

Independence was regained in 1991.

	Population	Area	Density
1995	1 487 000	45 227	35.1

FINLAND

	Population	Area	Density
1910	3 115 197	343 209	9.1
1920	3 364 807	343 209	9.8
1930	3 667 067	343 405	10.7
1942	3 887 217	343 405	11.3
1950	4 029 803	305 475	13.2
1960	4 446 222	305 475	14.6
1970	4 707 000	305 475	15.4
1980	4 787 778	305 475	15.7
1990	4 978 000	305 475	16.3
1995	5 101 000	305 475	16.7

FRANCE

	Population	Area	Density
1911 (excluding Alsace-Lorraine)	39 601 509	536 464	73.8
1921 (including) Alsace-Lorraine)	39 209 518	550 986	71.1
1931	41 834 923	550 986	76.0
1946	40 506 639	550 986	73.5
1954	42 777 174	551 601	77.6
1962	46 519 997	551 601	84.3
1968	49 778 540	551 601	90.2
1972	51 500 000	551 601	93.3
1975	52 655 802	551 601	97.0
1982	54 334 871	551 601	98.5
1990	56 647 000	543 965	104.1
1995	58 172 000	543 965	106.9

GEORGIA

	Population	Area	Density
1995	5 514 000	69 492	79.3

GERMANY (to 1940 and from 1990)

	Population	Area	Density
1910 (including Alsace-Lorraine)	64 925 993	540 740	120.1
1925 (after reduction at Versailles)	62 410 619	468 728	133.1
1933 (including Waldeck and Saarland)	66 030 491	470 600	140.3
1939 (including Austria and Sudetenland)	79 576 758	583 265	136.4
1990	79 112 831	357 041	221.6
1995	81 912 000	356 973	229.5

FEDERAL REPUBLIC OF GERMANY

	Population	Area	Density
1950	47 695 672	245 317	194.4
1971	61 502 500	248 593	247.4
1982	61 713 000	248 687	248.2
1989	62 679 035	248 706	252.0

393

GERMAN DEMOCRATIC REPUBLIC

	Population	Area	Density
1947	19 102 000	108 173	176.6
1950	17 313 734	108 173	160.1
1964	17 003 655	108 173	157.2
1971	17 042 363	108 178	157.5
1980	16 737 200	108 177	154.0
1989	16 433 796	108 333	151.7

GIBRALTAR

	Population	Area	Density
1911	19 586	6.5	3013.0
1921	17 160	6.5	2640.0
1931	17 613	6.5	2709.0
1951	23 232	6.5	3574.0
1961	24 075	6.5	3704.0
1968	26 007	6.5	4001.0
1970	26 833	6.5	4127.0
1981	28 719	6.5	4418.3
1990	30 861	6.5	4747.8
1993	28 051	6.5	4315.5

GREECE

	Population	Area	Density
1913	4 821 300	108 606	44.4
1920	5 536 375	108 606	51.0
1928	6 204 684	130 199	47.7
1940	7 347 002	132 561	55.4
1951	7 403 599	132 727	55.8
1961	8 388 553	131 944	63.6
1971	8 745 084	131 944	66.3
1981	9 740 417	131 986	73.8
1990	10 038 000	131 957	76.1
1995	10 496 000	131 957	79.5

HUNGARY

	Population	Area	Density
1910 (including Croatia and Slavonia)	20 886 787	324 773	64.3
1920	7 980 143	92 916	85.9

HUNGARY (*continued*)

	Population	Area	Density
1931	8 688 349	92 916	93.5
1941	14 670 000	92 916	157.9
1960	9 961 044	93 030	107.0
1970	10 314 152	93 030	110.9
1980	10 709 550	93 032	115.1
1990	10 437 000	93 032	112.2
1995	10 231 000	93 032	109.9

ICELAND

	Population	Area	Density
1901	78 000	102 968	0.76
1910	85 183	102 968	0.83
1920	94 679	102 846	0.92
1930	108 870	102 846	1.05
1940	121 618	102 846	1.18
1950	144 263	102 846	1.40
1960	177 292	102 819	1.72
1971	207 174	102 819	2.01
1981	231 958	102 819	2.27
1990	256 000	102 819	2.49
1995	269 000	102 819	2.62

IRELAND

	Population	Area	Density
1901	4 459 000	83 013	53.7
1911	4 390 800	83 013	52.9
1921	3 096 000	68 893	44.9
1936	2 968 420	68 893	43.1
1946	2 955 107	68 893	42.9
1956	2 898 264	68 893	42.1
1961	2 818 341	68 893	40.9
1971	2 971 230	68 893	43.1
1981	3 443 405	68 895	50.0
1991	3 494 000	68 895	50.1
1995	3 590 000	68 895	51.1

ITALY

	Population	Area	Density
1901	32 475 000	286 324	113.4
1911	35 441 918	286 324	123.8

ITALY (continued)

	Population	Area	Density
1921	37 143 102	305 573	121.5
1931	40 309 621	310 057	130.0
1936	42 024 584	310 189	135.4
1951	46 737 629	301 023	155.3
1961	50 463 762	301 225	167.5
1970	54 418 831	301 225	180.7
1981	56 243 935	301 245	187.0
1991	57 590 000	301 245	191.2
1995	57 386 000	301 245	190.5

LATVIA

	Population	Area	Density
1920	1 503 193	51 945	38.9
1935	1 950 502	51 945	37.5
1939	1 994 506	51 945	38.4

Independence was regained in 1991.

1995	2 515 000	64 610	38.9

LIECHTENSTEIN

	Population	Area	Density
1930	10 213	160	63.8
1960	16 628	160	103.9
1970	21 350	160	133.4
1981	26 130	160	163.3
1990	28 700	160	179.4
1995	30 900	160	193.1

LITHUANIA

	Population	Area	Density
1923	2 168 971	59 463	36.5
1940	2 879 070	66 119	43.5

Independence was regained in 1991.

1995	3 700 000	65 301	56.7

LUXEMBOURG

	Population	Area	Density
1900	236 000	2586	91.3
1916	263 824	2586	102.0
1950	298 578	2586	115.4
1970	339 848	2586	131.4
1980	365 100	2586	141.2
1990	379 000	2586	146.6
1995	409 000	2586	158.2

MACEDONIA

(Former Yugoslavia)

	Population	Area	Density
1995	2 104 000	25 713	81.8

MALTA

	Population	Area	Density
1911	211 864	305.6	693.3
1921	213 024	305.6	697.1
1931	244 002	316.0	772.2
1948	306 996	316.0	971.5
1957	319 620	316.0	1011.4
1967	314 216	316.0	994.4
1971	322 072	316.0	1019.2
1981	319 936	316.0	1012.5
1991	357 000	316.0	1129.8
1995	370 000	316.0	1171.0

MOLDOVA

	Population	Area	Density
1995	4 350 000	33 700	129.1

THE NETHERLANDS

	Population	Area	Density
1911	6 022 452	32 758	183.8
1920	6 865 314	32 587	210.7

THE NETHERLANDS (*continued*)

	Population	Area	Density
1930	7 935 565	32 580	243.6
1938	8 728 569	32 924	265.1
1947	9 625 499	33 328	288.8
1960	11 556 008	33 612	343.8
1970	13 119 430	33 686	389.4
1980	14 091 014	33 938	415.0
1990	14 934 000	33 937	440.1
1995	15 487 000	33 939	456.3

NORWAY

	Pupulation	Area	Density
1900	2 240 000	321 496	7.0
1910	2 391 782	321 496	7.4
1920	2 649 775	323 658	8.2
1930	2 814 194	322 683	8.7
1946	3 156 950	323 917	9.7
1950	3 278 546	323 917	10.1
1960	3 591 234	323 917	11.1
1970	3 866 468	323 878	12.6
1980	4 091 340	323 895	12.6
1990	4 246 000	323 878	13.1
1995	4 360 000	323 878	13.5

POLAND

	Population	Area	Density
1900	25 106 000	380 266	66.0
1921	27 092 025	380 266	71.2
1931	31 948 027	388 396	82.3
1950	24 976 926	311 732	80.1
1960	29 776 000	312 700	95.2
1970	32 670 000	312 700	104.5
1980	35 380 000	312 683	113.1
1990	38 064 000	312 683	121.7
1995	38 641 000	312 683	123.6

PORTUGAL

	Population	Area	Density
1900	5 423 000	89 329	60.7
1911	5 958 000	89 329	66.7

398

PORTUGAL (*continued*)

	Population	Area	Density
1920	6 032 991	89 329	67.5
1930	6 360 347	89 329	71.2
1940	7 722 152	89 329	86.4
1950	8 441 312	91 709	92.0
1960	8 889 392	91 641	97.0
1970	8 668 267	91 641	94.5
1981	9 833 014	91 631	107.3
1991	10 421 000	92 389	112.8
1995	9 906 000	91 831	107.9

ROMANIA

	Population	Area	Density
1912	7 235 000	. . .	. . .
1920	17 393 149	316 710	54.9
1930	18 025 037	316 710	56.9
1941	13 551 756	195 198	69.4
1948	15 872 624	237 428	66.9
1956	17 489 794	237 428	73.7
1966	19 103 163	237 428	80.5
1970	20 140 000	237 428	84.8
1975	21 559 910	237 428	89.9
1980	22 200 000	237 428	92.5
1990	23 265 000	237 428	98.0
1995	22 693 000	237 428	95.5

RUSSIA

	Population	Area	Density
1995	147 168 000	17 075 400	8.6

SAN MARINO

	Population	Area	Density
1963	17 000	61	278.7
1974	19 168	61	314.2
1980	21 300	61	349.2
1990	23 000	61	375.9
1995	24 900	61	406.9

SLOVAKIA

	Population	Area	Density
1995	5 355 000	49 036	109.2

SLOVENIA

	Population	Area	Density
1995	1 971 000	20 256	97.3

SPAIN

	Population	Area	Density
1900	18 594 000	504 488	36.9
1910	19 588 688	504 488	38.8
1920	21 303 162	504 488	42.2
1930	23 563 867	509 212	46.3
1940	25 877 971	492 229	52.5
1950	27 976 755	503 061	55.6
1960	30 430 698	503 545	60.4
1970	33 823 918	503 545	67.1
1981	37 746 260	504 750	74.0
1990	39 618 000	504 750	78.5
1995	39 188 000	504 750	77.6

SWEDEN

	Population	Area	Density
1900	5 137 000	447 749	11.5
1910	5 522 403	447 749	12.3
1920	5 904 489	448 161	13.2
1930	6 141 571	448 992	13.7
1940	6 370 538	449 101	14.2
1950	7 041 829	449 206	15.7
1960	7 495 129	449 793	16.7
1965	7 766 424	449 793	17.3
1970	9 076 903	449 793	20.1
1975	8 208 442	411 615	20.2
1980	8 320 438	411 615	20.2
1990	8 529 000	410 929	20.8
1995	8 826 000	410 929	21.5

SWITZERLAND

	Population	Area	Density
1900	2 315 000	41 378	55.9
1910	3 741 971	41 378	90.4
1920	3 880 320	41 378	93.8
1930	4 066 400	41 288	98.5
1941	4 265 703	41 288	103.3
1950	4 714 992	41 288	114.2
1960	5 429 061	41 288	131.5
1970	6 269 783	41 288	151.8
1980	6 365 960	41 288	154.0
1990	6 756 000	41 288	163.6
1995	7 039 000	41 288	170.5

TURKEY

	Population	Area	Density
1927	13 648 270	762 537	17.9
1935	16 158 018	762 537	21.2
1940	17 820 950	762 537	23.4
1950	20 936 524	767 119	27.3
1960	27 754 820	767 119	36.2
1965	31 391 421	767 119	40.9
1970	35 666 549	767 119	46.5
1980	44 736 957	767 119	58.3
1990	56 941 000	767 119	73.0
1995	62 526 000	767 119	80.2

UKRAINE

	Population	Area	Density
1995	52 003 000	603 700	86.1

USSR

	Population	Area	Density
1920	135 710 423	24 900 000	5.4
1926	147 013 609	21 300 000	6.9
1939	170 467 186	21 200 000	8.0
1959	208 826 000	22 400 000	9.3
1970	241 748 000	22 400 000	10.8
1980	264 500 000	22 400 000	11.8
1990	290 122 000	22 275 000	13.0

UNITED KINGDOM

	Population	Area	Density
1901	41 459 000	243 363	170.3
1911	45 222 000	243 363	185.8
1921	43 176 521	243 363	177.8
1931	44 937 444	243 363	185.1
1951	49 012 362	243 363	201.4
1961	51 435 567	243 363	211.4
1971	55 347 000	243 363	227.8
1981	55 775 650	243 363	229.2
1991	57 333 000	244 110	235.7
1995	58 586 000	244 110	240.0

YUGOSLAVIA

	Population	Area	Density
1921	12 017 323	248 987	48.3
1931	13 934 039	247 495	56.3
1953	16 927 275	256 393	66.0
1961	18 549 291	255 804	72.5
1970	20 529 000	255 804	80.3
1981	22 424 711	255 804	87.7
1990	24 107 000	255 804	94.2
1995[1]	10 555 000	102 173	103.3

[1] Serbia and Montenegro

11 NEW COUNTRIES
A Guide to the New States of the Post-Communist Era

ARMENIA

Republic of Armenia (Hayastani Hanrapetut'yun) is bounded in the north by Georgia, in the east by Azerbaijan and in the south and west by Turkey and Iran. Capital: Yerevan. In a referendum in 1991, 99% of the electorate voted for independence from the USSR, which was declared on 21 Sep 1991. In Dec 1991 it became a member of the Commonwealth of Independent States (CIS).

BELARUS

Republic of Belarus (Respublika Belarus) is bounded in the west by Poland, north by Latvia and Lithuania, east by Russia and south by Ukraine. Capital: Minsk. Belarus issued a declaration of state sovereignty on 27 Jul 1990 and on 25 Aug 1991 adopted a declaration of independence from the USSR. In Dec 1991 it became a member of the Commonwealth of Independent States (CIS).

BOSNIA–HERCEGOVINA

Republic of Bosnia and Hercegovina (Republika Bosna i Hercigovina) is bounded in the north and west by Croatia and in the east and southeast by Yugoslavia (Serbia and Montenegro). Capital: Sarajevo. On 15 Oct 1991 the National Assembly adopted a memorandum on sovereignty, against the wishes of the Serb Democratic Party. A referendum for independence was held 29 Feb–1 Mar 1992. The turn-out was 63%, largely boycotted by the Serbian population: there were 99.78% in favour. Bosnia-Hercegovina declared itself independent on 5 Apr 1992 and was recognized as an independent state by EU and USA on 2 Apr 1992. Fighting broke out between Serb, Croat and Muslim communities. UN-sponsored ceasefires were repeatedly violated. On 10 Apr 1994 NATO airstrikes were used. On 21 Nov 1995 the prime ministers of Bosnia, Croatia and Yugoslavia signed an agreement at Dayton, Ohio, USA to end hostilities. The terms were that (i) Bosnia would include a Serb state containing 49% of Bosnia territory and a Muslim–Croat Federation; (ii) a central government would represent all ethnic groups and deal with foreign, monetary and citizenship issues; and (iii) free elections would be held.

CROATIA

Republic of Croatia (Republika Hrvatska) is bounded in the north by Slovenia and Hungary and in the east by Yugoslavia and Bosnia–Hercegovina. Capital: Zagreb. In a referendum on 19 May 1991, 94.17% of the population on a turn-out of 82.97% voted for independence. Independence was declared in Jun 1991 and fighting broke out between Croatia and Serbia and continued until Jan 1992 when a ceasefire was declared.

CZECH REPUBLIC

The Czech Republic (Česká Republika) is bounded in the west by Germany, north by Poland, east by Slovakia and south by Austria. Capital: Prague. On 25 Nov 1992 the Czechoslovakian Federal Assembly voted for the dissolution of the Czech and Slovak Federal Republics and to form two sovereign states. This came into effect on 1 Jan 1993.

GEORGIA

Republic of Georgia (Sakartvelos Respublika) is bounded in the west by the Black Sea and south by Turkey, Armenia and Azerbaijan. Capital: Tbilisi. Following a referendum, 98.9% of the population voted for independence based on the Treaty of Independence of 26 May 1918. Independence was declared on 9 Apr 1991. In Jan 1992 there was an armed insurrection and the president was deposed. Georgia became a member of the Commonwealth of Independent States (CIS) by presidential decree on 22 Oct 1993 and this was ratified by parliament on 1 Mar 1994. South Ossetia, formerly an autonomous region, lost its autonomy on 11 Dec 1990. Fighting broke out between Georgian forces and those Ossetians who wished to unite with North Ossetia (part of the Russian Federation). In 1996 Russian forces keep the peace in a 7 km buffer zone.

MACEDONIA
Former Yugoslavia

Republic of Macedonia (Republika Makedonija, member of the United Nations as 'Former Yugoslavia Republic of Macedonia' which was acceptable to Greece) is bounded in the north by Yugoslavia, in the east by Bulgaria, in the south by Greece and in the west by Albania. Capital: Skopje. Macedonia declared its independence on 20 Nov 1992.

MOLDOVA

Republic of Moldova (Republica Moldova) is bounded in the east and south by the Ukraine and in the west by Romania. Formerly Moldavia. Capital: Chișinău. Sovereignty was declared in Jun 1990 and independence in Aug 1991. In Dec 1991, Moldova became a member of the Commonwealth of Independent States (CIS). The majority of the Romanian population wished to rejoin Romania. After some fighting the Russian and Ukrainian populations declared their independence from Moldova in Dec 1991 as the Transdneister Republic. The Moldovan government refused to recognize the republic and war continued during the early part of 1992 when a Russian CIS peacekeeping force was deployed.

RUSSIA

The Russian Federation (Rossiiskaya Federatsiya) is bounded in the north by the Arctic Ocean and the Berent Sea; in the west by Norway, the Gulf of Finland, Finland, Estonia, Latvia, Belarus and Ukraine; in the south by Georgia, Azerbaijan, the Black Sea, the Caspian Sea, Kazakhstan, China, Mongolia and North Korea; and in the east by the North Pacific and the Bering Strait. Capital: Moscow. The Federation consists of 89 members: 21 Republics, 10 Autonomous Areas (*okrug*), 49 Regions (*oblast*), 6 Autonomous Territories (*krai*), 2 cities with federal status (Moscow and St Petersburg) and one autonomous Jewish region, Birobijan.

With the break-up of the USSR in Dec 1991 Russia became one of the founding members of the Commonwealth of Independent States (CIS).

SLOVAKIA

The Slovak Republic (Slovenska Republika) is bounded in the northwest by the Czech Republic, north by Poland, east by the Ukraine, south by Hungary and south-west by Austria. Capital: Bratislava. On 25 Nov 1992 the Czechoslovakian Federal Assembly voted for the dissolution of the Czech and Slovak Federal Republics, and to form two sovereign states. This came into effect on 1 Jan 1993.

SLOVENIA

Republic of Slovenia (Republika Slovenija) is bounded in the north by Austria, in the north-east by Hungary, in the south-east by Croatia and in the west by Italy. Capital: Ljubljana. A declaration of sovereignty was declared by the Assembly on 2 Jul 1990. A referendum held on 23 Dec 1990 gave 88.5% voting for independence and this was declared on 26 Dec 1990. Federal Yugoslav troops moved into Slovenia on 27 Jun 1990 to 'secure Yugoslavia's external borders' but after a 10-day war, withdrew in Jul. Recognition as an independent state came from the Federal Republic of Germany 23 Dec 1991 and the European Union on 15 Jan 1992.

UKRAINE

Ukraine (Ukrayina) is bounded in the east by Russia; the north by Belarus; the west by Poland, Slovakia, Hungary, Romania and Moldova; and the south by the Black Sea and the Sea of Azov. Capital: Kiev (Kyyiv). On 5 Dec 1991 the Supreme Soviet unanimously repudiated the 1922 Treaty of Union and and declared Ukraine an independent state. This followed a referendum held 1 Dec 1991 when 90% of the electorate voted for independence. Ukraine was a founder-member of the Commonwealth of Independent States (CIS) in Dec 1991.

YUGOSLAVIA
Serbia and Montenegro

Federal Republic of Yugoslavia (Savezna Republika Jugoslavija) is bounded in the north by Hungary; north-east by Romania; east by Bulgaria; south by Macedonia and Albania; and west by the Adriatic Sea, Bosnia-Hercegovina and Croatia. Capital: Belgrade. On 27 Apr 1992 Serbia and Montenegro announced the formation of a federal republic of Yugoslavia constituted by themselves as the legal successor to the former Socialist Federal Republic of Yugoslavia (SFRY), but on 22 Sep 1992 the United Nations stated that the new republic could not automatically assume the seat of the former SFRY.

GLOSSARY OF TERMS

Action Française   French nationalist, monarchist, anti-semitic political organization founded in 1899 by Charles Maurras (1868–1952) which backed the Vichy regime and was banned after the 1944 Liberation.

Agadir Crisis   Diplomatic and military crisis in 1911 caused by arrival of German warship *Panther* in Moroccan port of Agadir. Supposedly sent to protect German residents, the main aim was to gain colonial concessions from the French elsewhere in Africa in exchange for recognition of the French interest in Morocco.

Agrogorod   (Russ. 'agro-town') Agricultural organization proposed by Nikita Khrushchev (1894–1971) under which farmers would live in flats and work on centrally-grouped private plots. A version was attempted in the Ukraine from 1959–65.

Anschluss   (Germ. 'union') Amalgamation of Germany and Austria forbidden by Versailles Treaty created on 13 Mar 1938 with entry of German troops after spurious request to maintain order by pro-Nazi Austrian Chancellor Seyss-Inquart.

Anti-Comintern Pact   *See* p. 369.

Apparatchik   Full-time paid officials working in the Soviet Communist party *apparat* (party machine).

Appeasement   Diplomatic attempt to avoid war by conceding demands, notably Anglo-French acquiescence in Hitler's seizure of the Rhineland (1936), Austria (1938) and the Czech Sudetenland (1938). Abandoned when Germany absorbed the remainder of Czechoslovakia in Mar 1939.

Arrondissement   In France, a subdivision of the larger political and administrative unit, the *département*.

Ausgleich (Germ. compromise)   Agreement reached between the Austrian government and moderate Hungarian politicians in 1867 which transformed the Austrian Empire into the Dual Monarchy of Austria-Hungary. The system remained in operation until 1918.

Austro-Marxism Revisionist Marxist trend which emerged in Austria in 1907. Its main figures were Max Adler, Otto Bauer and Rudolf Hilferding.

Autarchy Attempt by a state – *e.g.* pre-World War II Germany – to attain economic self-sufficiency by reducing imports and increasing home production.

Axis Term used by Mussolini on 1 Nov 1939 to describe alliance of Germany and Italy, extended in World War II to include Bulgaria, Hungary, Japan, Romania, and Slovakia.

Ballila Youth wing of the Italian Fascist Party.

Baltic States Term used for Estonia, Latvia and Lithuania, formerly part of the Soviet Union from 1940 to 1991. The Soviet Union had seized them in 1940 as part of the 1939 Nazi-Soviet Pact.

Barbarossa, Operation Code name for the 22 Jun 1941 German invasion of the USSR.

Benelux Customs union of Belgium, Netherlands and Luxembourg agreed at treaty of 3 Feb 1958, coming into effect on 1 Nov 1960.

Black Hand Popular name of the Serbian secret society (*Ujedinjenje ili Smrt*) formed in Belgrade in May 1911. Led by Colonel Dragutin Dimitriević, the society's main aim was the unifying of Serb minorities in Austria-Hungary and the Ottoman Empire with the independent state of Serbia.

Blackshirts Initially term for Italian Fascists because of their uniform; extended in 1930s to include German Schutzstaffeln (SS) and Mosley's British Union of Fascists.

Blank Cheque The verbal reply given on 5 Jul 1914 in response to a letter from Emperor Francis Joseph of Austria by Kaiser Wilhelm II to Count Hoyos, an Austrian Foreign Ministry official, guaranteeing German support if Austria attacked Serbia.

Blitzkrieg (Germ. 'lightning war') Military tactic of heavy air bombardment followed by rapid armoured advance, effectively used in Poland (1939) and Western Europe (1940).

Bloody Sunday Term used of the massacre in St Petersburg on Sunday 22 Jan 1905. A procession of workers and their families led by Father George Gapon was fired on by troops guarding the Winter Palace in St Petersburg. Over one hundred people were killed and several hundred wounded, an event which helped to spark off the 1905 Russian Revolution.

Bolshevik (Russ. 'larger') Militant majority under Lenin which emerged from a split in the Russian Social Democratic Party in 1903 (the Mensheviks made up the minority) and which seized power in October 1917.

Brezhnev Doctrine The ideological basis of the Warsaw Pact invasion of Czechoslovakia in August 1968. Leonid Brezhnev pronounced a doctrine of 'limited sovereignty' denying East European states the right to diverge widely from the Soviet model, and asserting the legitimacy of intervention.

Bundesrat West German federal council elected by members of the ten state (Länder) governments and which had restricted veto powers on Bundestag legislation. Joined in 1990 by the five former East German Länder.

Bundestag German Federal Parliament established on 23 May 49 and elected for a four-year fixed term. Prior to 1990, East Germany had its own parliament.

Bundeswehr Armed forces of the Federal Republic of Germany (West Germany prior to 1990).

Cadres Communist Party members with specific responsibility for organizing and politically educating the working class.

CAP Common Agricultural Policy, the mechanism for organizing European Community farming and primary production and for distributing agricultural subsidies.

Caudillo, El (Sp. 'the leader') Title taken in 1937 by General Francisco Franco (1892–1975), the leader of the successful right-wing rising against the Spanish Republic.

Central Powers Initially members of the Triple Alliance created by Bismarck in 1882, namely Germany, Austria-Hungary and Italy. As Italy remained neutral in the First World War, the term was applied to Germany, Austria-Hungary, their ally Turkey and later also Bulgaria.

409

Cetnik *See* Chetnik.

CGT Confédération Générale du Travail. The largest French trade union federation, formed in 1906 on a non-political syndicalist platform.

Charter '77 Charter demanding recognition by Czechoslovak government of 1975 Helsinki human rights declaration; signed by many Czechs despite harassment and victimization.

Cheka Secret political police established in Russia to defend regime internally through terror following Bolshevik seizure of power in Oct 17.

Chetnik Originally anti-Turkish Serbian nationalist guerrillas; in World War II initially active in anti-German resistance but their anti-Communism encouraged some to collaborate with German and Italian forces.

Christmas Revolution Term applied to the popular uprising in Romania in Dec 1989 against the Ceauçescu dictatorship. Sometimes called the 'winter revolution'.

Cohabitation Term used to describe the political situation in France following the 1986 parliamentary election when the socialist President Mitterrand and the conservative government went on to tolerate and work alongside each other.

Cold War Post-World War II tension between capitalist states – led by the USA – and Communist states – led by the USSR – which thawed following Gorbachev's emergence as Soviet leader in 1985 and appeared effectively over with East European Communism's collapse in 1989–90.

Colons French colonial settlers, particularly in Algeria.

Cominform Communist Information Bureau formed in Feb 1947 to organize Communist activity in Europe, dissolved by Khrushchev in Apr 1956 as conciliatory gesture to the West.

Comintern Communist International formed in Mar 1919 to co-ordinate international revolutionary Communist activity but which developed into an arm of Soviet foreign policy. Dissolved in May 1943 by Stalin to allay Western allies' fears.

Commissar Head of a government department in the USSR; political commissars in the Red Army had responsibility for ideological education.

410

Conducator Title taken by Nicolae Ceauçescu (1918–89), dictator of Romania from 1967 until his overthrow and execution on 25 Dec 1989.

D-Day The Allied invasion of Normandy, launched 6 Jun 1944.

Destalinization Criticism of Stalin's policies and attempt at reform following his death in 1953. Khrushchev denounced his 'cult of personality' and 1930s purges at the 1956 20th Party Congress; Stalin's role was increasingly attacked in post-glasnost USSR.

Deutsche Arbeiterfront (Germ. 'German Labour Front') Nazi organization formed in Nov 1933 replacing banned trade unions to unite all workers and employers in national rather than class interest.

Deuxième Bureau (Fr. 'Second Bureau') French military intelligence.

Dirigisme Post-World War II French policy of state intervention in the free enterprise economy without centralized socialist planning.

Drang nach Osten (Germ. 'thrust to the east') Historic German wish to expand into Eastern Europe.

Dual Alliance Also known as the Dual Entente. An alliance between Russia and France which lasted from 1893 until the Bolshevik Revolution of Oct 1917.

Duce Il (It. 'the leader') Title of Benito Mussolini (1883–1945), Italian Prime Minister from Oct 22, outright Fascist dictator from 1926.

Duma Russian parliament established by the Tsar in 1905 in response to demands which emanated from the abortive revolution of 1905.

Eastern Bloc Pre-1990 Communist states of Eastern Europe: Bulgaria, Czechoslovakia, East Germany, Hungary, Poland, USSR, and which also included – despite their differences –Albania, Romania and Yugoslavia.

Eastern Front Battle lines between Germany and Russia in World War I and II.

Eastern Question The title given to the various problems of international, and especially European, relations created by the gradual decline of the Ottoman Empire in the late nineteenth and early twentieth centuries.

EFTA *See* p. 23.

Einsatzgruppen (Germ. 'special service squads') Forces attached to German army to repress population in World War II occupied territories; responsible for killing of Jews, Communists, and anti-Nazi resistance members.

ELAS National People's Army of Liberation formed by Communists in Greece following Apr 1941 German occupation. After liberation fought unsuccessful civil war against Western-backed monarchists, changing name to Democratic Army of Greece.

Enosis (Gk. 'to unite') Greek Cypriot movement seeking union of Cyprus and Greece.

Entente Cordiale (Fr. cordial agreement) Term first used in the 1840s to describe the special relationship between Britain and France. Revived in the Anglo-French Entente of 8 Apr 1904 and a similar agreement with Russia in Aug 1907.

EOKA (Gk. Ethniki Orgánosis Kypriakoú Agnósos, 'National Organization of Cypriot Struggle') Anti-British Greek-Cypriot guerrilla force founded by George Grivas (1898–1974) active from 1955–9; remained in existence following 1960 Cypriot independence seeking union with Greece.

Épuration Purge of collaborators conducted in 1944–5 after liberation of France; 767 were legally executed following trial but 30 000 were believed killed.

Ersatz (Germ. 'substitute') Goods produced in wartime to replace unobtainable items, *e.g.* coffee made from acorns.

Estado Novo The 'new state' in Portugal, the fascist regime established in 1926 and which was for long ruled after 1932 by António de Oliveira Salazar.

ETA Separatist terrorist movement seeking to re-establish Basque republic of Euzkadi (*q.v*) which existed in Northern Spain from Oct 1936–Jun 1938.

Ethnic cleansing Euphemism which emerged in the break-up of the former Yugoslavia in 1992 to describe attempts to remove minority ethnic groups by persuading communities to flee through threats and near-genocidal violence. Most often used to describe Serb actions against the Muslim community in Bosnia.

Eurocommunism West European Communist parties' attempt to distance themselves from USSR and to seek power through parliamentary democracy and within own national traditions.

European Nuclear Disarmament (END) Movement formed in 1980 initially to agitate for a nuclear-free Europe, going on to seek an end to US and Soviet power in Europe.

Euzkadi Autonomous state in Northern Spain established by Basques in Oct 1936; cultural and political suppression followed its occupation by Franco's forces in Jun 1938.

Falange The only political party permitted in Franco's Spain.

February Strike Communist-organized General Strike in Amsterdam on 25 Feb 1941 in protest against transportation of 425 Jews to concentration camps, provoking German imposition of a state of siege.

Festung Europa (Germ. 'fortification of Europe') Hitler's World War II plans to create a Reich impregnable to Allied invasion.

Fifth Republic French Republic established under influence of Gen. Charles de Gaulle (1890–1970, President 1958–69), with a strong Presidency and a weak legislature.

Final Solution Nazi euphemism for their genocidal plans to destroy the Jews.

Force de frappe French strategic nuclear strike force.

Fourteen Points A peace programme put forward by President Woodrow Wilson to the US Congress on 8 Jan 1918 and accepted as the basis for an armistice by Germany and Austria-Hungary. Later it was alleged that the allied powers had violated the principles embodied in the Fourteen Points, especially in relation to the prohibition of Anschluss, the union of Germany with Austria.

Fourth International Communist organization formed in 1934 by Leon Trotsky (1879–1940) because of his antagonism towards the Stalin-dominated Third International (Comintern).

Fourth Republic   The French Republic from 1946 to 1958.

Francistes   Blue-shirted French fascist movement formed by Marcel Duchard in 1934, initially financed by Italy and then by Nazi World War II occupation forces.

Free French   Forces Françaises Libres, World War II anti-German and anti-Vichy forces led by a French National Committee under Gen. Charles de Gaulle (1890–1970); renamed Forces Françaises Combatantes (Fighting French Forces) in Jul 1942.

Führer   (Germ. 'leader') Title taken by Hitler following appointment as German Chancellor in Jan 1933.

Gastarbeiter (Germ. 'guestworker')   Overseas labour, predominantly Greek, Turkish and Moroccan, recruited to meet the needs of West German industry in the 1960s and 1970s.

GATT   General Agreement on Tariffs and Trade, a United Nations agency formed in 1948 to weaken national tariff barriers and encourage international trade.

Gauleiter   Nazi official responsible for economic, political and civil defence organization in his Gau, a Nazi administrative area.

Gaullists   Political followers in France of Gen. Charles de Gaulle (1890–1970, President 1958–69), mainly organized in the Rassemblement du Peuple Français (1947–55) and the Union pour la Nouvelle République (formed 1958).

Generalissimo   Italian and Spanish title for the supreme commander of a military and naval force. Used especially to refer to Spanish dictator Franco.

Gestapo   (Germ. 'Geheime Staats Polizei') Nazi secret police force established on 26 Apr 1933 to arrest and murder opponents, expanding and becoming a wing of the SS (*q.v.*) under Heinrich Himmler (1900–45).

Glasnost   (Russ. 'openness') Soviet political and intellectual liberalization following appointment of Mikhail Gorbachev as Communist Party Secretary in 1985, encouraging a questioning which ultimately weakened Party authority.

Gosplan   Soviet State Planning Commission created centrally to control Stalin's economic programmes from 1924 to 1953.

Grand Coalition   West German government from 26 Nov 1966 to 27 Sep 1969 with Christian Democrat Kurt Kiesinger as Chancellor and Social Democrat Willy Brandt as deputy and Foreign minister, formed to face developing economic problems.

Grundgesetz   The post-war constitution (*i.e.* the Basic Law) of (originally) West Germany. It came into force in 1949.

Gulag   The forced labour camps of the former Soviet Union, established by Stalin in 1930. Their infamous record (of perhaps 8 million deaths) was immortalised by Aleksandr Solzhenitsyn in *The Gulag Archipelago*.

Habsburgs   The house of Habsburg-Lorraine, an Austrian royal dynasty which ruled from 1282 to 1918. The murder of the heir to the Austrian Habsburg throne in 1914, Francis Ferdinand, led to the outbreak of the First World War, and the last Emperor, Charles I, was forced to abdicate in 1918.

Herrenvolk   (Germ. 'master race') Allegedly racially superior Aryans in Nazi ideology.

Historic compromise   Term used to describe the support given by the Italian Communist Party (PCI) to the governing Christian Democrats after 1976. The support marked the end of more than a generation of Communist exclusion from the governing coalitions of modern Italy and reflected the need to form a strong base with which to deal with growing problems of inflation and terrorism.

Hohenzollern   German royal dynasty which provided the three German emperors, 1871–1918. Originally the Prussian royal house, the monarchy was finally brought to an end by the abdication of Kaiser Wilhelm II in November 1918.

Holocaust   Nazi genocide against the Jewish race through murder in concentration camps during World War II.

International Brigades   Left-wing and Communist volunteers from many countries who fought for the Spanish Republic in the 1936–9 Civil War.

Iron Curtain   Post-war dividing line through Central Europe between Communist and non-Communist states which collapsed in 1989–90.

Irredentism   Demand by a country for the return of territory formerly in its possession; from 19th-century Italian Irredenta party.

July Conspiracy   Abortive plot to murder Hitler in Jul 1944.

Kadets   (Russ. Konstitutsionnye Demokraty, 'Constitutional Democrats') Russian liberal party formed after 1905 Revolution which proposed a democratic republic after 1917 Revolution; banned by the Bolsheviks in 1918.

Kaiser (Germ. Caesar, *i.e.* Emperor)   Title assumed by the Prussian King Wilhelm I following the unification of Germany and the creation of the German Empire. Wilhelm accepted the crown of a united Germany in Dec 1870.

Kapp Putsch   Attempted overthrow of Weimar Republic in Mar 1920 by journalist Wolfgang Kapp (1868–1922) with right-wing support; failed after general strike and because army officers refused backing.

KGB   (Russ. Komitet Gosudarstvennoe Bezopasnosti, 'Committee of State Security') Soviet secret police founded in Mar 1954 with responsibility for internal security, espionage and counter-espionage.

Komsomol   (Russ. Kommunisticheski Soyuz Molodezki, 'Communist Union of Youth') Communist Party of the Soviet Union's youth wing.

Kremlin   (Russ. 'citadel') Soviet government centre in Moscow; by extension the Soviet government itself.

Kulak   (Russ. 'tight-fisted person') Relatively prosperous peasants; millions were deported or murdered because of their opposition to Soviet agricultural collectivisation between 1928 and 1932.

Länder   States in the Weimar Republic from 1919–33; the title was restored in the post-World War II Federal Republic of Germany.

Landtag   Legislatures in the states (Länder) of Austria and the Federal Republic of Germany.

League of Nations   *See* p. 6.

Little Entente   *See* p. 369.

Maginot Line   French defensive fortifications against Germany reaching from Luxembourg to the Swiss border, constructed 1929–34, named after War Minister André Maginot (1877–1932). The Maginot Line was circumvented by the German offensive of 1940.

Maquis   World War II French anti-German resistance.

Marshall Plan   United States Plan for the economic reconstruction of Europe, named after secretary of state General George C. Marshall. The Organization for European Economic Cooperation was established to administer the aid in Apr 1948.

May Events   The events of May 1968 when French students, demonstrating against education cuts in Paris, precipitated a political crisis in France. The strikes and riots went on into June, but the government eventually defused the situation by promising educational reform, and wage increases to the workers.

Mein Kampf   (Germ. 'My Struggle') Book written in prison in 1923 by Adolf Hitler (1889–1945) setting out his political programme of German expansion, anti-communism and anti-semitism.

Menshevik   (Russ. 'the minority') Moderate wing emerging from the 1903 split in the Russian Social Democratic Party; outlawed by the Bolsheviks in 1922.

Moroccan Crisis   A European crisis precipitated by German attempts to break up the Anglo-French Entente of 1904. Wilhelm II's landing at Tangier and his expression of German support for Moroccan independence led to acrimonious relations between Germany and France. The Algeciras Conference of Jan–Apr 1906 recognized French predominance in Morocco and represented a defeat for the German stand.

National schism   Term for the bitter division between Constantine I, King of Greece, and his leading minister, Venizelos, over which side Greece should support int he First World War.

NATO   *See* p. 371.

Nazi   (Germ. Nationalsozialistische Deutsche Arbeiter Partei, German National Socialist Workers' Party) Member of the party formed in Oct 1920, led by Adolf Hitler (1889–1945) who became Chancellor in Jan 1933 and ruled until his suicide in Apr 1945.

NEP   New Economic Policy; relative liberalization of Bolshevik policy introduced in Mar 1921 allowing growth of small businesses, limited private agriculture, and freer internal trade.

New Order   World War II Nazi plans for a Europe united under German control.

Night of the Long Knives   Murder of the Nazi SA leaders, many of their followers, and other potential political rivals, on 29–30 Jun 1934, ordered by Hitler on grounds that the SA was plotting against his regime. This action consolidated Hitler's power.

November criminals   Abusive term current in Germany from 1918 to 1945, blaming politicians who negotiated Germany's surrender in 1918 for the nation's defeat.

Nuremberg Rallies   Mass propaganda Nazi rallies organized at the Party's Nuremberg congresses from 1933–38.

October Revolution   Bolshevik overthrow of Provisional Government and seizure of power on 6–7 Nov 1917 led by Vladimir Lenin (1870–1924). (Under the old Julian calendar then in operation in Russia, the month was October.)

OGPU   Soviet counter-revolutionary security police formed in 1922 as GPU (State Political Administration), renamed OGPU (Unified State Political Administration) in 1923. Replaced by the NKVD in 1934.

Ostpolitik   (Germ. 'eastern policy') German Federal Republic policy from 1970s of improving relations with East European Communist states, recognizing German Democratic Republic, and acknowledging post-war boundaries.

Outremer   (Fr. 'overseas') France's overseas colonies from the 17th to 20th centuries.

OVRA   Italian Fascist secret police formed in 1927.

Pact of Steel   Military alliance concluded between Germany and Italy in Berlin on 22 May 1939.

Panslavism   The name given to the various movements for closer union of peoples speaking Slavic languages in the nineteenth and early twentieth centuries.

Panzer   German expression for an armoured fighting vehicle, extended to describe an armoured division.

Partisans Guerrilla groups fighting behind enemy lines, *e.g.* in World War II German-occupied Russia, Albania, Greece, Slovakia and Yugoslavia.

Perestroika (Russ. 'restructuring') Attempt at radical reform of Soviet economy introduced by Mikhail Gorbachev, Communist Party leader from 1985, involving increasing replacement of central control by market forces.

Phoney War Period of military inactivity on the Western Front between the declaration of war on Germany in Sep 1939 and the German advance of Apr 1940.

Pogrom (Russ. 'destruction') Organized massacre in Russia, particularly involving attacks on Jews, the first of which was authorized by the Tsarist authorities in 1881.

Politburo The leading Party committee in Communist controlled states.

Popular Front Communist tactic of allying with socialists and liberals to confront common fascist enemy in the 1930s. Popular Front governments were formed in France and Spain.

Poujadist Supporter of the Union de Défence des Commercants et Artisans, militant right-wing party active in France from 1954–8, formed by Pierre Poujade.

Prague Spring Czechoslovak liberalization after the appointment of Alexander Dubček as Communist Party Secretary on 5 Jan 1968 and the adoption of a reform programme on 5 Apr. Warsaw Pact invasion ended the experiment on 20/21 Aug.

Provisional government The government of Russia between Mar and Oct 1917. Brought to power after the deposition of the monarchy, the Provisional government was made up of members of the Duma (*q.v.*) but had to share power in Petrograd with the Workers' and Soldiers' Soviet.

Putsch (Germ. 'revolt') Overthrow of a government by conspiracy, *e.g.* the failed right-wing attempt led by Wolfgang Kapp in 1920 to oust the Weimar Republic.

Quai d'Orsay The embankment in Paris where the French Foreign Office is situated.

Quisling   Collaborator with an occupying power, from Vidkun Quisling (1887–1945), a Norwegian Nazi who led a German puppet government during the 1940–5 occupation.

Rapacki Plan   Proposal by Polish Foreign Minister Adam Rapacki on 2 Oct 1957 to ban nuclear weapons production and deployment in Czechoslovakia, Poland, East and West Germany; rejected by the West because the USSR would have retained conventional superiority.

Red Brigades   Italian 1970s left-wing terrorist group which kidnapped and murdered former Prime Minister Aldo Moro in 1976; a core remained active into the 1980s.

Refuseniks   Predominantly Jewish Soviet citizens refused permission to emigrate from the USSR by the authorities.

Reich   (Germ. 'empire') The First Reich was the medieval Holy Roman Empire; the Second from German unification in 1871 until the 1918 defeat; the Third the period of Nazi rule from 1933 to 1945.

Reichsbanner   The Reichsbanner Schwarz-Rot-Gold (The Weimar Republic's colours), mainly Social Democratic unarmed force formed in May 24 to defend the Weimar Republic. Outlawed by Hitler in 1933.

Reichstag   German Parliament building in Berlin from 1871 until its destruction by arson in Feb 1933.

Rentenmark   German currency introduced in 1923 by Chancellor Gustav Stresemann (1878–1929) to restore financial confidence following massive inflation and the French occupation of the Ruhr.

Reparations   Compensation for war damage demanded by victors from a defeated power, most notably the post-World War I figure of £6600 million (largely unpaid) imposed on Germany in Apr 1921.

Resistance   Armed opponents of German occupation in World War II Europe, particularly in France, who attacked enemy installations and personnel.

Revisionist   Term applied by orthodox Marxists to one who attempts to reassess the basic tenets of revolutionary socialism. Originating in Germany in the 1890s and 1900s, its chief exponents were Edouard Bernstein and Karl Kautsky. Regarded as heresy in the Soviet Union.

Romanov The family name of the Russian royal house whose dynasty was ended by the deposition of Tsar Nicholas II in 1917 after the Russian Revolution.

SA (Germ. Sturmabteilung, 'storm-troopers') Brownshirted Nazi private army founded in 1920–1; 400 000 strong by 1933. SA 'socialist' tendencies provoked Hitler into killing its leaders and weakening its influence in 1934.

Sajudis The Lithuanian nationalist movement which declared Lithuania independent in 1990.

Samizdat Dissident literature criticizing the Communist regime in the Soviet Union circulated secretly by its opponents.

Schlieffen Plan German military plan for offensive action named after Chief of German General Staff, Count Alfred von Schlieffen, and first produced in 1905. In spite of constant revision, the plan was the basis for the German attack in the west in Aug 1914.

Scrap of Paper German Chancellor Bethmann-Hollweg's description of the 1839 Treaty of London, a five-power guarantee of Belgian neutrality which Germany violated by invasion on 4 Aug 1914, provoking a British declaration of war. He told the British ambassador that 'just for a scrap of paper, Great Britain is going to make war on a kindred nation which desires nothing better than to be friends with her.'

Second Front Allied invasion of Western Europe demanded by Stalin from 1941 to relieve German pressure on Soviet Union; opened with Anglo-American landings in Normandy on 6 Jun 1944.

Second International Formed in Paris in 1889 and based on membership of national parties and trade unions, the Second International was a loose federation which held periodic international congresses. It stood for Parliamentary democracy and thus rejected anarchist ideas, but also reaffirmed the commitment to Marxist ideas of the class struggle.

Second Reich The German Empire 1871–1918 also known as the *Keiserreich*; the period after German unification when Wilhelm I, king of Prussia was offered the throne of the Empire. The last Kaiser, Wilhelm II was forced to abdicate after the German army refused to support him at the end of the First World War.

Securitate Romanian secret police during dictatorship of Nicolae Ceauçescu (1918–89).

SHAPE Supreme Headquarters, Allied Powers in Europe; headquarters of the North Atlantic Treaty Organization, initially at Fontainebleau, then from 1966 in Brussels.

Show Trial Political trials held for propaganda effect with generally pre-determined verdict, the most notorious of which were held during Stalin's 1930s purges and in post-war Eastern Europe.

Siegfried Line German defensive line on Western Front in 1918; then the fortifications built by Germany against the French Maginot Line in the 1930s.

Social charter The European Union (EU) Charter of Social Rights of Workers, setting out a pattern for a European labour law. Largely the work of Jacques Delors and his colleagues. Opposed by right-wing Conservatives, especially in Britain.

Social fascist Abusive Communist epithet in early 1930s to describe Labour and Social Democratic competitors for working class support.

Solidarity Widely supported Polish free trade union formed on 8 Sep 1980; banned under martial law in Dec 1981. Formed government in 1989 with Tadeusz Mazowiecki as prime minister but appeared close to split over presidential candidate in 1990. Its leader, Lech Walesa, was eventually elected president.

Soviet (Russ. 'council') Workers' and soldiers' councils which emerged in the 1905 and 1917 Russian revolutions.

Sovkhoz (Russ. sovetskoe khozyaistvo, 'soviet farm') State-owned farm in the USSR.

Spartacists German radical socialists – named after Spartacus, the leader of a Roman slave revolt – led by Rosa Luxemburg and Karl Liebknecht who formed the German Communist Party in 1918.

'Splendid Isolation' Phrase used to describe Britain's diplomatic position in the latter part of the nineteenth century and, more generally, during the nineteenth century as a whole when Britain stood aside from entanglement in European alliances.

SS (Germ. Schutz Staffeln, 'guards detachment') Hitler's black uniformed bodyguard formed in 1928, led by Heinrich Himmler (1900–45), which by 1936 controlled Germany's police force, guarded concentration camps, and created an elite military Waffen SS in 1939.

State capitalism Term used by Vladimir Lenin (1870–1924) to describe the combination of central economic control and compromise with private financial interests in 1918 to preserve Bolshevik rule. More latterly a description of pre-1990 East European regimes.

Stormtroopers *See* SA.

Straits Question The issue of rights of passage through the Dardanelles and the Bosphorus which was disputed between the Great Powers and Turkey at several points in the nineteenth and twentieth centuries.

Third Reich Period of Nazi power in Germany from 1933–45, following upon the First Reich of the medieval Holy Roman Empire and the Second Reich from unification in 1871 until the defeat in 1918.

Third Republic Persistently weak French Republic from 1870 to 1946, but which effectively collapsed when Germany invaded in 1940, after having had 108 governments in 70 years.

Tripartism Name given to the joint governments of Christian Democrats, Socialists and Communists formed in France and Italy in the immediate aftermath of the Second World War. Tripartism lasted in Italy until Apr 1947 and France until 1947.

Triple Alliance Alliance formed between Germany, Austria-Hungary and Italy in 1882.

Triple Entente Agreement between Britain, France and Russia to resolve their outstanding colonial differences; it became a military alliance in 1914.

Trizonia Combined zones of American, British and French occupation in immediate post-World War II West Germany.

Trotskyist Followers of Leon Trotsky (1879–1940) who believed Stalin had betrayed the Russian Revolution and called for renewed socialist world revolution; briefly fashionable among student activists in the 1960s and 1970s.

Union Sacrée (Fr. Sacred Union)   Government formed in France at the outbreak of the First World War which included, for the first time and as a symbol of national unity, two Socialists among its members.

Ustase   Croatian nationalist terrorist organization formed in 1929 which assassinated King Alexander of Yugoslavia in 1934 and formed a collaborationist Croatian state during the World War II Axis occupation.

Vatican 2   Year-long Roman Catholic Church Council called by Pope John XXIII which sat from 11 Oct 1962; sought friendlier relations with non-Catholic churches and appeared to promise a degree of liberalization.

Velvet Chancellors   First post-war Chancellors of the Federal Republic of Germany (West Germany), notably Konrad Adenauer (1876–1967), Chancellor from 1949 to 1963.

Velvet Divorce   The division on 1 Jan 1993 of Czechoslovakia into the separate states of the Czech Republic and Slovakia. So called because of the apparent amicable nature of the separation, but also an ironic reference to the 1989 Velvet Revolution (see below) which overthrew Communist rule.

Velvet Revolution   Term used for the revolution which ended the Communist regime in Czechoslovakia in 1989.

Volkshammer   Parliament in East Berlin until 1990 of the German Democratic Republic (East Germany).

Waffen SS   World War II elite military wing of the German SS, finally 40 divisions strong, made up of 'Aryans' from Germany and occupied European countries.

Walloons   French-speaking minority in industrial southern Belgium, making up 45% of the population. The Mouvement Populaire Walloon seeks autonomy.

War Communism   Bolshevik policy from 1918–21 to preserve regime in Russian Civil War, included seizure of agricultural produce, nationalization of industry, and harsh labour discipline.

War Guilt Clause   Art. 231 of the 1919 Versailles Treaty by which Germany acknowledged responsibility for World War I and which provided a legal basis for Allied reparations demands.

Warsaw Pact *See* p. 371.

Weimar Democratic German Republic from 1919–33, named after the town in which a National Constituent Assembly met in Feb 19 and drew up a constitution in Jul 1919.

Weltpolitik (Germ. lit. world politics) A new trend in German foreign policy at the end of the nineteenth century. The Kaiser Wilhelm II determined to transform Germany into a first-rank global power. Ultra-nationalistic pressure combined with social and economic forces to support new interest in colonial expansion, the scramble for territory in China and Africa, and the establishment of a powerful navy.

White Russians Anti-Bolshevik monarchist forces in the 1917–21 Russian civil war, many of whom went into exile following the Red Army victory.

Winter War War fought from 30 Nov 1939 to 12 Mar 1940 following the Soviet invasion of Finland.

Yezhovschina Stalinist purges in the 1930s, term coming from the head of the Soviet secret police. N. I. Yezhov (1894–1939).

Young Plan Proposal by American businessman Owen D. Young (1874–1962) to reduce German war reparations by 75% and extend payment period to 1988. Accepted by Germany in 1929 but Hitler abandoned payments in 1933.

Young Turks Liberal reform movement among young army officers in the Ottoman Empire, active between 1903 and 1909.

Zimmermann Telegram Coded message of 19 Jan 1917 from the German foreign minister, Arthur Zimmermann, to the German minister in Mexico, urging the conclusion of a German–Mexican alliance in the event of a declaration of war on Germany by America when Germany resumed unrestricted submarine warfare against shipping on 1 February.

INDEX

Abyssinian War, 360
Action Française, 407
Afghanistan, Soviet Invasion of, 361
Agadir Crisis, 407
Agrogorod, 407
Algerian Revolutionary War, 361
Anglo–German Naval Agreement, 369
Anglo–Italian 'Gentleman's Agreement', 370
Anglo–Soviet Treaty, 370
Anschluss, 407
Anti-Comintern Pact, 369
Apparatchik, 407
Appeasement, 407
Armed Conflicts 1900–1996, Principal European, 356–9
Armed Conflicts (outside Europe) in which European Powers participated 1900–1996, Principal, 359–62
Armed Forces, NATO, 26
Armed Forces, Warsaw Pact, 26
Armenia, 403
Arrondissement, 407
Assembly (League of Nations), 9
Auditors (EU) Court of, 22
Ausgleich, 407
Austrian State Treaty, 372
Austro-Marxism, 408
Autarchy, 408
Axis, 408

Baghdad Pact, 371
Balkan Pact, 371
Balkan Wars, 356
Ballila, 408
Baltic States, 408
Bank for International Settlements, 10–11
Barbarossa, Operation, 408
Belarus, 403

Benelux, 408
Black Hand, 408
Blackshirts, 408
Blank Cheque, 408
Blitzkrieg, 408
Bloody Sunday, 409
Bolshevik, 409
Bosnia-Hercegovina, 403
Boxer Rebellion, 359
Brest-Litovsk, Treaty of, 363
Brezhnev Doctrine, 409
British–French–Turkish Agreement, 370
British–Polish Treaty, 370
Brussels Treaty, 371
Bundesrat, 409
Bundestag, 409
Bundeswehr, 409

Cadres, 409
CAP (Common Agricultural Policy), 409
Caudillo, El, 409
Central Powers, 409
Cetnik, 410
CGT (Confederation Générale du Travail), 410
Charter '77, 410
Chechnya–Russia War, 359
Cheka, 410
Chetnik, 410
Christmas Revolution, 410
CMEA (Council for Mutual Economic Assistance), 27–9
Cohabitation, 410
Cold War, 410
Colons, 410
COMECON (CMEA), 27–9
Cominform, 410
Comintern, 410
Commissar, 410
Commonwealth of Independent States, 24–6

Conductor, 411
'Congress of Europe', 17
Conventional Forces in Europe
    Treaty, 372
Council (League of Nations), 8–9
Council for Mutual Economic
    Assistance, 27–9
Council of Europe, 17–19
Council of Ministers (EU), 21
Court of Auditors (EU), 22
Court of Justice (EU), 22
Croatia, 404
Cyprus, Turkish Invasion of, 358
Czechoslovakia, Invasion of, 358
Czech Republic, 404

D-Day, 411
Defence and Treaties, 356–72
Defence Community, European, 16
Defence Treaties and Agreements
    1900–1996, Outline of Principal
    European, 368–72
Dependencies, 373–88
  Belgium, 373–4
  Denmark, 374
  France, 374–9
  Italy, 379
  Netherlands, 380
  Norway, 380–1
  Portugal, 382–4
  Spain, 384–5
  United Kingdom, 385–8
Destalinization, 411
Deutsche Arbeiterfront, 411
Deuxième Bureau, 411
Dirigisme, 411
Drang nach Osten, 411
Dual Alliance, 411
Duce, Il, 411
Duma, 411
Dunkirk Treaty, 371

EAEC (European Atomic Energy
    Community), 19
Eastern Bloc, 411
Eastern Front, 411
Eastern Question, 411
Economic and Social Committee
    (EU), 22
Economic and Social Council (UN),
    3–4

ECSC (European Coal and Steel
    Community), 19, 21
EEC (European Economic
    Community), 19
EFTA (European Free Trade Area),
    23
Einsatzgruppen, 411
Elections, 163–277
  Albania, 163–4
  Armenia, 164–5
  Austria, 165–7
  Belarus, 168
  Belgium, 168–71
  Bosnia-Hercegovina, 171–2
  Bulgaria, 172–5
  Croatia, 175–6
  Cyprus (Greek), 176
  Cyprus (Turkish), 176
  Czechoslovakia, 177–82
  Czech Republic, 182
  Danzig, 237–8
  Denmark, 182–7
  Estonia, 187–8
  European Parliament, 188–98
  Finland, 200–3
  France, 203–6
  Georgia, 206
  German Democratic Republic,
      208–10
  Germany, 206–7
  Germany, Federal Republic of,
      198–200
  Greece, 210–12
  Hungary, 212–17
  Iceland, 217–19
  Ireland, 219–21
  Italy, 221–3
  Latvia, 224
  Lithuania, 224–5
  Macedonia, 225–6
  Malta, 226
  Moldova, 226–7
  Netherlands, 227–9
  Norway, 229–31
  Poland, 232–7
  Portugal, 238–41
  Romania, 241–7
  Russia, 247–9
  Slovakia, 250
  Slovenia, 250
  Spain, 251–3

Elections *cont.*
  Sweden, 253–7
  Switzerland, 257–61
  Turkey, 261–6
  Ukraine, 266
  United Kingdom, 269–74
  USSR, 266–9
  Yugoslavia, 274–7
END (European Nuclear
  Disarmament), 413
Enosis, 412
Entente Cordiale, 412
Entente, The Little, 369
EOKA ('National Organization of
  Cypriot Struggle'), 412
Épuration, 412
Ersatz, 412
Estado Novo, 412
ETA (Basque terrorists), 412
Ethnic cleansing, 412–13
ETUC (European Trade Union
  Confederation), 12
EU (European Union), 19–22
Euratom, 19, 21
Eurocommunism, 413
'Europe, Congress of', 17
European Atomic Energy
  Community, 19
European Bank for Reconstruction
  and Development, 30–1
European Coal and Steel
  Community, 19
European Court of Human Rights, 18
European Defence Community, 17
European Free Trade Association, 23
European Investment Bank, 22
European Monetary Institute, 22
European Organizations, Other, 23
European Parliament, 21
European Parliament, Elections to,
  188–98
European Trade Union
  Confederation, 12
European Union (EU), 19–22
Euzkadi, 413

Falange, 413
Falklands Conflict, 361
February Strike, 413
Festung Europa, 413
Fifth Republic, 413

Final Solution, 413
Force de frappe, 413
Fourteen Points, 413
Fourth International, 413
Fourth Republic, 414
Francistes, 414
Franco–Belgian Military Convention,
  368
Franco–Polish Treaty, 368
Franco–Russian Alliance, 369
Franco–Soviet Treaty, 371
Franco–West German Treaty, 372
Free French, 414
Führer, 414

Gastarbeiter, 414
GATT (General Agreement on
  Tariffs and Trade), 414
Gauleiter, 414
Gaullists, 414
General Assembly (UN), 1–2
Generalissimo, 414
Georgia, 404
German Democratic Republic
  Uprising, 358
Gestapo, 414
Glasnost, 414
Glossary of Terms, 407–25
Gosplan, 414
Grand Coalition, 415
Greco–Turkish War, 357
Greek Civil War, 358
Grundgesetz, 415
Gulag, 415
Gulf War, 362

Habsburgs, 415
Heads of State, 32–58
  Albania, 32
  Andorra, 33
  Armenia, 33
  Austria, 33–4
  Belarus, 34
  Belgium, 34
  Bosnia-Hercegovina, 34–5
  Bulgaria, 35
  Croatia, 35–6
  Cyprus, 36
  Czechoslovakia, 36
  Czech Republic, 37
  Denmark, 37

Estonia, 37–8
Finland, 38
France, 39
Georgia, 40
Germany, 40
Greece, 41–2
Hungary, 43
Iceland, 44
Ireland, 44
Italy, 45
Latvia, 45–6
Liechtenstein, 46
Lithuania, 46
Luxembourg, 47
Macedonia, 47
Malta, 47
Moldova, 48
Monaco, 48
Netherlands, 48
Norway, 48–9
Poland, 49
Portugal, 50
Romania, 50–1
Russia, 51
San Marino, 51
Serbia, 52
Slovakia, 52
Slovenia, 52
Spain, 53
Sweden, 53
Switzerland, 53–5
Turkey, 55
Ukraine, 55–6
United Kingdom, 57
USSR, 56
Vatican, 57
Yugoslavia, 57–8
Yugoslavia, Former, 58
Herrenvolk, 415
Historic Compromise, 415
Hohenzollern, 415
Holocaust, 415
Human Rights, European Court of,
18
Hungarian Uprising, 358

ICFTU (International Confederation
of Free Trade Unions), 12
ILO (International Labour
Organization), 11
International Brigades, 415

International Confederation of Free
Trade Unions, 12
International Court of Justice (UN),
5–6
International Federation of Christian
Trade Unions, 12
International Labour Organization
(ILO), 11
International Organizations, 1–31
Iron Curtain, 415
Irredentism, 415
Italo–Turkish War, 356

July Conspiracy, 416
Justice, 329–55
Albania, 329
Andorra, 329
Austria, 330
Austria-Hungary, 330
Belgium, 331
Bulgaria, 331
Cyprus, 331
Czechoslovakia, 332
Czech Republic, 332–3
Denmark, 333
Estonia, 333
European Union, 333–4
Finland, 334
France, 334–6
German Democratic Republic,
338–9
Germany, 336–7
Germany, Federal Republic of,
337–8
Gibraltar, 339
Greece, 339
Hungary, 339–40
Iceland, 340–1
Ireland, 341–2
Italy, 342–3
Latvia, 343
Liechtenstein, 343
Lithuania, 343
Luxembourg, 343–4
Macedonia, 344
Malta, 344–5
Monaco, 345
Netherlands, 345
Norway, 345–6
Poland, 346–7
Portugal, 347

Justice *cont.*
  Romania, 347–8
  Russia, 348
  San Marino, 348
  Serbia, 348
  Slovakia, 348–9
  Slovenia, 349
  Spain, 349–50
  Sweden, 350
  Switzerland, 351
  Turkey, 351–2
  United Kingdom, 353–4
  USSR, 352–3
  Yugoslavia, 354–5
  Yugoslavia, Former, 355
Justice (EU), Court of, 20–1
Justice (UN) International Court of,
  4–6
Justice (League of Nations),
  Permanent Court of
  International, 10

Kadets, 416
Kaiser, 416
Kapp Putsch, 416
KGB ('Committee of State Security'),
  416
Komsomol, 416
Korean War, 360
Kremlin, 416
Kulak, 416

Labour, World Confederation of, 12
Länder, 416
Landtag, 416
Lausanne, Treaty of, 364
League of Nations, 6–10
Locarno Treaties, 369
London and Paris Agreements, 371

Maastricht, Treaty of, 372
Macedonia, 405
Maginot Line, 416
Malayan Emergency, 360
Maquis, 417
Marshall Plan, 417
May Events, 417
Mein Kampf, 417
Menshevik, 417
Ministers, 100–62
  Albania, 100–1

Armenia, 101
Austria, 101–3
Belarus, 104
Belgium, 104–6
Bosnia-Hercegovina, 106
Bulgaria, 106–8
Croatia, 108
Cyprus, 108–9
Czechoslovakia, 109–11
Czech Republic, 111
Denmark, 111–13
Finland, 113–15
France, 115–19
Georgia, 119
German Democratic Republic, 121–2
Germany, 119–21
Germany, Federal Republic of, 121
Greece, 122–5
Hungary, 125–8
Iceland, 128–9
Ireland, 129–30
Italy, 130–2
Latvia, 132–3
Lithuania, 133
Luxembourg, 134
Macedonia, Republic of, 134
Malta, 135
Moldova, 135
Montenegro, 135–6
Netherlands, 136–7
Norway, 138–9
Poland, 139–41
Portugal, 141–4
Romania, 144–6
Russia, 146–7
Russian Federation, 147
Serbia, 147–8
Slovakia, 148
Slovenia, 148
Spain, 149–51
Sweden, 151–3
Switzerland, 153–4
Turkey, 155–7
Ukraine, 157
United Kingdom, 158–9
USSR, 160
Yugoslavia, 161
Ministers (EU), Council of, 21
Moldova, 405
Moroccan Crisis, 417
Munich Agreement, 370

National schism, 417
NATO (North Atlantic Treaty
    Organization), 14–16, 371
NATO Armed Forces, 26
Nazi, 417
Nazi–Soviet Pact, 370
NEP (New Economic Policy), 417
Neuilly, Treaty of, 364
New Economic Policy, 417
New Order, 418
Night of the Long Knives, 418
North Atlantic Treaty, 371
North Atlantic Treaty Organization
    (NATO), 14–16, 371
November criminals, 418
Nuremberg Rallies, 418

October Revolution, 418
OECD (Organization for Economic
    Co-operation and Development),
    13–14
OEEC (Organization for European
    Economic Co-operation), 13
OGPU (Soviet counter-revolutionary
    security police), 418
Ombudsman (EU), 22
Organization for Economic Co-
    operation and Development
    (OECD), 13–14
Organization for European Economic
    Co-operation (OEEC), 13
Organization for Security and
    Co-operation in Europe, 29–30
Osimo, Treaty of, 372
Ostpolitik, 418
Outremer, 418
OVRA (Italian fascist police), 418

Pact of Steel, The, 370, 418
Panslavism, 418
Panzer, 418
Parliament, European, 21–2
Parliament, European, Elections to,
    188–98
Parliaments, 59–99
  Albania, 59
  Armenia, 59
  Austria, 60–1
  Belarus, 61
  Belgium, 61–2
  Bosnia-Hercegovina, 62

  Bulgaria, 63–4
  Croatia, 64
  Cyprus, 64
  Czechoslovakia, 64–5
  Czech Republic, 66
  Denmark, 66–7
  Estonia, 67–8
  Finland, 68
  France, 69–70
  Georgia, 70–1
  German Democratic Republic,
      73–4
  Germany, 71
  Germany, Federal Republic of, 72
  Greece, 74–5
  Hungary, 76
  Iceland, 77
  Ireland, 77–8
  Italy, 78–80
  Latvia, 80
  Liechtenstein, 80–1
  Lithuania, 81–2
  Luxembourg, 82
  Macedonia, 82
  Moldova, 83
  Monaco, 83
  Netherlands, 84
  Norway, 84–5
  Poland, 85–7
  Portugal, 87–8
  Romania, 88–9
  Russia, 89–90
  Slovakia, 90
  Slovenia, 90–1
  Spain, 91–2
  Sweden, 92–3
  Switzerland, 93
  Turkey, 93–5
  Ukraine, 95
  United Kingdom, 97–8
  USSR, 95–7
  Yugoslavia, 98–9
Partisans, 419
Peace Treaties arising from World
    War I, 1918–23, 363–4
Perestroika, 419
Permanent Court of International
    Justice (League of Nations), 10
Phoney War, 419
Pogrom, 419
Polish–Federal German Treaty, 372

Polish–German Treaty, 369
Polish–Soviet Treaty, 369
Politburo, 419
Political Parties, 278–328
  Albania, 278–9
  Austria, 279–80
  Belarus, 280–1
  Belgium, 281–2
  Bosnia-Hercegovina, 282–3
  Bulgaria, 283–5
  Croatia, 285
  Cyprus, 286
  Czechoslovakia, 286–7
  Czech Republic, 287–8
  Denmark, 288–9
  Estonia, 289–90
  Finland, 290–1
  France, 291–3
  German Democratic Republic, 296
  Germany 1900–45, 294–5
  Germany, Federal Republic of, 295–6
  Greece, 297–8
  Hungary, 298–300
  Iceland, 300
  Ireland, 301
  Italy, 302–4
  Latvia, 304–5
  Liechtenstein, 305
  Lithuania, 305–6
  Luxembourg, 306–7
  Macedonia, 307
  Malta, 307–8
  Moldova, 308
  Netherlands, 308–10
  Norway, 310–11
  Poland, 312–13
  Portugal, 313–14
  Romania, 314–16
  Russia, 316–18
  Slovakia, 318
  Slovenia, 318–19
  Spain, 319–20
  Sweden, 320–1
  Switzerland, 321–2
  Turkey, 322–4
  Ukraine, 324–5
  United Kingdom, 325–7
  USSR, 325
  Yugoslavia, 327–8
Popular Front, 419
Population, 389–402
  Albania, 389
  Andorra, 389
  Armenia, 389
  Austria, 389
  Austrian Empire, 390
  Belarus, 390
  Belgium, 390
  Bosnia-Hercegovina, 390
  Bulgaria, 390–1
  Croatia, 391
  Cyprus, 391
  Czechoslovakia, 391
  Czech Republic, 392
  Denmark, 392
  Estonia, 392
  Finland, 392
  France, 393
  Georgia, 393
  German Democratic Republic, 394
  Germany, 393
  Germany, Federal Republic of, 393
  Gibraltar, 394
  Greece, 394
  Hungary, 394–5
  Iceland, 395
  Ireland, 395
  Italy, 395–6
  Latvia, 396
  Liechtenstein, 396
  Lithuania, 396
  Luxembourg, 397
  Macedonia, 397
  Malta, 397
  Moldova, 397
  Netherlands, 397–8
  Norway, 398
  Poland, 398
  Portugal, 398–9
  Romania, 399
  Russia, 399
  San Marino, 399
  Slovakia, 400
  Slovenia, 400
  Spain, 400
  Sweden, 400
  Switzerland, 401
  Turkey, 401
  Ukraine, 401
  United Kingdom, 402
  USSR, 401
  Yugoslavia, 402

Portugal's Wars in Africa, 361
Poujadist, 419
Prague Spring, 419
Provisional government, 419
Putsch, 419

Quai d'Orsay, 419
Quisling, 420

Rapacki Plan, 420
Rapallo, Treaty of, 369
Red Brigades, 420
Refuseniks, 420
Reich, 420
Reichsbanner, 420
Reichstag, 420
Rentenmark, 420
Reparations, 420
Resistance, 420
Revisionist, 420
Romanov, 421
Russia, 405
Russia–Chechnya War, 359
Russian Civil War, 356
Russo–Finnish War, 357
Russo–Japanese War, 359–60
Russo–Polish War, 357

SA (German 'storm-troopers'), 421
St Germain, Treaty of, 364
Sajudis, 421
Samizdat, 421
Schengen Agreement, 22
Schlieffen Plan, 421
Scrap of Paper, 421
Second Front, 421
Second International, 421
Second Reich, 421
Secretariat (UN), 6
Securitate, 422
Security Council, (UN), 3
Sèvres, Treaty of, 364
SHAPE (Supreme Headquarters,
    Allies Powers in Europe), 422
Show Trial, 422
Siegfried Line, 422
Slovakia, 405
Slovenia, 406
Social Charter, 422
Social Fascist, 422
Solidarity, 422

Soviet, 422
Soviet–Federal Germany Treaty,
    372
Sovkhoz, 422
Spanish Civil War, 357
Spartacists, 422
'Splendid Isolation', 422
SS (Hitler's bodyguard), 423
State capitalism, 423
Steel, Pact of, 370
Stormtroopers, 423
Straits Question, 423
Suez War, 361

Third Reich, 423
Third Republic, 423
Trade Union Confederation,
    European, 12
Trade Unions, International
    Confederation of Free, 12
Trade Unions, International
    Federation of Christian, 12
Trade Unions, World Federation of,
    12–13
Treaties, Agreements and Alliances
    between European Countries
    1900–1996, 365–8
Trianon, Treaty of, 364
Tripartism, 423
Tripartite Pact, 370
Triple Alliance, 423
Triple Entente, 423
Trizonia, 423
Trotskyist, 423
Trusteeship Council (UN), 4

Ukraine, 406
Union Sacrée, 424
United Nations, 1–6
Ustase, 424

Vatican, 2, 424
Velvet Chancellors, 424
Velvet Divorce, 424
Velvet Revolution, 424
Versailles, Treaty of, 363
Vietnam War, First, 360
Volkshammer, 424

Waffen SS, 424
Walloons, 424

433

War Communism, 424
War Guilt Clause, 424
Warsaw Pact, 26–7, 371
Warsaw Pact armed forces, 23
Weimar, 425
Weltpolitik, 425
Western European Union, 16–17
WEU (Western European Union), 16–17
White Russians, 425
Winter War, 425
World Confederation of Labour, 12–13
World Federation of Trade Unions, 12–13
World War I (Europe), 356

World War I European Belligerents, 362
World War I, Peace Treaties arising from, 1918–23, 363–4
World War II (Asia), 360
World War II (Europe), 357
World War II Principal European Belligerents, 362–3

Yezhovschina, 425
Young Plan, 425
Young Turks, 425
Yugoslavia, Former, 406
Yugoslavian Civil War, 358

Zimmermann Telegram, 425